Mirror on America

Short Essays and Images
from Popular Culture

Mirror on America

*Short Essays and Images
from Popular Culture*

SECOND EDITION

JOAN T. MIMS

Texas Education Agency

ELIZABETH M. NOLLEN

West Chester University

BEDFORD/ST. MARTIN'S   Boston ◆ New York

FOR BEDFORD/ST. MARTIN'S

Developmental Editor: Amanda Bristow
Senior Production Editor: Anne Noonan
Senior Production Supervisor: Joe Ford
Marketing Manager: Brian Wheel
Editorial Assistant: Karin Halbert
Production Assistant: Kerri Cardone
Copyeditor: Jane Zanichkowsky
Text Design: Claire Seng-Niemoeller
Cover Design: Terry Govan
Cover Art: The New York, NY Hotel and Casino. Courtesy of MGM Grand,
   Las Vegas, Nevada
Composition: Pine Tree Composition
Printing and Binding: RR Donnelley and Sons Company

President: Joan E. Feinberg
Editorial Director: Denise B. Wydra
Editor in Chief: Karen S. Henry
Director of Marketing: Karen Melton
Director of Editing, Design, and Production: Marcia Cohen
Managing Editor: Elizabeth M. Schaaf

Library of Congress Control Number: 2002112260

Manufactured in the United States of America.

8   7   6   5   4   3
f   e   d   c   b

For information, write: Bedford/St. Martin's, 75 Arlington Street,
Boston, MA 02116   (617-399-4000)

ISBN: 0–312–39933–2

ACKNOWLEDGMENTS

Lorraine Ali. "Do I Look Like Public Enemy Number One?" From *Mademoiselle* (1999). Copyright © 1999. Reprinted by permission of the author. "Same Old Song: Controversy over pop
   music is as old as Elvis, but now we're in a cultural arms race." From *Newsweek*, October 9,
   2000, p. 68. Copyright 2000 Newsweek, Inc. All rights reserved.
Julia Alvarez. "I Want to Be Miss America." From *Something to Declare* by Julia Alvarez. Copyright © 1998 by Julia Alvarez. Published by Algonquin Books of Chapel Hill, 1998. Reprinted
   by permission of Susan Bergholz Literary Services, New York. All rights reserved.

*Acknowledgments and copyrights are continued at the back of the book on pages 383–85,
which constitute an extension of the copyright page. It is a violation of the law to reproduce
these selections by any means whatsoever without the written permission of the copyright holder.*

*This one is for my mom, who has been telling me
for years, "You should write a book!"
And as always, for Paul and Derek, who are the story of my life.*

J. T. M.

*To my husband Dennis, for appreciating and supporting
my work through the years.*

*To Laura and Julia, my in-house popular culture consultants,
for making me proud to be your mother.*

*To the rest of my family and those friends who
have nurtured my mind, body, and soul.*

*And to all those students who have made teaching
a pleasure and have taught me so much.*

E. M. N.

Preface for Instructors

If popular culture is a kind of mirror that reflects society and its values and preferences, it also forms one of the largest arenas for communication among all members of that society, irrespective of age, gender, ethnicity, or social standing. *Mirror on America: Short Essays and Images from Popular Culture,* Second Edition, gives students the context they need to understand this public dialogue and the critical thinking and writing skills necessary to participate intelligently. Composed primarily of short, high-interest essays and striking, thought-provoking images, the text's eight thematic chapters present material, which may already be familiar to students, in new and thoughtful ways. The text guides their responses to the material and helps them think and write critically about the popular culture surrounding them.

After teaching for many years, we became frustrated in our search for a reader that would at once interest and challenge students. Many writing texts underestimate the social awareness and critical thinking capability of first-year students. *Mirror on America* attempts to address this misconception by coupling thought-provoking editorial guidance with highly readable yet challenging selections of various types and difficulty levels including articles from popular periodicals, essays, cartoons, photographs, and advertisements.

Beginning with a student-friendly introduction, *Mirror on America* defines popular culture as "that collection of objects, people, events, and places that serves to mirror society and its members and to reflect their values and preferences." Also discussing the importance of reading and writing about popular culture, the introduction stresses that although all components of pop culture may not be of equal quality, they play a crucial role in our daily lives as well as in our shared social history.

Nine Chapters on Popular Culture

The first chapter, "Active, Involved Reading and the Writing Process: Establishing the Connection," demonstrates the essential link between the reading and writing processes by teaching students to read thoughtfully and to recognize such fundamental concerns as audience, tone, and purpose. We think that students who are able to recognize these essentials are more likely to consider them in their own writing. In this chapter we out-line for students the various types of questions accompanying each selec-tion and guide them through a sample reading. The second half of Chap-ter 1 guides the student step by step from active reading to self-generated writing and concludes with a new student essay written in response to a new professional essay.

Following the initial chapter are eight chapters on specific areas of popular culture. Chapters 2, 3, and 4, titled "Mars and Venus: How Cul-ture Shapes Gender Identity," "Mirror, Mirror: Cultural Reflections on Body Image," and "Melting Pot or Salad Bowl? How Cultural Identity Shapes Self-Image" deal with the ways popular culture affects us person-ally. These are followed by five chapters that deal with areas of culture that affect us in a more global sense:

- Chapter 5: "It's All about the Look: Fashion Trends and the Sig-nals They Send"
- Chapter 6: "Fantasies for Sale: Marketing American Culture"
- Chapter 7: "Flickering Illusions: Television and Movie Messages"
- Chapter 8: "What's That Sound? How Music and Culture Mix It Up"
- Chapter 9: "Are We Having Fun Yet? Sports and Leisure in Con-temporary Culture"

Readable, High-Interest Selections

Like the chapter topics, selections were chosen for their currency, high in-terest, challenging ideas, and readability. They were also chosen with an eye to their ability to generate engaging discussion and writing activities. Selected from sources such as newspapers, magazines, webzines, and essay collections, the readings range from three to five pages—about the same length as the papers that students will be asked to write. Well-known au-thors including Julia Alvarez, Stephen King, and John Leo write on topics such as American standards of beauty, the appeal of horror movies, and the strategies of advertising.

Striking Visuals

More accurately than other, more traditional texts, *Mirror on America*, Second Edition, reflects the students' world by including a wealth of im-ages such as magazine covers, advertisements, photographs, and cartoons. Every chapter opens with a striking image. These opening visuals are unique because they are accompanied by questions and prompts for criti-cal thinking that encourage students to approach the chapter with a criti-cal eye. The "Focusing on Yesterday, Focusing on Today" visuals at the end of each chapter ask students to examine their current culture by comparing and contrasting it with the culture of the past.

Helpful Guidance for Students

Abundant editorial apparatus in *Mirror on America,* Second Edition, guides students through the discovery process by asking them important questions and by offering them valuable context before and after every chapter and every selection.

At the beginning of each chapter you will find the following:

- A caption and questions accompany the chapter-opening visual to stimulate discussion or writing.
- "Gearing Up" questions ask students to reflect briefly in writing about the topic for that chapter. This feature may be used as a homework assignment or as an in-class preparation for discussion.
- A brief, attention-grabbing introduction provides valuable context for the chapter's selections and focuses student attention more fully on the chapter's topic.
- "Collaborating" activities introduce students to major concerns of the chapter and give them a chance to exchange ideas with their classmates.

Each reading selection is preceded by the following:

- An informative introduction to the selection provides students with cultural context as well as a brief biographical sketch about the selection's author.
- "Thinking Ahead" questions ask students to reflect briefly about the topic of that selection.
- "Increasing Vocabulary" gives students a prereading list of some unfamiliar words to look up and incorporate into their personal vocabularies.

Each reading selection is followed by four sets of questions:

- "Exercising Vocabulary" questions ask students to derive the meanings of especially interesting words from their context and to apply and compare those meanings to usage in other contexts.
- "Probing Content" questions call for students to engage in thoughtful discussion of the selection's subject.
- "Considering Craft" questions require students to focus on particular techniques used by the writers to accomplish their goals.
- "Responding to the Writer" questions ask students to reflect on some aspect of the reading and to question and comment on the writer's message while connecting it to their own experiences.

Finally, each chapter concludes with several student activities, including the "Focusing on Yesterday, Focusing on Today" activities discussed earlier as well as several writing suggestions, which take two forms:

- "Reflecting on the Writing" questions ask students to connect ideas from the essays within or across chapters and to draw their own conclusions.
- "Connecting to the Culture" questions ask students to reflect on personal experiences similar to those represented in the readings and to consider how their own life experiences are connected to popular culture in general.

What's New in the Second Edition

TEXT SELECTIONS

To keep pace with the ever-changing rhythm of American popular culture, there are now fifty-eight provocative readings, more than half of which are new. Although this edition includes fewer short essays than the first, there is still an ample selection to use as models for student writing assignments. The inclusion of longer essays exposes students to more elaborate, fully developed arguments, thus enriching their composition experience. Students will read fresh new writers such as Lorraine Ali ("Same Old Song"), as she writes about the role of rebellion in contemporary rock music; George Felton ("Wrestling with Myself"), as he extols the merits of the WWF; Naomi Klein ("The Brand Expands"), as she questions the logo phenomenon; and Damien Cave ("The Tyranny of 'Abercrappie'"), as he bashes the Abercrombie & Fitch clothing line.

We eliminated the chapter on technology and added a chapter concerning body image to bring the discussion of popular culture and its effects closer to home. Increasingly, our culture has become obsessed with the attainment of impossible body ideals, and we find that even within seemingly disparate aspects of popular culture such as music and sports, focus on body image dominates the conversation.

Every chapter now includes paired selections — two readings with different, but not necessarily opposite, points of view — showing students that every topic can be approached from at least two perspectives. We think you'll find these readings will generate lively discussion in your classroom. New "Drawing Connections" questions appear before the end of each chapter, asking students to compare and contrast the strategies the authors of the paired readings use to explain their points of view.

A new "Rhetorical Table of Contents" (p. 379) organizes the readings in this book into rhetorical modes.

IMAGE SELECTIONS

Nineteen images are new to this edition, and since our students' lives are media saturated, the ability to analyze this ever-present source of information is essential. Chapter 1 now ends with a new selection called "Deconstructing Media," which guides students through the process of "reading" a variety of visuals including a photograph and a cartoon. "Focusing on Yesterday, Focusing on Today" images at the end of each chapter have been carefully paired to generate discussion about the relationship between the images. For example, the chapter on movies pairs such images as a movie still from Hitchcock's classic thriller *Psycho* with an image from the contemporary thriller *Scream,* and the chapter on music pairs a photograph of a gyrating Elvis with an equally titillating photograph of Britney Spears.

NEW ESL GLOSSES

In addition to the glosses already available for each reading, there are now new glosses for students whose first language is not English. ESL glosses throughout the readings explain terminology that might be unfamiliar to this growing student population.

EVALUATING AND DOCUMENTING SOURCES

A new section on evaluating and documenting sources offers brief but essential coverage of MLA documentation style. This section features MLA citation models, as well as an annotation of a Web page and an assignment showing students how to document this multimedia source.

Companion Web Site at Bedfordstmartins.com/mirror

New Web links throughout the text connect to the new companion Web site, where you and your students will find useful on-line resources, including *TopLinks*—a dynamic database of annotated links that relate to each topic in the book and that provide opportunities for further exploration and possible essay ideas. Students may use the on-line Reading Quizzes to test themselves on the content of each reading. Each quiz offers feedback and immediate scoring, and instructors can track their students' progress.

Abundant Resources for Instructors

Included with *Mirror on America,* Second Edition, is the instructor's manual, *Resources for Teaching* MIRROR ON AMERICA: SHORT ESSAYS AND IMAGES FROM POPULAR CULTURE, Second Edition. We wrote this instructor's manual as a practical ancillary to the text to offer additional ways to present the material effectively. As with the apparatus, we have designed the exercises in the instructor's manual to offer imaginative alternatives that work well in the classroom. We do not claim to offer all the alternative teaching strategies and resources here. Instead we hope that those we do offer lead to stimulating classroom experiences.

After a brief essay on strategies for teaching Chapter 1, the instructor's manual offers the following material for each chapter and selection of the text:

- A brief chapter introduction from the instructor's point of view
- A short discussion of the chapter-opening material
- "Questions for Discussion"
- "Group Activities
- "Out of Class Projects"
- "Additional Writing Assignments"
- "Additional Resources"

Through class-testing many of the selections, writing suggestions, and activities in the text, we have found reading and writing about contemporary popular culture to be a highly effective means of teaching students to connect to larger cultural and discourse communities through their own reading and writing. We sincerely hope that you have equally successful classroom experiences as you use *Mirror on America: Short Essays and Images from Popular Culture,* Second Edition, with your own students.

Acknowledgments

We would like to thank Barbara Heinssen for signing this book, thus making our affiliation with Bedford/St. Martin's possible. We have found it a privilege to work with a team of highly competent people at Bedford, one of the last publishing houses to truly take the time to develop its writers. We wish especially to thank Bedford's past president, Chuck Christensen; its president, Joan Feinberg; and its editor in chief in Boston, Karen Henry, for sharing our vision and allowing us to share it with others. Special thanks also go to Aron Keesbury, developmental editor for the first edition, and his editorial assistant (now editor), Ellen Thibault. Their insight, inventiveness, and general good humor made our collaboration productive and enjoyable.

Two other people have been instrumental in the writing of this text. Amanda Bristow, developmental editor for this edition, lent a fresh, vibrant perspective to the daunting task of updating and transforming the first edition into an even more relevant and usable textbook. Her creative suggestions and constant encouragement played a major role in shaping the text. Her editorial assistant, Karin Halbert, proved invaluable by ably assisting with this edition from its earliest stages, by locating hard-to-find images graciously and speedily, and by masterfully managing the flow of manuscript materials among all of us. We appreciate the efforts of the production team headed by Anne Noonan who skillfully engineered and guided the production process. Copyeditor Jane Zanichkowsky's many suggestions were invaluable. We also wish to recognize the hard work of Elizabeth Bristow and Rose Corbett Gordon, who found and cleared permissions for all of the thought-provoking images you see in this book. We would like to thank Jeannine Thibodeau, who did biographical research, and Sandy Schechter, who cleared permissions for the book. We would also like to thank Lauren Brackbill, a talented writer and student in one of Elizabeth Nollen's classes, who provided the student essay for Chapter 1.

We owe a debt of gratitude to a group of people who were instrumental in the revision of this book. We thank our reviewers for their many helpful suggestions: Greg Ahrenhoerster, University of Wisconsin; Steven R. Chalk, Ball State University; Kathleen Chapman, Valencia Community College; Phyllis Davis, J. Sargeant Reynolds Community College; Susana de la Penã, Rio Hondo College; Sara Eaton, North Central College; Gerald Gems, North Central College; Katherine L. Hall, Roger Williams University; Matthew Henry, Richland College; Marilyn Kennedy, Orange Coast College; Seema Kurup, William Rainey Harper College; Steven R. Luebke, University of Wisconsin; Lisa Mott, Santa Rosa Junior College; Patricia A. Pallis, Naugatuck Valley Community College; Inez Schaechterle, University of Nevada; Lisa Rogers Sykes, Emory and Henry College; and Carmen Wong, John Tyler Community College. Finally, this book never would have been written had it not been for the many students we have taught over the years in our composition classrooms. With them, we have tested many of the topics, strategies, and activities that comprise this text, and from them we have learned much of what we know about teaching writing and about popular culture today.

Introduction for Students

This is not your usual English textbook. The material focuses on reading and writing about things in your world, like television, movies, music, and sports, often called *popular culture*. Why read and write about popular culture? In order to answer this question, we first need to understand what popular culture is and why it is important.

To arrive at a working definition, we can break the term down into its two components: *popular* and *culture*. In the most general sense, *popular* means "of the people"—the common people or the population at large, not the elite or chosen few. But more often, *popular* suggests choice, or preference. We usually use this term when we mean something or someone that many ordinary people prefer or value. When you think of popular culture, then, think of the People's Choice Awards as opposed to the Academy Awards.

That brings us to the second term, *culture*. Broadly defined, *culture* refers to the body of beliefs, behaviors, values, and thoughts that influence us every day. It contains not only the good, but also the bad—the high and the low. We normally associate the word *culture*, however, not with the masses—the ordinary man and woman on the street—but with the educated and financially privileged. We think of *Masterpiece Theatre,* not of *Friends*. If a person is cultured, we generally think she possesses good taste, is refined and educated, and is also probably upper class. If *popular* usually means "chosen by the common people," and *culture* is often associated with the chosen few, then what do these two seemingly contradictory terms mean when they are used together?

We may borrow the Cotton Institute slogan from television commercials to help us arrive at a working definition of popular culture: It is "the fabric of our lives." Pop culture is made up of all the objects, people, events, and places to which most of us readily relate and which comprise a society at any given time, past or present. The objects and people that are widely recognized as symbols of our culture are often referred to as cultural icons. The four components of pop culture—objects, people, events, and places—can be real or imagined. Let's look at some examples:

1. Objects as cultural icons include Barbie dolls, rap songs, television shows, clothing, advertisements, and even Cinderella's glass slipper.

2. People as cultural icons include such popular celebrities as Britney Spears, Julia Roberts, Freddy Krueger, Tiger Woods, Bugs Bunny, and the Energizer Bunny.

3. Events, activities, or rituals in popular culture are those that large groups of people participate in or can relate to, including Woodstock, the Super Bowl, the World Series, and the Grammys.

4. Places in pop culture are settings that hold special shared meaning for many people and include shopping malls, amusement parks, Las Vegas, Hollywood, the White House, and the Statue of Liberty.

These four elements of popular culture form a mirror in which each of us, as members of a common society, can see ourselves reflected as part of an interconnected, greater whole. At the same time, pop culture not only reflects our tastes and preferences at any given time, past or present, but also plays a role in determining future fads and trends. From the time we get up in the morning until the time we go to bed, and from the time we enter this world until the time we leave it, we are immersed in popular culture. We may agree that not all of its components are of the highest quality or in the best taste, but we would all have to concede that they play an integral part in our daily lives, as well as in our shared social history. Popular culture is part of what makes us all Americans.

It is important to remember that pop culture is not fixed in time. The popular or mass culture of the past may become the high or elite culture of the present, and that same elite culture may simultaneously be repopularized as it is once again embraced by the masses. Consider the case of William Shakespeare. If you read *Macbeth* or *Hamlet* in high school, you probably did not associate those difficult-to-read plays with pop culture. Remember, however, that Shakespeare's plays, much like blockbuster movies today, were extremely popular during the time they were written and enjoyed wide attendance by large, enthusiastic audiences. Shakespeare was tuned in to those audiences, which were made up of all segments of society, from the educated nobility to the illiterate "groundlings," so named because they sat on the ground near the stage. Thus, during his time, Shakespeare's plays were seen as popular entertainment. It was only in later years that his plays were appropriated by learned scholars in universities who sought to analyze them word by word as they continue to do today.

Interestingly enough, as evidence of Shakespeare's popular appeal in the second half of the twentieth century and into the new millennium, entertainment moguls have sought to revitalize his plays by taking them out of the hands of university professors and giving them back to the masses. Not only serious students of Shakespeare but also people who have never read a word of his plays can now enjoy his works. First there was the Broadway triumph of *West Side Story,* which recasts *Romeo and Juliet* as a musical set in a Puerto Rican neighborhood of New York City. For the past several years, Shakespeare's plays have been presented free to the public in New York's Central Park, often showcasing such movie celebrities as Kevin Kline and Denzel Washington. A 1996 movie version of *Romeo and Juliet* starring Leonardo DiCaprio and Claire Danes features tough modern gangs, a cross-dressing Mercutio, and a powerful musical score performed by contemporary artists. The 1999 Academy Awards were dominated by the Hollywood blockbuster *Shakespeare in Love*, a rollicking spoof featuring a young Shakespeare with writer's block, played by Joseph Fiennes, who is lovestruck by a beautiful woman played by Gwyneth Paltrow. Since then, there have been several other popular reincarnations of Shakespeare classics set in contemporary America, featuring young stars like Julia Stiles, Heath Ledger, Jet Li, and Aaliyah. These films, which target the teenage market, include *O*, a modern-day retelling of *Othello*; *10 Things I Hate about You*, based on *The Taming of the Shrew*; and *Romeo Must Die*, yet another retelling of the classic love story *Romeo and Juliet*. Thus Shakespeare is once again finding his way back to the masses. Since academics are already studying and writing scholarly articles on the impact of rap music, soap operas, and movies, which contemporary composers and screenwriters do you think will someday take their place alongside Shakespeare?

Popular culture, then, is that collection of objects, people, events, and places that serves to mirror society and its members and to reflect their values and preferences. Ironically, the study of popular culture, although still somewhat controversial, is becoming increasingly accepted in academic circles as worthwhile. By studying pop culture, you gain valuable new insights about yourself and make richer connections to all aspects of the society in which you live. Finally, we hope that you find it not only fulfilling but also fun to read and write about popular culture, a subject with which you are intimately connected every day of your life.

Contents

6. Fantasies for Sale: Marketing American Culture   205

CHAPTER 1

Active, Involved Reading
and the Writing Process
Establishing the Connection

If this is a writing course, why are there so many things to read in this text? Why is reading the first thing we want to discuss with you?

It's simple, really. People who write well read often. They read to find ideas, both for what to write about and for how to write. Reading makes us think, and good writing requires thought beforehand, during, and afterwards. Reading helps us identify things we'd like to model in our own work and things we'll never do, no matter what. Reading opens windows and doors to the world we share and offers mirrors in which we can look at our culture and ourselves.

Reading with a Difference

The kind of reading this discussion involves may not be the kind of reading you are used to. If you think of reading as a sit-still, passive, try-to-stay-awake-until-the-end-of-the-chapter event, you'll need to rethink. Real reading means really getting involved with the text, whether the text is song lyrics, a magazine or newspaper item, a poem, a chapter in a chemistry book, or an essay in this text. The more of your five senses you involve, the better.

Getting into Reading

This text includes some things that should make the reading–writing experience more manageable for you and more interesting, too. Each unit begins with something like a poster, a cartoon, or a copy of an advertisement. This **opening visual** gives you a first glimpse of the chapter's topic and helps you begin to think about the topic. Next are a few sentences called **Gearing Up.** This section is a journal and discussion prompt to help you reflect on your previous involvement with that chapter's topic and to get you started writing. Next is introductory text that provides some background thoughts about the chapter and raises some questions to help

1

you relate your own experiences to the topic for reading and discussion. Finally, each chapter includes a **Collaborating** section, an opening activity that suggests questions for you and your classmates to brainstorm about together before you begin to read and discuss the individual selections in each chapter.

Now you are ready to move on to the reading selections in the chapter. Before each essay is a brief **headnote** about the subject matter, the writer, and when and where the material was first published. Next is a journal prompt called **Thinking Ahead**. Unlike the journal prompt **Gearing Up** at the beginning of each chapter, the one before each reading selection deals not with the entire topic but with only the aspect of that topic that that particular reading selection covers. Following this is a list called **Increasing Vocabulary**, which contains some vocabulary words that you may find unfamiliar. Looking up definitions for these words and writing those dictionary definitions in your own words in a vocabulary notebook will help you to expand the number of words at your command when you write or read. The **reading selection** is next. This may be an essay, an article, or a column from a newspaper, magazine, or a Webzine.

Immediately following the selection are sets of questions: **Exercising Vocabulary** gives you a chance to explore the use and meaning of some especially interesting words. **Probing Content** asks questions about the writer's subject matter. **Considering Craft** questions are about why and how the writer has put together the selection as he or she has chosen to do. **Responding to the Writer** allows you to examine your own reactions and respond to issues the writer has raised. **Drawing Connections** questions ask you to compare strategies writers in the paired essays use to make theirs points about similar topics.

To understand how all these parts work together, let's look at a sample essay. First, read the brief introduction to the essay's subject and author. Many readers may be tempted to skip right over this information because it isn't part of the body of the essay, but that's a mistake. To see why, let's work with the headnote to a sample essay called "Playing in the Shadows: Popular Culture in the Aftermath of Sept. 11" by Teresa Wiltz.

Playing in the Shadows

Teresa Wiltz

What becomes of a nation when an irreversible event happens in an instant, as it did on September 11, 2001? Some people think that the events of that day permanently altered our national mindset: Our usual ironic, cynical outlook was replaced by a feeling of earnest patriotism. Others, like Teresa Wiltz, are not so sure. In "Playing in the Shadows," which first appeared in the *Washington Post* on November 19, 2001, Wiltz writes, "A change is gonna come. Or will it?" Speculating on September 11's effect on popular culture, she looks at the entertainment industry for clues. What do the music charts and box office figures from the weeks following the attack tell us about the direction in which popular culture is heading? How can the peddlers of pop culture show patriotism without appearing to be profiteers? Although she provides illuminating answers to these questions, in the end, Wiltz admits, "Most likely, it will be years before our culture is ready to deconstruct the events of September."

Wiltz currently writes for the Arts section of the *Washington Post*. She has also worked as a professional modern dancer, a staff writer for the *Cedar Rapids Gazette*, and a columnist for the *Chicago Tribune*. In addition to her work as a newspaper journalist, Wiltz has contributed articles to *Essence* magazine and coauthored *Andre Talks Hair!* (1997) with Oprah Winfrey's personal hairstylist, Andre Walker.

This headnote contains several important pieces of information. First, it outlines the overall effect of September 11, and raises interesting questions about how pop culture will—or won't—be affected by such a catastrophic event. It supplies a few general statements about Wiltz's stance, opening the way for the essay to supply details. Finally, it tells us when and where the article first appeared and a little information about its author, so that we can accurately think about her perspective on her subject and her original intended audience. How does the background information for this essay influence your reading?

Thinking Ahead

Following our sample essay's headnote are a few sentences under the heading "Thinking Ahead." This journal and discussion prompt helps you focus your initial thoughts about the essay's subject. If you have never kept a journal before, you'll find that it's a good way to learn to transfer your thoughts and ideas to paper. Don't worry too much about grammar and spelling as you write in your journal; the important thing here is just to get started writing. These journal notes may be seeds for your more formal essays later. Let's look at a sample journal prompt and one possible response for "Playing in the Shadows."

Now here is a journal entry written in response to this prompt:

I didn't know anyone who died on September 11, so I wasn't as personally affected as those who lost family or friends. I remember being glued to the TV — I wanted to go somewhere else, to stop seeing the Towers collapsing and those people running and screaming over and over again, but I couldn't make myself stop watching. Other people in my dorm were crying and cussing, but I just felt frozen. The whole thing just looked so much like a Bruce Willis movie. But there wasn't anyone to save the day. At least, not right away.

For a while after that people seemed to be more aware of each other. Things like the Emmys got postponed, and they delayed releasing a few movies because they had terrorist-type violence. Lots of musicians jumped on the patriotism idea. Old songs like Bruce Springsteen's "Born in the USA" and Neil Diamond's "Coming to America" suddenly got lots of airtime again. Flags were everywhere — in yards, on cars, on businesses — and everyone wore those little flag pins.

But by now that's kind of wearing off. It's like people just want to forget about it and get on with the ordinary stuff. But September 11 will always be there. It changed things, not just in New York, where people see the empty space every day on their way to work and school. I wonder when something else will happen. Will people I know have to fight in Afghanistan? I don't feel as safe anymore.

Remember that everyone's journal response will be different. The task of the journal prompt is to get you to think about a subject in a way that you might not have before, so the writing in your journal won't be a finished product. Your response will just be your ideas transferred from your head onto the paper.

Increasing Vocabulary

The next thing included for our sample essay is a list of vocabulary words. Following each word in parentheses is the part of speech that tells how the word is used in context—for example, noun, verb, adjective, or adverb—so you'll know where you might use this word in a sentence. Next is a number in parentheses; this is the paragraph number in the essay where the word appears. This allows you to see where and how the writer has used this word. The words aren't defined; keep a vocabulary list in your notebook with definitions that you put in your own words after reading the dictionary definition. Don't be tempted to just copy words from the dictionary onto your notebook page, however; that may give you penmanship practice, but your personal vocabulary won't grow. Think about building blocks. Someone with more building blocks can build a more complete castle than someone else with fewer blocks. Words are the building blocks of essays and conversations. Read what the dictionary has to say and write down a definition that makes sense to you. Then go back and reread the word in context to make sure your definition fits the author's intent. The objective is for you to be able to use this new word in your own conversations and writing.

Our vocabulary list may not cover all the words in the selection that you find unfamiliar; some unfamiliar words or names, which you probably would not use in your own writing or conversation, are defined for you at the bottom of the page where they are used so you don't miss what the author is trying to say. Always feel free to add to the list in your notebook additional words you'd like to master from each essay.

Here is our vocabulary list for "Playing in the Shadows," with some working definitions that a student might supply:

INCREASING VOCABULARY

flux (n.) (3) *constant change*
sartorial (adj.) (4) *referring to clothing or style of dress*
invincible (adj.) (6) *not capable of being defeated*
fickle (adj.) (7) *likely to change*
cataclysmic (adj.) (7) *sudden and violent*
unprecedented (adj.) (9) *never before experienced*
empathetic (adj.) (9) *identifying with someone else's feelings and thoughts*
perpetual (adj.) (15) *continuing forever*
murky (adj.) (20) *not clear*
combustible (adj.) (20) *able to catch fire and burn*
incremental (adj.) (21) *added on*

invulnerability (n.) (22) *a condition of not being able to be harmed*
irrevocable (adj.) (23) *cannot be changed*
succor (n.) (27) *help, comfort, or relief*
construed (v.) (33) *interpreted*
trivializes (v.) (39) *making something seem unimportant*
protracted (adj.) (41) *long and drawn out*
wistful (adj.) (41) *marked by longing or yearning*

Reading a Sample Essay

Once you have read the introduction, responded to the journal prompt, and defined the vocabulary, you are ready to read the selection itself. But reading doesn't mean you become a spectator. You don't learn about playing a sport just by watching, and you don't learn everything a text has to offer by just letting your eyes wander over the lines. That's why annotating is essential for really involved reading. Annotating means to read with highlighter, pencil, or pen in hand. When you annotate, you open up a dialogue between reader and text; you communicate.

Here's how annotating works. Circle any unfamiliar vocabulary words so you can look them up later; some may be in our list, but some may not. Underline or highlight important sentences, especially the thesis, or main idea, and the topic sentences for each paragraph. Mark sentences or phrases that just appeal to you or seem especially well worded. Jot down questions in the margin. Draw connections between the author's experiences and your own. Put question marks by whatever you don't accept as true or just don't understand. React to what you're reading!

Here is a copy of our sample essay, "Playing in the Shadows" with annotations. Don't worry if you would have marked different words and phrases and recorded different comments; that's fine. This is just to show you how one reader has actively read and annotated this essay.

Playing in the Shadows:
Popular Culture in the Aftermath of Sept. 11

TERESA WILTZ

In the first few weeks following *that day*, once we'd stopped reeling from the initial shock, there was a collective throat-clearing, and then came tumbling forth the pronouncements: 1

Whose vanity?

Not to offend people?

Vanity had taken a hit. Irony, so beloved by smarty-pants, was on life support. Comedy would be careful.

Such declarations are the punditocracy equivalent of calling the Super Bowl—three seasons in advance.

What does this mean?

Interesting definition

Popular culture, that which shapes how we see ourselves and how others see us, is in a state of flux. A change is gonna come. Or will it?

My professor would correct this!

German?

It is true, of course, that a certain earnestness has crept into the national zeitgeist, blotting out—for now, at least—our normal, unique brand of optimistic cynicism. In her latest video, blue-eyed soul singer Pink urges us all to "Get This Party Started" as she dances against the backdrop of a giant flag. Celebs attending the Emmy Awards earlier this month were asked to tone down the sartorial glitz. And just a week ago Sunday, in a much-publicized gathering, movie execs met with White House officials—again—to suss[2] out just what Hollywood could do for the war-on-terrorism effort.

Aren't these opposites?

Didn't happen at Oscars! Or did it?

What could H. do?

But amid the earnestness, there is contradiction. A couple of weeks ago, the No. 1 CD in the nation was a *God Bless America* compilation. New Agey popster Enya's feel-good CD, *A Day Without Rain*, ranked No. 2. The following week, both CDs were nudged out by gangsta rapper DMX's downtrodden CD *The Great Depression*. And last week Michael Jackson's latest CD, *Invincible*, reigned, followed by Enrique Iglesias's *Escape*—that is until midweek, when Britney Spears wiggled her way to the top of the charts.

accurate verb!

So what does it say that we go from blessing America to wallowing in the great depression to feeling invincible but desperately in need of escape?

That we're fickle, sure. But more importantly: Even a national tragedy of cataclysmic proportions can alter our cultural DNA by only so much. Popular culture is, as one observer put it, a daily Rorschach test,[3] a peek into the American id[4] as it flips and flops about. It's also a business, a huge one, arguably our biggest international export. And as with any business, it is the consumer who has the ultimate say.

Thesis!!

ink blots?

Freud term—check psych. text

Culture as business

Says Robert Thompson, professor of media and culture at Syracuse University and past president of the International Popular Culture Association: "We may be surprised at how capable American popular culture is of dissolving even the most horrible of historical events."

This makes Americans sound really shallow. Are we?

And now, in the wake of an unprecedented home front attack, peddlers of pop are grappling for ways to appear relevant. To strike just the right notes: empathetic yet resolved; patriotic but not profiteering.

But they are profiting!

If they've found the answers, they're not telling. Entertainers and execs contacted by *The Washington Post* were, for the most part, zipping lips. When asked about how their work would be affected by Sept. 11, most of them, from Steven Spielberg to Dr. Dre, decided to pass on the question. Some pleaded busy schedules; others, like Conan O'Brien, frankly admitted that they weren't stepping anywhere near *that* date.

Why?

But talk shows do bin Laden jokes—

Then there's Jack Valenti, chairman of the Motion Picture Association of America, who's more than happy to offer up his

---

[1] **zeitgeist:** The general intellectual, moral, and cultural climate of an era.
[2] **suss:** To investigate or figure out.
[3] **Rorschach test:** A personality and intelligence test in which a subject interprets inkblot designs.
[4] **id:** Source of unconscious and instinctive impulses.

Wow! How cold!

take on the future of popular culture. Which is to say, he doesn't see it changing much: As long as there's a great story to tell, he doesn't see a problem if somewhere along the way a building or two is blown up. Forget about forecasting trends in entertainment. The public's desire to be entertained is a constant.   — *True*

True

Valenti does see, however, among the American public a   12
strong yearning for escape, a desire reflected by the impressive box office figures ($156.7 million) of Disney's *Monsters, Inc.*, an animated flick about facing one's worst fears.   — *That's timely.*

"Show him the money!"

"It's spiritually beautiful," says Valenti, fresh from his meet-   13
ing with studio and White House officials. "That box office take is spiritually beautiful."   *profit from tragedy*

As Valenti sees it, box office takes will continue to be beau-   14
tiful—and the opening weekend totals for *Harry Potter and the Sorcerer's Stone* (a record-setting $93.5 million) indicate likewise.

This is always true—

"In times of peril, in times of uncertainty, people don't want   15
to be in a constant state of perpetual anxiety," he says. "People want to enjoy storytelling, which for a couple of hours at least will transport them away."

Even so, storytellers, like the rest of us, are faced with how   16
to interpret the recent life-changing turn of events.

"It's affected me personally," says mystery writer Walter   17
Mosley, who recently published *Futureland*, a "pre-apocalyptic"[5]

Find this to read!

collection of sci-fi stories with echoes of Sept. 11.

"It happened right outside my window; I watched it happen.   18   *Lots of people feel*
I don't even yet know what that means. On the other hand, my   *this way—unsure*
work has kind of gone on the way it has before.   *how to respond*

"I don't know what will happen next," he says. "But what's   19   *over time*
happened so far, as terrible as it is, is not enough to change the

What would? WWIII?

nature of the course of the nation. . . . Our concept of how the world works hasn't really been altered as of yet. We're still thinking people should be going out spending money and making capitalism function. There's a great desire, among the people and among our leaders, that life go back to normal. Whatever that is."

Indeed, "normal" is a murky concept for a nation with the   20   *Car commercials*

That's harsh!

attention span of a gnat, where race, class and religion often form   *using Beamer's*
a combustible mix, where box office numbers are "spiritual" and   *quote [good idea*
Madison Avenue pledges to "keep America rolling." With zero-   *for essay!]*
percent financing, of course.

Todd Beamer

Comfort in Continuity

Great, sweeping cultural changes happen in waves, one in-   21
cremental change lapping over another microscopic blip, gradually building in intensity. It's only afterward that we look back and realize that we've been hit by a tsunami. After all, the '60s—   — *What?*
or what we like to think of as happening in the '60s—didn't occur all at once: First there was the civil rights movement, then the assassinations, Vietnam and eventually Watergate. Somewhere in all that came the pill, women's lib and a revolution in pop music. By the time the '60s were in full force, it was, well,   — *Slow evolution* —

Maybe an essay idea here —

1975.

"September 11 is what I'd call a 'second order change,'"   22

compare 9/11 to these changes

says futurist and psychological anthropologist Doug Raybeck, who describes the gradual changes of the '60s as "first order

---

[5] **pre-apocalyptic:** Occurring before the end of the world.
[6] **tsunami:** A great sea wave produced by earth movement or eruption under the sea.

changes." "It took us to a place we'd never been before. We've lost our innocence, lost our invulnerability, and we're in the process of losing our naivete."[7]

So, what happens to a culture when irrevocable change happens in an instant? 23

How so? Most of what we've seen post-Sept. 11 is quick and reactive. 24 *was well done*

Television was first to weigh in and, for the most part, 25 came off looking heavy-handed: NBC's *Third Watch* cobbled together a two-part episode about the World Trade Center attacks; *West Wing* creator Aaron Sorkin whipped out a quick treatise[8] on terrorism.

How much of this was just to attract viewers??

Pop singers and rappers, from U2's Bono to Alicia Keys to 26 Ja Rule, crammed into the studio to produce a remake of Marvin Gaye's "What's Going On?" (Proceeds originally were planned to benefit AIDS patients, but the WTC and Pentagon survivors and relatives were quickly added to the list of beneficiaries.) Movie studios pushed back the release dates or postponed the production of a few films deemed too violent or involving acts of terrorism.

9/11 replaces AIDS as trendy cause?

nice image But many folks found comfort in continuity, the succor 27 found in cultural chicken soup. The sitcom *Friends* has been extended for another season in the wake of its overwhelming popularity since the attacks. And those predictions that violent films would be offensive were wiped out by the success of movies like *13 Ghosts, From Hell, Training Day* and *The Heist*, all of which feature no small amount of bloodshed.

What's the connection to 9/11?

D. Washington won Oscar!

Perhaps it's the American way, to channel anger and grief 28 through a weird mix of violence and humor. . . . *Not a compliment!*

answers my question earlier But in the corporate arena of the nation's networks, Sept. 29 11-related humor seemed almost verboten[9] at first. Late-night hosts David Letterman and Jay Leno stayed off the air the first week after the attacks. Now Taliban jokes are a steady part of their patter—including dancing bin Ladens, much like the dancing Judge Itos from O.J. Simpson days. *Saturday Night Live* took a pointed jab at the government's handling of D.C.'s anthrax cases: In a mock news conference, Chris Kattan, playing the National Institutes of Health's Anthony Fauci, proclaimed, "We cleaned the State Department, the White House, the Supreme Court and the Capitol building with state-of-the-art decontamination equipment . . ." As for decontaminating post offices, Fauci says, "We've given each post office some baby wipes and a Dust-Buster."

more German? Is author German?

So far, smart-aleck humor prevails, as on the "America's 30 Mad as Hell Humor Page," which offers to provide "humor in a time of grief."

But there are few voices like the darkly sardonic[10] Internet 31 comic strip "Get Your War On," where cynics ponder which is worse, bin Laden as president or anthrax, and depressives wonder, "Maybe I should write a poem about my feelings since September 11; that might help! What rhymes with alcohol-saturated dread?"

That's depressing

Lockdown and Lock Step?

True. But we are at war! "How can we have popular culture if everyone is afraid to 32 say anything but 'God Bless America'?" observes Kevin Jones, a

---

[7] **naivete:** An unaffected simplicity.
[8] **treatise:** An argument in writing discussing facts and principles.
[9] **verboten:** Forbidden.
[10] **sardonic:** Disdainful or mocking.

former studio executive who produced the Gwyneth Paltrow film *Duets.* . . .

"In the public eye at this point, you better show some sort of sympathy or love for America or it will be construed wrong," says hip-hop journalist and Bay Area radio personality Dave "Davey D" Cook. "For artists, every gesture is scrutinized. The messages, whether intentional or not, have been delivered hard and fast to people. Line up, get in lock step and God help you if you aren't. 33

"I see a few songs that are on the whole 'Wave the flag, I love America' tip," Cook says. "The big question is: Is this the record company trying to capitalize on people's emotions? Or are the artists really feeling that way? Time will tell." . . . 34

Possible essay — Neil Diamond, what others?

Wait and See

Aren't we doing that now? Even in this essay!

Yet!

Most likely, it will be years before our culture is ready to deconstruct the events of September. 35

It is anyone's guess what will be. The war changes daily, events seemingly tumbling over one another. For now, with no new outbreaks of anthrax infections and last week's advances in Afghanistan, we are sleeping a little easier. For now. 36

People really feel better?

"Trying to predict the endgame[11] right now is the biggest mistake you can make," says Scott Donaton, editor of *Advertising Age*. "In New York, for a couple of days you could cross the street across the traffic and no one beeped. But life gets back to normal more quickly than you think. We can't boil it down to earnest patriotism. That's not what we are." 37

How abnormal!

Is this always positive??

TV talk show host Ananda Lewis says she already sees signs that some people are tiring of it all. She was surprised, she says, when television stations outside New York and Washington told her they weren't interested in more shows about Sept. 11. 38

"I really think everybody would be about the healing process right now," says Lewis. "That seems to be true of only the areas that were affected. Which is sad, because it trivializes something to just a news event." 39

Who says everyone has to heal the same way?

It won't be just a news event if the things get worse. Or another plane falls from the sky—and this time it's not an accident. Or smallpox hits Tulsa. Then perhaps you'll see a society in which no one wants to leave home and people find release instead through virtual ski trips: A specially rigged treadmill and some goggles and you're there, on the Alps. It could happen. 40

economic impact

scary thought! And sad, too

Or maybe last week's advances in Afghanistan will take a turn and tens of thousands of young men and women will die in a protracted ground war. Maybe we'll see civil liberties erode in the name of fighting the evildoers, until our rights are nothing more than a wistful thought. And then, perhaps, we'll see a new brand of protest music on MTV and BET. 41

How much will we give up? Possible essay

compare w/60s

Vietnam?

"Remember 'Hell no, we won't go'?" asks hip-hop impresario Russell Simmons, whose latest endeavor, "Def Poetry Jam," was picked up by HBO in the days after Sept. 11. "I'm hopeful that young people will have something to contribute. Three rappers are more important than three heads of states talking." 42

Debatable!

Maybe right now there's an aspiring rapper with a turntable in his bedroom trying to work through his fears. Or maybe next 43

---

[11]**endgame:** The final stage of a chess game.

What?

month, three geeks[12] in a storefront will get the corporate back-
ing for their video game "Crush al Qaeda." Or maybe in 10 years
some eager director will be maxing out her credit cards to make
an indie[13] flick. *Odo*

We're shape-shifting. 44

It's anyone's guess what that final shape will look like. 45

Nice wrap-up — Just like staking it all on the Redskins three years down the 46
back to idea from road in Super Bowl XXXIX, there are no sure bets.

beginning

Thinking about the Reading

After reading and annotating the piece of writing, you are ready to continue the conversation with the text, guided by several sets of questions.
The first set is called "Exercising Vocabulary." These questions are different from the vocabulary list you looked at before the reading selection.
There you were locating definitions and thinking about adding those
words to your own speaking and writing vocabulary. Here you examine
just a few words from the reading selection in closer detail. You are asked
to draw some conclusions and occasionally to do some detective work to
arrive at a meaning for an unfamiliar word.

Here is the "Exercising Vocabulary" section for "Playing in the Shadows." We have supplied possible answers so you can see how this section
works.

EXERCISING VOCABULARY

1. In paragraph 2, Wiltz creates a new word: *punditocracy*. Look up *pundit* to
   find out what this noun means. Then find out what the suffix *-cracy* means.
   What words do you already know that end in this same suffix? Apply these
   pieces of information to explain punditocracy. Why didn't Wiltz simply use
   an existing word?

   *A pundit is an expert or an authority, or somebody who makes judgments like he is
   an authority. "Cracy" on the end of a word means rule or government by whatever
   group is named in the first part of the word. For instance, democracy means rule
   (cracy) by the people (demo). So punditocracy means rule by those who are in a
   position to make judgments and be believed as experts.*

---

[12] **ESL** geeks: Overly serious people.
[13] indie: A shortened form of "independent."

2. When a writer deliberately pairs two seemingly opposite words, he or she cre-
    ates an *oxymoron*. Popular examples are "jumbo shrimp," "same difference," or
    "small crowd." In paragraph 4, Wiltz refers to the spirit in the United States
    prior to September 11 as one of "optimistic cynicism." Why are these two words
    not usually used together? What does she mean by combining them here?

    *An optimist is a person who expects the best to happen, and a cynic is someone who
    believes that people act only in their own selfish interests. These words appear to
    contradict each other. I think Wiltz means that before September 11, Americans
    realized we all are basically somewhat selfish but still hoped somehow that things
    would turn out okay in spite of it.*

3. In paragraph 35, Wiltz states, "it will be years before our culture is ready to
    deconstruct the events of September." You already know what *construct*
    means. What does it mean to deconstruct something? How can we decon-
    struct an event? What effect might that deconstruction have on our culture?

    *To deconstruct something means to take it apart, to look at the separate pieces that
    comprise it. To deconstruct an event like September 11, we would look at what actually
    happened, the causes, and the results — both immediate and long-term. Doing that
    might help us to deal with our anger and our grief, and it might help us to be better
    prepared if another national tragedy happens.*

The next set of questions is called "Probing Content," and these questions are designed to get you to examine closely what the writer is saying.
Often a second part to the question asks you to think more deeply or to
draw a conclusion. Be sure to answer all the parts of each question. You'll
remember answers to some of these questions from your first reading, but
for others you'll need to reread carefully. Here are "Probing Content"
questions for "Playing in the Shadows," with some suggested answers; of
course, you might think of equally good, but different, answers.

PROBING CONTENT

1. In paragraph 7, the author refers to popular culture as a business, and
    throughout the essay, she ties popular culture to the economy. In what
    sense is popular culture a business? How does it impact the American
    economy?

Because we the people determine what is popular and therefore what will sell, popular culture is like any other business; the consumer has some control. When people spend money to see popular movies or buy popular CDs, the economy benefits. She also calls our culture "our biggest national export," which means that other countries like to "buy American." If they didn't, there wouldn't be McDonald's in Paris, London, or Bangkok.

2. In paragraph 13, when Jack Valenti is quoted referring to one aspect of a movie as "spiritually beautiful," he isn't referring to the cinematography, the quality of the acting, or the movie's message. To what is he referring? How does he justify this attitude?

Valenti was referring to how much money the movie made. He feels that he is doing a service for the American people, allowing them to escape reality for a few hours.

3. How does Doug Raybeck distinguish between a "first order change" and a "second order change" in paragraph 22? What kind of change was September 11? What are the consequences of the kind of change September 11 brought?

First order changes take place over a period of time and may not be readily noticed as they are happening because they happen so gradually. Second order changes are big events that happen suddenly and really change things immediately, like September 11. The events of that day have made us feel less safe and more anxious about the future.

4. How did television respond to September 11? Have the terrorist attacks changed the subject matter of movies?

At first talk show hosts like Jay Leno stayed off the air; then they just avoided the subject. A few months later jokes about the Taliban and bin Laden were always part of their shows. Television dramas like Third Watch had special episodes about the attacks. Movie studios delayed releasing violent movies, but now such movies are just as popular as they were before the attacks.

While the "Probing Content" questions examine what the writer has to say about the subject, the next set of questions, "Considering Craft," encourages you to find out how the writer has packaged that information. You are asked to consider the writer's purpose, audience, language and tone, sentence structure, titles, introductions and conclusions, and organization—the very things you must consider when you write your own papers. Here are some sample "Considering Craft" questions for "Playing in the Shadows," with some possible answers.

CONSIDERING CRAFT

1. It is clear from some of the colorful language Wiltz chooses that she believes that the American public's opinion is easily swayed. Find an example and explain why she chooses that particular language. What is the message for your own writing?

   In paragraph 20, the author calls America "a nation with the attention span of a gnat." This language really gets your attention and makes you think about her meaning. Gnats are always in your face, they are annoying, but then they are gone in a second. She could have written, "Americans have a short attention span," but it wouldn't have been as interesting, and it wouldn't stay in your head like this phrase does. This means as a writer I should try to think of original ways to say things so that my readers will think about what I write and remember some especially good phrases.

2. When Wiltz makes a point, she immediately follows it up with several concrete examples to prove her assertion. Locate and comment on one such spot in this essay. What does Wiltz accomplish by using this approach?

   Wiltz states in paragraph 27 that the American people like to be comforted by continuity. Friends has been more popular than ever since the attacks, and the kinds of violent movies that studios thought people wouldn't want to go see anymore are just as popular.

3. The author begins the essay with an analogy that she returns to at the end. What is this analogy? Why does she use it? How effective is its use?

   In paragraph 2, Wiltz says trying to predict how popular culture would react to September 11 is like trying to announce who will win the Super Bowl three years from now. In the last paragraph of the essay, she restates this idea, saying that our culture is rapidly changing, and betting on its final shape is like betting on a Super Bowl game three years away. This analogy is very effective because no one would place a bet on a future Super Bowl; we don't even know who will be playing. So she is saying that anyone who is predicting the future of popular culture after 9/11 is just guessing. Using the same idea at the beginning and again at the end makes the essay seem very unified. It forms a kind of a frame around the essay.

The final section concluding each reading selection is called "Responding to the Writer." Here you are asked to react to something particular the writer has suggested. This helps you to clarify and sum up your thoughts on the topic you've been reading and thinking about. Here's a sample "Responding to the Writer" for our sample essay, with one possible response.

RESPONDING TO THE WRITER

Remember the character Odo on the science-fiction television series *Deep Space Nine*? He was a shape-shifter, an entity that could assume whatever shape he chose, anything from a human being to a bucket to a dog. Teresa Wiltz argues that our culture is shape-shifting (para. 44). Explain why you agree or disagree with her.

> *I agree with the author that our popular culture is changing all the time. You just have to listen to the radio to know that this is true — the musical groups that are popular today won't be heard tomorrow. They'll be replaced by new groups, who'll be replaced the next week by someone else. Even the kinds of music are always changing; five years ago you never heard songs in Spanish or by Spanish artists on the regular pop rock stations.*

After the paired selections in each chapter, you will find "Drawing Connections" questions that ask you to compare and contrast the strategies the authors of the paired selections use to explain their point of view on similar topics.

You'll move through the process described above for each reading selection that your instructor assigns. At the end of all the reading selections in a chapter are several additional selections about that chapter's subject called **Wrapping Up**. The next feature is called **Focusing on Yesterday, Focusing on Today**. This feature will show you two images, such as a poster and a photograph. One image is an example of popular culture from the past; the other image is an example of popular culture today that reflects some aspect of the chapter's subject. The accompanying questions will ask you to think and write about how these two images compare and contrast to one another.

Finally, at the end of each chapter are two types of writing suggestions for developing your own essays. Some of these writing prompts are called **Reflecting on the Writing**. They ask you to link selections within the chapter just completed and also selections from various chapters within the text as you develop your essay response. The final set of writing suggestions is called **Connecting to the Culture**. These writing prompts encourage you to use your own experiences and observations to express your ideas about some aspect of the chapter's topic.

Now it's time to apply the ideas you have been developing while you were reading and answering questions. It's time to write about all the things *you* have to say.

Writing with a Difference

Getting into Writing

Writing is often not easy. There are probably a few hundred people for whom writing is as easy as golf is for Tiger Woods. For most of us, though, writing is hard work. Like skillful golf shots, good writing takes practice.

For some of us, the hardest part is just getting started. There is something about blank sheets of paper or computer screens that is downright intimidating. So the first and most important thing is to put something on that paper or screen. If it loosens up your writing hand to doodle in the margins first, then doodle. But eventually (and sometime before 3 A.M. the day the paper is due), it's a good idea to get moving in the right direction.

If your creative juices are a little slow to flow, try *brainstorming*. This simply means that you commit to paper whatever ideas related to your topic pop into your head. You don't evaluate them—you just get them down on paper. You don't organize them or reflect on them or worry about spelling them correctly; you just write them down. There are several popular ways to brainstorm. Lots of people like to do *outlines*, with or without the proper Roman numerals. This method lets you list ideas vertically. Writers who think less in straight lines may want to try *clustering*, also called *webbing*. This is a lot like doodling with intent. Write your subject in the center of your blank page and circle it. Then draw lines radiating out from the center, and at the end of each line write some other words related to your subject. Each of these spokes can have words radiating from it, too. Let's return to our sample essay, "Playing in the Shadows." If a student were brainstorming to write an essay about September 11's impact on popular culture, one web might look like the one found on page 17.

Planning Purpose, Audience, and Attitude

Before trying to impose any kind of structure or judgment on all her random bursts of thought, a good writer has to consider several important things: (1) Why am I writing this paper? (2) For whom am I writing this paper? (3) What is my own attitude about this subject? How much do I want this attitude reflected in the tone of my paper?

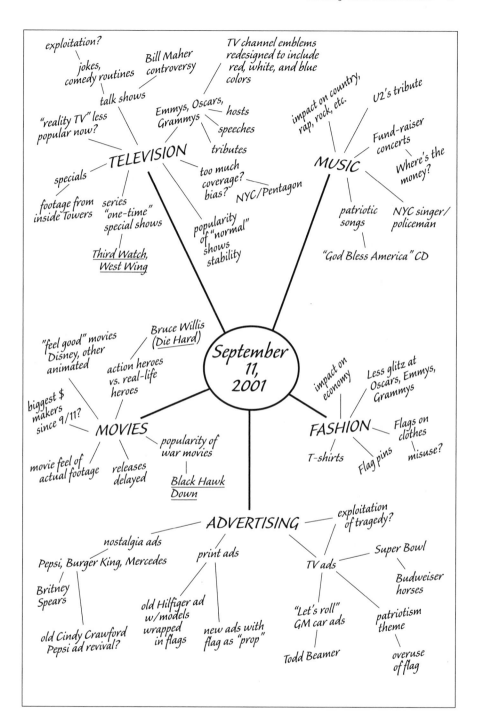

Let's think about your purpose for writing a paper. You think, "I am writing this because I am in this composition class, and the professor said to write a paper." Okay, true, but there's more to purpose than that. Are you hoping to entertain your audience? Inform them? Persuade them to take some action or change an opinion? Your answers to these questions determine how you approach your subject and develop your paper.

Something else that determines how you approach your writing is the intended audience. Who are they? How old are they? What are their interests? What do they already know about your topic, and what will you need to explain? Why should this group of people care about your topic? What attitudes do they already hold about this issue? The language you choose is affected by the audience that you expect to reach. An essay about rap music written for your peers won't need all the explanations that the same essay would need if written for forty-somethings.

Once you have determined your purpose and your audience, you are ready to determine what the tone of your essay will be. What is your own attitude toward your subject? To what extent should your writing reflect this attitude if you are to best achieve the purpose you have established for the particular audience you have identified? Do you want to be completely serious about your subject? Will injecting some humor make your audience more receptive? How formal or informal should the language of the essay be?

Hooking the Reader

Once you have some ideas and some sense of your purpose and audience, the next step is to write a draft. How do you start? Some order has to be made of this potentially useful chaos. Good essays begin with good introductions, so we'll talk about that first. But remember: The introduction doesn't have to be written at this point. Some very good authors write the whole essay and then write the introduction last. That's fine. The introduction has to be at the beginning eventually, but no law says it has to be there in the draft. Too many good essays remain locked in the creators' heads because their writers couldn't think up an introduction and so never started at all.

At whatever point you are ready to write your introduction, keep in mind one essential thing: If you don't get your audience's attention right away, you lose them. Students who are assigned to read your paper for peer editing will keep reading, and the professor who gets paid to read it will, but it's highly unlikely that any other reader will be receptive to your viewpoint and your ideas if that reader isn't involved, or hooked. Advertisers figure they have a precious few seconds to hook you as a potential customer, so they pull out all the stops to grab your attention before you flip that page in the magazine or punch that remote control. Gloria Borger, author of one of the essays in Chapter 3, sums it up: "Getting hooked early is what it's about." Likewise, as a writer, you have to pull out all the stops to hook your readers. What really nails a reader's attention? Of course, this depends on the reader, but some tried and true methods work on many readers:

1. First, you might start with a very brief story, also called an *anecdote*. We all love human interest and personal narrative. The reader must be made to want more information, to want answers, to have a real desire to know what else you'll say.

2. Interesting quotations make good openings, especially if they are somewhat startling or are attributed to someone famous. Statistics can be useful if they are really amazing. (As quotations, though, dictionary definitions are very difficult to use effectively as introductions.)

3. A thought-provoking or controversial question might be a good way to get a reader's attention.

Identifying a Thesis

Besides catching your reader's attention, your introduction may perform another important task: The introduction may house your *thesis statement.* This quick but thorough statement of the main point of the paper may be the first or last sentence of the first paragraph, but it could also be the last sentence of the essay. Where the thesis is located depends on your purpose for writing, your audience, and the effect you wish to create. If you begin with one of the attention-getters we've mentioned, you'll want to follow up your quotation or brief narrative with a few general statements about your topic, gradually narrowing the focus until you reach your specific thesis, possibly at the end of the first or second paragraph. If you have identified your audience as receptive to your attitude about your subject, then you may choose to state the thesis early in your paper and follow with supporting points that will have your readers nodding in agreement. However, if your purpose is to persuade a not-so-like-minded audience, then you will want to offer convincing proof first, offering your thesis later in the paper when a reader has already begun to agree with your opinion.

Wherever it occurs, a good thesis can go a long way toward making your essay effective. How do you recognize or create a good thesis statement? First, a good thesis is not simply a fact. Facts don't allow for a lot of fascinating development; they just are. A good thesis should be something about which more than one valid opinion exists. Next, your thesis must be focused. There's a difference between a subject and a thesis. A subject or topic is what the essay is about—for example, Barbie dolls. A thesis statement expresses the author's attitude about that subject: "Barbie dolls are an expression of society's misguided and demoralizing view of ideal womanhood," or "Barbie dolls are a positive influence on young girls because they indicate the wide variety of career choices available to women today." Everything in your essay must clearly relate to the development of this thesis or main idea.

Supporting the Thesis

The development of your thesis forms the body of your paper. The major points you wish to make about your thesis become the *topic sentences,* or one-sentence summaries, for various paragraphs. What information do you use for support? Where do you find this information? How much support is enough, and how much is too much?

It's important to recognize that all the support anyone can apply to any idea fits into one of two categories: The information is gathered either from personal experience or from a source outside the self. Personal experience knowledge is obviously whatever the writer has gathered through eyewitness encounters in which he has participated directly and personally. Outside source knowledge explains how we know everything else we know. Such outside source knowledge is often informal; we know that it would be painful to fall down a flight of stairs even though we've never had such an experience and never looked in a medical book to see which body parts would likely be damaged.

However, such outside source knowledge may also be formal and deliberately sought, as when we look up the salaries of professional athletes in *Sports Illustrated* or schedule an interview with the football coach to talk about whether college athletes should be paid. In your writing, you may often find it helpful to refer to ideas expressed in the essays in this text. In any case, you must avoid intellectual theft, called *plagiarism,* by carefully citing the source of the material you are using and by putting quotation marks around any wording taken directly from someone else, whether expressed in a few words or a few sentences or in written or oral form. There are several different methods of acknowledging sources; your instructor will let you know which method to use. In the appendix of this book, you'll find a section called "Evaluating Sources" to help you determine the validity of sources and how to document them correctly.

Organizing the Content

There are a number of different ways to arrange support material; the one that is best for your essay depends, once again, on your purpose and your audience. Some essays offer the most forceful point of support at once on the first page, and some other essays start softly and work up to a big crescendo of convincing examples or argument near the end. You might try sketching out your pieces of support in various arrangements on a sheet of paper to see which order feels most comfortable, but rest assured that there is rarely only one arrangement that will work. You are looking for whatever organization moves your thesis along best and seems most natural to you.

Connecting the Pieces

The best supporting information in the world won't move your thesis forward if the parts of the paper aren't unified so that your reader can follow your train of thought. Think of the paragraphs of your essay as links in a chain: Each link must be equally strong, no link can be open-ended, and each one must be connected to the link above and the link beneath. This connection comes from providing strong transitional words or phrases to smoothly carry the thesis idea and the reader from one topic sentence and one paragraph to the next one. Appropriate use of words like *however, nevertheless, furthermore, consequently,* and *in addition* facilitate this transition process. Another effective transition is to repeat a key word or brief phrase from the previous paragraph's last sentence in the first sentence of the new paragraph. Try to avoid the too-frequent use of very simple and obvious transitions like *first, next,* and *finally;* too many simple transitions may make your ideas seem simplistic.

Arriving at a Conclusion

Before you know it, you're ready to arrive at your conclusion. The most important rule about conclusions is to make sure there is one. Do not simply repeat something you have already said; this may lead your readers to believe that you hold their intelligence in very low esteem. However, it is a good idea not to forget that your reader best retains whatever she reads last. This means the conclusion is your chance to make sure some points you've raised really stick. Therefore, make sure that your main idea, your thesis, is central to your concluding paragraph. See how you stated the thesis earlier and word it a little differently. Some of the same advice that we discussed about introductions applies here: End on a memorable note. Make your essay the one the instructor is still pondering on the ride home.

Titling the Paper and Other Final Steps

If you haven't titled your paper already, you'll want to add a title now. A good title is not just a statement of the subject; it sheds light on what aspects of the subject are covered and how the subject is approached. Like an introduction, a good title also catches a reader's interest. Titles usually are not complete sentences.

Take time to present your paper well. You've spent quite a bit of time on the ideas; don't minimize the effect with sloppy margins, inaccurate page numbers, and other unusual printer misdeeds. Remember that your peers and your instructor are evaluating what you have produced, not your intentions.

Revising the Paper

After all this work, surely the paper is ready for the instructor. Not yet. What you have now is a first draft—a fairly complete first draft, admittedly, but still a first draft. You may think it's only the not-so-good writers who go through numerous drafts, but you'd be wrong: Good writers write and rewrite and revise and rewrite. Grammar and spelling errors that seem inconsequential by themselves may cause your reader to lose the train of ideas you have carefully prepared for the reader to follow. Thankfully, there is a logical pattern to the revising part of the writing process, too.

Start with the big things. It's tempting to spell check as the first revision step because that's easy and concrete, but that's a mistake for two reasons: (1) spell checking isn't revising, it's editing; and (2) you may decide to delete two of the paragraphs you just spent time spell checking. Ask yourself some hard questions. Does each paragraph contribute to the development of your thesis? If you find a paragraph that doesn't fit under that thesis umbrella, you have only two options: delete the paragraph or rewrite the thesis statement to make it wide enough to accommodate the additional material. Given your audience, are the degree of explanation and the level of language appropriate? Does each support paragraph carry its own weight, or do some of them seem skimpy and underdeveloped? Does your essay accomplish the purpose you established?

Read the last sentence of each paragraph followed directly by the first sentence of the next paragraph. Are your transitions smooth enough? Your reader should get a sense of moving up an escalator, not a sense of being bounced down a staircase, landing with a thud on each topic sentence.

Editing the Paper

Now you are ready to do some editing. Look at the sentences within each paragraph. Are there fragments masquerading as sentences? Are there incomplete thoughts? This is a good time to find a quiet spot and read your essay aloud. Once two senses are involved, you have twice as much opportunity to find something that's not just right yet. It's fine to run the spell checker at this stage, but remember, if your problem is with usage, like using *to* when you mean *too*, the spell checker cannot help you. It's best to keep a dictionary ready and be your own spell checker. Keep a grammar handbook handy to consult when you are unsure about matters like usage, punctuation, and sentence structure. And remember that your college or university probably has a tutoring or writing center where you can get help with revising and editing.

Peer Editing

Once you have completed your own initial revising and editing, your instructor may suggest that your class practice peer editing. No matter how good a writer you are, having someone else take a fresh look can be very beneficial. Here are some general suggestions for specific things to evaluate when you edit a classmate's paper.

1. Read only the first paragraph and stop reading. How interested are you in continuing to read? What about the introduction grabs your

attention? If you wouldn't be the least bit disappointed if someone took this paper away from you right now, your classmate needs a better introduction. What can you suggest?

2. Continue reading through the first page of the paper. Write down the essay's subject; then write down the main idea. If you can't find the thesis, make a note of that. If you are unsure of the thesis, write down what you think it might be. Take a minute now to check with the author. If you have identified the thesis correctly, that's fine. If you have identified the wrong message as the thesis, help the author clarify the main idea before you continue reading.

3. Continue reading. Is support for the thesis adequate? Are the examples specific enough? Detailed enough? Frequent enough? Is the thesis supported to your satisfaction?

4. What is the writer's attitude toward his subject? To what extent is the tone appropriate for the audience? Does the tone advance the writer's purpose or detract from it? When are changes in tone used appropriately or inappropriately?

5. Are there adequate transitions between sentences and paragraphs? Remember, this should feel like an escalator ride. What does the writer do to make sure ideas flow smoothly throughout the paper? Can you easily follow the forward progression of the author's train of thought?

6. Complete your reading of the essay. What about the final paragraph makes you feel a sense of completion? Is the essay finished, or does it just stop? How effective is the conclusion? What is memorable about it? What would make it stronger?

7. Review the paper now for mistakes in spelling or usage. Make a note of repetitive mistakes and comment on how awkward points of grammar are handled; don't attempt to note each error. Be especially alert for the kinds of errors that really disrupt the flow of a paper like fragments, run-ons, comma splices, or sentences that don't make sense.

8. Return the paper to its author and discuss your notes. Leave your notes with the author to be referred to as he does additional revising and editing. Evaluate the input you have received about your own paper. Resist the urge to be defensive; you are not obligated to make every change suggested, but you will want to honestly evaluate the comments and use those that seem justified to improve your work.

Gaining from the Effort

Writing is like almost anything else: The more you practice, the better you get. We've said the same thing about reading earlier: People who read often and actively read well. The same is true of writing. For some people, writing is fun. For other people, writing is anything but. In either case, good writing is hard work. But perhaps no other skill except speech says so much to others about who you are and has so much to do with how far and how fast you can travel up a career ladder. Writing is not just a college skill; writing is a life skill. Your willingness to better your writing ability is directly related to the impression you create, the salary you can expect to earn, and the level of advancement in life you can expect to attain.

Forget the five-paragraph boxes your writing may have been restricted to before now. Remember that formulas work well in math but just cramp your style in writing. Swear off procrastination and karate chop writer's block. There are no topics in this text that you don't already know something about. You have significant things to say. Start writing them down.

A Sample Student Essay

Here is a draft of a student essay written in response to a writing prompt associated with Teresa Wiltz's "Playing in the Shadows." Keep in mind that all the writing prompts can be approached from a number of different perspectives; this example reflects one student's decisions about purpose, audience, tone, and writing style.

CONNECTING TO THE CULTURE

Choose one medium—advertising, movies, magazines, television, or music—and examine how and why the events of September 11 have impacted this medium. Be sure to follow Wiltz's model and use specific examples to support your ideas. Based on your examples, predict how long and to what extent this influence will continue to be felt, seen, or heard.

Lauren M. Brackbill
Safety in Sales: Advertising after September 11th

It seems virtually impossible to turn on the television today or even flip through the pages of a magazine without encountering some information about what is weighing on the mind of almost every American: Sex. No, not anymore. "September 11th," "patriotism," "terrorism"-- these have become our society's new buzzwords. If it is newsworthy, it most likely involves one or more of these terms. The changes can certainly be felt in the content of the messages sent out by networks and newspapers, but they cannot be seen as obviously in the more idealized facets of popular culture: sitcoms, music, and advertising. The events of September 11th have altered the way many Americans live daily, but for the most part, they have not changed the strategies and appeals used by advertisers to persuade the consumers of our nation. It seems that, if anything, it is our perceptions of these values-- love, acceptance, security, and family-- that have been distorted.

There have been a handful of standout advertisements that have made direct statements about the events of that fateful day, but the general consensus from advertisers and companies seems to be that that is sacred ground. Of the few companies that have dared to cross that line between pre- and post-September 11th, even fewer have done so tastefully. While thousands of companies have donated time, energy, and money to helping the country recover from this disaster, others have decided to take this as an opportunity to cash in on the desire of every citizen to contribute to the cause. Echoing the words of hijacked passenger Todd Beamer, the "Keep America Rolling" campaign, launched by General Motors following the attacks, was met with some criticism. The American public is strongly opposed to anything that is even remotely close to profiting from this tragedy. Even the very respectful advertisement aired only once during the Super Bowl by the Anheuser-Busch company featuring the popular Clydesdale horses silently bowing before the broken cityscape was felt to be on the borderline of exploitation. If a message as intricate and heartfelt as that ad's could be seen as a risk, then it is clear why so few dared to walk that path.

Advertisers are using the same appeals to human needs for humor, sex, and affiliation that have been successful in the past to avoid having their ads be seen as exploiting the events or the victims of September 11th. While Wiltz predicts a shift in popular culture in the future to softer images that are more geared towards "positivity" and "hope" (more buzzwords), the same ads found for Calvin Klein's Eternity cologne that were spread throughout magazines on September 10th can still be found today, over six months later. Even though these messages are timeless and inoffensive, they are meant to sell the ideals of sex and love to a society that has always been interested in these values. If these advertisements had changed to a loving couple draped in the red, white, and blue of the American flag, rather than the classic black and white photos, people would notice and would, perhaps, have mixed feelings about that.

While it may seem that there are more advertisements today focusing on family values, nurturing, and security, these strategies are nothing new. It may be difficult to think of life before that day, but these values existed then as well. For example, in selling baby shampoo, the Johnson and Johnson company will always use adorable infants laughing and smiling to trigger parents' need to love and nurture their children. This strategy was successful prior to 9/11 and it seems that, although Johnson and Johnson has not changed to adapt to the changing times, the events of that day will only assure the success of the campaign in the future. Long before September 11th, MasterCard was airing a series of commercials that echoed the term "priceless." While the wholesome idea that "there are some things money can't buy" may be more of a reality to our now humble nation, the commercials were not adapted to suit the changing times. It seems that our harsh reality has forced us to view the world and our culture as we never have before -- a view that makes softer messages and images of families and happiness more important to us and, therefore, more noticeable.

It is obvious that these events have permanently changed our nation, but the advertisements themselves and the appeals targeted by them have not changed. For the most part, it is our perceptions of the ads that have been altered. We have become more aware of our forgotten values: love, nurturing, security, and belonging. As for blatant advertisements with direct messages about September 11th, it seems that, by this point, there are enough opportunities to remember that day: The lasting effects can be seen nearly everywhere else. The nation may find the static qualities of these familiar advertisements comforting; not everything is changing.

Deconstructing Media

We are a visual culture. Our vision is our primary way of receiving information from the world around us. Countless images brush past our eyes every day, yet we really pay attention to only a couple of them. There is so much to see that we filter out what we don't need or what doesn't grab our attention. Movie posters try to convince us to see a summertime blockbuster, magazine ads try to lure us into buying a particular product, and artists and photographers try to get us to feel a certain emotion, while billboards demand our attention no matter where we turn. All visual media compete to send us their messages. Choices we make, things we buy, even how we see and perceive ourselves are all affected by the images that are presented to us. You'll discover as you work through this book that American popular culture relies heavily on visual representation; even music is represented visually through the use of music videos. In this text you will see a number of images like those you encounter every day—advertisements, photographs, movie stills, comic strips, and cartoons. Learning to "read" these images and discovering what responses they are intended to provoke is an important part of understanding our culture.

The Message of Media

Let's picture an imaginary advertisement. The woman is beautiful and graceful. The man appears wealthy and sophisticated. The white sand beach is wide and private; the sparkling blue water looks cool and clear; tropical sunshine embraces the scene. The car in the foreground is a gold-colored luxury convertible. But why aren't the car's tires getting mired in the sand? Why aren't the woman's white shoulders sunburning? In reality, these might be issues you or I would have to think about, but this image has nothing to do with reality. This is advertising—that shadow world that separates us from our money by luring us into popular mythology.

What mythology? Here's how it goes: Unpopular? Popularity is as easy as changing the brand of jeans you wear. Unsuccessful? You must drive the wrong kind of car. Unattractive? Just get a new shade of lipstick. Misunderstood? It's not your personality; it's your poor cellular service.

We are in general a well-educated society. Why, then, are we so easily misled? Why do we buy the myths that advertising sells? We buy—and buy and buy and buy—because we desperately want the myths of advertising to be true.

For some time now, our culture has been as visual as we are verbal. We absorb images faster than our brains can process data, but the images remain imprinted in our minds. All those images influence our thoughts and the decisions we make in ways we may never have considered. From the time we begin to learn to read, we are encouraged to recognize the power of words—to interact with text, to weigh it for prejudice, to appreciate with discernment. But images are as powerful as words, and they communicate ideas and impressions we, as thinking individuals, should *question,* just as we question what we are told or what we read. How can the same skills we use to read be applied to "reading" images like billboards, photographs, political cartoons, drawings and paintings, and images on television, movie, and computer screens?

Asking the Right Questions

Effectively deconstructing media images involves taking those images apart and asking the right questions.

1. What do I see when I look at the image?

    How is color used?

    What is the significance of the layout?

    What are the relative sizes of the objects that compose the image?
2. What is the role of text (language)?
3. Where did I first see this image?
4. Who is the target audience?
5. What is the purpose of this image?
6. What is the message?

The easiest questions help solve the mystery of the more difficult ones, so let's think about the obvious. What do you see when you look at the photo, the ad, or the comic strip?

Taking It Apart

COLOR

Although none of the images you will see in this textbook are in color, most of the media representations you see around you make careful use of color. Is the eye drawn to a certain spot on the page by the strength of a color, by the contrast of colors, or by the absence of color? How is color being used to capture your eye and keep it on a certain part of the visual?

LAYOUT

Closely related to the use of color is the layout of the objects on the page. What relationships are established by the nearness of or distance between objects or people? What is your eye drawn to first because of its position? Sometimes the focal point will be right in the center of the ad or photo and therefore obvious. At other times, the object the composer of the image most wants you to appreciate, the one that is central to the image's message, may be easily overlooked by the casual glance. Because English is read from top to bottom and left to right, we tend to look first to the upper left-hand corner of a page. That spot is often used to locate the composer's focal point. At other times the eye may come to rest at the bottom right-hand corner of a page. Look at the Secret deodorant advertisement that opens Chapter 2 to see how this visual strategy works. To what point on the page is your eye drawn?

SIZE

The relative size of the people and objects in an image may also help its designer communicate his or her message. Our eye may be drawn to the largest object first, but that may not be where the message lies. To help you see how relative size of objects can communicate a strong message, look at the photograph titled "To Have and To Hold" at the end of Chapter 2.

TEXT

Deciding whether to include text with an image is another significant consideration for the photographer, artist, or ad designer. Sometimes the image may be so powerful on its own that text would be an irritating distraction. Think about the photograph of the Marines raising the flag on Iwo Jima or the shot of the three firefighters raising the flag at Ground Zero. These images speak for themselves. When text is included, other factors have to be examined. How much text is there? Where is it located? How big is the type? Is more than one font used? Does the text actually deliver the message? Does it enhance the message? Is part of the text a familiar slogan associated with the product (Burger King's "Have it your way," for example)? Is a well-known and easily recognized logo or symbol (like the Nike swoosh) part of the text? All of these considerations hinge upon the centrality of the text to the overall message of the image.

LOCATION

To properly evaluate an image, the reader must know where the image appeared. Did you see this image on a billboard? On the side of a bus? In the pages of a magazine? Images in *People* magazine may have a different purpose than those in *National Geographic*. This information will help determine the target audience.

TARGET AUDIENCE

For whom is this image intended? What are the characteristics of this target audience of viewers? What is the age range? What is their socioeconomic status? What work do they do? Where and how do they live? All this information must be taken into account by the photographer, artist, or designer if the image is to convey its intended message. For example, an ad for baby formula would most likely not hit its target audience if it were placed in *Spin* or *Rolling Stone*.

PURPOSE

Every image has a purpose. If the image is an advertisement, whether it appears on a billboard, on a Web site, or in a magazine, the most obvious question to ask is "What is this ad for?" In today's ads, the answer isn't always readily apparent. The actual object being sold may be a tiny speck on the page or may be completely absent. In the imaginary ad we invented earlier, the product might be the woman's alluring sundress, the man's starched khakis and sports shirt, or the convertible. Or maybe it's an ad for some exotic vacation spot. If the image is a photograph, its purpose may be to commemorate a special moment, object, or person or to illustrate an event or feeling. If the image is a cartoon, its purpose may be simply to entertain, or it may be designed to mask a political or social statement with humor.

MESSAGE

"What is the purpose of this image?" may be the most obvious question, but it isn't the most important one. The most important question is "What is the message of this image?"—and that's a very different question. That question challenges the viewer to probe beyond the obvious visual effects—color, shading, size of objects, text or lack of it, and relative placement of objects—to ferret out the message. This message always seeks to evoke a response from the viewer: wear this, drink this, click here, think this way, feel this emotion, affirm this value. Using all the information you have assembled by answering the earlier questions, answer this one.

Now you are prepared to decode or "read" the images that form such a large part of our popular culture.

Reading Images

Let's practice with two very different types of images: a photograph and a comic strip.

Look at the following image and consider some questions regarding the photograph. What do you see when you look at this image?

How is color used?   The colors in the original photograph not only help to highlight the photographer's choice of focal point but also work to help the viewer "read" the image. The mother's hair and sundress are very black, and there is an interesting and unexplained dark shadow across her back; this shadow is visible even in the black and white copy you see here. The baby's outfit is blue, and the liner for the baby seat is brightly patterned in red, yellow, blue, and green. All this color makes the baby the bright spot, more alive than anything else on the page. The sky is blue but marred by gray billowing smoke concentrated on the right side of the photograph. The cityscape in the background is a dreary gray. A red brick wall fills the extreme right side.

What is the significance of the layout?   Think about the layout and composition of this photograph. The mother and baby are the immediate focal point; the vast empty space behind them helps to call attention to them. The warm, nurturing appearance of the mother is in stark contrast to the barren concrete, metal, and brick of the rooftop. The smoky blur across the river seems very remote from the focal scene.

What is the relative size of the objects that compose the image?   The distant skyscrapers appear small, while the mother and baby, both in the foreground and therefore larger than anything else, are much more prominent. The large brick wall segment visible on the right appears to loom over the scene on the roof.

What is the role of text?   This photograph originally appeared in a magazine and was accompanied by this quotation from a minister: "We can't pass on a sense of hopelessness to generations to come." Underneath the quotation was a caption that read: "A mother comforts her child on a Brooklyn rooftop Sept. 11 as Manhattan burns in the distance." This caption reinforced the message of the quotation and both certainly supported the photograph's theme. However, at least in one regard, the visual is more powerful without any language; the text, which was located in the upper left corner, drew the viewer's eye away from the focal point of the mother and child.

What was the original location of the image?   This photograph appeared in *Time* magazine, a publication that over the years has been noted for publishing photographs that capture significant historical events.

Who is the target audience?   *Time* appeals to a wide and diverse audience, as does this photograph, since parenthood and coping with difficult events are integral facets of everyone's culture. It's a photograph for everyone who was touched by September 11 and for everyone who has been touched by war and tragic circumstances.

What is the purpose of this image?   Obviously this photograph commemorates a never-to-be-forgotten day in American history, an event that has impacted all aspects of our culture. Its intent is to make every viewer remember.

What is the message?   We know what we see when we look at this photograph, but what is it really about? What does it say? It is certainly thought-provoking, juxtaposing birth and death, new life with chaos and destruction. Atrocities smolder, but human life endures, and the photograph seems to ask us to remember hope, life, and the things that matter, as the quotation notes. The photograph asks us to consider two very different situations and to unify them. As we look at this photograph, we may feel a sense of comfort, even as the baby is comforted by its mother.

Now see the image at the bottom of this page. To conclude our introduction to this new type of reading, let's work on deconstructing a very different type of visual representation: a comic strip. What do you see when you look at this image?

With a comic strip, the viewer must allow his eyes to travel left to right across the panels, focusing on a number of frames, each of which may offer a visual, a text, or both. Often the strip's creator relies on a steady group of repeat readers who have learned to appreciate the personalities of the strip's characters and the subtle messages they deliver from the writer.

How is color used?   Although most strips appear in black and white in daily newspapers, many appear in color on Sundays, giving us a chance to learn more about the characters and the strip's designer. This Mallard Fillmore strip appeared in a Sunday newspaper with minimal but highly effective colorization. Against a light blue background, the duck is green with a yellow bill. The Sprite can is a lighter shade of green; we know it's a Sprite can only because Mallard says so. The human finger is peach-colored.

What is the significance of the layout?   To some extent, the layout of a cartoon strip is prescribed: It will be a series of panels. But this doesn't mean that the artist doesn't have a great deal of flexibility with layout within the various panels. The most interesting feature in this layout is the shifting view we have of Mallard the duck. At first we see his face, but he turns when addressed by the finger, and by the middle of the strip, he has his back to us, so that we viewers are made to feel outside the conversation, as though we are merely overhearing. By the last panel, Mallard has turned back to face the readers, making us a part of the scam he's pulling.

What is the relative size of objects that compose the image?   It's certainly no accident that the clearly recognizable "invisible finger of marketing" is every bit as large as Mallard's head in every panel except the final one, when Mallard has taken control of the situation. From time to time, as consumers, we may feel "under the thumb" of advertising; this comic strip offers a very graphic rendering of that concept.

What is the role of text?   As in many comic strips, the text here is the message. Generally, comic strips rely much more on text than ads or photographs do. The first significant language issue here arises in the title of the strip. Mallard Fillmore's name is a play on the name of an American president, Millard Fillmore, whose term of office reflected his own rather lackluster personality. A mallard is actually, of course, one type of duck. We'll pursue the rest of the text when we examine the message of the strip.

What was the original location of this image?   This comic strip is syndicated and appears regularly in many newspapers across the United States.

Who is the target audience?   The target audience is not children; although the character of the duck might catch their eye, the level of sophistication of the humor clearly places this strip beyond their interest. And certainly there is a degree of sophistication required to grasp the irony here. The reader needs to know something about popular culture—what's a Sprite? What are Nikes? Lugz? What's hip-hop? What's an icon? Knowing that the government has at times actually paid farmers not to grow certain crops (such as soybeans) in order not to flood the market and drive prices down explains the fifth panel. Bruce Tinsley, the strip's writer, is obviously not expecting everyone to agree with his take on advertising.

What is the purpose of this image?   Because this is a comic strip, we expect it to be entertaining or humorous. To determine if that is its only purpose, let's think about the message.

What is the message?   So what is Tinsley trying to say? Here is an ordinary duck, who might as well be either you or me, attempting to drink a popular beverage with a powerful marketing firm behind it. According to the finger of advertising, the entire ad campaign designed to elevate Sprite to a new level of "cool" could be devastated if Sprite were to be associated with this quite ordinary duck. The duck, however, represents the consumer, and he's not as dumb as he looks. He asks to be paid not to harm Sprite's fledgling coolness—he wants to be paid not to drink it. But what does he plan to do with the cash? He plans to buy Nikes or Lugz, thus succumbing to the lure of advertising. What a cycle! What a message: Manufacturers pay advertisers to create an image for a product, and that image is all-important, because it's often that image alone, not the product, that fuels our wants and loosens our wallets.

You'll have a chance to practice your media decoding skills throughout this text, from the images at the beginning of each chapter to paired images from the past and the present that bring each chapter to a close. Remember to ask yourself the questions we've identified. Look closely—and then look beyond what's on the page to see what's really being communicated.

Gearing Up to Read Images

Locate an ad, photograph, or comic strip that really appeals to you. Write a brief paragraph stating your initial reaction to the image. Then decode the image by applying the questions identified throughout this discussion. How did your initial impressions change after a careful study of the image?

Collaborating

Working with two or three other students, locate an image that communicates a significant message. Then plan and deliver a presentation to your classmates in which you decode the image you have selected.

Working in a small group, assemble a collection of various types of magazines: music, home and garden, news, sports, fashion, and so on. Cut out interesting images from each magazine and note where each image came from. Prepare to discuss the reasons why each image was placed in the particular publication from which it originated.

CHAPTER 2

Mars and Venus
How Culture Shapes Gender Identity

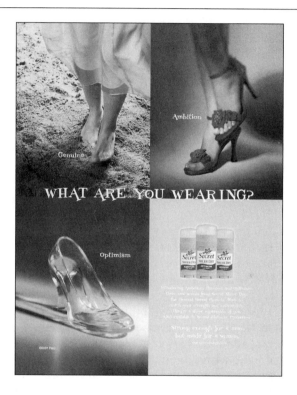

The words "Strong enough for a man, but made for a woman" have become famous in the advertising industry. In a recent ad campaign to launch the new Secret signature scents *Genuine, Ambition,* and *Optimism,* the familiar phrase is accompanied by the question "What are you wearing?"

- Why do the advertisers ask this question?
- Why are women's feet and shoes featured so prominently in an ad for deodorant?
- How do the words *Genuine, Ambition,* and *Optimism* relate to their respective visuals in the four different parts of this ad?
- What message about women's feelings and desires are we to take away from this ad?

Research this topic with TopLinks at www.bedfordstmartins.com/toplinks.

GEARING UP

One assumption in the study of popular culture is that each of us is constantly influenced by the cultural forces around us—objects, people,
events, and places. These influences begin with our home environment and,
as we grow older, move outward to such things as school, friends, books,
music, and television. As we are exposed to them, these influences help to
shape our sense of who we are, allowing us to develop a sense of cultural
identity, how we are both alike and different from others in our society.
Our gender identity—what it means to be male or female at this time in
this society—is a significant part of this cultural identity.

Make a list of some of the influences from your childhood and teenage
years that have taught you about who you are. Which have had the greatest influence on your image of yourself? Why was the force of these influences so powerful? How have you learned what our society expects of men
and women? Why do you think the expectations that go along with being
male or female may change over time? How have these expectations
changed from your grandparents' generation to yours?

From the time that we are first aware of our surroundings, many forces
play a part in defining our identity and creating our self-image: family,
peers, teachers, the media, and even the toys we like best. Although we are
generally unaware of these forces and spend little or no time thinking
about them, they are an important influence on our concept of ourselves.
An evaluation of their significance greatly enhances not only our understanding of ourselves but also our ability to mature in our relationships
with other people.

We often think about culture as something external—something outside us that goes on without our knowledge, permission, or concern.
However, we are each very much a part of the culture we live in. Even as
the popular culture around us is influencing us, we are influencing the direction in which that culture moves by making choices about what to buy,
which CDs to listen to, and which trends to follow.

One of the most significant factors in our developing self-awareness is
our realization of gender. Very young children recognize that boys and
girls are different, but these children learn only over time what difference
this difference makes. What does it mean to be a man or a woman in
today's society? In spite of legislation and our enthusiasm for equality, is
there still one set of rules for men and another for women? What factors
establish these unwritten rules? Who defines the gender roles we are each
expected to fulfill, and what standards measure how well each of us is succeeding? Just how much effect does our gender identity have on our vision
of our real and our ideal selves? How much does gender affect who we
can become and what we can accomplish? What happens when our care-

fully crafted personal self-image confronts, conflicts with, and sometimes collides head-on with the gender-based expectations of the larger society we live in?

The essays in this chapter are written by authors who differ in age, background, and perspective. The authors reveal their individual struggles to come to terms with our culture's view of gender-based privileges and responsibilities. Through their struggles and revelations, you'll learn more about your own continually developing self and the greater world that you influence and that influences you.

COLLABORATING

In small groups of four to six students, make a list of the major cultural influences on a child's or adolescent's developing gender identity and self-image. Consider such factors as toys, music, movies and television, advertising, families and friends, school and teachers, heroes and role models, and whatever else you can list. When your list is complete, choose the five influences that your group believes are the most significant for the largest number of people. Meet with other groups to discuss the similarities and differences in your lists.

The *"Fragile American Girl"* Myth

Christina Hoff Sommers

"It is simply irresponsible to argue that American women, as a gender, are worse off than American men," Christina Hoff Sommers asserts in the following selection adapted from remarks she delivered in December 1996 at the American Enterprise Institute Conference. Where does the notion come from that American women should be counted among this country's disadvantaged minorities? Sommers, author of the controversial 1994 book *Who Stole Feminism?: How Women Have Betrayed Women* and *The War Against Boys* (2000) has a definite answer. A contributor to such diverse periodicals as the *New Republic*, the *Wall Street Journal*, and the *New England Journal of Medicine*, Sommers is an associate professor of philosophy at Clark University. Her field is contemporary moral theory, and she has compiled two textbooks of readings on ethics.

THINKING AHEAD

Some people argue that in spite of the women's movement, American women still have fewer privileges, make lower salaries, have fewer opportunities in sports, and generally must work harder to achieve the same recognition as American men. Using examples from your own experience or the experiences of others, explain why you think such discrimination is real or imagined.

INCREASING VOCABULARY

statute (n.) (1)

redress (n.) (1)

demoralized (v.) (1)

epitomizes (v.) (4)

fixated (v.) (9)

deficits (n.) (12)

mendacious (adj.) (14)

D id you know that the United States Congress now categorizes 1
American girls as "a historical under-served population"? In a recent education statute, girls are classified with African Americans, Native Americans, the physically handicapped, and other disadvantaged minorities as a group in need of special redress. Programs to help girls who have allegedly been silenced and demoralized in the nation's sexist classrooms are now receiving millions of federal dollars. At the United Nations women's conference in Beijing, the alleged silencing and short-changing of American schoolgirls was treated as a pressing human rights issue.

Several popular books have appeared in recent years to build up the 2 notion that ours is a "girl-poisoning culture." That phrase is Dr. Mary Pipher's and her book, *Reviving Ophelia:*[1] *Saving the Selves of Adolescent Girls,* has been at the top of the *New York Times* best-seller list. According to Pipher, "Something dramatic happens to girls in early adolescence. Just as planes and ships disappear mysteriously into the Bermuda Triangle,[2] so do the selves of girls go down in droves. They crash and burn."

Where did she get this idea? Where did the United States Congress get the idea that girls are a victim group? How did the "silencing" of American schoolgirls become an international human rights issue?

3

To answer that, consider some highlights of what might be called the myth of the incredible shrinking girl. The story epitomizes what is wrong with the contemporary women's movement. First, a few facts.

4

The U.S. Department of Education keeps records of male and female school achievement. They reveal that girls get better grades than boys. Boys are held back more often than girls. Significantly fewer boys than girls go on to college today. Girls are a few points behind in national tests of math and science, but that gap is closing. Meanwhile, boys are *dramatically* behind in reading and writing. We never hear about that gap, which is not shrinking.

5

Many more boys than girls suffer from learning disabilities. In 1990, three times as many boys as girls were enrolled in special education programs. Of the 1.3 million American children taking Ritalin, the drug for hyperactivity, three-quarters are boys. More boys than girls are involved in crime, alcohol, drugs.

6

Mary Pipher talks about the "selves" of girls going down in flames. One effect of a crashing self is suicide. *Six times* as many boys as girls commit suicide. In 1992, fully 4,044 young males (ages fifteen to twenty-four) killed themselves. Among same-age females, there were 649 suicides. To the extent that there is a gender gap among youth, it is boys who turn out to be on the fragile side.

7

This is not to deny that some girls are in serious trouble or that we can't do better by girls, educationally and otherwise. What I am saying is, you cannot find any responsible research that shows that girls, as a group, are worse off than boys or that girls are an underprivileged class. So, where did that idea come from? Therein lies a tale.

8

The reality is, the contemporary women's movement is obsessed with proving that our system is rigged against women. No matter what record of success you show them, they can always come up with some example of oppression. Never is good news taken as real evidence that things have

9

---

[1] **Ophelia:** In William Shakespeare's *Hamlet,* daughter of Polonius who goes mad and commits suicide.
[2] **Bermuda Triangle:** Triangular area in the north Atlantic Ocean bordered by Bermuda, Florida, and Puerto Rico; site of numerous unexplained disappearances of ships and planes.

changed. The women's movement is still fixated on victimology. Where they can't prove discrimination, they invent it.

I, for one, do not believe American women are oppressed. It is simply   10
irresponsible to argue that American women, as a gender, are worse off than American men.

More women than men now go to college. Women's life expectancy   11
is seven years longer than men's. Many women now find they can choose between working full-time, part-time, flex-time,[3] or staying home for a few years to raise their children. Men's choices are far more constricted. They can work full-time. They can work full-time. Or they can work full-time.

The reason we hear nothing about men being victims of society or boys   12
suffering unduly from educational and psychological deficits is because the feminist establishment has the power to shape national discussion and determine national policy on gender issues.

Feminist research is advocacy research. When the American Associa-   13
tion of University Women released a (badly distorted) survey in 1991 claiming that American girls suffer from a tragic lack of self-esteem, a *New York Times* reporter got AAUW President Sharon Shuster to admit that the organization commissioned the poll to get data into circulation that would support its officers' belief that schoolgirls were being short-changed. Usually, of course, belief comes after, not before, data gathering. But advocacy research doesn't work that way. With advocacy research, first you believe and then you gather figures you can use to convince people you are right.

The myth of the short-changed schoolgirl is a perfect example of   14
everything that's gone wrong with contemporary feminism. It's all there: the mendacious advocacy research, the mean-spiritedness to men that extends even to little boys, the irresponsible victimology, the outcry against being "oppressed," coupled with massive lobbying for government action.

The truth is, American women are the freest in the world. Anyone   15
who doesn't see this simply lacks common sense.

EXERCISING VOCABULARY

1. In paragraph 1, Sommers informs us that girls are classified "as a group in need of special redress." Choose one of the other minorities mentioned in that same paragraph and tell what redress has been offered to that group's members.

---

[3] **ESL** **flex-time:** A work schedule that allows employees to work hours not within the standard 8:00 a.m. to 5:00 p.m. range.

2. Sommers accuses the women's movement of being "still fixated on victimology" (para. 9). What does she mean by the word *victimology*? The word *victim* is within the longer word. How is it related to Sommers's point?

PROBING CONTENT

1. At what age does Dr. Mary Pipher believe that "'. . . something dramatic happens to girls . . .'" (para. 2)? What happens? Why does Pipher hold society responsible?

2. Identify three or four specific facts from the writer that refute Pipher's argument. Why is it important that Sommers includes facts and not opinions?

3. What causes the writer to believe that "it is boys who turn out to be on the fragile side" (para. 7)? What does she mean by *fragile*?

4. How, according to Sommers, do the choices available to adult women differ from those of adult men? How does this information contradict the idea that American women are somehow held back by our society?

CONSIDERING CRAFT

1. What is the writer's main point (thesis)? Where does she state this in a thesis sentence? Why does she locate her thesis sentence where she does?

2. What is the effect of Sommers's beginning the essay with a question? What answer does the question elicit from readers? How does this put Sommers's opinion into perspective?

3. What tone does Sommers use in this essay? How does this tone further the author's purpose?

4. Sommers originally presented these ideas in a speech. Which presentation of this material do you think would be more effective, oral or written? Why?

RESPONDING TO THE WRITER

Now that you have read this essay, do you believe that American women should be included in a list of disadvantaged minorities? To what extent was Sommers successful in influencing your opinion? What specifically caused you to change your mind or reinforced the ideas you already had about this issue?

For a quiz on this reading, go to www.bedfordstmartins.com/mirror.

School, Girls, and the Information Age

MAGGIE FORD

Have you heard about the uproar caused by the talking Barbie doll who said, "Math is hard"? The controversy became so heated that the dolls were pulled from the shelves. Although the gender gap is narrowing in math and science, young female students are still far behind in highly technical fields like computer science. Since females are as fully capable of excelling in these subjects as males, what is holding the females back? Is it self-doubt, the classroom environment, or something at the societal level? Maggie Ford, as former president of the American Association of University Women Educational Foundation, is in a particularly good position to tackle these questions in her essay, which was published in the *Austin American-Statesman* on November 27, 1998.

THINKING AHEAD

Why are females still far behind in highly technological fields like computer science? Who or what is to blame? What can be done to alleviate this problem?

INCREASING VOCABULARY

imperative (adj.) (1)
consistently (adv.) (3)

mandatory (adj.) (5)
equitable (adj.) (6)

1   As the information age rapidly envelops every facet of our society, it is imperative that our schools not only integrate technology into the classroom but also ensure that girls and young women don't become bystanders in the computer-driven twenty-first century.

2   According to the report, "Gender Gaps: Where Schools Still Fail Our Children" by the American Association of University Women Educational Foundation, while girls have gained ground in math and science, they are falling behind in technology. For example, more girls enrolled in Algebra I and II, geometry, precalculus, trigonometry and calculus in 1994 than in 1990. On the other hand, girls make up only a small percentage of students in computer science classes. And, as recently as 1996, only 17 percent of Advanced Placement test-takers in computer science were girls.

3   Outside of school, boys enter the classroom with more prior experience with computers and other technology than girls. Girls are less interested and comfortable with computers than boys, consistently rating

themselves lower on computer ability. Girls encounter fewer powerful, active female role models in computer games and software. Thus, it comes as no surprise that girls of all ethnicities consistently rate themselves lower than boys on computer ability.

So what's keeping girls from computer science? Computer labs certainly aren't locked or have signs on them that say, "No Girls Allowed." Geoff Jones, principal of one of the nation's top public science and technology magnet high schools in Fairfax County, Va., says that even in a school like his where all students are required to take basic computer science, many girls steer clear of advanced courses in computer technology. According to Jones, the widespread perception that computer programming is a "boys' thing" starts at a very early age.

That is why Gender Gaps recommends that our schools take strong steps to prepare girls and young women for the Information Age. States should make Algebra I and geometry—the gatekeeper classes for college admissions and advanced study in math, science, engineering and computer science—mandatory for all students.

Schools should make sure that their software programs and classroom experiences do not send girls and young women subtle signals that computer technology is not really for them. Teacher training, too, should be improved. Teachers need to integrate technology into the curriculum in a challenging and equitable way to encourage both girls and boys to be "power users" of technology. Moreover, School-to-Work programs need to encourage girls to explore fields such as engineering so that they can compete in fields traditionally not open to them.

Since the AAUW Educational Foundation's landmark 1992 report "How Schools Shortchange Girls," public schools have made remarkable progress in targeted programs to help girls and young women improve in math and science. As a result, the gender gaps in math and science are narrowing. Now, our schools need to make similar efforts to prepare girls and young women to compete and succeed in the highly technical fields that will define the twenty-first century. What's at stake is not only the future of our daughters and granddaughters but our nation itself.

EXERCISING VOCABULARY

1. Ford says that "girls have gained ground in math and science" (para. 2). In what setting do people literally *gain ground*? What effect does this phrase have when Ford uses it?

2. What does *gatekeeper* mean? What does a gatekeeper do? How can Algebra I and geometry be "gatekeeper classes for college admissions" (para. 5)?

3. Think of several different usages for the word *integrate*. Then discuss how it is used by the writer in paragraph 6.

PROBING CONTENT

1. Why, according to Ford, do female students often avoid computer science courses? How do boys have advantages over girls in this area?

2. According to the writer, what does the AAUW Educational Foundation report recommend that schools do to prepare female students for the Information Age?

3. Why, according to the essay, is it imperative to narrow the gender gaps in highly technical fields? Who will benefit if we succeed?

CONSIDERING CRAFT

1. Describe Ford's tone in this essay. Does her position as former president of the American Association of University Women Educational Foundation influence her attitude toward her subject? Why do you think so?

2. Why does Ford refer to the "Gender Gaps" report twice and to another 1992 report once? How does she use these studies to get her point across?

RESPONDING TO THE WRITER

Do you think that female students have technophobia, a fear of technical subjects, or is Ford overstating the problem? Cite specific examples to either support or refute your position.

For a quiz on this reading, go to www.bedfordstmartins.com/mirror.

What Men Say When We're Not Around

NICK CHILES

"Silent," "uncommunicative," "emotionally barren": these are a few of the unflattering adjectives that women often use to describe the men in their lives. But do women *really* want to know what men think? Does women's criticism make it difficult for men to communicate? Are these accusations about men's uncommunicative nature deserved? What do men talk about when they're not with women? Nick Chiles takes on these questions in "What Men Say When We're Not Around," first published in *Essence* magazine in November 2001. Reporting on the different ways women and men communicate, Chiles finds that men are not as closed off as some women might think. In this insightful analysis, Chiles concludes that communication between the sexes is not hopeless. Though we express our feelings in different ways, "we forge ahead, finding ways to make our relationships work."

Chiles, a reporter for *Newsday*, has coauthored *Money, Power, Respect: What Brothers Think, What Sistahs Know* (2001), and *What Brothers Think, What Sistahs Know About Sex: The Real Deal on Passion, Loving, and Intimacy* (2000), along with his wife, Denene Millner. *Love Don't Live Here Anymore* (2002), their third book, is a novel that they took turns writing in alternating chapters.

THINKING AHEAD

In what ways does men's language differ from women's? How do men change their ways of communicating when women are not present?

INCREASING VOCABULARY

squabble (n.) (1)

brooding (adj.) (2)

barren (adj.) (2)

pontificate (v.) (2)

orate (v.) (2)

venerable (adj.) (5)

venue (adj.) (5)

machismo (n.) (6)

articulate (adj.) (9)

proliferation (n.) (11)

incarcerated (adj.) (11)

fend (v.) (13)

concede (v.) (17)

foster (v.) (17)

erosion (n.) (18)

adrenaline (n.) (21)

inhibitions (n.) (23)

stymied (adj.) (25)

bolsters (v.) (25)

Fortunately they don't come often, but come they do: draining, sharply worded conflicts with my beloved spouse. At some point after the anger but before the absolution, when we have no more words for each other, I often gaze into the mirror and make a discovery: I need a haircut. Or more specifically, I need to be surrounded by the comforting male spirit that flows through my barbershop—a spirit that will always take my side. There I will finally win the marital squabble—and my wife will never even know it.

When I'm confronted with the long list of unflattering adjectives that men get tagged with—"silent," "brooding," "uncommunicative," "emotionally barren"—my mind quickly jumps to Mahir's Barbershop in Montclair, New Jersey. In that place, amid the nappy[1] clumps scattered about and the wail of R&B[2] in the background, I see men reaching out to one another for support, reassurance, comfort. Yes, we talk. We pontificate. We orate. We discuss. We *communicate*. Some of us are even good at it.

But when we return to the presence of our women, something happens. We become more fragile, tentative. Deep down, we want our women to look at us with pride; we want to feel an ease about sharing intimacies, but often we don't know how to get to those places. So we close it down, keep our emotions on "mute."

In my most depressed moments, I sometimes grow hopeless about the state of love in our community. Take a gender that's told from infancy that strong, authoritative, decisive and unyielding is the only way for black women to be, then pair that ideal with a gender struggling from day one with eggshell-fragile egos. And—in a society that values black men less than any other group—one struggling with feelings of worthlessness, even despair. It's a coupling bound for conflict and pain. Yet we forge ahead, finding ways to make our relationships work. It's not easy.

But men *do* talk. Stroll to the corner basketball court or step into that venerable neighborhood barbershop; go into any venue where brothers[3] typically gather. This is the black-male court of public opinion, the therapeutic support group, the communal sounding board. No matter our income, our social standing, the number of letters after our name, in the company of just men, we can explore our latest theory on "the problem with women"; get much-needed reassurance that we were right and our lady was wrong; soothe our hurt when she runs out the door.

Yes, music, money and sports get their significant share of floor time in these forums, but we inevitably find our way back to the ladies. After all, Biggie[4] is still dead, we're still broke and even the Michael Jordan[5]

---

[1] **nappy:** Term used to describe coarse hair.
[2] ESL **R&B:** Rhythm and blues music.
[3] ESL **brothers:** An affectionate term used between African American men to refer to one another.
[4] ESL **Biggie:** Biggie Smalls, a popular rapper also known as Notorious B.I.G. He was shot and killed in 1997.
[5] ESL **Michael Jordan:** Famous basketball player.

will-he-or-won't-he-make-a-comeback debate gets tired eventually. Beneath the banter and bravado[6] and displays of machismo are meaningful exchanges that run deep.

I've often wished our women could hear us when we brothers open   7
up. So at the risk of scaring some sisters[7] — and in the hope of offering real insight — let me take you into the hearts and minds of some good black men. You'll find them at my barbershop: They're chillin'[8] in my living room; they're across the continent on the other end of my phone line. Listen in as we talk, brother to brother. You may be surprised.

Why We're Quiet Sometimes

Men have no problems expressing themselves — we just may not want to   8
do it on the woman's cue. And as barber Devon Philadelphia, twenty-two, asserts, many women don't really want to hear what we have to say. "They don't listen, or they don't let us talk," says Philadelphia, who is single. "They have it made up in their minds that they're right, so they don't need to listen to us."

Ron Elmore, Psy.D., forty-four, a southern California relationship   9
therapist and author of *How to Love a Black Man* (Warner), believes that women often close themselves off to men's nonverbal expressions as well. "The fact is that men can be very communicative and articulate; it's just that our language is not always nouns, verbs and adjectives," says Elmore, whose new book, *Outrageous Commitments* (HarperCollins), examines the self-sacrifice and compromise that it takes to transform a marriage into a relationship of enduring strength and substance. "As men, we express ourselves by what we do, don't do and commit never to do," Elmore continues. "If only women could become bilingual and see that love is a demonstrated language as well, and men are giving all kinds of communication of love every day. The more respect and appreciation a man gets for his nonverbal language, the more likely he is to give the other language, the verbal."

Sometimes our nonverbal communication is intended to be kind; we   10
want to be mindful not to say the wrong words. "Often our silence comes from a desire to shield our women from critical or overly negative thoughts," says Charles Watson, twenty-nine, Ph.D., a lecturer in the humanities at Stanford University. "In my case, the things that don't get said are the criticisms."

But if he did choose to speak up, what would he criticize? "There is   11
such a proliferation of unwed mothers," observes Watson, who is single and dating. "If black men are so bad, why is it that so many women seek

---

[6] **ESL   bravado:** Bold confidence.
[7] **ESL   sisters:** An affectionate term used between African American women to refer to one another.
[8] **ESL   chillin':** Relaxing.

out these thugs, these incarcerated men, and make them the new alpha male[9] they want? I question their choices in terms of the men who get celebrated. Malcolm X says you can tell a lot about the status of a culture by looking at the women." Strong opinions certainly, and yet when he's talking to women, Watson mostly keeps them to himself.

Elmore recognizes the instinct men have for not rocking the boat.[10]   12 It's all in the approach, he says, and when it comes to relationships, men tend to approach situations like a job to be mastered. "The main feature of that job is to make sure our women stay happily in love with us," Elmore explains. "We don't want to say anything that might make them cry or get angry because that would mean we failed at our job. So, no, I don't want to confront you or go to therapy, because I might say something that will make you less happy. Most men would rather not try a job than fail at it."

What We're Really Thinking

Of course, our silence, no matter how well-meaning, often draws a predictable response from sisters. We look too thoughtful, we gaze too long into the hazy distance and we know the question will come: "What are you thinking about?" To fend it off, too many of us have perfected the blank stare, the facial expression clearly meant to signal, Hey, there's nothing going on up here. Why, you ask, do we avoid the question? Because, to steal a line from Jack Nicholson in *A Few Good Men*, we know our women can't handle the truth.   13

"We often do bite our tongue;[11] they really don't want to know what   14 we're thinking," says Gregory Lee, Jr., twenty-seven, an assistant sports editor at *The Washington Post*. It's true that we men have learned to be very selective about what we share. "I think women only want to know certain things," says Ricco Keyes, thirty, a Web developer. "If it's something they will be happy about, you can tell them. But you cannot tell them everything. It's almost like you're doing them a favor and doing the relationship a favor too."

Even men like Malaney Hill, a twenty-nine-year-old consultant and   15 single father who tries to "keep it real and tell the truth," admits he has limits. "I try to keep it PC[12]; it's not going to be raw," he says. "I might be thinking, *She's really lazy,* but it might come out, 'You know what, I really don't like your lack of motivation; I don't think you've found your passion yet.' It still gets filtered."

And sometimes when we answer the "What are you thinking?" ques-   16 tion with a casual "Nothing," it could be we haven't completely worked

---

[9]**alpha male:** The dominant male of a pack.
[10] **ESL** **rocking the boat:** Causing upset or a disturbance.
[11] **ESL** **bite our tongue:** To refrain from communicating.
[12] **ESL** **PC:** Abbreviation for "politically correct."

out the answer for ourselves. "If I tell you what I'm thinking," says Elmore, "I might end up having to go down a long, dark road, defending myself, explaining myself, and I might not be ready to go. Men will only enthusiastically enter into something when we already know where we're headed."

Why We Don't Want to Fight

If there's anything growing up male has taught us, it's to avoid fights we can't win. The second we wake up in the morning, particularly when we look in the mirror, we begin our everyday ego maintenance—that is, doing whatever is necessary to avoid feeling terrible about ourselves. A fight with our lady falls squarely under the category of can't-win. So what do we do when she wants to fight? Run like hell—or concede victory, early and often. "The outcome is just not worth it," says writer and youth-development professional Shawn Dove, thirty-nine, who lives with his wife and two daughters in New Jersey. Dove says brothers know that if we put up too much of a fight, we won't be getting any of that special brand of intimacy we love so much later in the evening. And so, to foster marital harmony, Dove picks his battles. "I've learned that I don't have to be right all the time," he says. "The most empowering tool when I'm having a disagreement with my wife is four words: *You're right about that.*" 17

But for some men, conceding the field in a marital conflict feels too much like giving in to an erosion of male power and leadership. Certainly, when it comes to gender roles in male-female relationships, the rules of engagement[13] are murkier than they used to be. 18

"Things are more up in the air than when I was growing up," observes Jude Ezeilo, thirty-one, a financial analyst in south Florida who got married last year. "African American men had a certain role and were used to playing the leader in most situations. But women these days are not buying into that as much. They have their own ideas and opinions; they make their own money and want to do things their way. So there's a struggle; we're trying to figure out where we fit. If there's too much exertion from the male, then he's thought to be putting down his female counterpart. If there's too much dominance from the female, African American men are instantly turned off and feel their authority has been challenged. Neither of us knows where we're supposed to be, so there's tension." 19

Web developer Ricco Keyes, a divorced father, believes the confusion over gender roles has a lot to do with the collapse of the family unit in our community. "People are like fish out of water. They don't know what to do; they have no guides," says Keyes. "Women need to give men the opportunity to be men, to make the decisions for the family, unless they're making decisions that are ridiculous. Black women shouldn't compete with black men to be the leader." 20

---

[13] **ESL** **rules of engagement:** Terms of an encounter or conflict.

The truth is, even brothers who aren't hung up on being "the man of   21
the house" in the traditional sense still want to feel, well, like *men*. The
sentiment may sound simple, yet there's significant power behind it: We
want our women to be proud of us. We want to know they depend on us.
We want to feel that rush of adrenaline and warmth from the smile that
crosses her face when we report on an achievement or a job well done.
And we want her to know that when she denies us her approval and instead feeds us a steady diet of condemnation and attack, it affects the kind
of man we become.

"What some women don't always understand about us is the impact   22
of rejection," says Adeyemi Bandele, fifty-one, director of Men on the
Move, a spirit-based empowerment organization that holds conferences
across the country dedicated to uplifting men. Bandele, who is married to
talk-show host and best-selling author Iyanla Vanzant, says men carefully
monitor whether a woman will be receptive to what they have to say. "If
a man feels a woman is waiting to hear something she can pounce on,
then he won't give her that," he says. "He'll just say nothing. This is a
major piece a lot of women don't understand."

Ironically, black men's deep desire to find approval and be seen as   23
worthy creates its own set of inhibitions. "In our heart of hearts, we want
to be heroes and champions in our black women's eyes," says Dove. "The
problem comes when we want that but we're not quite sure how to get
there. What does it mean to be a hero? For some young people it's the
gang-banging hustler.[14] For others it's the husband working and providing for his family. We might be trying to give that, but when the criticism
comes, it knocks us down. It's our kryptonite.[15] There's more to us, so
much more, than a paycheck and a penis."

How We Put It All Together

In the end, we have to remember that women and men have very different   24
styles of communicating. "For men, talking is a declaration of our
thoughts, not a processing of our thoughts," explains Elmore. "After I
know, I speak. Women, on the other hand, speak to know. Men think it
through alone and come back with our bottom line. Women think we
didn't think, but we did, but they didn't see it or hear about it until the
bottom line was announced."

Sisters' ability to put feelings and thoughts into words with lightning   25
speed can leave a brother feeling stymied. "Sometimes talking to my wife,

---

[14] **ESL** **gang-banging hustler:** A person involved in criminal activity.
[15] **ESL** **kryptonite:** Fictional material that sapped the powers of Superman.

I become a blathering idiot," laughs Bandele. But, he adds, no one in the world appreciates us and bolsters us like a black woman.

Almost to a man, the brothers I talked to came to the same conclu-   26
sion: Black women will stick with us and shoulder our burdens, in addition to their own, when everyone else has left us in their dust. It's why barber Devon Philadelphia says of sisters, "We may not understand them, but we can't *be* without them." It's what prompts philosopher Charles Watson to observe, "Black women haven't given up on us. Even though they might have been done wrong four times in a row, the fifth time they're still willing to give some guy a chance." And it's why, after a rousing round of pontificating at Mahir's Barbershop, of winning points in the company of my brothers, I go home to my beloved wife and find the words that will bring us absolution.

EXERCISING VOCABULARY

1. In the opening and closing paragraphs of his essay, Chiles repeats the word *absolution*. What does it mean to give absolution to someone? In what context is this term normally used? How does the author use *absolution* in his essay? Who is absolving whom? How effective is his word choice? What is the effect of repeating this word at the end of the essay?

2. In paragraph 3, Chiles states that men keep their emotions on "mute." What does it mean to mute something? Give an example of something you might mute. What, then, is the author saying about his male friends' behavior when women are around?

3. In paragraph 5, Chiles says that any place where black men gather is the "black-male court of public opinion." What happens in a courtroom? What does the author mean when he says that barbershops and corner basketball courts are courts of public opinion?

PROBING CONTENT

1. How does the speech of the author and his friends change while women are present? Why does this happen?

2. According to the essay, why are men sometimes quiet? What role does nonverbal communication play in their relationships with women?

3. How does men's desire not to get into fights with women affect their communication? How have changing gender roles affected this communication? How do many black men still want to be seen by women?

4. What do almost all black men conclude about "sisters"? What role do these women play in the men's lives?

CONSIDERING CRAFT

1. Examine the title of the essay. To whom is it addressed? What does this tell you about the intended audience for the essay?

2. Chiles mentions Mahir's Barbershop several times and even quotes barber Devon Philadelphia. Find several places where he alludes to this setting. Why is this place important to the author? How does Chiles's emphasis on this setting relate to the content of the essay?

3. The author quotes a variety of sources in his essay. Locate several examples. What different kinds of people does he quote? Why does he do this? How effective is this writing strategy?

RESPONDING TO THE WRITER

Nick Chiles is an African American. In what ways does his argument about men's speech extend to society at large? What do you think of his assessment of the way men's communication is affected by the presence or absence of women?

For a quiz on this reading, go to www.bedfordstmartins.com/mirror.

Women's Magazines Flip Past Feminism

Alex Kuczynski

In the 1970s, mainstream women's magazines played an important role in pushing the feminist movement forward. They focused the nation's attention on feminist issues, featuring articles on topics including sexual harassment, date rape, and the gender gap in earnings. Today, however, most women's magazines display such interchangeable headlines as "Get a Better Body — for Sex," "What Men Think about Your Look," and "Sex Appeal: Do You Know Who He Finds Attractive?" "They're all breasts and lipstick and your performance in bed," says one critic. Do you agree? How do you feel about women's magazines like *Cosmopolitan* and *Glamour*? Are they empowering or demeaning? And what do they reveal about our attitudes toward feminism?

Alex Kuczynski, a media writer for the *New York Times*, raises these questions in the following essay. Kuczynski has also written for the Style section of the *New York Times*, and her work has been published in magazines including *Harper's Bazaar* and *Allure*. "Women's Magazines Flip Past Feminism" first appeared in the *New York Times* on April 4, 1999.

THINKING AHEAD

Think about some women's magazines you've looked at or heard about. What makes a magazine a "women's" publication? What kinds of articles and advertisements do you find in women's magazines? How do they differ from those found in men's magazines?

INCREASING VOCABULARY

blaring (v.) (1)

lust (n.) (1)

modulated (adj.) (2)

stridency (n.) (2)

staple (n.) (4)

vexes (v.) (5)

modified (adj.) (7)

convergence (n.) (8)

eludes (v.) (10)

thwarted (adj.) (10)

starkly (adv.) (11)

embodiment (n.) (11)

unshackled (v.) (11)

deplore (v.) (12)

concede (v.) (12)

mainstream (adj.) (14)

arguably (adv.) (17)

reigning (adj.) (17)

advocating (v.) (22)

overt (adj.) (25)

When the January issue of *Glamour* magazine reached its 2.2   1
million readers, some may have been surprised to find this line
blaring from the cover: "New for '99: You asked for it! Horo-
scopes. Psychic details you need for your love, lust and work life. Big Decisions!"

The magazine—once an influential voice in the feminist movement   2
because its gospel of modulated assertiveness appealed to a large audience
that was put off by the stridency of *Ms.* magazine—had dumped its
"Women in Washington" column, which covered political activity concerning women's issues. It had added astrology.

Glamour commonly ran articles like "Let's Stop Lying About Day   3
Care" and "Excuse Me, Are Women Equal Yet? 18 Reasons Why We Still
Need Affirmative Action."[1] Recently it featured an editorial on e-mail pri-
vacy titled "Why We Should All Get Down on Our Knees and Thank
Monica Lewinsky."[2]

Even the sexual advice, a staple of women's magazines since the hey-   4
day[3] of Helen Gurley Brown[4] at *Cosmopolitan*, has changed—from
instruction on maximizing female or mutual pleasure, to guidance on
pleasing men.

The change in *Glamour*, echoed in other women's magazines, is part   5
of a larger retreat—not a backlash of men against women but of women
against feminism—that vexes feminist theorists and cheers conservatives.

By virtue of the articles they choose to publish, youthful women's   6
magazines like *Cosmopolitan*, *Glamour* and *Marie Claire* seem to argue
that their reader doesn't want or need feminism; that she doesn't care
much about Washington or affirmative action and that she isn't terribly
angry about being cheated out of day care.

Marie Claire, which began publishing in 1996 with a modified feminist   7
tone and regular features on women's issues, now runs articles like these:
"How Do Men See You?" (September 1998); "Sex Appeal: Do You Know
Who He Finds Attractive?" (December 1998); "Men, Sex and You" and
"What Men Think About Your Look" (the current issue). One headline
announces, "Get a Better Body—for Sex." Tellingly, *Marie Claire* is one of
the great circulation successes of the women's magazine categories, shooting up from 400,000 in 1996 to more than twice that now.

The fact that American women seem to be buying these magazines in   8
increasing numbers points to an unsteady postfeminist convergence in
American attitudes toward feminism. The convergence brings together
magazine editors—mostly liberal-leaning women who consider them-

---

[1] **Affirmative Action:** A program that promotes the increase of numbers of women, minorities, and handicapped at all levels within the workforce.
[2] **ESL Monica Lewinsky:** White House intern famous for her affair with President Bill
Clinton.
[3] **ESL heyday:** Slang term to describe something at its best moment in the past.
[4] **Helen Gurley Brown:** Former controversial editor-in-chief of *Cosmopolitan* magazine.

selves feminists—and anti-feminists like the authors of two recent books that argue that feminism has made women unhappy.

In one of the books, *A Return to Modesty: Discovering the Lost Virtue* (Free Press), which was widely praised by conservatives, twenty-three-year-old author Wendy Shalit argues that the sexual liberty championed by the feminist movement is responsible for eating disorders and other female troubles, and that men respect women who won't accede to their sexual advances without putting up a fight.   9

In the other book, *What Our Mothers Didn't Tell Us: Why Happiness Eludes the Modern Woman* (Simon & Schuster), thirty-five-year-old Danielle Crittenden, who studied decades of women's magazines in preparation for her book, argues that if the truth about women can be found in the magazines they read, feminism was a bad career move. It taught women to expect to live freewheeling[5] sex lives, which have left her contemporaries "even more miserable and insecure, more thwarted and obsessed with men, than the most depressed, lithium-popping[6] suburban readers of the 1950s."   10

The political conservatives say the path to feminine fulfillment lies within the orderly rows of family, child-rearing and husband-pleasing. That view is starkly different from the one that emerges from the pages of the women's magazines, which hold up Lewinsky as the embodiment of the modern woman—an independent-minded mistress, unshackled from sexual modesty and constantly celebrating her healthy sensuality.   11

Yet authors such as Shalit and Crittenden, who attack the gains of feminism by saying it promoted female licentiousness,[7] have become unlikely comrades-in-arms against feminism with the magazine editors whose work they deplore. The editors concede they are products of feminism, while the conservatives say they are not. Yet both have dismissed it.   12

To be sure, some of the editors insist that feminism is alive and well in their pages.   13

Bonnie Fuller, forty-two, the editor-in-chief of *Glamour,* argues that the lessons of feminism are now so densely woven into the cultural fabric that readers don't need to revisit them, and that the mainstream magazines no longer need to provide monthly monitoring on the state of women's rights.   14

"I can't speak for all women's magazines," Fuller said, "but there are an enormous number of thought-provoking articles in women's magazines and very much so in *Glamour.* We assign investigative reporters, who do major articles on women's health issues every single month."   15

The March issue, for example, carried an editorial about domestic violence. And she pointed out that sexual advice is a product of the   16

---

[5] freewheeling: Carefree and irresponsible.
[6] ESL lithium-popping: Refers to people who take sedatives to calm their nerves.
[7] licentiousness: Disregard for rules or general morality.

women's movement. "It would be unempowering for women not to be able to read about sex as much as they wanted," she said.

But Gloria Steinem, the editor of *Ms.* and arguably the last reigning   17
symbol of 1970s feminism, said she has been observing what she considers to be a decadelong anti-feminist shift in women's magazines away from coverage of women's issues and politics and even high-quality fiction.

"Advertisers in women's magazines have more influence than ever and   18
don't want their ads to appear next to anything but stories about celebrity and sex," she said. (*Ms.*, which Steinem reintroduces this month, does not carry advertising.)

Steinem said such magazines offer sexual advice about pleasing men   19
as part of a larger movement toward making women feel bad about themselves, and then fixing those imagined ills in the pages of the magazines.

"So reading them becomes this self-fulfilling prophecy," she said.   20

Crittenden's description of these magazines is not very different. The   21
magazines she read from the early 1970s, she said, "were so intelligent it breaks your heart. They were packed with interesting things to read. It wasn't *The Atlantic Monthly,* but there were serious interviews and good writing." She added: "Magazines today, especially under an editor like Bonnie Fuller, sell beauty and sex and sex and more sex. That's all there is."

Shalit argues in her book that such magazines diminish female power   22
by advocating sexual helplessness and round-the-clock[8] availability.

"They're all breasts and lipstick and your performance in bed," said   23
Shalit, whose book cites articles in a half-dozen women's magazines, in-
cluding *Glamour* and *Mademoiselle.* "There's something so desperate about it. The thinking is that if you're not currently in a sexual relationship, you're a real weirdo."

Crittenden said Lewinsky is "a total product of *Cosmo* and *Glamour.*   24
She goes in there and does what she did and thinks she's a liberated woman."

So while conservatives may be pleased that women's magazines have   25
backed away from overt feminism, the Lewinskyization that has replaced it is not exactly what they had in mind.

EXERCISING VOCABULARY

1. In paragraph 5, Kuczynski speaks about a "backlash . . . of women against feminism." What does the word *backlash* mean? What image comes to mind when you see this word?

2. Kuczynski writes that according to political conservatives, "the path to femi-
nine fulfillment lies within the orderly rows of family, child-rearing and husband-pleasing" (para. 11). Think of a classroom in which the chairs are placed in orderly rows. What does this set-up suggest to you about the pro-

---

[8] **ESL** **round-the-clock:** Twenty-four hours a day.

fessor's teaching style? What does this image imply about the conservatives' view of women? How effective is this image?

3. The author quotes Bonnie Fuller, who argues that "the lessons of feminism are now so densely woven into the cultural fabric that readers don't need to revisit them" (para. 14). Describe what a densely woven fabric would look like. What does Fuller mean when she speaks of a cultural fabric? What relationship between feminism and culture is Fuller establishing in this figure of speech?

4. In paragraph 20, Kuczynski argues that reading current women's magazines is a "self-fulfilling prophecy." What is a prophecy? How can a prophecy be self-fulfilling?

CONSIDERING CRAFT

1. Examine the title of this essay. How does this title underline the author's message?

2. How does the author answer the opposition in her essay? Why does she include viewpoints opposed to her own?

3. Find several places where Kuczynski uses titles of articles taken from contemporary women's magazines. How do these examples affect your reading of the essay?

PROBING CONTENT

1. How has *Glamour* magazine changed in recent years? How does the author view these changes and similar ones in other popular women's magazines?

2. Who are Wendy Shalit and Danielle Crittenden? How do they view women's magazines? How do they view the feminist movement?

3. What was Gloria Steinem's role in the women's movement? What does she think of current women's magazines? How does *Ms.* magazine differ from these publications?

4. What is the relationship between the views of the conservatives and the current editors of women's magazines like Bonnie Fuller? In what sense are they "unlikely comrades-in-arms" (para. 12)?

RESPONDING TO THE WRITER

How do you respond to Kuczynski's claim that many women's magazines are contributing to negative, "unempowering" images of women? How much of an impact do popular publications like *Glamour* and *Cosmopolitan* have on women's behavior and self-image?

For a quiz on this reading, go to www.bedfordstmartins.com/mirror.

How Boys Become Men

JON KATZ

Are boys taught to endure pain rather than show fear? Do men receive little mercy as boys, making it difficult for them to show any themselves? Jon Katz explores these questions in "How Boys Become Men," first published in the January 1993 issue of *Glamour*. Drawing on an experience from his childhood, Katz shows how the lessons boys learn affect their behavior as men. According to Katz, it's the boyhood "Code of Conduct" — with its unspoken but unyielding rules about expressing emotion — that explains why some men may seem insensitive. "Boys are rewarded for throwing hard. Most other activities — reading, befriending girls, or just thinking — are considered weird. And if there's one thing boys don't want to be, it's weird," Katz writes. Do you think that this statement still applies to boys growing up today?

Katz has worked as an editor and reporter at the *Washington Post*, the *Boston Globe*, and the *Philadelphia Inquirer* and as a media critic for *New York* magazine and *Rolling Stone*. He has also written eleven books, most of which are mystery novels. His most recent book, *A Dog Year: Twelve Months, Four Dogs, and Me* (2002), is a memoir.

THINKING AHEAD

Think back to your childhood. Describe the ways in which little boys treated one another. In what ways were they kind or cruel to their playmates? Why do you think they behaved the way they did?

INCREASING VOCABULARY

whooshing (v.) (1)	wary (adj.) (18)
audible (adj.) (2)	intervening (v.) (18)
ethics (n.) (3)	balk (v.) (18)
remote (adj.) (4)	stigmatized (v.) (18)
ruthless (adj.) (5)	evolves (v.) (20)
empathy (n.) (5)	rumpled (adj.) (20)
resignedly (adv.) (7)	

Two nine-year-old boys, neighbors and friends, were walking 1 home from school. The one in the bright blue windbreaker was laughing and swinging a heavy-looking book bag toward the head of his friend, who kept ducking and stepping back. "What's the matter?" asked the kid with the bag, whooshing it over his head. "You chicken?"[1]

His friend stopped, stood still and braced himself. The bag slammed into the side of his face, the thump audible all the way across the street where I stood watching. The impact knocked him to the ground, where he lay mildly stunned for a second. Then he struggled up, rubbing the side of his head. "See?" he said proudly. "I'm no chicken."

No. A chicken would probably have had the sense to get out of the way. This boy was already well on the road to becoming a *man*, having learned one of the central ethics of his gender: Experience pain rather than show fear.

Women tend to see men as a giant problem in need of solution. They tell us that we're remote and uncommunicative, that we need to demonstrate less machismo and more commitment, more humanity. But if you don't understand something about boys, you can't understand why men are the way we are, why we find it so difficult to make friends or to acknowledge our fears and problems.

Boys live in a world with its own Code of Conduct, a set of ruthless, unspoken, and unyielding rules:

Don't be a goody-goody.[2]

Never rat.[3] If your parents ask about bruises, shrug.

Never admit fear. Ride the roller coaster, join the fistfight, do what you have to do. Asking for help is for sissies.

Empathy is for nerds.[4] You can help your best buddy, under certain circumstances. Everyone else is on his own.

Never discuss anything of substance with anybody. Grunt, shrug, dump on teachers, laugh at wimps,[5] talk about comic books. Anything else is risky.

Boys are rewarded for throwing hard. Most other activities—reading, befriending girls, or just thinking—are considered weird. And if there's one thing boys don't want to be, it's weird.

More than anything else, boys are supposed to learn how to handle themselves. I remember the bitter fifth-grade conflict I touched off by elbowing aside a bigger boy named Barry and seizing the cafeteria's last carton of chocolate milk. Teased for getting aced out by a wimp, he had to reclaim his place in the pack. Our fistfight, at recess, ended with my knees

---

[1] **ESL** **chicken:** A slang mocking term used to describe someone who is afraid of something.
[2] **ESL** **goody-goody:** A slang mocking term used to describe someone who is eager to please.
[3] **ESL** **rat:** A slang mocking term for giving away information.
[4] **ESL** **nerds:** A slang mocking term used to describe unpopular people.
[5] **ESL** **wimps:** A slang mocking term used to describe people who are afraid of doing something.

buckling and my lip bleeding while my friends, sympathetic but out of range, watched resignedly.

When I got home, my mother took one look at my swollen face and screamed. I wouldn't tell her anything, but when my father got home I cracked and confessed, pleading with them to do nothing. Instead, they called Barry's parents, who restricted his television for a week.   8

The following morning, Barry and six of his pals stepped out from behind a stand of trees. "It's the rat," said Barry.   9

I bled a little more. *Rat* was scrawled in crayon across my desk.   10

They were waiting for me after school for a number of afternoons to follow. I tried varying my routes and avoiding bushes and hedges. It usually didn't work.   11

I was as ashamed for telling as I was frightened. "You did ask for it," said my best friend. Frontier Justice has nothing on Boy Justice.   12

In panic, I appealed to a cousin who was several years older. He followed me home from school, and when Barry's gang surrounded me, he came barreling toward us. "Stay away from my cousin," he shouted, "or I'll kill you."   13

After they were gone, however, my cousin could barely stop laughing. "You were afraid of *them?*" he howled. "They barely came up to my waist."   14

Men remember receiving little mercy as boys; maybe that's why it's sometimes difficult for them to show any.   15

"I know lots of men who had happy childhoods, but none who have happy memories of the way other boys treated them," says a friend. "It's a macho marathon from third grade up, when you start butting each other in the stomach."   16

"The thing is," adds another friend, "you learn early on to hide what you feel. It's never safe to say, 'I'm scared.' My girlfriend asks me why I don't talk more about what I'm feeling. I've gotten better at it, but it will *never* come naturally."   17

You don't need to be a shrink[6] to see how the lessons boys learn affect their behavior as men. Men are being asked, more and more, to show sensitivity, but they dread the very word. They struggle to build their increasingly uncertain work lives but will deny they're in trouble. They want love, affection, and support but don't know how to ask for them. They hide their weaknesses and fears from all, even those they care for. They've learned to be wary of intervening when they see others in trouble. They often still balk at being stigmatized as weird.   18

Some men get shocked into sensitivity—when they lose their jobs, their wives, or their lovers. Others learn it through a strong marriage, or through their own children.   19

It may be a long while, however, before male culture evolves to the   20

---

[6] **ESL** shrink: A slang term for psychiatrist.

point that boys can learn more from one another than how to hit curve balls. Last month, walking my dog past the playground near my house, I saw three boys encircling a fourth, laughing and pushing him. He was skinny and rumpled, and he looked frightened. One boy knelt behind him while another pushed him from the front, a trick familiar to any former boy. He fell backward.

When the others ran off, he brushed the dirt off his elbows and walked 　21
toward the swings. His eyes were moist and he was struggling for control.

"Hi," I said through the chain-link fence. "How ya doing?" 　22

"Fine," he said quickly, kicking his legs out and beginning his swing. 　23

EXERCISING VOCABULARY

1. In paragraph 5, Katz writes that boys live by a set of "unyielding rules." What does it mean to yield? In what context do you normally see this word used? Examine the rules Katz lists. In what sense are these rules unyielding?

2. In paragraph 12, Katz compares the justice boys practice on each other to "Frontier Justice." Where was the American frontier? What kind of justice ruled there? Who made the laws and enforced them? In what ways are "Frontier Justice" and "Boy Justice" alike?

3. In paragraph 16, the author quotes a friend who says that for boys, "'It's a macho marathon from third grade up, . . .'" What does the word *macho* mean? What is the noun form of this adjective? What is a marathon? What then does Katz mean by the phrase "macho marathon"? How effective is this image?

PROBING CONTENT

1. Describe the "Code of Conduct" by which the author believes boys live. How do these rules affect boys' behavior?

2. What happened between the author and Barry? How did Katz's parents respond? What saved the situation?

3. How do "the lessons boys learn affect their behavior as men" (para. 18)? How do some men change their behavior when they become adults? What helps them to do so?

4. What happens to the little boy Katz saw on the playground? What does the boy's reaction imply about the future of male behavior?

CONSIDERING CRAFT

1. This essay was originally published in *Glamour*, a magazine for young women. Why do you think the author would choose a women's publication for his article? What message is he trying to relay to these readers?

2. The author opens and closes this essay with anecdotes, or short personal narratives. What message does Katz want the reader to take away from each of these
   anecdotes? How effective is this strategy for opening and closing his essay?

RESPONDING TO THE WRITER

How accurate do you find Katz's representation of boys' behavior? Do you agree
that "Men are being asked, more and more, to show sensitivity, but they dread
the very word" (para. 18)? Cite examples from personal experience to defend your
position.

For a quiz on this reading, go to www.bedfordstmartins.com/mirror.

X: A Fabulous Child's Story

LOIS GOULD

Lois Gould's fable "X: A Fabulous Child's Story," which first appeared as a "Story for Free Children" in the December 1972 issue of *Ms.* magazine, explores how gender shapes our self-identities from the time we are born. In the story, X is raised as neither boy nor girl, frustrating parents who demand that boys have typical "boy" characteristics (husky biceps) and girls have typical "girl" characteristics (dimples). What does this say about society's gender-based expectations? Would children be better off without these expectations? Who makes the rules that require girls and boys to look, dress, and act differently? What if someone breaks all the rules, as X does? In this clever exploration of how society shapes our gender roles, Gould provides some surprising answers to these questions.

Gould is known for what *Publishers Weekly* has called her "sharply etched presentation of a female viewpoint." The author of the "Hers" column for the *New York Times*, Gould has also written for *Newsday* and the *New York Times Magazine*. Her numerous books include the novels *La Presidente* (1982), *Subject Change* (1988), and *No Brakes* (1997), as well as a memoir of her mother, *Mommy Dressing* (1988).

THINKING AHEAD

Is it possible to think of children as genderless? What would be the advantages of this mindset? What problems could arise?

INCREASING VOCABULARY

husky (adj.) (6)	retrieving (v.) (23)
biceps (n.) (6)	disruptive (adj.) (50)
fret (v.) (11)	spooky (adj.) (59)
dainty (adj.) (12)	bewildered (adj.) (74)
huffily (adv.) (14)	mischievous (adj.) (87)
snarl (v.) (18)	

O nce upon a time, a baby named X was born. This baby was 1 named X so that nobody could tell whether it was a boy or a girl. Its parents could tell, of course, but they couldn't tell anybody else. They couldn't even tell Baby X, at first.

You see, it was all part of a very important Secret Scientifix 2 Xperiment, known officially as Project Baby X. The smartest scientists had set up this Xperiment at a cost of Xactly 23 billion dollars and 72 cents, which might seem like a lot for just one baby, even a very important Xperimental baby. But when you remember the prices of things like strained carrots and stuffed bunnies, and popcorn for the movies and booster shots[1] for camp, let alone twenty-eight shiny quarters from the tooth fairy,[2] you begin to see how it adds up.

Also, long before Baby X was born, all those scientists had to be paid to work out the details of the Xperiment, and to write the *Official Instruction Manual* for Baby X's parents and, most important of all, to find the right set of parents to bring up Baby X. These parents had to be selected very carefully. Thousands of volunteers had to take thousands of tests and answer thousands of tricky questions. Almost everybody failed because, it turned out, almost everybody really wanted either a baby boy or a baby girl, and not Baby X at all. Also, almost everybody was afraid that a Baby X would be a lot more trouble than a boy or a girl. (They were probably right, the scientists admitted, but Baby X needed parents who wouldn't *mind* the Xtra trouble.)

There were families with grandparents named Milton and Agatha, who didn't see why the baby couldn't be named Milton or Agatha instead of X, even if it *was* an X. There were families with aunts who insisted on knitting tiny dresses and uncles who insisted on sending tiny baseball mitts. Worst of all, there were families that already had other children who couldn't be trusted to keep the secret. Certainly not if they knew the secret was worth 23 billion dollars and 72 cents—and all you had to do was take one little peek at Baby X in the bathtub to know if it was a boy or a girl.

But, finally, the scientists found the Joneses, who really wanted to raise an X more than any other kind of baby—no matter how much trouble it would be. Ms. and Mr. Jones had to promise they would take equal turns caring for X, and feeding it, and singing it lullabies. And they had to promise never to hire any baby-sitters. The government scientists knew perfectly well that a baby-sitter would probably peek at X in the bathtub, too.

The day the Joneses brought their baby home, lots of friends and relatives came over to see it. None of them knew about the secret Xperiment, though. So the first thing they asked was what kind of a baby X was. When the Joneses smiled and said, "It's an X!" nobody knew what to say. They couldn't say, "Look at her cute little dimples!" And they couldn't say, "Look at his husky little biceps!" And they couldn't even say just plain "kitchy-coo." In fact, they all thought the Joneses were playing some kind of rude joke.

But, of course, the Joneses were not joking. "It's an X" was absolutely all they would say. And that made the friends and relatives very angry. The relatives all felt embarrassed about having an X in the family. "People

---

[1] **ESL** **booster shots:** Injections children receive to inoculate them against illness.
[2] **ESL** **tooth fairy:** A fictional fairy that leaves money under children's pillows when they lose their teeth.

will think there's something wrong with it!" some of them whispered. "There *is* something wrong with it!" others whispered back.

"Nonsense!" the Joneses told them all cheerfully. "What could possibly be wrong with this perfectly adorable X?"   8

Nobody could answer that, except Baby X, who had just finished its bottle. Baby X's answer was a loud, satisfied burp.   9

Clearly, nothing at all was wrong. Nevertheless, none of the relatives felt comfortable about buying a present for a Baby X. The cousins who sent the baby a tiny football helmet would not come and visit any more. And the neighbors who sent a pink-flowered romper suit[3] pulled their shades down when the Joneses passed their house.   10

The *Official Instruction Manual* had warned the new parents that this would happen, so they didn't fret about it. Besides, they were too busy with Baby X and the hundreds of different Xercises for treating it properly.   11

Ms. and Mr. Jones had to be Xtra careful about how they played with little X. They knew if they kept bouncing it up in the air and saying how *strong* and *active* it was, they'd be treating it more like a boy than an X. But if all they did was cuddle it and kiss it and tell it how *sweet* and *dainty* it was, they'd be treating it more like a girl than an X.   12

On page 1,654 of the *Official Instruction Manual,* the scientists prescribed: "plenty of bouncing and plenty of cuddling, *both.* X ought to be strong and sweet and active. Forget about *dainty* altogether."   13

Meanwhile, the Joneses were worrying about other problems. Toys, for instance. And clothes. On his first shopping trip, Mr. Jones told the store clerk, "I need some clothes and toys for my new baby." The clerk smiled and said, "Well, now, is it a boy or a girl?" "It's an X," Mr. Jones said, smiling back. But the clerk got all red in the face and said huffily, "In *that* case, I'm afraid I can't help you, sir." So Mr. Jones wandered helplessly up and down the aisles trying to find what X needed. But everything in the store was piled up in sections marked "Boys" or "Girls." There were "Boys' Pajamas" and "Girls' Underwear" and "Boys' Fire Engines" and "Girls' Housekeeping Sets." Mr. Jones went home without buying anything for X. That night he and Ms. Jones consulted page 2,326 of the *Official Instruction Manual.* "Buy plenty of everything!" it said firmly.   14

So they bought plenty of sturdy blue pajamas in the Boys' Department and cheerful flowered underwear in the Girls' Department. And they bought all kinds of toys. A boy doll that made pee-pee and cried, "Pa-pa." And a girl doll that talked in three languages and said, "I am the Pres-i-dent of Gen-er-al Mo-tors." They also bought a storybook about a brave princess who rescued a handsome prince from his ivory tower, and another one about a sister and brother who grew up to be a baseball star and a ballet star, and you had to guess which was which.   15

The head scientists of Project Baby X checked all their purchases and told them to keep up the good work. They also reminded the Joneses to see   16

---

[3] **ESL** **romper suit:** A baby's outfit worn during playtime.

page 4,629 of the *Manual,* where it said, "Never make Baby X feel *embarrassed* or *ashamed* about what it wants to play with. And if X gets dirty climbing rocks, never say 'Nice little Xes don't get dirty climbing rocks.'"

Likewise, it said, "If X falls down and cries, never say 'Brave little Xes   17
don't cry.' Because, of course, nice little Xes *do* get dirty, and brave little Xes *do* cry. No matter how dirty X gets, or how hard it cries, don't worry. It's all part of the Xperiment."

Whenever the Joneses pushed Baby X's stroller in the park, smiling   18
strangers would come over and coo: "Is that a boy or a girl?" The Joneses would smile back and say, "It's an X." The strangers would stop smiling then, and often snarl something nasty—as if the Joneses had snarled at *them.*

By the time X grew big enough to play with other children, the Joneses'   19
troubles had grown bigger, too. Once a little girl grabbed X's shovel in the sandbox, and zonked[4] X on the head with it. "Now, now, Tracy," the little girl's mother began to scold, "little girls mustn't hit little . . ." and she turned to ask X, "Are you a little boy or a little girl, dear?"

Mr. Jones who was sitting near the sandbox, held his breath and   20
crossed his fingers.

X smiled politely at the lady, even though X's head had never been   21
zonked so hard in its life, "I'm a little X," X replied.

"You're a *what?*" the lady exclaimed angrily. "You're a little b-r-a-t,   22
you mean!"

"But little girls mustn't hit little Xes, either!" said X, retrieving the   23
shovel with another polite smile. "What good does hitting do, anyway?"

X's father, who was still holding his breath, finally let it out, un-   24
crossed his fingers, and grinned back at X.

And at their next secret Project Baby X meeting, the scientists grinned,   25
too. Baby X was doing fine.

But then it was time for X to start school. The Joneses were really   26
worried about this, because school was even more full of rules for boys and girls, and there were no rules for Xes. The teacher would tell boys to form one line, and girls to form another line. There would be boys' games and girls' games, and boys' secrets and girls' secrets. The school library would have a list of recommended books for girls, and a different list of recommended books for boys. There would even be a bathroom marked BOYS and another one marked GIRLS. Pretty soon boys and girls would hardly talk to each other. What would happen to poor little X?

The Joneses spent weeks consulting their *Instruction Manual* (there   27
were 249½ pages of advice under "First Day of School"), and attending urgent special conferences with the smart scientists of Project Baby X.

The scientists had to make sure that X's mother had taught X how to   28
throw and catch a ball properly, and that X's father had been sure to teach X what to serve at a doll's tea party. X had to know how to shoot

---

[4] **ESL** zonked: Hit.

marbles and how to jump rope and, most of all, what to say when the Other Children asked whether X was a Boy or a Girl.

Finally, X was ready. The Joneses helped X button on a nice new pair of red-and-white checked overalls,[5] and sharpened six pencils for X's nice new pencilbox, and marked X's name clearly on all the books in its nice new bookbag. X brushed its teeth and combed its hair, which just about covered its ears, and remembered to put a napkin in its lunchbox. 29

The Joneses had asked X's teacher if the class could line up alphabetically, instead of forming separate lines for boys and girls. And they had asked if X could use the principal's bathroom, because it wasn't marked anything except BATHROOM. X's teacher promised to take care of all those problems. But nobody could help X with the biggest problem of all—Other Children. 30

Nobody in X's class had ever known an X before. What would they think? How would X make friends? 31

You couldn't tell what X was by studying its clothes—overalls don't even button right-to-left, like girls' clothes, or left-to-right, like boys' clothes. And you couldn't guess whether X had a girl's short haircut or a boy's long haircut. And it was very hard to tell by the games X liked to play. Either X played ball very well for a girl, or else X played house very well for a boy. 32

Some of the children tried to find out by asking X tricky questions, like "Who's your favorite sports star?" That was easy. X had two favorite sports stars: a girl jockey named Robyn Smith and a boy archery champion named Robin Hood. Then they asked, "What's your favorite TV program?" And that was even easier. X's favorite TV program was "Lassie," which stars a girl dog played by a boy dog. 33

When X said that its favorite toy was a doll, everyone decided that X must be a girl. But then X said that the doll was really a robot, and that X had computerized it, and that it was programmed to bake fudge brownies and then clean up the kitchen. After X told them that, the other children gave up guessing what X was. All they knew was they'd sure like to see X's doll. 34

After school, X wanted to play with the other children. "How about shooting some baskets in the gym?" X asked the girls. But all they did was make faces and giggle behind X's back. 35

"How about weaving some baskets in the arts and crafts room?" X asked the boys. But they all made faces and giggled behind X's back too. 36

That night, Ms. and Mr. Jones asked X how things had gone at school. X told them sadly that the lessons were okay, but otherwise school was a terrible place for an X. It seemed as if Other Children would never want an X for a friend. 37

Once more, the Joneses reached for their *Instruction Manual*. Under "Other Children," they found the following message: "What did you 38

---

[5] **ESL** **overalls:** Pants that include suspender straps and a front bib panel.

Xpect? *Other Children* have to obey all the silly boy-girl rules, because their parents taught them to. Lucky X — you don't have to stick to the rules at all! All you have to do is be yourself. P.S.[6] We're not saying it'll be easy."

X liked being itself. But X cried a lot that night, partly because it felt afraid. So X's father held X tight, and cuddled it, and couldn't help crying a little, too. And X's mother cheered them both up by reading an Xciting story about an enchanted prince called Sleeping Handsome, who woke up when Princess Charming kissed him.

The next morning, they all felt much better, and little X went back to school with a brave smile and a clean pair of red-and-white checked overalls.

There was a seven-letter-word spelling bee[7] in class that day. And a seven-lap boys' relay race in the gym. And a seven-layer-cake baking contest in the girls' kitchen corner. X won the spelling bee. X also won the relay race. And X almost won the baking contest, except it forgot to light the oven. Which only proves that nobody's perfect.

One of the Other Children noticed something else, too. He said, "Winning or losing doesn't seem to count to X. X seems to have fun being good at boys' skills *and* girls' skills."

"Come to think of it," said another one of the Other Children, "maybe X is having twice as much fun as we are!"

So after school that day, the girl who beat X at the baking contest gave X a big slice of her prizewinning cake. And the boy X beat in the relay race asked X to race him home.

From then on, some really funny things began to happen. Susie, who sat next to X in class, suddenly refused to wear pink dresses to school any more. She insisted on wearing red-and-white checked overalls — just like X's. Overalls, she told her parents, were much better for climbing monkey bars.[8]

Then Jim, the class football nut, started wheeling his little sister's doll carriage around the football field. He'd put on his entire football uniform, except for the helmet. Then he'd put the helmet *in* the carriage, lovingly tucked under an old set of shoulder pads. Then he'd start jogging around the field, pushing the carriage and singing "Rock-a-bye Baby" to his football helmet. He told his family that X did the same thing, so it must be okay. After all X was now the team's star quarterback.

Susie's parents were horrified by her behavior, and Jim's parents were worried sick about his. But the worst came when the twins, Joe and Peggy, decided to share everything with each other. Peggy used Joe's hockey skates, and his microscope, and took half his newspaper route. Joe

39

40

41

42

43

44

45

46

47

---

[6] **ESL** **P.S.:** Abbreviation for postscript; an addition, usually to a letter.
[7] **ESL** **spelling bee:** A spelling contest.
[8] **ESL** **monkey bars:** Children's climbing apparatus on a playground.

used Peggy's needlepoint kit, and her cookbooks, and took two of her three baby-sitting jobs. Peggy started running the lawn mower, and Joe started running the vacuum cleaner.

Their parents weren't one bit pleased with Peggy's wonderful biology experiments, or with Joe's terrific needlepoint pillows. They didn't care that Peggy mowed the lawn better, and that Joe vacuumed the carpet better. In fact, they were furious. It's all that little X's fault, they agreed. Just because X doesn't know what it is, or what it's supposed to be, it wants to get everybody *else* mixed up, too! 48

Peggy and Joe were forbidden to play with X any more. So was Susie, and then Jim, and then *all* the Other Children. But it was too late; the Other Children stayed mixed up and happy and free, and refused to go back to the way they'd been before X. 49

Finally, Joe and Peggy's parents decided to call an emergency meeting of the school's Parents' Association, to discuss "The X Problem." They sent a report to the principal stating that X was a "disruptive influence." They demanded immediate action. The Joneses, they said, should be *forced* to tell whether X was a boy or a girl. And then X should be *forced* to behave like whichever it was. If the Joneses refused to tell, the Parents' Association said, then X must take an Xamination. The school psychiatrist must Xamine it physically and mentally, and issue a full report. If X's test showed it was a boy, it would have to obey all the boys' rules. If it proved to be a girl, X would have to obey all the girls' rules. 50

And if X turned out to be some kind of mixed-up misfit, then X should be Xpelled from the school. Immediately! 51

The principal was very upset. Disruptive influence? Mixed-up misfit? But X was an Xcellent student. All the teachers said it was a delight to have X in their classes. X was president of the student council. X had won first prize in the talent show, and second prize in the art show, and honorable mention in the science fair, and six athletic events on field day, including the potato race. 52

Nevertheless, insisted the Parents' Association, X is a Problem Child. X is the Biggest Problem Child we have ever seen! 53

So the principal reluctantly notified X's parents that numerous complaints about X's behavior had come to the school's attention. And that after the psychiatrist's Xamination, the school would decide what to do about X. 54

The Joneses reported this at once to the scientists, who referred them to page 85,759 of the *Instruction Manual.* "Sooner or later," it said, "X will have to be Xamined by a psychiatrist. This may be the only way any of us will know for sure whether X is mixed up—or whether everyone else is." 55

The night before X was to be Xamined, the Joneses tried not to let X see how worried they were. "What if . . . ?" Mr. Jones would say. And Ms. Jones would reply, "No use worrying." Then a few minutes later, Ms. 56

Jones would say, "What if . . . ?" and Mr. Jones would reply, "No use worrying."

X just smiled at them both, and hugged them hard and didn't say   57
much of anything. X was thinking. What if . . . ? And then X thought: No use worrying."

At Xactly nine o'clock the next day, X reported to the school psychia-   58
trist's office. The principal, along with a committee from the Parents' Association, X's teacher, X's classmates, and Ms. and Mr. Jones, waited in the hall outside. Nobody knew the details of the tests X was to be given, but everybody knew they'd be *very* hard, and that they'd reveal Xactly what everyone wanted to know about X, but were afraid to ask.

It was terribly quiet in the hall. Almost spooky. Once in a while, they   59
would hear a strange noise inside the room. There were buzzes. And a beep or two. And several bells. An occasional light would flash under the door. The Joneses thought it was a white light, but the principal thought it was blue. Two or three children swore it was either yellow or green. And the Parents' Committee missed it completely.

Through it all, you could hear the psychiatrist's low voice, asking hun-   60
dreds of questions, and X's higher voice, answering hundreds of answers.

The whole thing took so long that everyone knew it must be the most   61
complete Xamination anyone had ever had to take. Poor X, the Joneses thought. Serves X right, the Parents' Committee thought. I wouldn't like to be in X's overalls right now, the children thought.

At last, the door opened. Everyone crowded around to hear the re-   62
sults. X didn't look any different; in fact, X was smiling. But the psychiatrist looked terrible. He looked as if he was crying! "What happened?" everyone began shouting. Had X done something disgraceful? "I wouldn't be a bit surprised!" muttered Peggy and Joe's parents. "Did X flunk the *whole* test?" cried Susie's parents. "Or just the most important part?" yelled Jim's parents.

"Oh, dear," sighed Mr. Jones.   63

"Oh, dear," sighed Ms. Jones.   64

"*Sssh*," ssshed the principal. "The psychiatrist is trying to speak."   65

Wiping his eyes and clearing his throat, the psychiatrist began, in a   66
hoarse whisper. "In my opinion," he whispered—you could tell he must be very upset—"in my opinion, young X here . . ."

"Yes? Yes?" shouted a parent impatiently.   67

"*Sssh!*" ssshed the principal.   68

"Young *Sssh* here, I mean young X," said the doctor, frowning, "is   69
just about . . ."

"Just about *what*? Let's have it!" shouted another parent.   70

". . . just about the *least* mixed-up child I've ever Xamined!" said the   71
psychiatrist.

"Yay for X!" yelled one of the children. And then the others began   72
yelling, too. Clapping and cheering and jumping up and down.

"*SSSH!*" SSShed the principal, but nobody did.   73

The Parents' Committee was angry and bewildered. How *could* X   74
have passed the whole Xamination? Didn't X have an *identity* problem?
Wasn't X mixed up at *all*? Wasn't X *any* kind of a misfit? How could it
not be, when it didn't even *know* what it was? And why was the psychiatrist crying?

Actually, he had stopped crying and was smiling politely through his   75
tears. "Don't you see?" he said, "I'm crying because it's wonderful! X has
absolutely no identity problem! X isn't one bit mixed up! As for being a
misfit—ridiculous! X knows perfectly well what it is! Don't you, X?" The
doctor winked, X winked back.

"But what *is* X?" shrieked Peggy and Joe's parents. "We still want to   76
know what it is!"

"Ah, yes," said the doctor, winking again. "Well, don't worry. You'll   77
all know one of these days. And you won't need me to tell you."

"What? What does he mean?" some of the parents grumbled suspi-   78
ciously.

Susie and Peggy and Joe all answered at once. "He means that by the   79
time X's sex matters, it won't be a secret any more!"

With that, the doctor began to push through the crowd toward X's   80
parents. "How do you do," he said, somewhat stiffly. And then he
reached out to hug them both. "If I ever have an X of my own," he whispered, "I sure hope you'll lend me your instruction manual."

Needless to say, the Joneses were very happy. The Project Baby X sci-   81
entists were rather pleased, too. So were Susie, Jim, Peggy, Joe, and all the
Other Children. The Parents' Association wasn't, but they had promised
to accept the psychiatrist's report, and not make any more trouble. They
even invited Ms. and Mr. Jones to become honorary members, which
they did.

Later that day, all X's friends put on their red-and-white checked   82
overalls and went over to see X. They found X in the back yard, playing
with a very tiny baby that none of them had ever seen before. The baby
was wearing very tiny red-and-white checked overalls.

"How do you like our new baby?" X asked the Other Children   83
proudly.

"It's got cute dimples," said Jim.   84

"It's got husky biceps, too," said Susie.   85

"What kind of baby is it?" asked Joe and Peggy.   86

X frowned at them. "Can't you tell?" Then X broke into a big, mis-   87
chievous grin. "*It's a Y!*"

EXERCISING VOCABULARY

1. What does the word *fabulous* mean in the title? What is a fable? How are
these two words related? How do these words relate to this story?

2. The Joneses buy X a storybook about "a brave princess who rescued a handsome prince from his ivory tower" (para. 15). What is the figurative definition of the term "ivory tower"? How does it relate to the fairytale definition?

3. In paragraphs 51 and 52, X is referred to as a "mixed-up misfit." What does the prefix "mis" mean? Then what is a misfit? List some other words that use the same prefix.

PROBING CONTENT

1. What is the goal of Project Baby X? Why was it so difficult for the scientists to select the perfect parents to take part in this experiment?

2. How did friends and relatives react when the Joneses would not reveal the gender of Baby X? Why did they react this way?

3. What were some of the problems the Joneses faced when purchasing clothing and toys for Baby X? What kinds of clothes and playthings did they buy? Why did they make the purchases they did?

4. What problems did X encounter in school? How did the other children respond to their new classmate? What impact did X have on them?

5. What was the X Problem? How was this problem resolved?

CONSIDERING CRAFT

1. From the second paragraph on, there are numerous examples of neologisms like Xperiment and Xactly in this story. What is a neologism? What effect do these words have on your reading? Why has the author chosen to include them?

2. What kinds of stories open with the words "Once upon a time . . ."? What are your expectations for the rest of this story after you have read the opening?

3. Who is the intended audience for this story? Consider the fact that it was first published in *Ms.* magazine, a feminist publication, in 1972.

4. How would you describe the author's tone in this story? How does she approach her topic? What about Gould's writing style? How difficult is the vocabulary? Does the author use figurative language? How effective is the story format in getting across her deeper message about gender roles?

RESPONDING TO THE WRITER

How has gender identity changed since Lois Gould wrote this story more than twenty years ago? What has stayed the same? In what ways does her fable still have relevance today?

For a quiz on this reading, go to www.bedfordstmartins.com/mirror.

Why Boys Don't Play with Dolls

KATHA POLLITT

Why is it that boys still like trucks and girls still like dolls, despite the feminist movement and the changes in traditional sex roles that women had hoped for? Do modern parents really want to change the ways they look at boys' and girls' roles? How would most mothers feel if their son begged to own a Barbie doll? Though studies have shown that children's toy preferences are genetically programmed, Katha Pollitt is not convinced by the research. In "Why Boys Don't Play with Dolls," which was first published in the *New York Times* on October 8, 1995, she asks whether we really have any control over the messages our children receive about what it means to be male or female.

Pollitt is both a respected journalist and an acclaimed poet. Her work has appeared in periodicals including the *Atlantic Monthly*, the *New Yorker*, *Mother Jones*, and the *New York Times Book Review*. Since 1982, Pollitt has been an editor of the *Nation* magazine. For *Antarctic Traveler* (1982), her collection of poetry, Pollitt won a National Book Critics Circle Award.

THINKING AHEAD

Why don't most boys play with dolls? And why don't most girls play with trucks? To what degree are gender differences inborn? How do popular culture and parental influence affect what it means to be male or female?

INCREASING VOCABULARY

robust (adj.) (1)

prenatal (adj.) (1)

cognitive (adj.) (2)

orienting (v.) (2)

invariably (adv.) (2)

innate (adj.) (4)

tentatively (adv.) (4)

ambivalently (adv.) (7)

grotesque (adj.) (7)

flouted (v.) (8)

macho (adj.) (8)

misstep (n.) (10)

psychic (adj.) (11)

paradox (n.) (13)

evoked (v.) (13)

aspire (v.) (14)

ideology (n.) (14)

converging (adj.) (14)

imposing (v.) (16)

inculcating (v.) (16)

It's twenty-eight years since the founding of NOW,[1] and boys still like trucks and girls still like dolls. Increasingly, we are told that the source of these robust preferences must lie outside society—in prenatal hormonal influences, brain chemistry, genes—and that feminism has reached its natural limits. What else could possibly explain the love of preschool girls for party dresses or the desire of toddler boys to own more guns than Mark from Michigan?

True, recent studies claim to show small cognitive differences between the sexes: He gets around by orienting himself in space; she does it by remembering landmarks. Time will tell if any deserve the hoopla[2] with which each is invariably greeted, over the protests of the researchers themselves. But even if the results hold up (and the history of such research is not encouraging), we don't need studies of sex-differentiated brain activity in reading, say, to understand why boys and girls still seem so unalike.

The feminist movement has done much for some women, and something for every woman, but it has hardly turned America into a playground free of sex roles. It hasn't even got women to stop dieting or men to stop interrupting them.

Instead of looking at kids to "prove" that differences in behavior by sex are innate, we can look at the ways we raise kids as an index to how unfinished the feminist revolution really is, and how tentatively it is embraced even by adults who fully expect their daughters to enter previously male-dominated professions and their sons to change diapers.

I'm at a children's birthday party. "I'm sorry," one mom silently mouths to the mother of the birthday girl, who has just torn open her present—Tropical Splash Barbie. Now, you can love Barbie or you can hate Barbie, and there are feminists in both camps. But *apologize* for Barbie? Inflict Barbie, against your own convictions, on the child of a friend you know will be none too pleased?

Every mother in that room had spent years becoming a person who had to be taken seriously, not least by herself. Even the most attractive, I'm willing to bet, had suffered over her body's failure to fit the impossible American ideal. Given all that, it seems crazy to transmit Barbie to the next generation. Yet to reject her is to say that what Barbie represents—being sexy, thin, stylish—is unimportant, which is obviously not true, and children know it's not true.

Women's looks matter terribly in this society, and so Barbie, however ambivalently, must be passed along. After all, there are worse toys. The Cut and Style Barbie styling head, for example, a grotesque object intended to encourage "hair play." The grown-ups who give that probably apologize, too.

[1] **NOW:** National Organization for Women.
[2] **hoopla:** Excited commotion.

How happy would most parents be to have a child who flouted sex   8
conventions? I know a lot of women, feminists, who complain in a comical,
eyeball-rolling way about their sons' passion for sports: the ruined weekends, obnoxious coaches, macho values. But they would not think of dis-
couraging their sons from participating in this activity they find so foolish.
Or do they? Their husbands are sports fans, too, and they like their husbands a lot.

Could it be that even sports-resistant moms see athletics as part of   9
manliness? That if their sons wanted to spend the weekend writing up
their diaries, or reading, or baking, they'd find it disturbing? Too antisocial? Too lonely? Too gay?

Theories of innate differences in behavior are appealing. They let par-   10
ents off the hook—no small recommendation in a culture that holds
moms, and sometimes even dads, responsible for their children's every
misstep on the road to bliss and success.

They allow grown-ups to take the path of least resistance to the domi-   11
nant culture, which always requires less psychic effort, even if it means
more actual work: Just ask the working mother who comes home exhausted and nonetheless finds it easier to pick up her son's socks than
make him do it himself. They let families buy for their children, without
too much guilt, the unbelievably sexist junk that the kids, who have been
watching commercials since birth, understandably crave.

But the thing the theories do most of all is tell adults that the *adult*   12
world—in which moms and dads still play by many of the old rules even
as they question and fidget and chafe against them—is the way it's supposed to be. A girl with a doll and a boy with a truck "explain" why men
are from Mars and women are from Venus, why wives do housework and
husbands just don't understand.

The paradox is that the world of rigid and hierarchical[3] sex roles   13
evoked by determinist[4] theories is already passing away. Three-year-olds
may indeed insist that doctors are male and nurses female, even if their
own mother is a physician. Six-year-olds know better. These days, something like half of all medical students are female, and male applications to
nursing school are inching upward. When tomorrow's three-year-olds
play doctor, who's to say how they'll assign the roles?

With sex roles, as in every area of life, people aspire to what is possible,   14
and conform to what is necessary. But these are not fixed, especially
today. Biological determinism may reassure some adults about their present, but it is feminism, the ideology of flexible and converging sex roles,
that fits our children's future. And the kids, somehow, know this.

That's why, if you look carefully, you'll find that for every kid who   15
fits a stereotype, there's another who's breaking one down. Sometimes
it's the same kid—the boy who skateboards *and* takes cooking in his

[3] **hierarchical:** Arranged according to levels of authority.
[4] **determinist:** One who believes that all events have sufficient natural causes.

afterschool program; the girl who collects stuffed animals *and* A-pluses in science.

Feminists are often accused of imposing their "agenda" on children.   16
Isn't that what adults always do, consciously and unconsciously? Kids aren't born religious, or polite, or kind, or able to remember where they put their sneakers. Inculcating these behaviors, and the values behind them, is a tremendous amount of work, involving many adults. We don't have a choice, really, about *whether* we should give our children messages about what it means to be male and female—they're bombarded with them from morning till night.

EXERCISING VOCABULARY

1. In paragraph 4, Pollitt notes "how tentatively [the feminist revolution] is embraced even by adults who fully expect their daughters to enter previously male-dominated professions and their sons to change diapers." What does it mean to embrace a person? What then does it mean to embrace a cause?

2. Pollitt argues that many adults "still play by many of the old rules [concerning gender roles] even as they question and fidget and chafe against them" (para. 12). What might cause a person to fidget and chafe? What does it mean to fidget and chafe against rules?

3. In paragraph 16, the author writes that children are constantly "bombarded" with messages about "what it means to be male and female." What does it mean to bombard something? What effect does Pollitt hope to achieve by using this word in this context?

PROBING CONTENT

1. According to Pollitt, what lesson can we learn by examining the way in which we raise children? How does she use Barbie and sports to support her argument?

2. How do theories of innate gender differences influence parents? What influence do these theories have on their behavior?

3. What is happening to rigidly differentiated sex roles, according to Pollitt? What evidence does the author offer to prove her point?

4. According to Pollitt, how does feminism "fit our children's future" (para. 14)? What do children know without our teaching them? Give some examples from the essay.

CONSIDERING CRAFT

1. Why does the author mention so many different kinds of Barbie dolls by name? How does this relate to her argument?

2. Paragraph 9 of Pollitt's essay is comprised of a series of rhetorical questions. What is a rhetorical question? How do they function here? Find another example of a rhetorical question in the essay and discuss its function.

3. In paragraph 12, Pollitt writes, "A girl with a doll and a boy with a truck 'explain' why men are from Mars and women are from Venus, why wives do housework and husbands just don't understand." How does this summary statement make use of vivid images? How does it relate to the main idea of the essay? Why is the word *explain* in quotation marks? How does its simple language differ from that of other passages in the essay? Which is more effective?

RESPONDING TO THE WRITER

Do you believe there will ever come a day when boys will play with dolls and girls will play with trucks and no one will notice? Explain your answer. Suppose that parents could successfully forget about the gender of their child. What would be the advantages of this? What would be the disadvantages?

For a quiz on this reading, go to www.bedfordstmartins.com/mirror.

DRAWING CONNECTIONS

1. How would Katha Pollitt ("Why Boys Don't Play with Dolls") respond to Project Baby X ("X: A Fabulous Child's Story")? What aspects of the experiment would she support? What aspects might cause her concern? Why?

2. Would the scientists in charge of Project Baby X in "X: A Fabulous Child's Story" pick any of the parents described in Katha Pollitt's essay "Why Boys Don't Play with Dolls"? Why or why not? How do the parents in Pollitt's essay differ from the Joneses?

FOCUSING ON YESTERDAY, FOCUSING ON TODAY

Describe what you see in this novelty wedding photograph by Jean-Christian Bourcart. What do the sizes and positions of the bride and groom imply about the relationship between the two? What is the message behind the bride's resemblance to either a Barbie doll or the tiny bride figurine poised on the top of a wedding cake? Would most modern brides find this pose an appealing one to place in their wedding albums?

To Have and To Hold

Notice how changing gender roles are reflected in this photograph of Laila Ali, the daughter of heavyweight champion Muhammed Ali and a championship boxer herself. We see this powerful woman sparring with John McClain as she prepares for her match with Karen Bill on April 8, 2000. Here is a daughter who has followed in her father's, not her mother's, footsteps, into a sport still dominated by men. How does her aggressive stance reflect the hard-won battles of the women before her who fought for equality? How have some women moved beyond traditional gender roles? How has the role of the "little woman," who was content to serve her husband and stay home to raise the children, been transformed into a figure like Laila Ali? What role have men played in the evolution of gender roles?

Like Father, Like Daughter (Laila Ali)

REFLECTING ON THE WRITING

1. Using material from the essays in this chapter, as well as your own observations and experiences, write an essay in which you either support or refute the idea that the kinds of toys a child plays with are a strong influence on developing gender identity and self-image.

2. Write an essay in which you prove or disprove Ford's assertion that a gender gap exists in highly technical fields like computer studies. Focus your essay on either school-aged students or college students. To strengthen your argument, you may interview friends and teachers as well as use facts and statistics from written reports.

3. Several of the essays in this chapter address the issue of feminism and its effect on how both men and women view themselves and the opposite sex. After carefully reading these texts, write an essay in which you explore the ways in which the feminist movement has impacted your life, directly or indirectly or both. To support your thesis, use material from the essays and from popular women's and men's magazines.

CONNECTING TO THE CULTURE

1. Based on your own observations and experience as well as information from this chapter, support or refute the idea that women in the United States are a disadvantaged minority group. As you develop your essay, you may reinforce your position by comparing and contrasting the position of women in this society with that of women in a different society.

2. Think about the people who have helped shape your ideas about what it means to be male or female in this society. These may be people you know personally or famous people you have never actually met. These people may have been positive role models for you, helping you to set goals for yourself. In other cases, their influence may have been negative, showing you what you did not want to become. Explore in an essay how one or several of these people have influenced you.

3. Pick an area of popular culture you would like to explore in more depth: music, sports, leisure, television, movies, fashion, or advertising. Write an essay in which you examine the role gender plays in your chosen area. Narrow your topic as much as possible. For example, if you were to pick leisure or television, you could write about the new breed of strong female characters in video games like Tomb Raider or on television shows like *Alias*.

CHAPTER 3

Mirror, Mirror
Cultural Reflections on Body Image

This is an advertisement for Altoids, a brand of British mints famous for their strong taste. The ad features a broadly smiling bodybuilder, complete with perfect teeth. The caption is a play on words. For someone so muscular, we usually would say, "Nice deltoids," referring to the large triangular muscles over the shoulders. However, the play on words is not what catches your eye first.

- What is the hook here?
- Why would a company that manufactures and sells breath mints choose this ad?
- How does this ad reflect our culture's ideas about male attractiveness?

Research this topic with TopLinks at www.bedfordstmartins.com/toplinks.

GEARING UP

Think about the forces that have shaped your impressions of what your body should look like. Then make a list of the major influences. These might include people you know, television and movie actors, models, advertisements, magazines, Web sites, or even songs. Then think about specific times during your teens when you were satisfied or dissatisfied with the way you looked. Why did you feel the way you did? How did these feelings affect you? To what extent do you feel the effects today?

We are aware of body image from the time we are toddlers. "What a pretty little girl" or "What a big strong boy" echoes in our ears and in our minds. At a very early age, we begin to realize that there are very specific feminine and masculine ideals of beauty. Although these can be somewhat culture-specific, all Americans, regardless of ethnicity, quickly discover that the dominant ideal is represented by a young, attractive man or woman who has a fit body, good hair and skin, and a winning smile. Think about the Abercrombie & Fitch models frolicking on the beach, the famous faces selling Revlon cosmetics, or the curvaceous Victoria's Secret models lounging in their sexy lingerie. Think too of the movie stars, television actors, and sports stars you watch and have possibly come to idolize. Can you help wondering how much their good looks contribute to their success? Hasn't research shown that attractive people have an edge over those judged less attractive when all other attributes are equal? Is it an accident that the great majority of American presidents have been more than six feet tall and that tall men are more successful in the world of business?

Obviously, most of us never have or never will look like these "beautiful" people. Luckily, for many of us, our appearance does not become a major lifelong problem. Even though we may have grown up playing with Barbie or Ken, we didn't grow up thinking we had to look like them or like Gwyneth or Brad. Even though most people find the teenage years difficult, since we were discovering then who we are, we have grown into fairly confident adults who are comfortable with our self-image, including our looks. Most of us have decided to make the most of our good features and to downplay or simply live with the less-than-perfect ones.

For some people, however, the search for the perfect body becomes a distracting, even life-threatening, obsession. In an effort to improve on what they were born with or to reverse the march of time, men and women alike have turned to fad diets and exercise programs, diet pills and steroids, anti-aging cosmetics, liposuction, botox and collagen injections, and cosmetic surgery to resculpt their bodies. Some even suffer from eating disorders or drug abuse. In this chapter, you will read selections by a variety of authors about their own struggles with or reflections on body image. Some of the essays are humorous, and some are very serious. All, however, should make you think about your own self-image and the cultural influences that have helped to form it.

COLLABORATING

In groups of four to six students, discuss the question "What makes people attractive?" Brainstorm a list of at least ten attributes each for both men and women. Now study your lists to determine how many of these qualities relate to body image. Share your observations with the rest of the class.

Venus Envy

Patricia McLaughlin

Do you think men today are just as stressed out as women about the way they look? Do the men you know obsess about a few extra pounds here, a little less muscle there, or whether a particular color or style is well suited to the image they want to show the world? In "Venus Envy," first published in the *Philadelphia Inquirer Magazine* on November 5, 1995, Patricia McLaughlin reports on the increasing importance of appearance to a man's self-image, popularity, and career success. In this analysis, McLaughlin draws candid and often humorous parallels with women's long-standing worries about their looks.

McLaughlin has written the "Style" column in the *Philadelphia Inquirer Magazine* since 1983, and her column "Ask Patsy" has appeared on the *TotalWoman.com* network since its launch in April 2000. Her syndicated column appears in over two hundred newspapers nationwide. She has also published feature stories and essays in the *Washington Post, Mirabella*, the *American Scholar*, the *New York Times Magazine*, and *Rolling Stone*.

THINKING AHEAD

How much does gender influence concern with personal appearance? Which specific things about appearance most concern men? Which things most concern women? Compare the amount of time you think men and women devote to looking their best.

INCREASING VOCABULARY

wince (n.) (2)   ogle (v.) (7)
vertiginous (adj.) (3)

It used to be that what mattered in life was how women looked and what men did—which, to many women and other right-thinking people, didn't seem fair. Now, thanks to the efforts of feminists (and a lot of social and economic factors beyond their control) what women do matters more. 1

Meanwhile, in a development that's almost enough to make you believe in the Great Seesaw of Being, how men look is also beginning to carry more weight. Men are having plastic surgery to get rid of their love handles[1] and tighten their eye bags and beef up their chins and flatten their bellies and even *(major wince)* bulk up their penises. They're dyeing 2

---

[1] **love handles:** Excess fat around a man's waist, also called a *spare tire*.

their hair to hide the gray. They're buying magazines to find out how to lose those pesky last five pounds.

Naturally, women who always envied the way men never had to suffer to be beautiful think they're making a big mistake. (What next: too-small shoes with vertiginous heels?) But maybe they don't exactly have a choice.

The key to how men feel about how they look, says Michael Pertschuk, who's writing a book about it, is social expectation: What do they think folks expect them to look like? And how far do folks expect them to go to look that way?

You think of anorexia and bulimia as disorders that strike teenage girls, but men get them, too—not many, but "a bit more" than used to, according to Pertschuk, a psychiatrist who sees patients (including men) with eating disorders. Because eating disorders virtually always start with a "normal" desire to lose weight and look slimmer, the increase among men suggests that men are worrying about their looks more than they used to.

Pertschuk has also worked with the dermatologists and plastic surgeons at the Center for Human Appearance at the University of Pennsylvania to screen candidates for cosmetic surgery, and he says "there are certainly more male plastic surgery patients," which suggests the same thing: "It's become more culturally accepted or expected for men to be concerned about their appearance."

And no wonder, when you look at the media. Stephen Perrine, articles editor at *Men's Health,* a magazine that in the last six years has built a circulation as big as *Esquire*'s and *GQ*'s put together, says the mass media "in the last five to seven years has really changed the way it portrays men." Whether you look at Calvin Klein's[2] underwear ads or that Diet Coke commercial where the girls in the office ogle the shirtless construction hunk, "men are more and more portrayed as sex objects. . . . So they're feeling the way women have for many, many years: 'Oh, that's what's expected of me? *That's* what I'm supposed to look like?'" And they—some of them, anyway—rush to live up to those expectations.

Which—wouldn't you know?—turns out to be a heck of a lot easier for them than it ever was for women: "It's easier for men to change their bodies," Perrine says, "easier to build muscle, easier to burn fat." Besides, the male physical ideal is more realistic to begin with: A man "who's healthy and works out . . . will look like Ken, but a woman can exercise till she's dead, and she's not going to look like Barbie," Perrine says.

Ken? Is that really what women want?

Maybe some women. Me, I get all weak in the knees when I see a guy running a vacuum, or unloading a dishwasher without being asked. Not that Calvin Klein is ever going to advertise his underwear on a cute guy with a nice big electric broom.

But what women want isn't the point.

---

[2] **ESL** Calvin Klein: A popular American fashion designer.

Used to be, Pertschuk says, men who had plastic surgery said they   12
were doing it for their careers: They wouldn't get promoted if they looked
old and fat and tired. Now they say the same thing women do: "I want to
feel better about myself." In other words, they look at their love handles
or eyebags or pot bellies or saggy chins and feel inadequate and ugly and
unworthy, just the way women have been feeling all along about their
hips, stomachs, thighs, breasts, wrinkles, etc.

That's new: For more men, self-regard has come to hinge not just on   13
what they do, but on what they see in the mirror. And it's easier to change
that than the values that make them feel bad about it.

EXERCISING VOCABULARY

1. What does the adjective *pesky* (para. 2) mean? This word sounds like the
   noun *pest.* What characteristics do pests and pesky things share? In what
   way could the last five pounds of a diet be pesky?

2. Check your "Increasing Vocabulary" definition for *vertiginous.* Using that definition as a starting point, explain what a person who suffers from vertigo
   fears. How does the phrase "too-small shoes with vertiginous heels" (para. 3)
   relate to what McLaughlin is saying here?

PROBING CONTENT

1. According to McLaughlin, what three changes in men's behavior show that
   they are worrying more about their looks than they used to? How are these
   changes a reaction to what is happening in our society?

2. Why does McLaughlin say it is easier for men to conform to a cultural ideal
   than it is for women? Where are these ideas about cultural ideals coming
   from?

3. According to Michael Pertschuk, in the past, why did men say they were alter-
   ing their appearance by such methods as plastic surgery? How have the reasons men give changed? What does this change mean?

CONSIDERING CRAFT

1. Who is Venus? How does knowing who she is help you to understand the
   deliberate play on words in this essay's title?

2. How does McLaughlin's quoting Michael Pertschuk and Stephen Perrine help
   make her point? If she wanted to use other sources, what would she gain by
   quoting them directly instead of just summing up their opinions?

3. What is the effect of having paragraphs 9 and 11 each be only one sentence
   long? What makes this strategy successful?

4. In her conclusion, McLaughlin restates her thesis. How does this kind of conclusion benefit the reader? How does it benefit the writer?

RESPONDING TO THE WRITER

To what extent does McLaughlin's essay persuade you that men and women suffer equally when it comes to agonizing about personal appearance? What in your
personal experience and your knowledge of the opposite sex causes you to either
support or doubt her position?

For a quiz on this reading, go to www.bedfordstmartins.com/mirror.

Barbie's Newest Values

GLORIA BORGER

One of the most widely recognized figures in the world doesn't belong to an athlete, a rock singer, or a movie star. It belongs to a doll. According to Douglas Kalajian, a reporter for the *Palm Beach Post*, by December 1998 the number of Barbies worldwide was close to one billion in 140 countries. An average of eight Barbies and friends reside in the home of each U.S. girl between the ages of three and eleven.

Most toys peak and fade. Where have all the Cabbage Patch Kids gone? The Pound Puppies? The Furbys? Barbie holds her own. She has experienced more careers and jumped into her pink convertible in more outfits than we can imagine. What explains her enormous popularity? Some people blame Barbie for creating an impossible standard of womanhood that no real woman can possibly achieve. Is this doll responsible for fostering impossible expectations about the female body? Has Barbie's figure caused young girls to resort to anorexia, bulimia, diet pills, and excessive exercise? Critics of Barbie fault her and her parent company, Mattel, for contributing to a social climate that overemphasizes looks at the expense of other qualities.

Taking such criticisms to heart, Mattel signed Barbie up for an extraordinary round of plastic surgery in 1998. Her breasts were reduced, her waist was enlarged, and her face was changed just a bit, all to produce a more "realistic" ideal. Just as she was undergoing her reinvention, however, Gloria Borger wrote this December 1, 1997, *U.S. News & World Report* article declaring that Barbie's figure wasn't ever the real issue in the first place. Borger is a Barbie owner, a contributing editor for *U.S. News & World Report*, a CBS News analyst, and a frequent panelist on PBS's popular *Washington Week in Review*. Here she argues a position that may surprise you.

THINKING AHEAD

Of the toys you played with as a child, which ones were your favorites? Why? Did these toys influence your ideas about what girls should do or be or what boys should do or be? In what ways? Were certain toys, games, and activities presented to you because you were a boy or a girl (for example, girls receive toy kitchens and boys trains and airplanes)? Or were you free to choose any toy to play with?

INCREASING VOCABULARY

replenish (v.) (1)   elitist (n.) (6)

I was all set to write something nasty about Iraq when a headline on the front page of the *Wall Street Journal* trumpeted some news not to be disregarded: "Top-Heavy Barbie Is Getting Body Work." And more. The headline also reveals this new line of Barbie dolls will have a new face, too. "When Plastic Surgery Is Done, She Will Be 'Really Rad,'" which happens to be her new name, as in "radical." All told, Barbie is getting new breasts (smaller), a new waist (wider), and a different mouth (closed). The folks at Mattel Inc. hope that little girls will (a) find this makeover awesome and (b) be struck with a sudden urge to replenish their collections.

Enough already. Every time Mattel tries to update Barbie, it turns into a PC nightmare. Remember the Teen Talk Barbie who said, "Math class is tough"? Feminists revolted. The wheelchair of Barbie's recently invented disabled friend, Share a Smile Becky, didn't fit inside Barbie's two-story pink mansion. Advocates for the disabled protested. And now the toy maker is changing Barbie's buxom, leggy figure partly out of "sensitivity" to those who say that girls grow up wanting to look like Barbie, whose measurements would make it impossible for her to stand upright in real life. The other (real) reason is so Barbie can look good in her new hip-huggers.[1]

Don't get me wrong: I'm no Barbie hater. I once owned one, or ten. I believe it's a good thing that Barbie is now available in an assortment of races, hair colors, and professions. And maybe Barbie's upcoming effort at physical correctness will inspire a whole generation of female plastic surgeons. Or patients.

But Barbie's bosom aside, let's be clear about something: Six-year-olds are not protesting that Barbie is too glamorous or too tacky. It's the self-indulgent gen X-ers who complain that Barbie has hurt their self-image. (Thereby forcing them into their nose-ring phase?) And it's the narcissistic (and aging) baby boomers[2] who still believe they determine every fashion and cultural trend—even Barbie's style. (What's next? Barbie in Birkenstocks?[3] Totally Cellulite[4] Barbie?)

All of this, however, misses a more important point: It's not Barbie's figure that's the big problem. It's her values. Whatever size blouse Barbie wears, she lately seems to be ordering most of her clothes from the likes of Ralph Lauren, Bill Blass, Bob Mackie, and Christian Dior. These designers are a part of a line of Barbie collectibles that are groomed to appeal to those upwardly[5] mobile baby boomer moms who thought Barbie looked too cheap for their children. "When I grew up, I thought Barbie was middle class," says Democratic pollster Celinda Lake. "I thought she

[1] **ESL** **hip-huggers:** Pants cut low on the hips.
[2] **ESL** **baby boomer:** People born between the years 1946 to 1964.
[3] **ESL** **Birkenstocks:** A popular brand of sandal.
[4] **ESL** **cellulite:** Bumpy or dimpled skin on the thighs or arms due to fat deposits under the skin.
[5] **ESL** **upwardly mobile:** A term applied to those who desire a higher economic status.

was like us." No more. Now Barbie is into labels, and she's not shopping at outlet[6] malls.

Alas, Barbie has become a snob. While she was mod[7] in the '60s and disco[8] in the '70s, by 1980, "she had the taste of a lottery winner," says M. G. Lord, author of *Forever Barbie*. "At the core of this change is class." Mattel spokeswoman Lisa McKendall says this is rubbish, since these upwardly mobile dolls — which start at about $65 a pop—are designed for grown-ups to play with. Please. What about a recent ad for Bloomingdale's[9] Ralph Lauren Barbie, which claims to be "the most sophisticated Barbie ever." What adult is this aimed at? Barbie's makers also say they want more realism in their dolls, and maybe that's what we're getting: You're never too young to become an elitist.

As the mother of young sons, I've never had lengthy wardrobe discussions. Boys into Power Rangers[10] do not feel the need to find shoes to match their laser guns. But wait. Like those girls begging for Barbie's glen plaid Ralph Lauren handbag, my boys have shown an increasing fondness for Nike-brand items—shorts, shirts, and sneakers. Getting hooked early is what it's about, and we make it easy. After all, insecure baby boomers teach their kids to constantly strive upward. Class warfare, once a Democratic party line, is definitely not a boomer gig. Class coding is. And the marketers know it.

Of course, it's easy to overstate the impact of Barbie. She's a fantasy doll for girls, not a real role model for women. (Some of us, however, await the Madeleine Albright[11] diplomatic collection, featuring a secretary of state who finally knows how to accessorize.) As for the controversy over Barbie's new body, there's one more hidden lesson for little girls who want to be big girls: No matter how her measurements evolve, Barbie will always be a smallish size—as long as she's wearing expensive clothes. In real life, designers reduce sizes all the time, making size-8 baby boomers feel like a young size 6 again. Surely they'll do it for Barbie, too.

EXERCISING VOCABULARY

1. Identify the age groups who make up the populations Borger calls "the self-indulgent gen X-ers" and the "narcissistic (and aging) baby boomers" (para. 4). What does her choice of adjectives tell you about how Borger views each group?

---

[6] **ESL** **outlet malls:** A large plaza of brand-name stores that offer discount prices on brand merchandise.

[7] **ESL** **mod:** An abbreviated term for *modern* that refers to a style trend of the 1960s.

[8] **ESL** **disco:** A form of dance, dance-music, and nightclub from the 1970s made popular by the movie *Saturday Night Fever* starring John Travolta.

[9] **ESL** **Bloomingdales':** A large, Manhattan-based department store.

[10] **ESL** **Power Rangers:** A popular children's action television show featuring multi-colored, multi-gendered humans dressed as robot warriors.

[11] **ESL** **Madeleine Albright:** 64th U.S. Secretary of State, from 1997–2001.

2. What does an *elitist* believe? If you were an elitist, how would you react to the idea that every high school basketball player on the school team should have equal playing time on the court?

PROBING CONTENT

1. Why does Mattel say that it made physical changes to Barbie? What does the writer believe is the real reason?

2. Give an example of "a PC [politically correct] nightmare" (para. 2) already associated with Barbie. If Mattel's intentions were to include more young girls in Barbie's world, how have the plans backfired?

3. Borger doesn't believe that the problems with Barbie center around her impossible figure. What does Borger think the real problem is? What evidence supports her position?

4. Borger's sons have no interest in Barbies, yet Borger sees a certain awareness of class and status in their preferences, too. How do her sons reflect the influence of carefully aimed advertising? What does this have to do with Barbie and Borger's thesis?

CONSIDERING CRAFT

1. Evaluate the writer's tone in this essay, citing a few specific sentences to support your evaluation. What assumptions does she make about her audience? Would these assumptions be true of most people who read *U.S. News & World Report*, the publication in which this essay first appeared?

2. What does Borger do to grab the reader's attention at the opening of her essay? What about the first paragraph encourages you to keep reading?

RESPONDING TO THE WRITER

To what extent has Borger accurately reflected Barbie's influence on our culture? How do Barbie's "values" reflect our own?

For a quiz on this reading, go to www.bedfordstmartins.com/mirror.

My Inner Shrimp

GARRY TRUDEAU

Garry Trudeau's humorous essay "My Inner Shrimp" examines the impact of body image on the fragile self-esteem of a teenager. As a short high school student, Trudeau tried everything to overcome this dilemma: hanging from door frames, sleeping on his back, and doing floor exercises. His sense of self became so wrapped up in his appearance that he attributed all his normal teenage problems to his height. Even though Trudeau had a delayed growth spurt and is now over six feet tall, he admits that he still has the "soul of a shrimp." Do you, like Trudeau, believe that adolescent insecurities follow us into adulthood? Do you still see yourself as others saw you in your high school years?

Trudeau is well known for his comic strip *Doonesbury*, for which he won a Pulitzer Prize in 1975. He has contributed articles to *The New Yorker*, *The New Republic*, *Harper's*, the *Washington Post*, *Time*, and the *New York Times*. "My Inner Shrimp" first appeared in the *New York Times Magazine* on March 31, 1997.

THINKING AHEAD

Describe a time when you have been dissatisfied with the way you look, when your "inner" and "outer" body image have been at odds. How did this affect you?

INCREASING VOCABULARY

diminutive (adj.) (1)	perverse (adj.) (9)
harrowing (adj.) (1)	compelling (adj.) (9)
flukish (adj.) (1)	contingent (n.) (10)
warren (n.) (2)	ignominiously (adv.) (10)
ascended (v.) (3)	taunt (v.) (10)
excruciatingly (adv.) (3)	ancillary (adj.) (11)
resolutely (adv.) (4)	calamities (n.) (12)

For the rest of my days, I shall be a recovering short person. Even from my lofty perch of something over six feet (as if I don't know within a micron), I have the soul of a shrimp. I feel the pain of the diminutive, irrespective of whether they feel it themselves, because my visit to the planet of the teenage midgets was harrowing, humiliating, and extended. I even perceive my last-minute escape to have been flukish, somehow un-earned—as if the Commissioner of Growth Spurts had been an old class-mate of my father.

My most recent reminder of all this came the afternoon I went hunting for a new office. I had noticed a building under construction in my neighborhood—a brick warren of duplexes, with wide, westerly-facing windows, promising ideal light for a working studio. When I was ushered into the model unit, my pulse quickened: The soaring, twenty-two-foot living room walls were gloriously aglow with the remains of the day. I bonded immediately.

Almost as an afterthought, I ascended the staircase to inspect the loft, ducking as I entered the bedroom. To my great surprise, I stayed ducked: The room was a little more than six feet in height. While my head technically cleared the ceiling, the effect was excruciatingly oppressive. This certainly wasn't a space I wanted to spend any time in, much less take out a mortgage on.

Puzzled, I wandered down to the sales office and asked if there were any other units to look at. No, replied a resolutely unpleasant receptionist, it was the last one. Besides, they were all exactly alike.

"Are you aware of how low the bedroom ceilings are?" I asked.

She shot me an evil look. "Of course we are," she snapped. "There were some problems with the building codes. The architect knows all about the ceilings.

"He's not an idiot, you know," she added, perfectly anticipating my next question.

She abruptly turned away, but it was too late. She'd just confirmed that a major New York developer, working with a fully licensed architect, had knowingly created an entire twelve-story apartment building virtually uninhabitable by anyone of even average height. It was an exclusive high-rise for shorties.

Once I knew that, of course, I couldn't stay away. For days thereafter, as I walked to work, some perverse, unreasoning force would draw me back to the building. But it wasn't just the absurdity, the stone silliness of its design that had me in its grip; it was something far more compelling. Like some haunted veteran come again to an ancient battlefield, I was revisiting my perilous past.

When I was fourteen, I was the third-smallest in a high school class of one hundred boys, routinely mistaken for a sixth grader. My first week of school, I was drafted into a contingent of students ignominiously dubbed the "Midgets," so grouped by taller boys presumably so they could taunt us with more perfect efficiency. Inexplicably, some of my fellow Midgets refused to be diminished by the experience, but I retreated into self-pity. I sent away for a book on how to grow tall, and committed to memory its tips on overcoming one's genetic destiny—or at least making the most of a regrettable situation. The book cited historical figures who had gone the latter route—Alexander the Great, Caesar, Napoleon (the mind involuntarily added Hitler). Strategies for stretching the limbs were suggested—hanging from door frames, sleeping on your back, doing assorted floor exercises—all of which I incorporated into my daily routine (get up, brush teeth, hang from door frame). I also learned the importance of meeting girls early in the day, when, the book assured me, my rested spine rendered me perceptibly taller.

For six years, my condition persisted; I grew, but at nowhere near the rate of my peers. I perceived other problems as ancillary, and loaded up the stature issue with freight shipped in daily from every corner of my life. Lack of athletic success, all absence of a social life, the inevitable run-ins with bullies—all could be attributed to the missing inches. The night I found myself sobbing in my father's arms was the low point; we both knew it was one problem he couldn't fix.   11

Of course what we couldn't have known was that he and my mother already had. They had given me a delayed developmental timetable. In my seventeenth year, I miraculously shot up six inches, just in time for graduation and a fresh start. I was, in the space of a few months, reborn—and I made the most of it. Which is to say that thereafter, all of life's disappointments, reversals, and calamities still arrived on schedule—but blissfully free of subtext.   12

Once you stop being the butt, of course, any problem recedes, if only to give way to a new one. And yet the impact of being literally looked down on, of being *made* to feel small, is forever. It teaches you how to stretch, how to survive the scorn of others for things that are beyond your control. Not growing forces you to grow up fast.   13

Sometimes I think I'd like to return to a high-school reunion to surprise my classmates. Not that they didn't know me when I finally started catching up. They did, but I doubt they'd remember. Adolescent hierarchies have a way of enduring; I'm sure I am still recalled as the Midget I myself have never really left behind.   14

Of course, if I'm going to show up, it'll have to be soon. I'm starting to shrink.   15

EXERCISING VOCABULARY

1. Trudeau refers to himself in the opening sentence as a "recovering short person." What type of person do you usually think of when you hear the word *recovering*? How does the author's word choice prepare you for the subject of this essay?

2. In paragraph 12, Trudeau explains that when he was seventeen, "all of life's disappointments, reversals, and calamities still arrived on schedule — but blissfully free of subtext." What is a subtext? What is the subtext to which the author is referring in this sentence?

3. Trudeau states that "Adolescent hierarchies have a way of enduring" (para. 14). What is a hierarchy? Give an example. What does he mean when he refers to adolescent hierarchies? Give some examples from your own experience to explain your response.

PROBING CONTENT

1. What effect did the author's visit to the new apartment building have on him? Why did it affect him this way?

2. What problem did Trudeau have in high school? How did he react to the nickname he was given? How did his reaction differ from that of others with the same problem? How did he attempt to overcome this problem?

3. What happened when Trudeau was seventeen? How did this affect Trudeau's outlook on life?

4. Has Trudeau completely overcome his high school anxiety? Support your response with material from his essay. What does he mean when he says, "I'm starting to shrink" in the final paragraph?

CONSIDERING CRAFT

1. Trudeau is a well-known cartoonist. Describe his tone in this essay. How does he use humor in this essay to drive home his argument? Refer to several specific examples, including the title.

2. The author makes use of alliteration in paragraphs 2, 4, and 10. What is alliteration? How does the use of it affect your reading of the essay?

3. Trudeau's use of irony often enhances his writing. In paragraph 10, he writes, "some of my fellow Midgets refused to be diminished by the experience." How is this statement ironic? What effect does he achieve by using irony here?

RESPONDING TO THE WRITER

How do you respond to Trudeau's obsession with his "inner shrimp"? Do you empathize with him? If so, why? Or do you think he makes too much of his "problem," especially since many will say he should have "grown out of it"? Explain your response.

For a quiz on this reading, go to www.bedfordstmartins.com/mirror.

"Going Thin" in Fiji
Now That Television Has Arrived

ELLEN GOODMAN

How does television's unrealistic portrayal of how women "should" look affect young women? In the following essay, Ellen Goodman examines American television's effect on Fiji's teenagers. Before 1995 — the year that American television arrived in Fiji — "going thin" was undesirable. Instead, being big was considered beautiful. But soon after American television programming invaded the island nation, almost three-quarters of Fiji's teenage girls felt "too big" or "too fat" at some time. What does this say about the entertainment industry and its expectations of women? Is insecurity about body image the United States' number one export?

Goodman's Pulitzer Prize–winning editorial commentary appears in more than 450 newspapers nationwide. Currently an associate editor and columnist at the *Boston Globe*, she has also been a staff writer at *Newsweek* and the *Detroit Free Press*. Goodman has published six collections of her essays, including *Value Judgments* (1993), *Making Sense* (1989), and *Keeping in Touch* (1985). "'Going Thin' in Fiji Now That Television Has Arrived" first appeared in the *Boston Globe* on May 27, 1999.

THINKING AHEAD

How do television actors, both male and female, affect our cultural ideals of beauty? Name several actors that you believe have influenced your or your peers' ideas about body image. How have they done this? What specific changes in appearance have you or your friends made or considered because of this influence?

INCREASING VOCABULARY

satire (n.) (3)	subsistence (adj.) (9)
imperative (n.) (4)	robust (adj.) (10)
rites (n.) (4)	disparity (n.) (13)
anorexia (n.) (8)	ample (adj.) (14)
bulimia (n.) (8)	massacre (n.) (16)

First of all, imagine a place women greet one another at the market with open arms, loving smiles, and a cheerful exchange of ritual compliments: 1

"You look wonderful! You've put on weight!" 2

Does that sound like dialogue from Fat Fantasyland? Or a skit from 3 fat-is-a-feminist-issue satire? Well, this Western fantasy was a South Pacific fact of life. In Fiji, before 1995, big was beautiful and bigger was more beautiful—and people really did flatter one another with exclamations about weight gain.

In this island paradise, food was not only love, it was a cultural imperative. Eating and overeating were rites of mutual hospitality. Everyone worried about losing weight—but not the way we do. "Going thin" was considered to be a sign of some social problem, a worrisome indication the person wasn't getting enough to eat.   4

The Fijians were, to be sure, a bit obsessed with food; they prescribed herbs to stimulate the appetite. They were a reverse image of our culture. And that turns out to be the point.   5

Something happened in 1995. A Western mirror was shoved into the face of the Fijians. Television came to the island. Suddenly, the girls of rural coastal villages were watching the girls of *Melrose Place* and *Beverly Hills 90210.*   6

Within 38 months, the number of teenagers at risk for eating disorders more than doubled to 29 percent. The number of high school girls who vomited for weight control went up five times to 15 percent. Worse yet, 74 percent of the Fiji teens in the study said they felt "too big or fat" at least some of the time and 62 percent said they had dieted in the past month.   7

This before-and-after television portrait of a body image takeover was drawn by Anne Becker, an anthropologist and psychiatrist who directs research at the Harvard Eating Disorders Center. She presented her research at the American Psychiatric Association last week with all the usual caveats.[1] No, you cannot prove a direct causal link between television and eating disorders. Heather Locklear[2] doesn't cause anorexia.   8

Fiji is not just a Fat Paradise Lost. It's an economy in transition from subsistence agriculture to tourism and its entry into the global economy has threatened many old values.   9

Nevertheless, you don't get a much better lab experiment than this. In just 38 months, and with only one channel, a television-free culture that defined a fat person as robust has become a television culture that sees robust as, well, repulsive.   10

"Going thin" is no longer a social disease but the perceived requirement for getting a good job, nice clothes, and fancy cars. As Becker says carefully, "The acute and constant bombardment of certain images in the media are apparently quite influential in how teens experience their bodies."   11

Speaking of Fiji teenagers in a way that sounds all-too familiar, she adds, "We have a set of vulnerable teens consuming television. There's a huge disparity between what they see on television and what they look like themselves—that goes not only to clothing, hairstyles, and skin color, but size of bodies."   12

[1] **caveats:** Warnings.
[2] **ESL Heather Locklear:** An actress in television series including *Melrose Place* and *Spin City.*

In short, the sum of Western culture, the big success story of our en-   13
tertainment industry, is our ability to export insecurity: We can make any
woman anywhere feel perfectly rotten about her shape.

I'm not surprised by research showing that eating disorders are a cul-   14
tural byproduct. We've watched the female image shrink down to Calista
Flockhart[3] at the same time we've seen eating problems grow. But Hollywood hasn't been exactly eager to acknowledge the connection between
image and illness.

Since the Columbine High[4] massacre, we've broken through some de-   15
nial about violence as a teaching tool. It's pretty clear that boys are literally learning how to hate and harm others.

Maybe we ought to worry a little more about what girls learn: To   16
hate and harm themselves.

EXERCISING VOCABULARY

1. In paragraph 4, Goodman states that before 1995 food was a "cultural imperative." What is an imperative? How important did this make food? In what
   sense is food cultural?

2. In paragraph 5, Goodman describes the Fijian culture before 1995 as "a reverse
   image" of our own. What is a reverse image? How did the Fijian ideal of female beauty fit this description?

PROBING CONTENT

1. How did women greet each other in Fiji before 1995? What does this tell you
   about Fijian women's body image prior to this date?

2. How did Fijian women's body image change after 1995? What does Goodman
   believe is responsible for this change? What did "going thin" imply to other
   Fijians?

3. According to Goodman, what did the tragedy at Columbine High teach us
   about young men? What does she think we should learn about young
   women from the Fijian women's response to television?

CONSIDERING CRAFT

1. Why does Goodman quote Anne Becker in paragraphs 11 and 12 and cite various statistics in paragraph 7? How does this strategy advance the author's
   argument?

---

[3] **ESL** **Calista Flockhart:** Star of *Ally McBeal*, noted for her thin frame.
[4] **ESL** **Columbine High:** Littleton, Colorado, site of fatal school shooting that occurred on
    April 20, 1999.

2. Goodman refers to the titles of specific television shows and actors in her essay. Locate several examples. What purpose do these references serve for the author?

3. Goodman says that in 1995, "A Western mirror was shoved into the face of the Fijians" (para. 6). Explain what she means by this metaphor.

RESPONDING TO THE WRITER

Consider possible ways to confront the problem posed by Goodman in the last line of her essay. How do you think she would get girls to quit hating and harming themselves? What would you suggest?

For a quiz on this reading, go to www.bedfordstmartins.com/mirror.

Dying to Be Bigger

H. D.

The potentially devastating effects of anabolic steroids and other performance-enhancing drugs continue to receive media attention. From Olympic medalists to high school football players, some athletes seem drawn to these so-called wonder drugs. Some people even insist that Mark McGwire's use of such substances tarnished his otherwise stellar baseball record in 1998 for the most home runs in a single season. Why do athletes, who perhaps value their bodies much more than the rest of us, place their most valuable asset at such potentially disastrous risk? Is the quest to be the biggest, the fastest, the buffest, the best really worth the possible consequences?

In "Dying to Be Bigger," a young man recounts his own frightening experiences with steroids. While the abuse of steroids is not solely a male concern, many young men have been seduced by this supposedly fast track to physical prowess and optimal performance. H. D., who was born in 1970, wrote this personal account while he was a university undergraduate. He graduated in August 1993 with plans to pursue a doctorate in clinical psychology. His essay was first published in *Seventeen* magazine in December 1991.

THINKING AHEAD

Have you ever been tempted to take radical steps to enhance your physical attractiveness? Have you known others who have sought to change their bodies through the use of steroids, diet pills, plastic surgery, rigid dieting, or excessive exercise? What do people who take such steps expect to achieve? How significant are the risks? Why are some people willing to accept the possible negative consequences?

INCREASING VOCABULARY

maiming (v.) (1)

cocky (adj.) (2)

perversion (n.) (7)

equine (adj.) (13)

plummeted (v.) (16)

celibacy (n.) (17)

ramification (n.) (21)

depleted (v.) (21)

fluctuated (v.) (22)

I was only fifteen years old when I first started maiming my body with the abuse of anabolic steroids.[1] I was always trying to fit in with the "cool" crowd in junior high and high school. Willingly smoking or buying pot when offered, socially drinking in excess, displaying a macho

---

[1] **anabolic steroids:** Group of usually synthetic hormones used by athletes in training to temporarily increase muscle size and metabolism.

image—and, of course, the infamous "kiss and tell" were essentials in completing my insecure mentality.

Being an immature, cocky kid from a somewhat wealthy family, I wasn't very well liked in general. In light of this, I got beat up a lot, especially in my first year of public high school. 2

I was one of only three sophomores to get a varsity letter in football. At five-foot-nine and 174 pounds, I was muscularly inferior to the guys on the same athletic level and quite conscious of the fact. So when I heard about this wonderful drug called steroids from a teammate, I didn't think twice about asking to buy some. I could hardly wait to take them and start getting bigger. 3

I bought three months' worth of Dianobol (an oral form of steroids and one of the most harmful). I paid fifty-five dollars. I was told to take maybe two or three per day. I totally ignored the directions and warnings and immediately started taking five per day. This is how eager I was to be bigger and possibly "cooler." 4

Within only a week, everything about me started to change. I was transforming mentally and physically. My attention span became almost nonexistent. Along with becoming extremely aggressive, I began to abandon nearly all academic and family responsibilities. In almost no time, I became flustered and agitated with simple everyday activities. My narcissistic ways brought me to engage in verbal as well as physical fights with family, friends, teachers, but mostly strangers. 5

My bodily transformations were clearly visible. In less than a month, I took the entire three-month supply. I gained nearly thirty pounds. Most of my weight was from water retention, although at the time I believed it to be muscle. Instead of having pimples like the average teenager, my acne took the form of grotesque, cystlike blood clots that would occasionally burst while I was lifting weights. My nipples became the size of grapes and hurt severely, which is common among male steroid users. My hormonal level was completely out of whack.[2] 6

At first I had such an overload of testosterone that I would have to masturbate daily, at minimum, in order to prevent having "wet dreams." Obviously these factors enhanced my lust, which eventually led to acute perversion. My then almost-horrifying physique prevented me from having any sexual encounters. 7

All of these factors led to my classification as a wretched menace. My parents grew sick and tired of all the trouble I began to get in. They were scared of me, it seemed. They cared so much about my welfare, education, and state of mind that they sent me to a boarding school that summer. 8

I could not obtain any more steroids there, and for a couple of months it seemed I had subtle withdrawal symptoms and severe side effects. Most of the time that summer I was either depressed or filled with intense anger, both of which were uncontrollable unless I was in a state of intoxication from any mind-altering drug. 9

---

[2] **ESL** **out of whack:** Not normal.

After a year of being steroid-free, things started to look promising for me, and I eventually gained control over myself. Just when I started getting letters from big-name colleges to play football for them, I suffered a herniated disc. I was unable to participate in any form of physical activity the entire school year.

In the fall, I attended a university in the Northeast, where I was on the football team but did not play due to my injury. I lifted weights with the team every day. I wasn't very big at the time, even after many weeks of working out. Once again I found myself to be physically inferior and insecure about my physique. And again came into contact with many teammates using steroids.

My roommate was a six-foot-three, 250-pound linebacker who played on the varsity squad as a freshman. As the weeks passed, I learned of my roommate's heavy steroid use. I was exposed to dozens of different steroids I had never even heard of. Living in the same room with him, I watched his almost daily injections. After months of enduring his drug offerings, I gave in.

By the spring of my freshman year, I had become drastically far from normal in every way. My body had stopped producing hormones due to the amount of synthetic testosterone I injected into my system. At five-foot-eleven, 225 pounds, disproportionately huge, acne-infested, outrageously aggressive, and nearing complete sterility, I was in a terrible state of body and mind. Normal thoughts of my future (not pertaining to football), friends, family, reputation, moral status, etc., were entirely beyond me. My whole entire essence had become one of a primitive barbarian. This was when I was taking something called Sustunon (prepackaged in a syringe labeled "For equine use only") containing four types of testosterone. I was "stacking" (a term used by steroid users which means mixing different types) to get well-cut definition along with mass.

It was around this time when I was arrested for threatening a security guard. When the campus police came to arrest me, they saw how aggressive and large my roommate and I were. So they searched our room and found dozens of bottles and hundreds of dollars' worth of steroids and syringes. We had a trial, and the outcome was that I could only return the next year if I got drug-tested on a monthly basis. I certainly had no willpower or desire to quit my steroid abuse, so I transferred schools.

After a summer of even more heavy-duty abuse, I decided to attend a school that would cater to my instinctively backward ways. That fall I entered a large university in the South. Once again I simply lifted weights without being involved in competition or football. It was there that I finally realized how out of hand I'd become with my steroid problem.

Gradually I started to taper down my dosages. Accompanying my reduction, I began to drink more and more. My grades plummeted again. I began going to bars and keg parties on a nightly basis.

My celibacy, mental state, aggressiveness, lack of athletic competition, and alcohol problem brought me to enjoy passing my pain onto others by means of physical aggression. I got into a fight almost every time I drank. In the midst of my insane state, I was arrested for assault. I was in really deep this time. Finally I realized how different from everybody else I'd become, and I decided not to taper off but to quit completely.

The average person seems to think that steroids just make you bigger.   18
But they are a drug, and an addictive one at that. This drug does not put you in a stupor or in a hallucinogenic state but rather gives you an up, all-around "bad-ass" mentality that far exceeds that of either normal life or any other narcotic I've tried with not taking steroids. Only lately are scientists and researchers discovering how addictive steroids are — only now, after hundreds of thousands may have done such extreme damage to their lives, bodies, and minds.

One of the main components of steroid addiction is how unsatisfied   19
the user is with his overall appearance. Although I was massive and had dramatic muscular definition, I was never content with my body, despite frequent compliments. I was always changing types of steroids, places of injection, workouts, diet, etc. I always found myself saying, "This one oughta do it" or "I'll quit when I hit 230 pounds."

When someone is using steroids, he has psychological disorders   20
that increase when usage stops. One disorder is anxiety from the loss of the superior feeling you get from the drug. Losing the muscle mass, high energy level, and superhuman sensation that you're so accustomed to is terrifying.

Another ramification of taking artificial testosterone over time is the   21
effect on the natural testosterone level (thus the male sex drive). As a result of my steroid use, my natural testosterone level was ultimately depleted to the point where my sex drive was drastically reduced in comparison to the average twenty-one-year-old male. My testicles shriveled up, causing physical pain as well as extreme mental anguish. Thus I desired girls less. This however did lead me to treat them as people, not as objects of my desires. It was a beginning step on the way to a more sane and civil mentality.

The worst symptoms of my withdrawal after many months of drug   22
abuse were emotional. My emotions fluctuated dramatically, and I rapidly became more sensitive. My hope is that this feeling of being trailed by isolation and aloneness will diminish and leave me free of its constant haunting.

EXERCISING VOCABULARY

1. How does H. D.'s use of such words as *maiming, grotesque, perversion, wretched,* and *depleted* help the reader form a clear impression of the author's self-image?

2. In Greek mythology, who is Narcissus? What happened to him? Why is the adjective derived from his name, *narcissistic* (para. 5), particularly suitable for this narrative?

PROBING CONTENT

1. When did the writer begin taking anabolic steroids? Why did he believe that doing so was necessary?

2. What physical changes did H. D.'s body undergo? How were these physical changes related to what happened to him mentally?

3. Why did H. D. resume steroid use after his drug-free summer at boarding school? Why did he keep changing his dosage, the type of steroids, and where he injected himself? How much steroid use would the writer have considered "enough"?

4. What triggered the writer's decision to stop using steroids for good? What withdrawal symptoms did he experience? Compare H. D.'s self-image at the beginning of this essay with his self-image at its conclusion.

CONSIDERING CRAFT

1. What does *dying* mean in the essay's title? How could H. D.'s use of this word mean more than one thing? How does this title reflect the main idea of the essay?

2. The writer includes many graphic and painful details about his condition. What purpose do these details serve? Why are they necessary in this essay?

3. What is H. D.'s purpose in telling his own story? Why does he not use his full name? What reaction might H. D. hope his readers will have?

4. How would you characterize the writer's attitude toward his use of steroids? How does this tone change throughout the narrative? By the end, how do you feel toward H. D.?

5. This essay was originally published in *Seventeen* magazine. Who makes up the usual audience for this magazine? How does knowing this affect your understanding of the essay?

RESPONDING TO THE WRITER

How would you have responded if H. D.'s story had been shared with you by a friend as his or her personal experience? Would you have felt sympathetic? Judgmental? What advice would you give your friend or H. D.?

For a quiz on this reading, go to www.bedfordstmartins.com/mirror.

Thigh Anxiety

LAURA FRASER

In "Thigh Anxiety" Laura Fraser looks at a whole new group of cosmetic surgery candidates — men. Marketed as a way to make men more attractive, powerful, and masculine, cosmetic surgery has been attracting a growing number of males; from 1992 to 1997, the number of liposuction procedures performed on men tripled, and the number of face lifts doubled. Do these figures mean that more men are now feeling the same intense pressure to be thin and attractive that women have faced for years? Will an increasing number of men develop the same "body and appearance neuroses" that have plagued women? Will women be sympathetic to this new male plight, as the author asserts?

Fraser first published "Thigh Anxiety" in the March–April 1999 issue of *Mother Jones*. She has written for *Vogue, Glamour, Self,* and *Elle* and was a contributing editor at *Health* and *Good Housekeeping*. She is the author of *An Italian Affair* (2001), a travelogue and memoir about escaping heartbreak through a trip to Italy. She also wrote *Losing It: America's Obsession with Weight and the Industry That Feeds on It* (1997), an exposé of manipulative tactics used by the diet industry.

THINKING AHEAD

Think about people who have had cosmetic surgery. Are they personal acquaintances or celebrities? Are they men or women? How old were they when they had their surgery? What do you think about their decisions to "remake" themselves? Would you ever consider cosmetic surgery? Explain your reasons.

INCREASING VOCABULARY

virile (adj.) (1)
domain (n.) (3)
vibrant (adj.) (5)
aesthetic (adj.) (7)
validates (v.) (7)

pectoral (adj.) (7)
promoted (v.) (11)
intrusive (adj.) (12)
neuroses (n.) (14)

On a Web site advertising the Beverly Hills–based Barron Centers Body Recontouring and Male Enhancement Clinic, a virile-looking man reclines on the grass as he embraces a lovely young woman. The site is promoting liposuction[1] and penile enlargement

1

---

[1] **liposuction:** Surgical removal of local fat deposits especially for cosmetic purposes.

surgery. "The positive results are the same for virtually every person: greater self-esteem, a new level of self-confidence, the ability to feel your best," promises the copy. "This improved self-image is evident not only in your sexual life, but in most other arenas." Below that, a large banner announces: "New Lower Fees."

Talk about a hard sell.   2

Welcome to the macho world of cosmetic surgery. Once the hush-   3
hush domain of aging society women, the fast-growing market for cosmetic procedures now increasingly draws male baby boomers. From 1992 to 1997, the number of men having liposuction has tripled, according to the American Society of Plastic and Reconstructive Surgeons, and the number having face-lifts has doubled. In 1997, men spent almost $130 million on liposuction, face-lifts, nose reshaping, and eyelid surgery combined—up from $88 million in 1992.

"It's definitely a growing trend," says San Francisco–based plastic sur-   4
geon Corey Maas. "After all these years of guys walking around with big beer bellies and wrinkly faces while women are looking better and better, finally, men are catching on."

Cosmetic surgery, with ads promising quick and easy high-tech re-   5
sults, is being marketed to men the way sports cars and stereo equipment are sold—as accessories to make them more attractive, powerful, and masculine. "It's extremely important for the working man or woman to appear energetic and youthful," says the Palm Beach Plastic Surgery Center's Web site. "You may feel young and 'ready to go,' but your sagging lids, loose neck, or thinning hair may portray a less vibrant impression than you would like." As one male UC-Berkeley professor who has had plastic surgery puts it, "If it's available, and it makes me look better, and I have the money, why not? It's not any stupider than buying a Jaguar."[2]

Also, women are no longer settling for chubby, balding executives.   6
They don't have to. "It used to be that men responded to physical beauty and women responded to power and status," says David Sarwer, a psychologist at the University of Pennsylvania's Center for Human Appearance. "Now women have their own power and status, and they're looking for more attractive men."

In some ways, this new aesthetic surgery trend among men validates   7
what women have always known: Looking good is hard work. But it's also ironic. Feminists who once hoped that gaining equality in the workplace would mean they could stop worrying so much about appearance are now finding that men are worrying more about their own looks—and presumably haven't learned any lessons from their female colleagues' struggle. Of the millions of people diagnosed with anorexia nervosa, bulimia, and other eating disorders each year, almost 10 percent are men. Silicone calf and pectoral implants—used to beef up the less-than-muscular leg or chest—are becoming more common.

---

[2] **ESL** **Jaguar:** An expensive luxury automobile.

Still, men continue to be far less anxious than women about their   8
looks. "There's definitely more emphasis on men's looks, bodies, and
weight than in any time in the past, but I don't think men will ever feel the
intense pressure to be trim and attractive that women face every day,"
says Debbie Then, a California-based social psychologist who studies appearance. But now that popular men's magazines are filling up with ads
for plastic surgery and ab-tightening machines, it won't be long before
men start taking their physical imperfections to heart.

Psychologists also have identified in men a disorder known as body   9
dysmorphia, which involves extreme, exaggerated dissatisfaction with
body parts and appearance. For men that often means body build, hair
loss, and genital size.

Whether or not the problem is between men's ears, cosmetic surgeons   10
are doing their best to help men improve what's on top of their heads—
and between their legs. In 1996 alone, men spent about $12 million on pe-
nile enlargements. Privately, many plastic surgeons say the results are
rarely impressive—and often dangerous. Martin Resnick, chair of the Department of Urology at Case Western Reserve University and secretary of
the American Urological Association, says that "penile enlargement has
not been shown to give patients the degree of enlargement they desire.
And in some cases, the procedure has led to infection and deformity."

A more common procedure is liposuction for love handles. While li-   11
posuction is promoted as safe, a recent study by doctors in California
showed that one patient in five thousand dies, usually after a surgeon re-
moves a large volume of fat. Robert del Junco, a head and neck surgeon
who leads the Medical Board of California's commission to investigate
cosmetic surgery, says some doctors now operate after only a weekend
seminar's worth of training.

Despite the risks, it's likely that more men will undergo cosmetic   12
surgery in the future, especially as the technology shortens recovery times
and the procedures become less intrusive. Some men are even seeking
lunchtime fixes: a quick collagen injection[3] to smooth out wrinkles, a
speedy dermabrasion[4] to reduce blemishes.

The effort to look young and attractive is going beyond gender, as our   13
culture becomes more androgynous. Obsession with appearance is likely to
become less a matter of gender than of class; people, no matter what their
sex, are likely to spend whatever they can afford to enhance their looks.

Inevitably, more men will develop the kinds of body and appearance   14
neuroses that many women have suffered for years: eating disorders, body
dysmorphia, and general self-loathing for not measuring up to an impossible ideal. It may disappoint women, who have always thought men would
be less obsessive about facial flaws and extra pounds—real or imagined.
But we'll be sympathetic. We know how it feels.

---

[3] **collagen injection:** An injection into the face or lips for cosmetic purposes.
[4] **dermabrasion:** Surgical removal of skin blemishes or imperfections such as scars or tattoos.

EXERCISING VOCABULARY

1. Fraser says that cosmetic surgery was "once the hush-hush domain of aging society women" but is now a "macho" world (para. 3). What does she mean by the terms "hush-hush" and "macho"? How do these terms reflect the changes in cosmetic surgery in recent years? How effective is the author's description of these changes?

2. In paragraph 13, Fraser asserts that our culture is becoming more "androgynous." What does the word *androgynous* mean? What relevance does this term have for Fraser's position in this essay?

3. In paragraph 7, Fraser describes the growing trend of cosmetic surgery for men as "ironic." What is irony? Why does she use this term here? In what sense is this trend ironic?

PROBING CONTENT

1. What is the latest trend in cosmetic surgery? What evidence does Fraser give to support her assertion?

2. How is cosmetic surgery being marketed to men? How do the advertisers play on the "macho" desires of some men (para. 3)?

3. What has changed in the lives of women that has led more men to seek cosmetic surgery?

4. What kinds of cosmetic surgery are men having? Why?

5. What long-term effects does Fraser fear cosmestic surgery will have for men? How may women react?

CONSIDERING CRAFT

1. Carefully examine the title of this essay. How does it reflect the subject under examination? How does the author play on words here?

2. In her essay, Fraser quotes both advertisements and authorities. Find several examples. How do these quotations affect your reading of the essay?

RESPONDING TO THE WRITER

In the final paragraph of the essay, Fraser gives us her thoughts on how both men and women will respond to the increase in men's cosmetic surgery. To what extent do you agree with her conclusion? Explain your answer.

For a quiz on this reading, go to www.bedfordstmartins.com/mirror.

The Ugly Truth about Beauty

DAVE BARRY

Dave Barry, humor columnist based at the *Miami Herald*, is convinced that men's involvement with their appearance is restricted to only the most basic concerns. In fact, Barry contends, "Most men, I believe, think of themselves as average-looking. Men will think this even if their faces cause heart failure in cattle at a range of 300 yards." He also believes that women seriously over-inflate how much men notice how women look. Nevertheless, he cautions men everywhere to think carefully before responding to a woman's casual question, "How do I look?" Although Barry's tone is humorous and his purpose here is to entertain, he raises some significant issues about the ways men and women view themselves. Why do these differences exist? What is responsible for them? Can the differences in our gender-driven concerns about appearance really be attributed to He-Man action figures and Barbie dolls?

Barry's witty and thought-provoking essay was published on February 8, 1998, in the *Philadelphia Inquirer Magazine*. Barry has written numerous books, including *Babies and Other Hazards of Sex: How to Make a Tiny Person in Only Nine Months, with Tools You Probably Already Have Around the House* (1984); *Bad Habits: A 100% Fact Free Book* (1987); *Dave Barry Hits Below the Beltway* (2001); and *My Teenage Son's Goal in Life Is to Make Me Feel 3,500 Years Old and Other Thoughts on Parenting* (2001). His humorous observations won him the Pulitzer Prize for commentary in 1988, and his column is syndicated in over 150 newspapers nationwide.

THINKING AHEAD

In your experience, how much attention do men pay to the appearance of women? What do men notice? What are women looking for when they look at men? Are men or women more likely to approach someone simply because that person "looks good"? What specifically makes you think this is true?

INCREASING VOCABULARY

regimen (n.) (5)	demeaning (adj.) (9)
mutation (n.) (8)	bolster (v.) (9)

If you're a man, at some point a woman will ask you how she looks. 1

"How do I look?" she'll ask. 2

You must be careful how you answer this question. The best tech- 3
nique is to form an honest yet sensitive opinion, then collapse on the floor
with some kind of fatal seizure. Trust me, this is the easiest way out. Because you will never come up with the right answer.

The problem is that women generally do not think of their looks in 4
the same way that men do. Most men form an opinion of how they look
in seventh grade, and they stick to it for the rest of their lives. Some men
form the opinion that they are irresistible stud muffins,[1] and they do not
change this opinion even when their faces sag and their noses bloat to the
size of eggplants and their eyebrows grow together to form what appears
to be a giant forehead-dwelling tropical caterpillar.

Most men, I believe, think of themselves as average-looking. Men will 5
think this even if their faces cause heart failure in cattle at a range of 300
yards. Being average does not bother them; average is fine, for men. This
is why men never ask anybody how they look. Their primary form of
beauty care is to shave themselves, which is essentially the same form of
beauty care that they give to their lawns. If, at the end of his four-minute
daily beauty regimen, a man has managed to wipe most of the shaving
cream out of his hair and is not bleeding too badly, he feels that he has
done all he can, so he stops thinking about his appearance and devotes his
mind to more critical issues, such as the Super Bowl.

Women do not look at themselves this way. If I had to express, in three 6
words, what I believe most women think about their appearance, those
words would be: "not good enough." No matter how attractive a woman
may appear to be to others, when she looks at herself in the mirror, she
thinks: woof. She thinks that at any moment a municipal animal-control
officer is going to throw a net over her and haul her off to the shelter.

Why do women have such low self-esteem? There are many complex 7
psychological and societal reasons, by which I mean Barbie. Girls grow up
playing with a doll proportioned such that, if it were a human, it would be
seven feet tall and weigh 81 pounds, of which 53 pounds would be bosoms.
This is a difficult appearance standard to live up to, especially when you
contrast it with the standard set for little boys by their dolls . . . excuse me,
by their action figures. Most of the action figures that my son played with
when he was little were hideous-looking. For example, he was very fond of
an action figure (part of the He-Man series) called "Buzz-Off," who was
part human, part flying insect. Buzz-Off was not a looker. But he was extremely self-confident. You could not imagine Buzz-Off saying to the other
action figures: "Do you think these wings make my hips look big?"

But women grow up thinking they need to look like Barbie, which for 8
most women is impossible, although there is a multibillion-dollar beauty
industry devoted to convincing women that they must try. I once saw an

---

[1] **ESL** **stud muffins:** Men who are particularly attractive to women.

Oprah[2] show wherein supermodel Cindy Crawford dispensed makeup tips to the studio audience. Cindy had all these middle-aged women applying beauty products to their faces; she stressed how important it was to apply them in a certain way, using the tips of their fingers. All the women dutifully did this, even though it was obvious to any sane observer that, no matter how carefully they applied these products, they would never look remotely like Cindy Crawford, who is some kind of genetic mutation.

I'm not saying that men are superior. I'm just saying that you're not   9
going to get a group of middle-aged men to sit in a room and apply cosmetics to themselves under the instruction of Brad Pitt,[3] in hopes of looking more like him. Men would realize that this task was pointless and demeaning. They would find some way to bolster their self-esteem that did not require looking like Brad Pitt. They would say to Brad: "Oh YEAH? Well what do you know about LAWN CARE, pretty boy?"

Of course many women will argue that the reason they become ob-   10
sessed with trying to look like Cindy Crawford is that men, being as shallow as a drop of spit, WANT women to look that way. To which I have two responses:

1. Hey, just because WE'RE idiots, that does not mean YOU have to   11
be; and

2. Men don't even notice 97 percent of the beauty efforts you make   12
anyway. Take fingernails. The average woman spends 5,000 hours per year worrying about her fingernails; I have never once, in more than 40 years of listening to men talk about women, heard a man say, "She has a nice set of fingernails!" Many men would not notice if a woman had upward of four hands.

Anyway, to get back to my original point: If you're a man, and a   13
woman asks you how she looks, you're in big trouble. Obviously, you can't say she looks bad. But you also can't say that she looks great, because she'll think you're lying, because she has spent countless hours, with the help of the multibillion-dollar beauty industry, obsessing about the differences between herself and Cindy Crawford. Also, she suspects that you're not qualified to judge anybody's appearance. This is because you have shaving cream in your hair.

EXERCISING VOCABULARY

1. Can a man's daily "beauty" routine accurately be called a *regimen* (para. 5)? Why or why not? How does this choice of words contribute to Barry's main idea?

2. The words *genetic mutation* are often applied to creatures in horror movies or to aliens on *The X-Files*. In what sense does Barry apply them to supermodel Cindy Crawford (para. 8)? What does he accomplish by using these

---

[2] **ESL** **Oprah:** Oprah Winfrey, star of a popular television talk show.
[3] **ESL** **Brad Pitt:** Popular American film actor that has appeared in such films as *Thelma and Louise, Fight Club, Meet Joe Black,* and *Spy Game.*

words in this ironic way? (*Irony* is the use of words in a way other than their literal meaning, often done for humor or to make a point.)

PROBING CONTENT

1. What toys does Barry accuse of magnifying gender differences in self-image? How does he justify his accusations?

2. What does Barry say to women who blame their obsession with looks on the need to satisfy men's expectations? How valid are his responses?

3. Why, according to Barry, is it impossible for a male to respond correctly to a woman's question, "How do I look?" By saying that it is impossible, what is Barry implying about women?

CONSIDERING CRAFT

1. Barry is best known for his humorous approach to current topics. Give several examples of his humorous tone in this essay. What impact does the humor here have on the effectiveness of his support for his thesis?

2. For what audience is Barry writing? How does he make clear his awareness of this audience? Cite specific examples, words, and phrases.

3. What does Barry add to his essay by mentioning such popular people as Cindy Crawford and Brad Pitt?

4. Barry concludes his final paragraph by revisiting a point from earlier in the essay. How does Barry's return to this point provide an appropriate and effective ending for his essay?

RESPONDING TO THE WRITER

Summarize Barry's opinions of men and women as detailed in this essay. Support or refute his contentions based on your own observations and experience.

For a quiz on this reading, go to www.bedfordstmartins.com/mirror.

DRAWING CONNECTIONS

1. What would Dave Barry say to the men described by Laura Fraser who are having cosmetic surgery?

2. With whom do you empathize—the men described by Barry who care little for their looks or those described by Fraser who seek to change them surgically? How would you respond to these two different groups? What advice would you offer to each?

3. How do Fraser and Barry represent women in their essays? According to these two authors, how do women relate to men?

Wrapping Up Chapter 3

REFLECTING ON THE WRITING

1. Using material from the essays in this chapter as well as your own observations and experiences, write an essay in which you either support or refute the idea that the kinds of toys a child plays with are a strong influence on his or her ideas about desirable body image.

2. Compare McLaughlin's ("Venus Envy") and Fraser's ("Thigh Anxiety") viewpoints about men's increased concern with their appearance with the viewpoint of Barry ("The Ugly Truth about Beauty"). Which of these writers makes the most accurate observations? Explain your response.

3. People often go to extreme, even dangerous, measures to attain a certain ideal body or look. Using essays from this chapter and your own experience and observations, identify a dangerous trend like steroid abuse, cosmetic surgery, or eating disorders that you would like to research further. Then write an essay in which you examine this trend and its effects on your peers.

4. Trudeau and H. D. chronicle the struggles adolescents have with body image. Using their essays, others from this chapter, or examples from the media, write an essay in which you relate your own difficulties with growing up in a culture that privileges a certain nearly impossible ideal of beauty.

CONNECTING TO THE CULTURE

1. If, as McLaughlin ("Venus Envy") and Fraser ("Thigh Anxiety") argue, men are now more concerned than ever before with their appearance, what elements in our society are most responsible for this heightened awareness? To what extent are the media (television, movies, magazines, and the Internet) responsible? What consequences do you expect? What changes in advertising or new products support this thesis?

2. Think about the people who have helped shape your self-image, both "inner" and "outer." These may be people you know personally or celebrities you have never actually met. These people may have been positive role models for you, helping you to set goals for yourself, or negative influences showing you what you did not want to become. In an essay, explore how one or several of these people have influenced you.

3. Different cultures have different ideals of beauty. Do some research on another country whose beauty ideals are different from those in the United States. In an essay, examine the differences you have found and relate how the standard of beauty affects the members of the culture you selected.

4. Ideals of beauty have changed throughout history in the United States. Pick a specific historical period and research how beauty was defined for men or women during that time. Then write an essay in which you compare the ideal body image of the historical period to today's ideal of beauty. Use specific examples and visuals from the time period you have researched.

FOCUSING ON YESTERDAY, FOCUSING ON TODAY

In the early twentieth century when French Impressionist Auguste Renoir painted this nude, big was indeed beautiful. An ample, full-bodied woman was the feminine ideal; a thinner figure was suspect and suggested an impoverished existence. Interestingly, in the 1990s Body Shop ad, we return to the luscious curves of Renoir's beauty. However, this time we are no longer looking at a human model but at a plus-sized Barbie doll.

How has female body image changed since the Barbie doll was first introduced in 1959?

What do most supermodels look like today? How does today's feminine ideal of beauty differ from that presented in these two visuals? What message is The Body Shop, a body products company, sending by using this unique image? What target audience is The Body Shop hoping to reach?

When Big Was Beautiful

A Real-Life Barbie Doll

CHAPTER 4

Melting Pot or Salad Bowl?
How Cultural Identity Shapes Self-Image

At first thought, this question would appear to be simple enough. It's a question anyone might ask a chat room friend or a potential blind date in a phone conversation. What are we really asking when we ask this question?

- Who is KiKi1?
- Describe the boy's expression in the second panel.
- Why is the little boy uncertain about his response to the question?
- What does this cartoon imply about communication in an electronic age?
- What is the message here about ethnic labels?

Research this topic with TopLinks at www.bedfordstmartins.com/toplinks.

GEARING UP

Think about what forces — objects, people, events, and places — helped shape your sense of who you are, your awareness of the culture of your ancestors, and your ethnic identity. How have these forces influenced you? What special things about your ethnic heritage were you aware of as a child? What additional aspects have you become aware of as an adult?

How do I look to other people? Do I fit in? Do I want to fit in? Will I find my own place in the world? What should I call myself? Just who am I?

These are questions that all people ask themselves at some time in their lives. Many factors affect people's self-image. One is biological: our physical appearance as determined by our genetic makeup. The other is cultural and is composed of two segments: the culture of our ancestors and the larger contemporary culture that we participate in, better known as popular culture.

Cultural diversity has become a hot — and sometimes heated — topic in the United States. Should we learn about and celebrate the differences between people of different ethnicities and cultural heritages? Or should we deemphasize those differences and concentrate on the similarities between people? Many people reject the notion that the United States is a melting pot where everyone is simply an "American." Instead they see America as a salad bowl containing a mix of ethnicities that complement one another and that deserve to maintain their cultural diversity within the larger U.S. popular culture. But can too much attention be paid to cultural diversity? Does an appreciation of other ethnic groups unite or further divide us as a people?

What happens to members of minority groups when the ideals of their own culture collide with those of the dominant American popular culture? The media is gradually becoming a more accurate reflection of the actual U.S. population, as witnessed by the increasing numbers of models and actors of varying ethnicities. However, many Americans still feel separated from society's mainstream because they do not resemble the models or actors that stare out at them from the pages of glossy fashion magazines or from television or movie screens. When certain members of society do not look like those role models or have the privileged lifestyle that the media seems to take for granted, the self-esteem of those citizens may suffer.

The writers in this chapter come from diverse ethnic backgrounds at different points in their lives. They detail individual struggles toward self-awareness and appreciation of the cultures of their ancestors. Reading their essays will help you to reflect on what goes into the continual reevaluation and reshaping of your own cultural identity.

COLLABORATING

In groups of four to six students, spend fifteen to twenty minutes discussing the major cultural influences on an individual's self-image as a child and as an adolescent. Consider such influences as ethnicity, gender, home life, peers, teachers, and the media. Make a list of the major influences and then discuss them as a class.

Black and Blue

Carolyn Edgar

What does it mean to be a woman of African American and Native American descent in a society whose standards of beauty are derived from the white majority? In "Black and Blue," Carolyn Edgar, an attorney in New York City, attempts to answer this question. By taking us into her family, Edgar traces her own painful battle with self-image. From her childhood, through high school and college, and finally on the verge of her own motherhood, the author details her battles with both the black and white societies' ideals of beauty. This essay was first published in 1994 in *Reconstruction*, a scholarly publication concerned with race issues.

THINKING AHEAD

Every culture has its own ideals of beauty. What are some of those ideals for your particular culture? What conflicts have arisen for you in trying to live up to those standards?

INCREASING VOCABULARY

rabid (adj.) (1)	generic (adj.) (16)
shrouded (adj.) (3)	deemphasized (v.) (17)
lamented (v.) (4)	castigated (v.) (17)
wistfully (adv.) (7)	tantamount (adj.) (18)
ranted (v.) (8)	vying (v.) (22)
revert (v.) (9)	inconsequential (adj.) (23)
repress (v.) (11)	advent (n.) (25)
approximated (v.) (11)	derisive (adj.) (25)
submissive (adj.) (15)	skewed (v.) (26)

I was born in the mid-sixties to Southern parents who thought Malcolm X[1] was a rabid fool and that "black pride" was a lot of nonsense. My parents were suspicious of folks with big Afros and dashikis[2] who changed their names to letters.

They were not alone. In the midst of the Black Power movement, many black people in Detroit and elsewhere still placed a premium on light skin and curly hair. When I was a child, Afrocentricity never made its way to the pages of Detroit's black newspaper, the *Michigan Chronicle*.

[1] **ESL** **Malcolm X:** Militant black civil rights activist of the 1960s.
[2] **dashikis:** Loose-fitting African pullover garments that are usually brightly colored.

We were supposed to be black and proud, yet light-skinned men and women were photographed for the society pages of the *Chronicle* nearly to the exclusion of all others, especially if the featured event was an Alpha Kappa Alpha or Delta Sigma Theta sorority function. Dark-skinned women usually were absent from the society pages, except in photographs of church events or Zeta Phi Beta sorority balls.

My mother blamed my father for any of our undesirable physical features and personality traits, with the sole exception of his curly hair, which my second oldest sister Caroletta inherited. So, of course he was responsible for our big lips, which neither Mama nor any of her brothers or sisters had. The rest of our good features came from my mother's side of the family. My mother's father—Granddaddy, as we called him—was born of mixed parentage. Though I'm not sure of the exact combination, I think one parent was black and Indian, and the other was white and Indian. Like many things in Mississippi, the white part and the Indian part remain shrouded in mystery. Ignorance was passed from generation to generation because to explain where the hair color and eye color came from would have required grown folks to discuss openly with children rape and babies born out of wedlock, topics rarely even discussed among themselves except for those rare moments when they thought the children were asleep.

My grandfather died when I was seven, so my memories of him are vague. I recall only a pale man who must have shocked many people by marrying a beautiful, dark woman with warm brown eyes. Mama often told us she thought her mother was the most beautiful woman in the world and tried to copy her every move. Yet she seemed obsessed with finding evidence in her six children, not of her mother but of her father. Sometimes, we would sit down and name which of my cousins had inherited some of my grandfather's features. My light-skinned brothers were "red" like Granddaddy. My oldest sister, Cheryl, had a light complexion, but it didn't have that "Indian red" tint to it. My mother lamented that none of us had the high Indian cheekbones she'd inherited from him.

Like all mothers, mine was fond of telling her children what they were like as babies—which of her six babies was the easiest, the hardest, the most stubborn, the smartest, and the prettiest. I hated when she went on about her pretty babies. They were, of course, my three light-skinned, green-eyed siblings: Cheryl and my brothers, Gregory and Robert. Robert, we were told, was especially pretty. "His eyes were so clear then!" she was fond of saying. "People used to ask me if he was blind." I found that particular story depressing. It saddened me that my mother found such beauty in eyes that looked as though they could not see.

Mama even dared to put her feelings about her beautiful pale babies in a paper she wrote for an English course at a local community college. Caroletta and I nearly gagged as we read about the joy my mother felt when she held her lovely, pale, blond-haired, gray/green-eyed babies in her arms for the first time. We darker-skinned children—William, my oldest brother; Caroletta; and I—weren't even in the paper! We were old enough by then to laugh about the paper and make fun of my mother's writing style. Nevertheless, we were hurt because we believed that my mother's failure to write about her brown-skinned children meant that the emotion she felt holding us for the first time either was something less than joy or else wasn't worth writing about.

Not that Mama never said I was a pretty baby. For a few short months of my life that I don't even remember, I was a beautiful little dream child with blue eyes and thick, wavy hair. But the things my mother appeared to treasure most in a pretty baby deserted me before I ever got a chance to enjoy them. Mama would talk about my blue eyes and say wistfully, "I hoped your eyes would stay blue, but they just changed." I would ask, "So what happened?" She would respond, "I don't know. They just changed." I used to wonder what I'd done to make the blue eyes and the curly hair go away. I would stare at my eyes in the mirror for several minutes at a time, trying to imagine what I would look like if they were still blue.

Compared to my sisters, I thought I was nothing special. Cheryl had it all—green eyes *and* light skin that stayed light throughout the summer, unlike mine, which would prompt my mother to say, "Girl, when did you get so BLACK!?" Cheryl's light, light skin and green eyes confused some of her teachers into thinking that one of her parents was white. My light-skinned sister was still the "fine"[3] one of the girls, the one my brothers' friends tripped over themselves staring at as they made their way through our house. My brothers' friends always ranted about how fine my two sisters were, but I don't think they ever noticed I was alive.

Caroletta was the one with "good" hair. Though I teased her about being dark (her skin was about a quarter-shade darker than mine), I was openly envious of her long, wavy, reddish-brown hair. No matter how straight Mama pressed my hair, it never hung longer than Caroletta's did, even after her hair was newly trimmed. Caroletta never had to endure the pain of the pressing comb[4], or sleep on foam rollers for curls that would wilt and revert to kinks[5] by midday. Strangers often asked my sister if she was West Indian, whatever that meant.

Strangers never mistook me for anything other than what I was—a black girl who looked like a black girl.

Because my hair was not as wavy and silky as Caroletta's, it had to be pressed. Usually, I would wash my hair on a Friday or Saturday and wear it braided until Sunday, when my mother would work her magic with the pressing comb. For everyday wear, I had to be satisfied with a warm combing—just enough heat applied to it with the pressing comb to smooth out some of the kinks. "Bone-straight" pressings were rare, re-

7

8

9

10

11

---

[3] **ESL** **fine:** Pretty or attractive.
[4] **ESL** **pressing comb:** A hot comb used for smoothing and straightening hair.
[5] **ESL** **kinks:** Bends or curls in hair.

served only for picture-taking days and Easter. Winters were okay, because my hair would hold a press for a week between washings, but summers were awful. I couldn't hold even a hard press more than an hour. More to the point, I sweated so much in the summer heat that my hair was impossible to repress. Any activity that caused me to sweat was out. I still don't swim well because of my hair. I signed up for a class in high school to learn how to swim, assuming that a good swim cap would protect my hair. I wasn't as worried about the chlorine as I was about getting my hair wet. The first day we swam, I thought I had hair protection down to a science: I wore a plastic cap under my rubber swim cap and hopped confidently into the water. I instantly regretted it. There was nothing I could do about the water that seeped under the rubber and plastic and turned my hair into raw wool. After that, I spent as little time as possible with my head anywhere near the water, choosing instead to hang out in the shallow end, laughing with my friends (who also didn't want to get their hair wet). Swimming, or doing anything that approximated swimming, was out of the question.

I begged my mother to let me get a relaxer[6] so I wouldn't have to worry about the pressing comb, but she refused. She claimed that relaxers were for people with truly nappy[7] hair, and that my hair, with its natural curl (hidden underneath the kinks) was too good to perm. Mama claimed that relaxers had ruined Cheryl's hair—she insisted that Cheryl's hair turned nappy after she started getting it relaxed. She also maintained a healthy distrust for beauticians, claiming that they only wanted to chop off long hair. And in response to my complaints about my "nappy" hair, my mother offered the consolation that my hair wasn't "bad," that although it wasn't as "good" as Caroletta's, and even though it had to be pressed, it wasn't that "cantcha-doncha" stuff (you can't comb it, and dontcha try). I don't think it was an accident that most of the girls on the high school swim team either had very short hair or naturally straight or wavy hair.   12

Even in second grade, competition was fierce among the long-haired, light-skinned girls in my second-grade class for the attention of boys. Those of us who weren't quite light enough to join the contest watched from the sidelines. The boys played with the silkier ponytails of the lighter-skinned girls, but called me "cat eyes" and pulled my ponytails to be mean, not to flirt. The best I could do was to befriend the "bald-headed" girls: the dark-skinned, short-haired female bullies in my class who admired my longer hair, even if it was kinky.   13

At home, I constantly fought with my sisters. When it came to name-calling, Cheryl was always a "yellow" something or other, and Caroletta, whose skin was just barely darker than mine, was always a "black skillet." I learned that my mother generally believed my word against my sisters',   14

---

[6] **ESL** **relaxer:** A chemical product used to straighten hair.
[7] **ESL** **nappy:** An African style of hair, referring to kinky or curly hair.

and I used her trust to tattle on them. I never hesitated to invent a good story or add facts that did not exist, especially when I knew my stories would get them into trouble. I always made up with Caroletta because she was the only real playmate I had, but Cheryl and I fought as often as possible, for any reason and usually for no reason at all. None of the fighting improved my satisfaction with what I saw when I looked in the mirror.

Growing up in an era in which the only Africans we saw were in   15
Tarzan[8] movies, there was nothing at all desirable about being of African descent. African men, we were told, were crazy and liked their women submissive; they were no better than the "A-rabs" who owned all the convenience stores near our house. Plus, in my family's view, there was something wrong with great big noses and great big lips. None of us really had big noses, but as babies, we all had our noses pinched. My mother believed that pinching kept a nose from spreading all over a baby's face.

But most important were those damned "gray eyes" — my mother's   16
generic term for anything other than brown eyes. I eventually gave up on blue, because I knew THAT wasn't coming back. But my eye color changed so often that green wasn't impossible. My heart skipped a beat every time my mother would ask me, "Are your eyes changing color again?" I would look in the mirror for several minutes, staring at my irises until my eyes crossed, looking for a sign that the faint green outer circle was widening to envelop the large brown inner circle. Yet, no matter how close my brown eyes got to green (and they still change color according to my mood), Mama would only tell me that my eyes were "turning" green, never that they'd actually made it.

The African part of our heritage was definitely deemphasized in com-   17
parison to our amorphous[9] Indian blood, but not even my grandfather's mixed ancestry distinguished me from the pack. Every black person I know claims to be part Indian, and those claims are probably historically accurate. But all the while we were trying to be Indian, we castigated those who were too close to white. The sprinkling of half-white kids in my elementary, middle, and high schools were openly teased and called "half-breeds" or worse. Even in my family, we didn't talk about where those prized eyes came from.

Caroletta and I had an opportunity to separate ourselves from the rest   18
of our part-Indian black friends and classmates when we started receiving what we termed "Indian surveys" at school. These were one-page questionnaires from THE GOVERNMENT, designed to identify persons of Native American ancestry in the Detroit Public School system. Since none of my part-Indian friends at school received these surveys, I figured that my mother's stories about her father's heritage had to be true, especially if the federal government knew about it. Why else would we be singled out,

---

[8] **ESL** **Tarzan movies:** The hero of Edgar Rice Burroughs' novel about a boy raised by apes in the African jungle.
[9] **ESL** **amorphous:** Of no particular type or character; unorganized; formless.

when our birth certificates listed our race only as Negro? Caroletta and I always returned our surveys promptly, each time trying to figure out, based on our grandfather's half-Indian blood and my parents' not-so-distant blood relationship (they were second cousins, but didn't know it until after they were married), what percentage Indian blood we could claim on the form. We were never told the purpose of the Indian surveys, or how the information we religiously submitted each year was used. Nor did we bother to ask until we found out that filling out a survey for the Detroit Public Schools was not tantamount to registering ourselves as members of a federally recognized Indian tribe to qualify for Native American scholarship programs. It wasn't until Caroletta found out that you had to be recognized as an Indian by the federal government that the "Indian survey" began to look like a public school system scam[10]. Yet we were so busy trying to be something more than just blacks that we just continued to fill out the surveys without question, and probably would have continued to do so if we had been able to get some scholarship money out of it. Caroletta once talked of researching our ancestry to see if we actually qualified for any of the federal scholarship programs — after all, *Roots*[11] was still fresh in our memories — but somehow, it never happened. Over time, the surveys simply stopped coming.

Without the Indian surveys, I was back to being a regular black girl.   19
In high school, I was neither light enough to be cute nor rich enough to be popular. I kept my hair pressed so it would fall past my shoulder blades, but long, kinky hair and eyes that I now called "hazel-green" were no match for yellow girls with wavy hair whose daddies were doctors instead of spray booth attendants at Ford Motor Company, girls who drove their own cars to school instead of being dropped off every morning in a rusty Ford Fairmont. Coach purses and Calvin Klein jeans were the fashion standard of the day; my whatever-was-on-sale purses and clothes didn't stand up. Most of the "beautiful people" had money, and almost all of those with money were also fair-skinned. The people who lived south of Six Mile Road (McNichols) were rarely invited to the parties given by those who lived closer to Southfield, and the price of entry into that closed circle was more dear than I was willing to pay. To get in, you had to date a popular boy, or suck up to one of the popular girls (required for access to the popular boys). I thought about sex, wrote about sex, and dreamed about sex, but lived out my personal fantasies through the exploits of my fair-skinned best friend Melanie, who was considered cute because she was light-skinned and who was popular because she dated a guy on the football team.

Until I left college, I never got along well with other black women. I   20
simply didn't like most of the girls in high school for one reason (too cute)

---

[10] **scam:** A scheme to cheat or swindle.
[11] **ESL** *Roots:* Popular novel by Alex Haley and subsequent television miniseries describing the struggles of several generations of a black family from the days of slavery.

or another (too cute AND too stupid). When I started college at the University of Michigan, I decided to change my attitude. Even though Ann Arbor was only thirty-five miles from Detroit, it might as well have been thirty-five hundred miles away since I had neither a car nor money for a bus or train back home on weekends, and my parents firmly believed that coming home from school was something you only did on school breaks. I tried being friendly to the other black women in my dorm, believing that they wouldn't be as class- or color-struck as my high school classmates had been.

It didn't take me long to find out that living with snobs[12] was even worse than just going to school with them. There was little difference between the high school scene and the college scene. Unlike high school, you could go to any party you wanted to as long as you had the cash; like high school, the only way to have fun at parties was to be part of the "in" crowd, which meant belonging to the black Greek[13] sororities and fraternities. And the only way to be Greek was to be light enough or rich enough or willing to kiss enough ass to make up for too much skin pigment and too little money. 21

The black social scene at Michigan was ruled by the black fraternities, Alpha Phi Alpha and Kappa Alpha Psi, and the sororities Delta Sigma Theta and Alpha Kappa Alpha. As in high school, class and color played a large part in determining who was chosen to be part of the popular crowd. Some freshman females were invited almost immediately to join the Kappa and Alpha Sweethearts, the little-sister groups of the two fraternities which, as everybody knew, was a good way to make contact with and eventually become part of the entire Greek scene. I wasn't even approached. At Greek parties, the Deltas and AKAs stood on opposite sides of the room, talking about each other and vying for the attention of the fraternity men. Unless you were Greek, a Greek follower, or small enough and light enough that it didn't matter, your dance partner was likely to be either your male buddy from the dorm or some creep who had been rejected by all the fine (read: light and long) women. I got tired of working up my courage to ask a guy to dance, only to get rejected and watch him on the floor moments later with some Delta or AKA with a heavy Coach bag slung over one shoulder, barely moving to keep from sweating. When I realized I was never going to be a Delta, I stopped going to Greek parties and started hanging out with my white dorm hallmates. Pretty soon, the same people who shut me out of the "in" black crowd began to call me "Oreo" because I was frequently seen in the company of whites. 22

Since I had convinced myself that I wasn't pretty, I was determined to be smart. Mama, despite her concern with the color of our eyes, preached independence over beauty and warned her girls "not to sit around waiting for a man to give you anything." Being beautiful or pretty or cute or even 23

---

[12] **ESL** **snobs:** People who think they are superior to others.
[13] **ESL** **Greek:** A member of a fraternity or sorority.

attractive was inconsequential compared to being smart. And being smart didn't just mean "book knowledge," but having common sense as well. My father, the ultimate judge of common sense, preached a daily sermon: "You got all kinds of book smarts, but you ain't got *no* common sense." I prided myself on being the A student, the child with real potential, the one "most likely to succeed," and I took excessive pride in the way my mother raved over my grades and scholarships. It was my only advantage over my two sisters, who still had more men flocking after them than I did.

Unfortunately, success is no substitute for love, and the black woman   24 who gets the most attention from black men is often the sister with light skin, long hair, and light eyes. No matter how well-educated and "down" they supposedly are, black men still go for light and long. The few times I've gone to clubs with my sisters, I've found myself left at the table with my drink while they were on the dance floor.

But other times, I am the "honey with the light eyes" that other black   25 women sneer at. When I tell other women about my family and how unattractive I felt as a child, they usually respond, "Are you kidding? You'd be the favorite in most families!" No matter how much time I spend in the sun trying to stay brown, my women friends always include me in the category of "light-skinned" women who attract all the male attention at the parties we attend. And the advent of colored contact lenses has made me the frequent target of derisive comments from strangers who assume I bought my hazel-green eyes from an optician. A woman once approached me in a department store and said, "You have really pretty eyes — for what you paid for them." As a child, I never would have guessed that by the time I turned twenty-five and started relaxing my hair, other black women would be spending thousands of dollars for hair weaves the texture of my hair and contact lenses the same color as my eyes.

My perception of male beauty was skewed for years by what I found   26 unattractive about myself. Until recently, my ideal man was a tall, light-skinned brother with wavy hair like my father. He would even have light-colored eyes so we would produce beautiful little blue- or green-eyed children. Ironically, this tall, light-skinned, wavy-haired man of my romantic fantasies looked just like the same boys who rejected me in high school. I cringe to think of how many good men I rejected because they were too short or too dark or otherwise fell short of my damned-near-white ideal. Until I took a good look at Denzel Washington[14] and Wesley Snipes,[15] the only thing a brown- or dark-skinned brother could do for me was give me his light-skinned friend's phone number.

I know I must resolve this issue within myself before I bring a child   27 into the world. I am afraid of innocently inflicting pain upon my own children as my mother innocently inflicted pain upon me. My sisters have suffered their own pain; yet I also hear their voices dripping sweetly

---

[14] **ESL** **Denzel Washington:** A black actor who won the "Best Actor" Oscar in 2002.
[15] **ESL** **Wesley Snipes:** An African American Actor who has starred in such films as *New Jack City, White Men Can't Jump,* and *Blade II.*

about so-and-so's baby who's so pretty, with her long ponytails and light-colored eyes. When my older brothers and sisters began to marry and have children (sometimes in that order, sometimes not), Mama told us, "You pick your boyfriends and girlfriends, but I pick my grandchildren." Yet almost all of my siblings picked walnut-brown mates, and Granddaddy's genes were no match for those of my in-laws. Mama couldn't help loving her little, brown, kinky-haired grandchildren. But so far, none of my brothers or sisters have brought my mother that light-eyed grandbaby I know she'd love to have. Despite the pain I've suffered from my family's obsession with hair texture, skin complexion, and eye color, I now also feel that the job of producing the good-haired, fair-skinned, light-eyed grandchild has fallen to me. No matter what my future mate looks like, I know I will spend a couple of anxious months waiting to see from which side my first baby takes its coloring, its hair, its eyes. And if Granddaddy's genes can stand up to those of my future husband and my children get the blue eyes I lost long ago, I know I will feel as though I have finally "won."

EXERCISING VOCABULARY

1. Edgar's parents thought Malcolm X was a "rabid fool" (para. 1). How does *rabid* describe their perception of Malcolm X? How is this word more commonly used?

2. What does *Afrocentricity* mean in paragraph 2? What other words use the suffix *-centricity* or *-centric*? How are they related to *Afrocentricity*?

3. Edgar writes about black people who "placed a premium on light skin and curly hair" (para. 2). How do these people feel about light skin and curly hair? What other meanings of *premium* do you know?

PROBING CONTENT

1. Describe Edgar's physical appearance. How does it differ from that of her brothers and sisters? How does the writer feel about her appearance as compared to Cheryl's and Caroletta's? How do these feelings affect her interactions with others?

2. Why are the Indian surveys important to the author and her sister?

3. In high school, how is the writer different from the "beautiful people"? What advantages do "beautiful people" have, according to Edgar?

4. Describe the writer's college experience and then compare it to her high school one.

5. What characteristics does Edgar consider beautiful in males? In what ways do Edgar's negative feelings about her looks affect her perception of male beauty?

CONSIDERING CRAFT

1. To what does the phrase in the title refer? How do the different meanings of this phrase affect your understanding of Edgar's attitudes?

2. Edgar uses both formal and informal language, including slang. Identify two places where she uses formal language and two places where she uses informal language. What effect do her choices have on you?

3. Why does Edgar end the essay with a discussion of her own unborn child and her and her family's reaction to that child?

RESPONDING TO THE WRITER

Describe your feelings about how you looked while you were growing up. Think about times when you compared yourself unfavorably with family members or friends. How did your perception of your looks affect your self-esteem?

For a quiz on this reading, go to www.bedfordstmartins.com/mirror.

The Eye of the Beholder

GRACE SUH

Have you ever been tempted to completely remake yourself? Did you want to look especially good for that special event or person, or were you just tired of the same old you? When Grace Suh, a Korean American, treats herself to a makeover at Neiman Marcus, a luxury department store, she gets much more than she bargains for. As a result of her experience, Suh makes a crucial discovery about what it means to be an Asian American woman in a society that values Western ideals of beauty. By reading Suh's candid and funny description of her disastrous makeover, which first appeared in *A. Magazine* in 1992, we become passengers on her journey to selfhood.

Grace Suh is a native of Seoul, Korea, but she was raised in Wisconsin and Chicago. She now lives in New York City where she works in academic publishing and is a poetry editor for the *Asian Pacific American Journal.*

THINKING AHEAD

Reflect on a time when you have done something just to fit in with a certain group. What was the outcome? In what ways did your efforts achieve the desired effect?

INCREASING VOCABULARY

stark (adj.) (2)   wafted (v.) (9)

renounced (v.) (3)   impeccably (adv.) (10)

dogeared (adj.) (3)   reverie (n.) (11)

imperious (adj.) (6)   mannequin (n.) (11)

aloof (adj.) (6)   distorted (v.) (20)

scrutiny (n.) (9)   recessed (v.) (25)

Several summers ago, on one of those endless August evenings when the sun hangs suspended just above the horizon, I made up my mind to become beautiful.   1

It happened as I walked by one of those mirrored glass-clad office   2
towers, and caught a glimpse of my reflection out of the corner of my eye. The glass on this particular building was green, which might have accounted for the sickly tone of my complexion, but there was no explaining away the limp, ragged hair, the dark circles under my eyes, the facial blemishes, the shapeless, wrinkled clothes. The overall effect—the whole being greater than the sum of its parts—was one of stark ugliness.

I'd come home from college having renounced bourgeois[1] suburban values, like hygiene and grooming. Now, home for the summer, I washed my hair and changed clothes only when I felt like it, and spent most of my time sitting on the lawn eating mini rice cakes and Snickers[2] and reading dogeared back issues of *National Geographic*.

But that painfully epiphanous[3] day, standing there on the hot sidewalk, I suddenly understood what my mother had been gently hinting these past months: I was no longer just plain, no longer merely unattractive. No, I had broken the Unsightliness Barrier. I was now UGLY, and aggressively so.

And so, in an unusual exertion of will, I resolved to fight back against the forces of entropy.[4] I envisioned it as reclamation work, like scything down a lawn that has grown into meadow, or restoring a damaged fresco.[5] For the first time in ages, I felt elated and hopeful. I nearly sprinted into the nearby Neiman Marcus.[6] As I entered the cool, hushed, dimly lit first floor and saw the gleaming counters lined with vials of magical balm, the priestesses of beauty in their sacred smocks, and the glossy photographic icons[7] of the goddesses themselves—Paulina, Linda, Cindy, Vendella—in a wild, reckless burst of inspiration I thought to myself, Heck, why just okay? Why not BEAUTIFUL?

At the Estée Lauder[8] counter, I spied a polished, middle-aged woman whom I hoped might be less imperious than the aloof amazons at the Chanel counter.

"Could I help you?" the woman (I thought of her as "Estée") asked.

"Yes," I blurted. "I look terrible. I need a complete makeover—skin, face, everything."

After a wordless scrutiny of my face, she motioned me to sit down and began. She cleansed my skin with a bright blue mud masque and clear, tingling astringent and then applied a film of moisturizer, working extra amounts into the rough patches. Under the soft pressure of her fingers, I began to relax. From my perch, I happily took in the dizzying, colorful swirl of beautiful women and products all around me. I breathed in the billows of perfume that wafted through the air. I whispered the names of products under my breath like a healing mantra:[9]cooling eye gel, gentle exfoliant,[10] night time neck area reenergizer, moisture recharging intensi-

---

[1] **bourgeois:** Middle class.
[2] **ESL** **Snickers:** Candy bar.
[3] **epiphanous:** Characterized by a sudden flash of recognition.
[4] **entropy:** In physics, the tendency of things toward disorder.
[5] **ESL** **fresco:** A painting on fresh plaster that, when dry, produces a unique effect of depth.
[6] **ESL** **Neiman Marcus:** Expensive department store.
[7] **ESL** **icons:** Images, usually religious.
[8] **ESL** **Estée Lauder:** Popular manufacturer of expensive cosmetics.
[9] **ESL** **mantra:** A sacred formula chanted repeatedly in prayer or incantation.
[10] **ESL** **exfoliant:** A mixture that causes peeling off in layers.

fier, ultra-hydrating complex, emulsifying[11] immunage. I felt immersed in femininity, intoxicated by beauty.

I was flooded with gratitude at the patience and determination with which Estée toiled away at my face, painting on swaths of lip gloss, blush, and foundation. She was not working in vain, I vowed, as I sucked in my cheeks on her command. I would buy all these products. I would use them every day. I studied her gleaming, polished features—her lacquered nails, the glittering mosaic of her eyeshadow, the complex red shimmer of her mouth, her flawless, dewy skin—and tried to imagine myself as impeccably groomed as she.

Estée's voice interrupted my reverie, telling me to blot my lips. I stuck the tissue into my mouth and clamped down, watching myself in the mirror. My skin was a blankly even shade of pale, my cheeks and lips glaringly bright in contrast. My face had a strange plastic sheen, like a mannequin's. I grimaced as Estée applied the second lipstick coat: Was this right? Didn't I look kind of—fake? But she smiled back at me, clearly pleased with her work. I was ashamed of myself: Well, what did I expect? It wasn't like she had anything great to start with.

"Now," she announced, "Time for the biggie—Eyes."

"Oh. Well, actually, I want to look good and everything, but, I mean, I'm sure you could tell, I'm not really into a complicated beauty routine . . ." My voice faded into a faint giggle.

"So?" Estée snapped.

"Sooo . . ." I tried again, "I've never really used eye makeup, except, you know, for a little mascara sometimes, and I don't really feel comfortable—"

Estée was firm. "Well, the fact is that the eyes are the windows of the face. They're the focal point. An eye routine doesn't have to be complicated, but it's important to emphasize the eyes with some color, or they'll look washed out."

I certainly didn't want that. I leaned back again in my chair and closed my eyes.

Estée explained as she went: "I'm covering your lids with this champagne color. It's a real versatile base, 'cause it goes with almost any other color you put on top of it." I felt the velvety pad of the applicator sweep over my lids in a soothing rhythm.

"Now, being an Oriental, you don't have a lid fold, so I'm going to draw one with this charcoal shadow. Then, I fill in below the line with a lighter charcoal color with a bit of blue in it—frosted midnight—and then above it, on the outsides of your lids, I'm going to apply this plum color. There. Hold on a minute . . . Okay. Open up."

I stared at the face in the mirror, at my eyes. The drawn-on fold and dark, heavy shadows distorted and reproportioned my whole face. Not

10

11

12

13

14

15

16

17

18

19

20

---

[11] **emulsifying:** Making a suspension of two liquids that do not mix, such as oil and water.

one of the features in the mirror was recognizable, not the waxy white skin or the redrawn crimson lips or the sharp, deep cheekbones, and especially, not the eyes. I felt negated; I had been blotted out and another face drawn in my place. I looked up at Estée, and in that moment I hated her. "I look terrible," I said.

Her back stiffened. "What do you mean?" she demanded.   21

"Hideous. I don't even look human. Look at my eyes. You can't even   22
see me!" My voice was hoarse.

She looked. After a moment, she straightened up again, "Well, I'll   23
admit, the eyeshadow doesn't look great." She began to put away the pencils and brushes. "But at least now you have an eyelid."

I told myself that she was a pathetic, middle-aged woman with a boring   24
job and a meaningless life. I had my whole life before me. All she had
was the newest Richard Chamberlain[12] miniseries.

But it didn't matter. The fact of the matter was that she was pretty,   25
and I was not. Her blue eyes were recessed in an intricate pattern of folds
and hollows. Mine bulged out.

I bought the skincare system and the foundation and the blush and the   26
lip liner pencil and the lipstick and the primer and the eyeliner and the
eyeshadows—all four colors. The stuff filled a bag the size of a shoebox.
It cost a lot. Estée handed me my receipt with a flourish, and I told her,
"Thank you."

In the mezzanine[13] level washroom, I set my bag down on the counter   27
and scrubbed my face with water and slimy pink soap from the dispenser.
I splashed my face with cold water until it felt tight, and dried my raw
skin with brown paper towels that scratched.

As the sun sank into the Chicago skyline, I boarded the Burlington   28
Northern Commuter[14] for home and found a seat in the corner. I set the
shopping bag down beside me, and heaped its gilt boxes and frosted glass
bottles into my lap. Looking out the window, I saw that night had fallen.
Instead of trees and backyard fences I saw my profile—the same reflection, I realized, that I'd seen hours ago in the side of the green glass office
building. I did have eyelids, of course. Just not a fold. I wasn't pretty. But
I was familiar and comforting. I was myself.

The next stop was mine. I arranged the things carefully back in the   29
rectangular bag, large bottles of toner and moisturizer first, then the short
cylinders of masque and scrub and powder, small bottles of foundation
and primer, the little logs of pencils and lipstick, then the flat boxed compacts of blush and eyeshadow. The packages fit around each other clev-

[12] **Richard Chamberlain:** British born actor made popular in the mid-late 1960s by the television program *Dr. Kildare* and the film, *Shogun,* and by the television mini-series *The Thorn Birds.*

[13] **mezzanine:** A low-ceilinged story between two main stories of a building.

[14] **Burlington Northern Commuter:** A type of suburban commuter train that operated out of Chicago.

erly, like pieces in a puzzle. The conductor called out, "Fairview Avenue," and I stood up. Hurrying down the aisle, I looked back once at the neatly packed bag on the seat behind me, and jumped out just as the doors were closing shut.

EXERCISING VOCABULARY

1. How is Suh's day of beauty "painfully epiphanous" (para. 4)? What lessons does she learn?

2. Suh says in paragraph 4 that she "had broken the Unsightliness Barrier." What other phrase does this remind you of? What effect does this have on your reading of Suh's words?

3. Suh refers to famous models in paragraph 5 as "goddesses" and to their pictures as "icons." How are these two words used in a religious sense? How does that affect your reading of Suh's paragraph?

PROBING CONTENT

1. What causes Suh to get a makeover? What feelings lead her to this decision?

2. On which facial feature does Estée focus? What is the significance of this? What does it say about Estée's idea about beauty?

3. What is the writer's reaction to the makeover? According to Suh, whom does she look like now?

4. What causes the writer to leave the makeup behind her on the commuter train? What does she feel like after she does this?

5. What lesson do you think Suh learns from her experience at Neiman Marcus?

CONSIDERING CRAFT

1. Of what common phrase does the title of the essay remind you? How does this phrase relate to the general message of the essay?

2. How does Suh's tone or attitude change as she begins to describe the cosmetic counters at Neiman Marcus? Why does it change? Why does Suh call the saleswomen "priestesses of beauty" (para. 5)? How does this reflect about her opinion of them? Of the culture as a whole?

3. Reread paragraphs 9 and 10, in which Suh uses many examples of specialized language, or jargon, from the beauty industry — including "exfoliant," "ultra-hydrating complex," and "emulsifying immunage." What effect does Suh's use of such language have? Describe in detail how Suh communicates her "reverie" in paragraphs 9 and 10.

4. The saleswoman calls Suh an "Oriental" (para. 19). What does Suh achieve by using this word? Why doesn't she use the more culturally acceptable term *Asian American?*

5. Find several examples of dialogue in this essay. What effect do they have?

RESPONDING TO THE WRITER

What is your response to Suh's makeover? What do you feel as you read the essay? How do you feel at the end after she scrubs off the makeup?

For a quiz on this reading, go to www.bedfordstmartins.com/mirror.

Let's Be Chromatically Correct

MAX FRANKEL

What advantages or disadvantages might result from replacing ethnic labels such as *blacks* and *whites* with more descriptive labels such as "ebonies, chocolates, . . . pinks, [or] taupes"? Would such changes be merely politically correct, or could they bring us all closer together? Recurring media stories about Thomas Jefferson fathering at least one child with his African American slave Sally Hemings and interviews with the pair's descendants focus the spotlight on such questions. In this essay, originally published in the "Word and Image" section of the December 6, 1998, *New York Times Magazine,* Max Frankel provides some possible answers to questions like these.

Frankel was born in Gera, Germany, in 1930 and became a U.S. citizen in 1948. He began his career at the *New York Times* in 1952 as a reporter. From 1963 to 1976, he served in different capacities for the *Times,* including diplomatic correspondent, White House correspondent, Washington bureau chief, Sunday editor, and executive editor from 1986–1994. He currently writes the *Times'* Sunday magazine column "Word and Image" and recently published a memoir entitled *Max Frankel: The Times of My Life and My Life with the Times* (2000). In 1973, he was awarded the Pulitzer Prize for international reporting.

THINKING AHEAD

In what ways do the names people use for cultural and ethnic groups reflect certain attitudes toward those groups? What do ethnic or cultural labels reveal about those who use them?

INCREASING VOCABULARY

simplistically (adv.) (1)	decennial (adj.) (8)
chromatically (adv.) (5)	nomenclature (n.) (9)
miscegenation (n.) (2)	facetious (adj.) (11)
boon (n.) (6)	anachronistic (adj.) (12)
miscreants (n.) (6)	degradation (n.) (13)

Americans who are simplistically called people of color seem to have had none of the difficulty felt by the allegedly uncolored in absorbing the evidence that Thomas Jefferson[1] sired at least one of Sally

---

[1] **ESL** **Thomas Jefferson:** Third president of the United States.

Hemings's children. "Everybody knew that already," Fareed Thomas told a *Times* reporter, referring to his like-minded African American classmates in a Los Angeles high school.

The reporter, Don Terry, readily accepted this testimony and inserted a charming autobiographical note. He said that adult African Americans, too, have never doubted that Jefferson and many other of their ancestors practiced miscegenation freely. 2

"They believed it every time they traced the black and white branches of their own family trees," Terry wrote. "They believed it every time they held a family reunion, and Aunt Wakara, her skin the color of coffee with cream, showed up along with dark-skinned Uncle Noah, espresso-colored cousin Henry, brown sister Julie and baby Nia, who was smack dab in the middle." 3

Without even a wink of irony, Terry went on to quote Fareed's teacher, Fahamisha Butler: "Look at the black people in this class. We are the color of the rainbow. Our ancestors didn't come over from Africa this way." 4

They sure didn't. But neither did they ever call the rainbow black. Or white, for that matter. The Terry dispatch suggests that a faster way to escape some of America's racial and ethnic muddles may be for all of us to sharpen our vision and make our speech chromatically correct. 5

The police and the news media could help by becoming much more discriminating about skin color. Just as they have always distinguished among people's black, brown, red, yellow, gray or white hair and their blue, brown, green, gray or hazel eyes, let them offer a rich array of skin shades. What a boon to social harmony and effective police work if we all shed the sloppy habit of identifying achievers and miscreants as merely blacks or whites, and instead called them ebonies, chocolates, cocoas, coffees, lattes and creams on the one hand, and pinks, ivories, taupes and eggshells on the other. 6

Think how liberating it would be to read, "The gunman, a six-foot ocher, fired twice at the frail, russet shopkeeper before two elderly neighbors, one buff, one milky, wrestled him to the ground." Or, "Muhammed Jefferson Akeem, the first umber ever elected to the House of Representatives, is being actively wooed by both the Melanic and Earthtone caucuses." And how helpful it would be to detectives if police artists rendered their portraits of wanted suspects in truly descriptive shadings. 7

An even larger social benefit could be achieved in the national census in 2000. America's mating habits have confused and distorted the decennial population counts since Jefferson's time because the racial classifications have forced so many inhabitants to make an intolerable choice between "black" and "white." 8

At the least, the census should have provided a registry long ago for "mulattoes" and "quadroons," and for their descendants—as "octone- 9 gral" and "octocaucasal" or some such. In still later generations, of course, this would lead to a wholly unpronounceable nomenclature, without clearing up the additional confusions created by the remaining census racial categories — American Indian, Eskimo and Aleut and Asian and Pacific Islander. Worse, the Census Bureau then divides all these arbitrary racial groupings into Hispanic and non-Hispanic subsets, looking to document racial and ethnic strength rather than facial coloration.

Whatever may be the residual political and sociological value of these categories, they should not dominate our thought and speech. They cry out for refinement in the next century. Modern printing and computer technologies would make it easy for all of us to be given a new census form that includes a vivid color chart depicting the planet's full range of skin shades. That chart would be held up against every face to determine the closest match. 10

Such a supplementary survey would finally produce a record that looks like America. The results could be filed and published both graphically and in a new vocabulary of designer colors: mahogany, saffron and zinc, among others. Barring any change in our mating habits, what may still strike conservative minds as facetious in 2000 will, I think, appear not only sensible but also downright necessary by 2100. 11

As we correct our speech and thoughts chromatically, why not begin to clean them up historically, too? Unvarnished color consciousness requires that we abandon African American, Hispanic and Caucasian as anachronistic exaggerations or falsehoods. 12

Jefferson, who believed that the starkest sort of race mixing produces a "degradation of human character," obviously judged Sally Hemings as sufficiently pale (that is, un-African) to bear his child, but still dark enough (African) to remain his slave. Most of his American contemporaries probably saw no contradiction in such bifurcated[2] reasoning. Even a man of great intellect and democratic conviction could love and own a woman simultaneously. Nowadays, we ascribe that attitude to a "timebound" racism — not unlike the timebound sexism that we blame for preserving the ideal of wifely obedience into our century's marriage vow. 13

Finding this dusty furniture in the mind's attic can be both shocking and illuminating. Just as we now wonder how otherwise enlightened people could trade in dark-skinned bodies or demand and accept female subservience, future generations are bound to marvel at how so many of their forebears could routinely feast while others went hungry, or how some ancestors could amass fortunes while others went begging. Like slavery and male domination in their time, the inequalities of our day are 14

[2] **bifurcated:** Divided into two parts.

justified even in the most progressive circles as not only tolerable but also actually essential to economic growth and social harmony.

Our descendants will shake their heads in disbelief. But in that distant   15
time, like Jefferson, we will surely want it said that things were never so black and white.

EXERCISING VOCABULARY

1. How is the word *liberating* used in paragraph 7? How is this meaning related to other meanings of the term?

2. What does the phrase "without even a wink of irony" mean in paragraph 4? What does *winking* have to do with *irony*?

3. What does the term "unvarnished color consciousness" mean in paragraph 12? If you possess this, why does the author say you can no longer use the terms African American, Hispanic, and Caucasian?

PROBING CONTENT

1. Though the writer doesn't explicitly mention who "people of color" are (para. 1), he presumes that they have no trouble believing that Thomas Jefferson fathered at least one child by his slave Sally Hemings. On what does he base this presumption?

2. Who, according to the writer, could help make our speech and thought chromatically correct? How does the writer suggest they could help? What good would it do for us to follow his suggestions?

3. List some advantages the writer mentions of making our speech and thought chromatically correct.

4. What does Frankel mean by "anachronistic exaggerations or falsehoods" (para. 12)? How would cleaning up our historical speech and thoughts help remove these? What would be the benefit of doing this?

CONSIDERING CRAFT

1. Frankel opens his essay with people's reactions to the relationship between Thomas Jefferson and Sally Hemings. How does reading about their reactions affect your understanding of the essay?

2. Find several examples of chromatically correct speech in the essay. How do they help the writer get his point across?

3. At the end of the essay, what does the writer refer to with the expression "black and white" (para. 15)? How is it appropriate here?

RESPONDING TO THE WRITER

Do you think the writer is being realistic in suggesting that we refer to people as "ebonies, chocolates, . . . pinks, [or] taupes"? What might opponents of Frankel's idea say?

For a quiz on this reading, go to www.bedfordstmartins.com/mirror.

Do I Look Like Public Enemy Number One?

LORRAINE ALI

"Do I Look Like Public Enemy Number One?" is Lorraine Ali's personal account of growing up Arabic in the United States and the prejudices she's faced while living an almost double life—as both an American and an Arab. In her teenage years, Ali realized that "an entire race of people was judged by its most violent individuals" and that she would be "identified as part of a culture that America loved to hate." As she recalls her struggle to appreciate her ethnic heritage, Ali raises some important questions. How can an American of a different ethnic background forge an identity between two cultures? How does prejudice caused by racial stereotypes affect a person's self-image?

Ali is a general editor at *Newsweek* who primarily covers music for the magazine's Arts and Entertainment section. She has written about everything from Christian alternative rock to Latino Lone Star rap and has also occasionally covered Arab American culture and Middle Eastern affairs. In addition to her work for *Newsweek*, Ali has contributed stories to the *New York Times*, *GQ*, and *Rolling Stone*. She is currently working on a book about Arab American life in the United States. "Do I Look Like Public Enemy Number One?" was first published in *Mademoiselle* in 1999.

THINKING AHEAD

Since the attack on America on September 11, 2001, Arab Americans have been under uncomfortable scrutiny and often unwarranted suspicion. Have terrorist actions by a radical few forever affected our ability to treat all people as the individuals they are? What repercussions will such a shift in thought have on the American way of life?

INCREASING VOCABULARY

stock (adj.) (1)	shoddy (adj.) (6)
retort (n.) (2)	mesmerized (v.) (7)
composite (n.) (2)	subversive (adj.) (7)
outmoded (adj.) (3)	forge (v.) (15)
pundit (n.) (3)	

"You're not a terrorist, are you?" That was pretty much a stock   1
question I faced growing up. Classmates usually asked it after they heard my last name: "Ali" sounded Arabic; therefore, I must be some kind of bomb-lobbing religious fanatic with a grudge against Western society. It didn't matter that just before my Middle Eastern her-

itage was revealed, my friend and I might have been discussing the merits of rock versus disco, or the newest flavor of Bonne Bell Lip Smacker.[1]

I could never find the right retort; I either played along ("Yeah, and I'm going to blow up the math building first") or laughed and shrugged it off. How was I going to explain that my background meant far more than buzz words like *fanatic* and *terrorist* could say? Back in the '70s and '80s, all Americans knew of the Middle East came from television and newspapers. "Arab" meant a contemptible composite of images: angry Palestinian refugees, irate Iranian hostage-takers, extremist leaders like Libya's Muammar al-Qaddafi or Iran's Ayatollah Khomeini, and long gas lines at home. What my limited teenage vernacular couldn't express was that an entire race of people was being judged by its most violent individuals.

Twenty years later, I'm still trying to explain. Not much has changed in the '90s. In fact, now that Russia has been outmoded as Public Enemy Number One, Arabs have been promoted into that position. Whenever a disaster strikes without a clear cause, fingers point toward Islam. When an explosion downed TWA Flight 800, pundits prematurely blamed "Arab terrorists." Early coverage following the Oklahoma City bombing featured experts saying it "showed Middle Eastern traits." Over the next six days there were 150 documented hate crimes against Arab Americans; phone calls to radio talk shows demanded detainment and deportation of Middle Easterners. Last fall, *The Siege* depicted Moslems terrorizing Manhattan, and TV's *Days of Our Lives* showed a female character being kidnapped by an Arabian sultan, held hostage in a harem, and threatened with death if she didn't learn how to belly dance properly. Whatever!

My Childhood Had Nothing to Do with Belly Dancing

Defending my ethnicity has always seemed ironic to me because I consider myself a fake Arab. I am half of European ancestry and half Arab, and I grew up in the suburban sprawl of Los Angeles' San Fernando Valley. My skin is pale olive rather than smooth brown like my dad's, and my eyes are green, not black like my sisters' (they got all the Arab genes). Even my name, Lorraine Mahia Ali, saves all the Arab parts for last.

I also didn't grow up Moslem, like my dad, who emigrated from Baghdad, Iraq's capital, in 1956. In the old country he wore a galabiya (or robe), didn't eat pork, and prayed toward Mecca five times a day. To me, an American girl who wore short-shorts, ate Pop Rocks,[2] and listened to Van Halen,[3] his former life sounded like a fairy tale. The Baghdad of his childhood was an ancient city where he and his brothers swam in the Tigris River, where he did accounting on an abacus[4] in his father's tea shop, where his mother blamed his sister's polio on a neighbor's evil eye,

[1] **ESL** **Bonne Bell Lip Smacker:** A brand of flavored lip gloss.
[2] **ESL** **Pop Rocks:** A type of fizzy candy made popular in the 1970s.
[3] **ESL** **Van Halen:** A rock/metal musical group that gained popularity in the 1980s.
[4] **abacus:** ancient device for calculating arithmetic.

where his entire neighborhood watched Flash Gordon[5] movies projected on the side of a bakery wall.

My father's world only started to seem real to me when I visited Iraq   6 the summer after fifth grade and stayed in his family's small stucco house. I remember feeling both completely at home and totally foreign. My sister Lela and I spoke to amused neighbors in shoddy sign language, sat cross-legged on the floor in our Mickey Mouse T-shirts, rolling cigarettes to sell at market for my arthritic Bedouin[6] grandma, and sang silly songs in pidgin[7] Arabic with my Uncle Brahim. Afterward, I wrote a back-to-school essay in which I referred to my grandparents as Hajia and Haja Hassan, thinking their names were the Arab equivalent of Mary Ellen and Billy Bob. "You're such a dumb-ass," said Lela. "It just means grandma and grandpa." But she was wrong too. It actually meant they had completed their Haj duty—a religious journey to Mecca in Saudi Arabia that millions of Muslims embark on each year.

At home, my American side continued to be shamefully ignorant of all   7 things Arab, but my Arab side began to notice some pretty hideous stereotypes. Saturday-morning cartoons depicted Arabs as ruthless, bumbling, and hygienically challenged. I'd glimpse grotesque illustrations of Arab leaders in my dad's paper. At the mall with my mom, we'd pass such joke items as an Arab face on a bull's-eye. She tried to explain to me that things weren't always this way, that there was a time when Americans were mesmerized by Arabia and Omar Sharif[8] made women swoon. A time when a WASP[9] girl like my mom, raised in a conservative, middle-class family, could be considered romantic and daring, not subversive, for dating my dad. In effect, my mom belonged to the last generation to think sheiks were chic.

Not so in my generation. My mother tells me that when my oldest sister was five, she said to a playmate that her dad "was an Arab, but not a bad one." In elementary school, we forced smiles through taunts like, "Hey, Ali, where's your oilcan?" Teachers were even more hurtful: During roll call on her first day of junior high, Lela was made to sit through a twenty-minute lecture about the bloodshed and barbarism of Arabs toward Israel and the world. As far as I knew, Lela had never shed anyone's blood except for mine, when she punched me in the nose over a pack of Pixie Sticks.[10] But that didn't matter. As Arabs, we were guilty by association, even at the age of twelve.

---

[5] **ESL** **Flash Gordon:** Hero of a comic book series that originated in 1934 about a space traveler battling evildoers.

[6] **Bedouin:** Tent dweller of the desert; a wanderer.

[7] **pidgin:** A simplified form of a language.

[8] **ESL** **Omar Sharif:** Egyptian actor, best known for his charismatic performances in the films *Lawrence of Arabia,* and *Doctor Zhivago.*

[9] **ESL** **WASP:** Slang term for White Anglo-Saxon Protestant.

[10] **ESL** **Pixie Sticks:** A type of powdered candy that comes in a paper straw.

By High School, I Was Beginning to Believe the Hype

It's awful to admit, but I was sometimes embarrassed by my dad. 9

I know it's every teen's job to think her parents are the most shameful 10
creatures to walk the planet, but this basic need to reject him was exacerbated[11] by the horrible images of Arabs around me. When he drove me to
school, my dad would pop in a cassette of Quran suras (recorded prayers)
and recite the lines in a language I didn't understand, yet somehow the
twisting, weaving words sounded as natural as the whoosh of the Santa
Ana winds through the dusty hills where we lived. His brown hands
would raise off the steering wheel at high points of the prayer, the sun illuminating the big white moons of his fingernails. The mass of voices on
tape would swell up and answer the Mezzuin[12] like a gospel congregation
responding to a preacher. It was beautiful, but I still made my dad turn it
down as we approached my school. I knew I'd be identified as part of a
culture that America loved to hate.

My dad must have felt this, too. He spoke his native tongue only in 11
the company of Arabic friends and never taught my sisters or me the language, something he would regret until the day he died. His background
was a mystery to me. I'd pester him for answers: "Do you dream in English or Arabic?" I'd ask, while he was busy doing dad work like fixing
someone's busted Schwinn[13] or putting up Christmas lights. "Oh, I don't
know," he'd answer playfully. "In dreams, I can't tell the difference."

Outside the safety of our home, he could. He wanted respect; there- 12
fore, he felt he must act American. Though he truly loved listening to
Roberta Flack[14] and wearing Adidas sweatsuits, I can't imagine he enjoyed making dinner reservations under pseudonyms[15] like Mr. Allen. He
knew that as Mr. Ali, he might never get a table.

Desert Storm Warning

Fifteen years later, "Ali" was still not a well-received name. We were at 13
war with the Middle East. It was January 16, 1991, and Iraq's Saddam
Hussein had just invaded Kuwait. I will never forget the night CNN's
Bernard Shaw lay terrified on the floor of his Baghdad hotel as a camera-
man shot footage of the brand-new war outside his window. I was
twenty-six and working for a glossy music magazine called *Creem*. When
the news broke that we were bombing Baghdad in an operation called
Desert Storm, I went home early and sat helpless in my Hollywood apart-

---

[11] **exacerbated:** To make more harsh or bitter.
[12] **Mezzuin:** An Islamic cantor.
[13] ESL **Schwinn:** A popular bicycle manufacturer.
[14] ESL **Roberta Flack:** A soul singer who gained popularity in the mid-1970s.
[15] **pseudonym:** A fictitious name used by an author.

ment, crying. Before me on the TV was a man dressed in a galabiya, just like the kind my dad used to wear around the house, aiming an ancient-looking gun turret toward our space-age planes in the sky. He looked terrified, too. With every missile we fired, I watched the Baghdad I knew slip away and wondered just who was being hit. Was it Aunt Niama? My cousin Afrah?

Back at work, I had to put up with "funny" faxes of camels, SCUD 14 missiles, and dead Arabs. To my colleagues, the Arabs I loved and respected were now simply targets. Outside the office, there was a virtual free-for-all of racist slogans. Arab-hating sentiment came out on bumper stickers like "Kick Their Ass and Take Their Gas." Military footage even documented our pilots joking as they bombed around fleeing civilians. They called it a turkey shoot. A turkey shoot? Those were people.

Arabs bleed and perish just like Americans. I know, because two years 15 before we started dropping bombs on Baghdad, I watched my father die. He did not dissolve like a cartoon character, nor defy death like a Hollywood villain. Instead, chemotherapy shrunk his 180-pound body down to 120, turned his beautiful skin from brown to ashen beige, and rendered his opalescent[16] white fingernails a dull shade of gray. When he finally let go, I thought he took all the secrets of my Arabness with him, all the good things America didn't want me to know. But I look in the mirror and see my father's wide nose on my face and Hajia's think lines forming between my brows. I also see my mom's fair skin, and her mother's high cheekbones. I realize it's my responsibility to somehow forge an identity between dueling cultures, to focus on the humanity, not the terror, that bridges both worlds.

EXERCISING VOCABULARY

1. In paragraph 2, the author regrets "what my limited teenage vernacular couldn't express." What does *vernacular* mean? What is the purpose of a group having its own vernacular?

2. What does it mean to possess and to give the "evil eye"? How does Ali's inclusion of this phrase in paragraph 5 contribute to your understanding of the gap between her life and the early life of her father?

3. Ali states that "now that Russia has been outmoded as Public Enemy Number One, Arabs have been promoted into that position" (para. 3). What is ironic about her use of the word *promoted* in this context?

---

[16] **opalescent:** Reflecting an iridescent light.

PROBING CONTENT

1. In Ali's opinion, how did television enhance the image of the "bad Arab"?

2. What elementary school experience stimulated Ali's awareness of her family's cultural heritage? How did that experience color her everyday thinking?

3. What examples does the author provide to show how carefully she and her family tried to keep their two cultures from clashing?

CONSIDERING CRAFT

1. In paragraph 5, what strong images does Ali choose to represent her American childhood? What images represent her father's childhood? How does her inclusion of these images convey the gap between her father's culture and the one in which she was raised?

2. How does Ali use her personal experience to make a broad statement about how people of one culture relate to those from a different background? How effective is this writing strategy?

RESPONDING TO THE WRITER

Explain how Ali's phrase "dueling cultures" (para. 15) has taken on a very different meaning since this essay was first published in 1999. In light of recent events, what would you say to Ali about her effort to "focus on the humanity, not the terror" (para. 15) that bridges Middle Eastern and American culture?

For a quiz on this reading, go to www.bedfordstmartins.com/mirror.

I Want to Be Miss America

JULIA ALVAREZ

In "I Want to Be Miss America," Julia Alvarez examines an American tradition from an outsider's point of view. After moving to the United States from the Dominican Republic at the age of ten, Alvarez desperately wanted to belong. Watching the Miss America pageant for clues about how to look more "American," she and her sisters learned more than just how to "translate our looks into English." Coming from a culture where girls were expected only to grow up and become housewives, Alvarez learned that girls could excel in other areas — Miss America could be beautiful *and* succeed as a doctor, for example. Nevertheless, the pageant presented a limited vision of what was considered beautiful and made Alvarez feel insecure, as if she could never be a "Made-in-the-U.S.A. beauty" like the women on television.

A prolific writer, Alvarez has published ten books, including *How the Garcia Girls Lost Their Accents* (1991), winner of the PEN/Oakland award, and *In the Time of Butterflies* (1994), a National Book Critics Circle finalist. Alvarez, who currently teaches creative writing at Middlebury College in Vermont, most recently published *In the Name of Salome* (2001), a novel about a mother and daughter from the Dominican Republic. Her essays, stories, and poems have appeared in the *New York Times Magazine, Allure, The New Yorker, Hispanic Magazine,* and *USA Weekend.* "I Want to Be Miss America" was first published in her collection of essays *Something to Declare* (1999).

THINKING AHEAD

Within every culture, there are some firmly held beliefs about what constitutes "beauty." How are these ideals a reflection of the values of the culture? When have you questioned any of the beauty ideals in your own culture? What caused you to begin to question them?

INCREASING VOCABULARY

acute (adj.) (5)
sallow (adj.) (9)
gawk (v.) (11)
sashayed (v.) (14)
inane (adj.) (18)

aspirations (n.) (18)
prodigies (n.) (19)
sappy (adj.) (20)
diaphanous (adj.) (21)
gratifying (adj.) (22)

A s young teenagers in our new country, my three sisters and I   1
searched for clues on how to look as if we belonged here. We col-
lected magazines, studied our classmates and our new TV, which
was where we discovered the Miss America contest.

Watching the pageant became an annual event in our family. Once a   2
year, we all plopped down in our parents' bedroom, with Mami and Papi
presiding from their bed. In our nightgowns, we watched the fifty young
women who had the American look we longed for.

The beginning was always the best part—all fifty contestants came on   3
for one and only one appearance. In alphabetical order, they stepped forward and enthusiastically introduced themselves by name and state. "Hi!
I'm! Susie! Martin! Miss! Alaska!" Their voices rang with false cheer. You
could hear, not far off, years of high-school cheerleading, pom-poms,
bleachers full of moon-eyed boys, and moms on phones, signing them up
for all manner of lessons and making dentist appointments.

There they stood, fifty puzzle pieces forming the pretty face of Amer-   4
ica, so we thought, though most of the color had been left out, except for
one, or possibly two, light-skinned black girls. If there was a "Hispanic,"
she usually looked all-American, and only the last name, López or
Rodríguez, often mispronounced, showed a trace of a great-great-grand-
father with a dark, curled mustache and a sombrero charging the Alamo.[1]
During the initial roll-call, what most amazed us was that some contestants were ever picked in the first place. There were homely girls with
cross-eyed smiles or chipmunk cheeks. My mother would inevitably shake
her head and say, "The truth is, these Americans believe in democracy—
even in looks."

We were beginning to feel at home. Our acute homesickness had   5
passed, and now we were like people recovered from a shipwreck, looking
around at our new country, glad to be here. "I want to be in America,"
my mother hummed after we'd gone to see *West Side Story*,[2] and her four
daughters chorused, "OK by me in America." We bought a house in
Queens, New York, in a neighborhood that was mostly German and Irish,
where we were the only "Hispanics." Actually, no one ever called us that.
Our teachers and classmates at the local Catholic schools referred to us as
"Porto Ricans" or "Spanish." No one knew where the Dominican Republic was on the map. "South of Florida," I explained, "in the same general
vicinity as Bermuda and Jamaica." I could just as well have said west of
Puerto Rico or east of Cuba or right next to Haiti, but I wanted us to
sound like a vacation spot, not a Third World country, a place they would
look down on.

---

[1] **ESL** **the Alamo:** Former Franciscan mission in San Antonio, Texas, that was the site of
the most heroic battle of the Texan war of independence against Mexico.
[2] **ESL** *West Side Story:* Film and Broadway musical that featured 1950s clashes between
Latin American culture and U.S. culture in the context of a modern-day Romeo and
Juliet story.

Although we wanted to look like we belonged here, the four sisters,   6
our looks didn't seem to fit in. We complained about how short we were,
about how our hair frizzed, how our figures didn't curve like those of the
bathing beauties we'd seen on TV.

"The grass always grows on the other side of the fence," my mother   7
scolded. Her daughters looked fine just the way they were.

But how could we trust her opinion about what looked good when   8
she couldn't even get the sayings of our new country right? No, we knew
better. We would have to translate our looks into English, iron and tweeze
them out, straighten them, mold them into Made-in-the-U.S.A. beauty.

So we painstakingly rolled our long, curly hair round and round,   9
using our heads as giant rollers, ironing it until we had long, shining
shanks, like our classmates and the contestants, only darker. Our skin was
diagnosed by beauty consultants in department stores as sallow; we definitely needed a strong foundation to tone down that olive. We wore tights
even in the summer to hide the legs Mami would not let us shave. We
begged for permission, dreaming of the contestants' long, silky limbs. We
were ten, fourteen, fifteen, and sixteen—merely children, Mami explained. We had long lives ahead of us in which to shave.

We defied her. Giggly and red-faced, we all pitched in to buy a big   10
tube of Nair[3] at the local drugstore. We acted as if we were purchasing
contraceptives. That night we crowded into the bathroom, and I, the most
courageous along these lines, offered one of my legs as a guinea pig. When
it didn't become gangrenous or fall off as Mami had predicted, we
creamed the other seven legs. We beamed at each other; we were one step
closer to that runway, those flashing cameras, those oohs and ahhs from
the audience.

Mami didn't even notice our Naired legs; she was too busy disapprov-   11
ing of the other changes. Our clothes, for one. "You're going to wear *that*
in public!" She'd gawk, as if to say, What will the Americans think of us?

"This *is* what the Americans wear," we would argue back.   12

But the dresses we had picked out made us look cheap, she said, like   13
bad, fast girls—gringas without vergüenza, without shame. She preferred
her choices; fuchsia skirts with matching vests, flowered dresses with
bows at the neck or gathers where you wanted to look slim, everything
bright and busy, like something someone might wear in a foreign country.

Our father didn't really notice our new look at all but, if called upon   14
to comment, would say absently that we looked beautiful. "Like Marilina
Monroe." Still, during the pageant, he would offer insights into what he
thought made a winner. "Personality, Mami," my father would say from
his post at the head of the bed, "Personality is the key," though his favorite contestants, whom he always championed in the name of personality, tended to be the fuller girls with big breasts who gushed shamelessly

---

[3] **ESL Nair:** A brand of hair-removal lotion.

at Bert Parks[4]. "Ay, Papi," we would groan, rolling our eyes at each other. Sometimes, as the girl sashayed back down the aisle, Papi would break out in a little Dominican song that he sang whenever a girl had a lot of swing in her walk:

> Yo no tumbo caña,
> Que la tumba el viento,
> Que la tumba Dora
> Con su movimiento!

> ("I don't have to cut the cane,
> The wind knocks it down,
> The wind of Dora's movement
> As she walks downtown.")

My father would stop on a New York City street when a young woman swung by and sing this song out loud to the great embarrassment of his daughters. We were sure that one day when we weren't around to make him look like the respectable father of four girls, he would be arrested. 15

My mother never seemed to have a favorite contestant. She was an ex-beauty herself, and no one seemed to measure up to her high standards. She liked the good girls who had common sense and talked about their education and about how they owed everything to their mothers. "Tell that to my daughters," my mother would address the screen, as if none of us were there to hear her. If we challenged her—how exactly did we *not* appreciate her?—she'd maintain a wounded silence for the rest of the evening. Until the very end of the show, that is, when all our disagreements were forgotten and we waited anxiously to see which of the two finalists holding hands on that near-empty stage would be the next reigning queen of beauty. How can they hold hands? I always wondered. Don't they secretly wish the other person would, well, die? 16

My sisters and I always had plenty of commentary on all the contestants. We were hardly strangers to this ritual of picking the beauty. In our own family, we had a running competition as to who was the prettiest of the four girls. We coveted one another's best feature: the oldest's dark, almond-shaped eyes, the youngest's great mane of hair, the third oldest's height and figure. I didn't have a preferred feature, but I was often voted the cutest, though my oldest sister liked to remind me that I had the kind of looks that wouldn't age well. Although she was only eleven months older than I was, she seemed years older, ages wiser. She bragged about the new kind of math she was learning in high school, called algebra, which she said I would never be able to figure out. I believed her. Dumb and ex-cute, that's what I would grow up to be. 17

As for the prettiest Miss America, we sisters kept our choices secret until the very end. The range was limited—pretty white women who all 18

---

[4] **ESL** **Bert Parks:** Long-time host of the Miss America Pageant.

really wanted to be wives and mothers. But even the small and inane set of options these girls represented seemed boundless compared with what we were used to. We were being groomed to go from being dutiful daughters to being dutiful wives with hymens intact. No stops along the way that might endanger the latter; no careers, no colleges, no shared apartments with girlfriends, no boyfriends, no social lives. But the young women on-screen, who were being held up as models in this new country, were in college, or at least headed there. They wanted to do this, they were going to do that with their lives. Everything in our native culture had instructed us otherwise: girls were to have no aspirations beyond being good wives and mothers.

Sometimes there would even be a contestant headed for law school   19
or medical school. "I wouldn't mind having an office visit with her," my father would say, smirking. The women who caught my attention were the prodigies who bounded onstage and danced to tapes of themselves playing original compositions on the piano, always dressed in costumes they had sewn, with a backdrop of easels holding paintings they'd painted. "Overkill," my older sister insisted. But if one good thing came out of our watching this yearly parade of American beauties, it was that subtle permission we all felt as a family: a girl could excel outside the home and still be a winner.

Every year, the queen came down the runway in her long gown with a   20
sash like an old-world general's belt of ammunition. Down the walkway she paraded, smiling and waving while Bert sang his sappy song that made our eyes fill with tears. When she stopped at the very end of the stage and the camera zoomed in on her misty-eyed beauty and the credits began to appear on the screen, I always felt let down. I knew I would never be one of those girls, ever. It wasn't just the blond, blue-eyed looks or the beautiful, leggy figure. It was who she was—an American—and we were not. We were foreigners, dark-haired and dark-eyed with olive skin that could never, no matter the sun blocks or foundation makeup, be made into peaches and cream.[5]

Had we been able to see into the future, beyond our noses, which we   21
thought weren't the right shape; beyond our curly hair, which we wanted to be straight; and beyond the screen, which inspired us with a limited vision of what was considered beautiful in America, we would have been able to see the late sixties coming. Soon, ethnic looks would be in. Even Barbie, that quintessential white girl, would suddenly be available in different shades of skin color with bright, colorful outfits that looked like the ones Mami had picked out for us. Our classmates in college wore long braids like Native Americans and embroidered shawls and peasant blouses from South America, and long, diaphanous skirts and dangly earrings from India. They wanted to look exotic—they wanted to look like us.

[5] **ESL** **peaches and cream:** A complimentary description of Caucasian skin color.

We felt then a gratifying sense of inclusion, but it had unfortunately   22
come too late. We had already acquired the habit of doubting ourselves as
well as the place we came from. To this day, after three decades of living
in America, I feel like a stranger in what I now consider my own country.
I am still that young teenager sitting in front of the black-and-white TV in
my parents' bedroom, knowing in my bones I will never be the beauty
queen. There she is, Miss America, but even in my up-to-date, enlightened
dreams, she never wears my face.

EXERCISING VOCABULARY

1. Define *quintessential* and then explain why Alvarez calls Barbie "that quintessential white girl" in paragraph 21.

2. In her final sentence, why does Alvarez refer to her adult dreams as enlightened? How have her dreams changed since her childhood? How truly "enlightened" are her dreams?

PROBING CONTENT

1. How does the Miss America pageant that Alvarez watches support or deny
   her mother's assertion that "'. . . Americans believe in democracy — even in
   looks.'" (para. 4)?

2. When Alvarez explained where her family came from, what geographic reference points did she use to help friends locate the Dominican Republic? Why
   did she choose these landmarks instead of others?

3. Why don't the Alvarez girls trust the opinion of their mother about what
   looks good? Why is their father's opinion also suspect?

4. What hopes for the future were Julia Alvarez and her sisters expected to
   have? How were these expectations at odds with the plans of some of the
   Miss America contestants? How did this difference make the girls feel?

5. How did a change in the appearance of Barbie dolls mirror what Alvarez saw
   at college? How does Alvarez feel about this development?

CONSIDERING CRAFT

1. Why does Alvarez put exclamation points between every word of the contestant's introduction in paragraph 3? What does this unusual punctuation
   achieve?

2. How does Alvarez's concluding paragraph differ in tone from the first paragraph of her essay? What message does this difference in tone convey to the
   reader?

3. In paragraph 4, Alvarez writes, "There they stood, fifty puzzle pieces forming the pretty face of America . . . though most of the color had been left out." How does this figurative language reinforce the main idea of her essay?

RESPONDING TO THE WRITER

Do you identify with the strong need of Alvarez and her sisters "to look as if we belonged" (para. 1)? Why are some people so motivated not to express and celebrate their differences but to simply "fit in"?

For a quiz on these readings, go to www.bedfordstmartins.com/mirror.

They've Got to Be Carefully Taught

SUSAN BRADY KONIG

This essay is a mother's humorous account of Cultural Diversity Month at her daughter's preschool. Through humor, Susan Brady Konig ponders very serious questions: Can too much emphasis on cultural diversity actually do more harm than good? Does it serve to confuse rather than to clarify, to separate rather than to unify?

Konig was born in Paris, France, in 1962 but was educated in the United States. She has written articles for such wide-ranging publications as *Us, Travel & Leisure, Ladies' Home Journal*, and the *National Review*. She has worked as an editor for *Seventeen* magazine, as a writer for the "Style" section of the *Washington Post*, and currently writes an opinion column for the *New York Post*. "They've Got to Be Carefully Taught" originally appeared in the September 15, 1997, issue of the *National Review*.

THINKING AHEAD

Think back to your early school days. How was the issue of cultural diversity handled? What special occasions were held to highlight diversity issues? How did these events affect your own cultural awareness?

INCREASING VOCABULARY

badgered (v.) (6)	culmination (n.) (21)
decidedly (adv.) (14)	disparity (n.) (21)
opted (v.) (20)	concerted (adj.) (24)

At my daughter's preschool it's time for all the children to learn that 1
they are different from one another. Even though these kids are at
that remarkable age when they are thoroughly color blind, their
teachers are spending a month emphasizing race, color, and background.
The little tots are being taught in no uncertain terms that their hair is different, their skin is different, and their parents come from different places.
It's Cultural Diversity Month.

I hadn't really given much thought to the ethnic and national back- 2
grounds of Sarah's classmates. I can guarantee that Sarah, being two and
a half, gave the subject absolutely no thought. Her teachers, however, had
apparently given it quite a lot of thought. They sent a letter asking each
parent to contribute to the cultural-awareness effort by "providing any information and/or material regarding your family's cultural background.

For example: favorite recipe or song." All well and good, unless your culture isn't *diverse* enough.

The next day I take Sarah to school and her teacher, Miss Laura, anxious to get this Cultural Diversity show on the road, begins the interrogation.   3

"Where are you and your husband from?" she cheerily demands.   4

"We're Americans," I reply—less, I must confess, out of patriotism than from sheer lack of coffee. It was barely 9:00 A.M.   5

"Yes, of course, but where are you *from*?" I'm beginning to feel like a nightclub patron being badgered by a no-talent stand-up comic.[1]   6

"We're native New Yorkers."   7

"But where are your *people* from?"   8

"Well," I dive in with a sigh, "my family is originally Irish on both sides. My husband's father was from Czechoslovakia and his mother is from the Bronx, but her grandparents were from the Ukraine."   9

"Can you cook Irish?"   10

"I could bring in potatoes and beer for the whole class."   11

Miss Laura doesn't get it.   12

"Look," I say, "we're Americans. Our kids are Americans. We tell them about American history and George Washington and apple pie and all that stuff. If you want me to do something American, I can do that."   13

She is decidedly unexcited.   14

A few days later, she tells me that she was trying to explain to Sarah that her dad is from Ireland.   15

"Wrong," I say, "but go on."   16

"He's *not* from Ireland?"   17

No, I sigh. He's from Queens. I'm from Ireland. I mean I'm Irish—that is, my great-grandparents were. Don't get me wrong, I'm proud of my heritage—but that's entirely beside the point. I told you we tell Sarah she's American.   18

"Well, anyway," she smiles, "Sarah thinks her Daddy's from *Iceland!* Isn't that cute?"   19

Later in the month, Miss Laura admits that her class is not quite getting the whole skin-color thing. "I tried to show them how we all have different skin," she chuckled. Apparently, little Henry is the only one who successfully grasped the concept. He now runs around the classroom announcing to anyone who'll listen, "I'm white!" Miss Laura asked the children what color her own skin was. (She is a light-skinned Hispanic, which would make her skin color . . . what? Caramel? Mochaccino[2]?) The kids opted for purple or orange. "They looked at me like I was crazy!" Miss Laura said. I just smile.   20

---

[1] **ESL** **stand-up comic:** A type of comedian who performs standing on a stage at a comedy club.

[2] **mochaccino:** A frothy coffee beverage made from espresso, steamed milk, and chocolate syrup.

The culmination of Cultural Diversity Month, the day when the par-   21
ents come into class and join their children in a glorious celebration of
multicultural disparity, has arrived. As I arrive I see a large collage on the
wall depicting the earth, with all the children's names placed next to the
country they are from. Next to my daughter's name it says "Ireland." I
politely remind Miss Laura that Sarah is, in fact, from America and suggest that, by insisting otherwise, she is confusing my daughter. She reluctantly changes Sarah's affiliation to USA. It will be the only one of its kind
on the wall.

The mom from Brazil brings in a bunch of great music, and the whole   22
class is doing the samba[3] and running around in a conga line.[4] It's very
cute. Then I get up to teach the children an indigenous folk tune from the
culture of Sarah's people, passed down through the generations from her
grandparents to her parents and now to Sarah — a song called "Take Me
Out to the Ballgame." First I explain to the kids that Sarah was born right
here in New York — and that's in what country, Sarah? Sarah looks at me
and says, "France." I look at Miss Laura, who just shrugs.

I stand there in my baseball cap and sing my song. The teacher tries to   23
rush me off. I say, "Don't you want them to learn it?" They took long
enough learning to samba! I am granted permission to sing it one more
time. The kids join in on the "root, root, root" and the "1, 2, 3 strikes
you're out," but they can see their teacher isn't enthusiastic.

So now these sweet, innocent babies who thought they were all the   24
same are becoming culturally aware. Two little girls are touching each
other's hair and saying, "Your hair is blonde, just like mine." Off to one
side a little dark-haired girl stands alone, excluded. She looks confused as
to what to do next. She knows she's not blonde. Sure, all children notice
these things eventually, but, thanks to the concerted efforts of their teachers, these two- and three-year-olds are talking about things that separate
rather than connect.

And Sarah only knows what she has been taught: Little Henry is   25
white, her daddy's from Iceland, and New York's in France.

EXERCISING VOCABULARY

1. What does Konig mean when she describes the children in her daughter's
   class as "color blind" (para. 1)? How does this expression acquire additional
   meaning when used in the context of this essay?

2. What does Konig's description of Miss Laura's questions as an "interrogation"
   (para. 3) suggest about the writer's attitude toward the teacher? What kinds of
   situations or settings do you think of when you hear the word *interrogation*?

[3] **samba:** A Brazilian dance of African origin; also, the music for this dance.
[4] **conga line:** A Cuban dance of African origin performed by a group, usually in single file,
   involving three steps followed by a kick.

3. Why does the writer call "Take Me Out to the Ballgame" an "indigenous folk tune" (para. 22)? What does *indigenous* mean? What kinds of songs are usually referred to as indigenous folk tunes?

PROBING CONTENT

1. For what reasons does the writer disagree with Miss Laura's strategy? What does she think the students are learning or not learning as a result of their classroom activities on diversity?

2. The words *American* or *Americans* are repeated four times in paragraph 13. What does the writer mean when she says that her family is American? To what else besides the geographical location of their home is she referring?

3. Describe the effect of Cultural Diversity Month on the students. From Konig's description, what do the children appear to learn? What positive lessons do they fail to learn?

CONSIDERING CRAFT

1. Find several examples of the writer's use of dialogue in this essay. How do they change your attitudes about the characters?

2. Describe the writer's tone or attitude in this essay. Why does she choose this tone? What kind of response is she hoping to get as a result?

RESPONDING TO THE WRITER

Explain why you agree or disagree with Konig's idea that too much emphasis on cultural diversity may actually separate people of different ethnicities and cultures rather than bring them together.

For a quiz on this reading, go to www.bedfordstmartins.com/mirror.

Is There an American Tribe?

LEWIS LAPHAM

Is democracy weakened when people cling to communities based on common interests, ethnicity, sexual preference, or social class? This excerpt from Lewis Lapham's article "Is There an American Tribe?" explores the growing tendency to place an adjective before the word *American* (female American, African American, gay American). Does this trend mean it is becoming more important to belong to a select group than to the all-inclusive group of Americans as a whole? According to Lapham, this elitist view runs counter to the democratic spirit of America.

Since 1983, Lapham has been an editor at *Harper's*. He writes a monthly essay for the magazine called "Notebook" and in 1995 won a National Magazine Award for three of those essays. Known as one of America's most respected and insightful contemporary journalists, Lapham has also written for *Life, Commentary, National Review*, the *Yale Literary Magazine, Elle, Forbes, Vanity Fair*, the *London Observer*, the *New York Times*, and the *Wall Street Journal*. He has published six collections of essays, including *Waiting for the Barbarians* (1997) and *Money and Class in America* (1988). "Is There an American Tribe?" first appeared in the January 1992 issue of *Harper's* magazine.

THINKING AHEAD

In an earlier age, when the United States was being populated by emigrants from all over the world, the greatest desire of those new citizens was to be called Americans. Today, however, many feel the need to qualify *American* with particular adjectives that set one subgroup apart from another. What has caused this shift? Is it beneficial or detrimental to us as a country? Support your opinion with several examples.

INCREASING VOCABULARY

premise (n.) (1)	buttress (v.) (5)
canon (n.) (2)	repudiate (v.) (7)
guild (n.) (3)	assimilation (n.) (7)
elitist (adj.) (4)	

Were I to believe what I read in the papers, I would find it easy to think that I no longer can identify myself simply as an American. As a plain American I have neither voice nor authentic proofs of existence. I acquire a presence only as a female American, a white American, an old American, a rich American, a black American, a gay American, a poor American, a native American, a dead American.

1

The subordination of the noun to the adjectives makes a mockery of both the American premise and the democratic spirit.

These days, the news is full of arguments in the arenas of cultural opinion that echo the same bitter refrain. The ceaseless quarrels about the canon of preferred texts pick at the scab of the same questions. Who and what is an American? How and where do we find an identity that is something other than a fright mask? When using the collective national pronoun ("we the people," "we happy few," etc.) whom do we invite into the club of the we?

Do we really believe that the American achieves visible and specific meaning only by reason of his or her association with the political guilds of race, gender, age, ancestry, or social class?

That assumption is as elitist as the view that only a woman endowed with an income of $1 million a year can truly appreciate the beauty of money and the music of Cole Porter.[1] Comparable theories of grace encourage the belief that only black people can know or teach black history, that no white man can play jazz piano, that blonds have a better time, and that Jews can't play basketball.

America was founded on precisely the opposite premise. We were always about becoming, not being; about the prospects for the future, not about the inheritance of the past. The man who rests his case on his color makes a claim to special privilege not unlike the divine right of kings. The pretensions might buttress the cathedrals of our self-esteem, but they run counter to the lessons of our history.

The American equation rests on the habit of holding our fellow citizens in thoughtful regard not because they are exceptional (or famous, or beautiful, or rich) but simply because they are our fellow citizens. If we abandon the sense of mutual respect, we abandon the premise as well as the machinery of the American enterprise.

Among all the nations of the earth, America is the one that has come most triumphantly to terms with the mixtures of blood and caste,[2] and maybe it is another of history's ironic jokes that we should wish to repudiate our talent for assimilation at precisely the moment in time when so many other nations in the world (in Africa and Western Europe as well as the Soviet Union) look to the promise of the American example. The jumble of confused or mistaken identities that was the story of nineteenth-century America has become the story of a late twentieth-century world defined by a vast migration of people across seven continents and as many oceans. Why, then, do we lose confidence in ourselves and grow fearful of our mongrel freedoms?

---

[1] **ESL** **Cole Porter:** American songwriter (1891–1964) noted for sophisticated lyrics.
[2] **caste:** Hereditary social divisions of some societies.

EXERCISING VOCABULARY

1. What is the relationship between two people or things if one of them is subordinated to the other? What point is Lapham making in paragraph 1 when he talks about "the subordination of the noun to the adjectives" in phrases like "an old American, a rich American, a black American"?

2. What is a mongrel? With what kind of animal is the word usually associated? Why does Lapham describe the freedoms we enjoy as Americans as "mongrel freedoms" (para. 7)?

PROBING CONTENT

1. Lapham asserts that if he referred to himself as "a plain American" (para. 1), he would lack two important things. What are these things? Why are they significant?

2. In paragraph 2, what is "the club of the we"? Which groups have historically been excluded from this club?

3. Name several of the "elitist" theories that Lapham believes are contrary to the American spirit. What is your opinion of these theories?

CONSIDERING CRAFT

1. What is the significance of the title Lapham chose? How effective is this choice? Why?

2. To what extent does Lapham answer his own question: "Who and what is an American" (para. 2)?

3. Lapham uses figurative language often in this brief essay: "quarrels about the canon of preferred texts pick at the scab of the same questions" (para. 2), "the cathedrals of our self-esteem" (para. 5), "the machinery of the American enterprise" (para. 6). How does his use of such language affect you as a reader? Why do you think authors sometimes choose such complex language to convey their message?

RESPONDING TO THE WRITER

Lapham asserts that Americans should hold their fellow citizens "in thoughtful regard . . . simply because they are our fellow citizens" (para. 6). If all Americans accepted this premise, how might our society change?

For a quiz on this reading, go to www.bedfordstmartins.com/mirror.

DRAWING CONNECTIONS

1. How would Lewis Lapham respond to Sarah's teacher's efforts to teach cultural diversity in "They've Got to Be Carefully Taught"?

2. What are the difficulties shared by Lewis Lapham and Susan Brady Konig in trying to be "plain Americans"?

3. What aspects of the future might Lapham fear if all children accepted Sarah's teacher's point of view? How justified would these fears be?

Wrapping Up Chapter 4

REFLECTING ON THE WRITING

1. Several of the selections in this chapter are written by members of minority communities. Drawing on two or more of those selections, write an essay in which you compare the writers' problematic experiences developing their self-images in a culture that they believe extends more privileges to people who look like members of the majority group.

2. Pick the selection or selections from this chapter with which you most closely identify to use as a starting point. Write a paper in which you describe your experience with cultural identity or that of someone you know well. You might want to use one or more selections to get ideas for the approach, structure, or tone of your paper.

3. In her autobiographical essay, Edgar details her family's situation and relates it to the larger situation of being an African American woman in a largely white society. Pick out portions of her essay that deal with her experience; then pick out portions that deal with the larger African American experience. Examine and compare these two different approaches to her subject.

4. Like Alvarez, Suh, and Edgar, you may have wanted to change certain of your features when you were growing up. What features would you have changed, if possible? How did you think your life would have been improved by such changes? Now that you are an adult, have you reevaluated your desire for those alterations?

CONNECTING TO THE CULTURE

1. Think about celebrities who have helped to shape your cultural self-image. They might be models, sports figures, musicians, or television personalities. They might have had positive, negative, or mixed influences on you. Write an essay in which you trace the influence these people have had on your cultural self-image.

2. Since you have been attending college, what new cultural influences have you experienced? Have they been positive, negative, or mixed? To what extent have you been influenced? In what ways have these influences changed you?

3. What influence has your particular cultural group had on the formation of your self-image?

4. As a current or future parent, identify some negative cultural influences on the formation of self-image in children and detail how you would attempt to curb those influences.

5. What role do you think television plays in shaping and reinforcing our ideas about people of cultures or races different from our own? Cite specific examples of television shows to support your points.

FOCUSING ON YESTERDAY, FOCUSING ON TODAY

Norman Rockwell's art for *The Saturday Evening Post* has long been considered a staple of American popular culture. He rendered the everyday moments that defined our society, catching our humanity and our frailty in a way that everyone could relate to and few other artists can match. In this 1940s painting Rockwell captures a wide range of ethnicities and ages. The people stand close together and yet are clearly distinct from each other, each dressed in clothing that identifies a unique cultural heritage. By contrast, the stresses of

Do Unto Others

a "melting pot" culture are clearly revealed in the cover photograph from this 1999 *National Geographic*. While the mother's dress reflects her heritage, the daughter's sleek jumpsuit makes a bold statement about her own cultural affiliation.

What changed in the fifty years between these images to redefine the way we read cultures? How would you interpret the facial expressions in the Norman Rockwell image? In the *National Geographic* photo? How does the text enforce the message of the Norman Rockwell image?

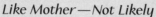

Like Mother—Not Likely

CHAPTER 5

It's All about the Look
Fashion Trends and the Signals They Send

This tongue-in-cheek cartoon, which first appeared in the *Utne Reader*'s March/April 1998 edition, makes an important and not-so-subtle point about the pervasive role of logos, or advertising symbols and slogans, in our lives.

- Where is the scene in this cartoon set?
- How would you interpret the expression on the face of the woman in the bed?
- Why does the cartoonist include so few details in his drawing?
- What might persuade a parent to "logo-ize" a baby?

Research this topic with TopLinks at www.bedfordstmartins.com/toplinks.

We are all consumers. Some of us buy only the bare necessities. Some of us regard shopping as an enjoyable pastime. Some of us are "shopaholics" whose uncontrollable shopping sprees threaten our financial and emotional well-being. In whichever category we fall, we are all consumers of everything from the food we eat and the clothes we wear to the shampoo we use, the CDs we listen to, and the books we read. Among all the products we consume, fashion items are among the closest to our hearts, not to mention our bodies. While we cannot live without clothing, many of us want and often buy more, and more expensive, clothes than we need to shelter us from the elements and maintain our modesty. Why do our travel plans often include a stop at the local Hard Rock Cafe to buy a T-shirt we can show off when we get home? Do we buy different brands of jeans to portray certain images? What will people say if we get that extra piercing? How do we know what's "in"? Will it still be "in" next month? Why do we care? How are we, as fashion consumers, manipulated by those advertising and marketing executives who follow and create the latest trends? The essays in this chapter explore such questions and lead you to some answers about your own consumer behavior and the consumer standards we accept.

The Motorcycle Jacket

MICK FARREN

Motorcycle jackets have long been worn by the famous and not-so-famous alike. Movie icons James Dean, Marlon Brando, and John Travolta have sported them. So have television stars like the Fonz from the 1970s sitcom *Happy Days* and musicians as diverse as Elvis Presley, Bruce Springsteen, Billy Idol, and Madonna. Today, many different kinds of people, from Hell's Angels and grandmothers riding Harley-Davidsons on weekend excursions to fashionable young men and women on the street, wear motorcycle jackets. What image do they convey? What significance do the jackets have to those that wear them? Like white T-shirts and blue jeans, the motorcycle jacket means many things to many people and now is an icon of American fashion. For more than fifty years, its shiny black leather, zippers, and silver studs have sent diverse messages—everything from macho intimidation and violent criminality to dangerous sex appeal and counterculture hipness. In the following essay, which first appeared in the February 1998 issue of *Icon Thoughtstyle Magazine*, Mick Farren traces the history and analyzes the significance of this staple of American pop fashion. The subtitle of his essay, "How a Functional Piece of Protective Gear Came to Represent the Best and the Worst in Us," gives you a hint of what lies ahead in your reading.

Farren has written several pop-culture publications, including three books on Elvis Presley, *Jim Morrison's Adventures in the Afterlife: A Novel* (1995), and *Conspiracies, Lies, and Hidden Agendas* (1999). Farren was also lead vocalist with the pop band the Deviants in the late 1960s.

THINKING AHEAD

Describe some people you've seen wearing motorcycle jackets, either in real life or on television or in the movies. What do you think of when you see someone wearing a motorcycle jacket? Why do you have this reaction? Under what circumstances would you wear a motorcycle jacket? What statement would you be making?

INCREASING VOCABULARY

laconic (adj.) (1)
seminal (adj.) (1)
belligerently (adv.) (1)
immaculate (adj.) (1)
codified (v.) (3)
sociopathic (adj.) (3)
disaffected (adj.) (3)
instigate (v.) (4)
incite (v.) (4)

credential (n.) (5)
sinuous (adj.) (9)
transcends (v.) (9)
brandishing (v.) (14)
disengagement (n.) (15)
empathy (n.) (15)
mutant (adj.) (15)
ludicrous (adj.) (16)

"You get your first leather jacket and you put it on and go, 'Uh-huh,   1
that's it, now I'm really *baaad.*'" This laconic summation comes
from Lemmy of Motörhead, the seminal metal band that, for more
than twenty years, has been instructing callow[1] would-be outlaws in the
finer points of desperado attitude. Motörhead's music may sound like a B-
52 powering for a bombing run, but their renegade image has always been
belligerently immaculate. Thus when Lemmy Kilmister, an intimate of
both the Hell's Angels[2] and the late Sid Vicious, states that the motorcycle
jacket was, is, and always will be a crucial item in the panoply[3] of any aspiring hoodlum,[4] you can take his word for it.

In 1955, songwriters Jerry Leiber and Mike Stoller, who would later   2
compose "Jailhouse Rock" and "If You're Looking for Trouble" for Elvis
Presley, penned the lines, "He wore black denim trousers and motorcycle
boots/A black leather jacket with an eagle on the back/. . . that fool was
the terror of Highway 101." This forgotten jukebox gem, "Black Denim
Trousers," was the one-hit wonder for a vocal group called The Cheers,
but it also foreshadowed Lemmy's statement by four decades and as many
cultural upheavals.

The song, however, was hardly the first pop-culture reference to the   3
motorcycle jacket. In the previous year, Marlon Brando had starred in
Laslo Benedek's *The Wild One.* As Johnny, Brando codified what would
remain the primary style of the sociopathic youth for the rest of the twentieth century: blue jeans, engineer boots, sideburns, a sneer, and the
almighty *pièce de résistance*[5]—the motorcycle jacket, splendid in its zippers, studs, and heavy black leather. It may not have instilled terror, but
at the least it communicated a threatening and disaffected sexual potency.
Brando's costume—for which, by most contemporary accounts, the actor
himself was largely responsible—was lifted directly from the street fashion of the early '50s hipster/motorcycle subculture. It took *The Wild One,*
though, to establish it in the mass mindset.

Brando himself was as "surprised as anyone" at the impact of *The*   4
Wild One and that, almost a half century later, young men and women
would still walk the walk in the same costume. In his autobiography,
Songs My Mother Taught Me, he recalls: "There was a scene in which
somebody asks my character what I was rebelling against, and I answered,
'Whaddya got?' But none of us involved in the picture ever imagined it
would instigate or encourage youth rebellion. A few nuts even claimed
The Wild One was part of a Hollywood campaign to loosen morals and
incite young people to rebel against their elders. Sales of leather jackets
soared."

---

[1] **callow:** Lacking sophistication, experience, judgment, or perception.
[2] **ESL** **Hell's Angels:** A motorcycle club from the 1960s and 1970s that occasionally en-
     gaged in violent activities.
[3] **panoply:** Ceremonial attire.
[4] **ESL** **hoodlum:** Gangster or member of a gang.
[5] *pièce de résistance:* The outstanding item of a group.

The other image of '50s rebellion was, of course, James Dean. Although   5
Dean posed for publicity stills astride a Brando-style 500cc Triumph in a
classic Schott motorcycle jacket, he never actually wore one on the big
screen. In Nicholas Ray's 1955 classic teen-alienation movie, *Rebel Without
a Cause*, Dean wore a bright red windbreaker, mainly so he'd stand out
from Dennis Hopper, Nick Adams, and the rest of the leather-clad supporting cast. In the wake of *The Wild One* and the James Dean cult, the leather
jacket became irremovable from the pop-fashion wardrobe. Its recycling
was endless. Greasers[6] in the '50s and Black Panthers[7] and iconoclastic[8]
white radicals in the '60s all made it their own. Seventies punks couldn't attend a Clash concert without one. It became an '80s credential for
Madonna, Bruce Springsteen, and Ken Wahl in the TV series *Wiseguy*,
while grunge kids wore it over their plaid lumberjack shirts in the '90s. The
image of the dominatrix[9] — bike jacket over corset, fishnets, and boots (with
or without whip or riding crop) — is celebrated over and over in private fantasy and behind the closed portals of a thousand commercial dungeons.

When Bob Dylan wanted to defect from folk protest to Stratocaster,[10]   6
he donned a black leather jacket to make his point. Jim Morrison wrote
anthems to his own Lizard King image: "She was a princess, queen of the
highway/He was a monster, black dressed in leather. . . ." Elvis Presley, in
the 1968 TV special that salvaged his career, looked to leather to confirm
that he'd left the Hollywood beach party and come home to Heartbreak
Hotel. When The Ramones made their initial mark at CBGB, they selected
the tried-and-true bike jackets with ripped jeans. Billy Idol shredded his
with a razor for a post-apocalyptic[11] road warrior chic, the artist then
known as Prince played a tiny Brando-Barbie in *Purple Rain*, and even
Michael Jackson, in his *Bad* period, covered a customized bike jacket with
self-awarded decorations. All instinctively knew they'd locked into a powerful symbolism, but even Dylan would have been hard-pressed to specifically define the symbol.

On the surface, the leather motorcycle jacket is a comparatively simple   7
creation. It comes in two basic designs: The plainer of the two is a single-
breasted version with two vertical side pockets and a center zipper. However, Brando, Dean, and a million lookalikes have always favored the
more exotic (and original) double-breasted number with an asymmetrical
front zipper to provide the wearer with a double layer of chest protection,
created by the Schott Brothers leather company in 1928 and copied ad
infinitum[12] ever since. "Grandpa Schott was commissioned by Harley-

---

[6] **ESL** Greasers: Term applied to 1950s car aficionados who wore grease in their hair.

[7] **ESL** Black Panthers: An all-African American progressive political organization of the
    1960s that moved to enact social change in the United States.

[8] iconoclastic: That which attacks established ideals, beliefs, customs, or institutions.

[9] dominatrix: Female sexual persona characterized by physical and verbal control.

[10] Stratocaster: A brand of electric guitar.

[11] post-apocalyptic: After the Apocalypse or the end of the world.

[12] ad infinitum: Into infinity; forever.

Davidson to come up with a jacket for bikers—there was nothing made specially for bikers before then," says Roz Schott, the company's vice president. Both styles have two short zips on the sleeve that can close the cuffs tight on the wrists to prevent ballooning and protect the arms in a wipeout.

The legitimate motorcyclist's jacket is constructed from heavyweight cowhide with a semigloss, water-resistant "chrome" finish. It has a quilted lining, in red or black silk, that tends to wear out while the rest of the garment is still going strong. The real bike jacket should come off the rack so stiff as to be virtually unwearable and need a month or more of breaking in before it looks anything but embarrassingly new. (And if some fool suggests a new jacket can be distressed by soaking it in water or rubbing it with a brick, ignore him. All you get is a new jacket that looks like it's been rubbed with a brick.) Costing between $100 and $600, the cheaper lines are made from a lighter, glossier, and more user-friendly leather. They look good from the get-go but tend to have a shorter life span.

Back in the mid-'60s, designer Mary Quant cited the motorcycle jacket and Levi's as benchmark garments "so perfectly utilitarian they could never be improved on." The cut of the motorcycle jacket, by its very function of protecting the wearer from slipstream[13] and mishaps on the highway, conforms closely to an idealized human body shape. On a man, it classically broadens the shoulders and narrows the waist—but don't expect it to entirely hide a biker beer gut. On a woman, it adds a macho masculinity to all of the above. The semi-reflective surface flatters the bodyline and makes movement appear more deliberate and sinuous. But that's hardly the whole story; the bike jacket's endurance and adaptability indicates that its impact transcends functionality, a tendency to flatter, or even its pop-icon pedigree.

And that's some pedigree to transcend. On one level, the idea of wearing leather can be looked on as a throwback to atavistic[14] prehistory, when to wear the hide of a dead animal was to assume that creature's unique spiritual power. The studded leather armor of Roman gladiators, berserker[15] Vikings, and Attila's Huns are echoed in the implied threat of biker chic, as are the somber garbs of the medieval executioner, the Caribbean pirate, and the western gunfighter. Observe closely and you may even perceive Count Dracula's red cape there in the lining.

The true roots of the motorcycle jacket lie with World War I German air aces like Hermann Goering and Manfred von Richthofen, the notorious Red Baron. While the foot soldiers died in filth and carnage, these early

---

[13] **slipstream:** Area of reduced air pressure and forward suction found immediately behind rapidly moving vehicles.

[14] **atavistic:** Primitive.

[15] **berserker:** An ancient Scandinavian warrior reputed to be invulnerable, enormously strong, and wildly frenzied in battle.

aviators, literally above it all, were able to maintain the illusion that, as knights of the air, they were a throwback to an age of chivalry—and they instructed their tailors accordingly. Their original combat-issue, ankle-length leather coats were cut down, first to a nifty three-quarter length and ultimately to the short hussar-style jacket that was only a short hop from Dean and Brando.

When U.S. soldiers came home from World War II, some, unable to 12 settle to the conformity of family and factory, looked for excitement in a Harley-Davidson, a case of Pabst Blue Ribbon, and a bugs-in-your-teeth hostility to being told what to do. The most notoriously violent—and fashion conscious—of the motorcycle outlaws were the Booze Fighters, the Market Street Commandoes, and, of course, the heavily publicized Hell's Angels, who helped solidify the image of the black-jacketed thug. These restless vets were the motorcycle misfits that Brando would glamorize in a double-breasted Schott.

One of the paradoxes of the bike jacket is how it's favored by law en- 13 forcement and outlaws alike. From German motorcycle cops to the LAPD, police departments, sheriff's deputies, and state troopers all prize their leather jackets as highly as any Hell's Angel (or Patti Smith fan) and go to as many extremes to decorate and accessorize them. At riot, bust, or rumble, the black leather jacket has shown up simultaneously on both sides of the law. Is what we're talking about here a symbol of raw and basic power?

This seems to have been the theory of Nazi Propaganda Minister 14 Joseph Goebbels. From their red-and-black swastika banners to the sinister, Busby Berkeley[16] choreography of their mass rallies, the Nazis treated their symbolism with a mystical intensity. When the Panzer divisions of the Waffen SS and the fighter pilots of the Luftwaffe put on their leather jackets or the Gestapo[17] swooped in the dead of night in long black leather trenchcoats, they appeared as dark twentieth-century Teutonic[18] knights brandishing absolute, dehumanizing power. Marshall McLuhan, in his book *The Mass Psychology of Fascism*, makes the argument that wearing a uniform such as the black leather jacket divorces human beings from their individuality and sense of personal responsibility.

Freud might have viewed the wearing of leather armor as a disengage- 15 ment from empathy, enabling the wearer to engage in actions more outrageous and perverse than would be possible without the psychic protection. This was certainly one of the directions of designer Vivienne Westwood's thinking as she developed what would eventually be identified as punk style: "As we researched motorbike wear, we also became interested in rubber and fetish clothing. We started to put zips where they shouldn't

[16]**Busby Berkeley:** Director and choreographer for many of the big dance production numbers in movies of the 1930s and 1940s.
[17] **ESL Gestapo:** Nazi Germany's secret police.
[18] **ESL Teutonic:** German.

logically be. After all, there were all sorts of sexy associations to zips. We added multiple chains to jackets, or sadomasochistic flourishes and accessories. We got a lot of criticism from feminists who said our designs were degrading to women. They never thought that women might feel in control through these clothes, that they might feel empowered." It's no exaggeration to say that the bulk of the more outré[19] S&M[20] costumes are the mutant offspring of traditional bike couture, from Diana Riggs's leather catsuit in *The Avengers* to the tongue-stud kids who pushed the rubber envelope at Hollywood's Club Fuck.

If any other proof is needed of the bike jacket's symbolism, look no   16
further than the response of those in authority. From the '50s onward, the kid in leather was the one your parents didn't want you to hang with. School dress codes specifically prohibited them. Until the coming of punk, nightclub door policy put leather on the wrong side of the velvet rope. One of the most absurd examples of this resistance came when the sitcom *Happy Days* was first going into production. To imagine the Fonz without a leather jacket seems ludicrous, but initially ABC's Department of Standards and Practices, the network's in-house censors, specifically vetoed it: A character in a bike jacket "could not appear in a sympathetic role in a show aimed primarily at children." In their opinion, a leather jacket had "unacceptably strong overtones of violence, criminality, and homosexuality." Actor Henry Winkler was forced to wear a baby-blue nylon windbreaker for half of the first season of *Happy Days*. Garry Marshall, the show's creator, pleaded that the audience would be worried about Fonzie injuring himself on his motorcycle if he wore nylon. ABC compromised: To wear leather, the Fonz had to be accompanied by his motorcycle. So Marshall sent out a secret memo to the entire crew telling everyone to put the motorcycle in all Fonzie scenes. "By the time the network figured out what we were doing," says Marshall, "Fonzie was too popular to change."

And in 1981, Mayor Ed Koch and Police Commissioner Robert   17
Maguire phased out the leather jacket as part of the NYPD uniform, replacing it with dark blue nylon. The idea was to give New York's finest a kinder, gentler image and avoid the "occupying army syndrome" that later would cause many of Los Angeles's law enforcement problems.

Will the bike jacket ultimately dilute its power by becoming so widely   18
accepted that it's merely conventional? Claude Montana designs leather dresses with biker echoes, Calvin Klein and Ralph Lauren flirt with fetish, and over on the wild side, it's no longer Westwood and Betsey Johnson but gangsta fashion: jeans and T-shirts voluminous enough to hide an AK-47. The veteran punk or biker can, however, take comfort that the bike jacket has never made its way inside the Washington Beltway. The new

---

[19] outré: French for *daring.*
[20] S&M: Sadomasochistic, that which associates sexual pleasure with the infliction of pain on both others and oneself.

generation of baby-boom politicians, the Al Gores and Bill Clintons, may have embraced less offensive generational garb—blue jeans, cowboy boots, sweats, and Nikes—but you'll never see one of them in a black leather bike jacket. Their handlers would instantly eighty-six the image as too dangerous and alienating. About the only politician I ever saw wearing a motorcycle jacket was Ann Richards, the Harley-riding ex-governor of Texas, but she was always a serious maverick.

So what about all the ex-yuppies[21] walking around dressed like   19
Johnny Thunders?

"It's just a fad. They'll get over it," says Legs McNeil, author of   20
Please Kill Me, an oral history of punk. "You can still tell the real people who are going to spit in your face and ask, 'Whaddya got?'"

EXERCISING VOCABULARY

1. In paragraph 18, the writer says that Calvin Klein and Ralph Lauren "flirt with fetish." Define *fetish.* You know what *flirt* means. What then does it mean when these two designers "flirt with fetish"?

2. In paragraph 18, Farren says that Al Gore and Bill Clinton's "handlers would instantly eighty-six" the motorcycle jacket-wearing image. You know what *handle* means in relation to an object. What then would *handlers* mean here? What does *eighty-six* mean when used as a verb?

3. In paragraph 8, Farren discusses ways to distress a bike jacket. What does *distress* usually mean? How does Farren use the word here?

PROBING CONTENT

1. According to Farren, who and what established the motorcycle jacket "in the mass mindset" (para. 3)? What did it represent as a fashion icon at that time?

2. Give several examples of people the essay identifies as wearing the motorcycle jacket. What did it represent to the public when each of these people or groups of people wore it?

3. Describe the bike jacket designed for Harley-Davidson by the Schott Brothers. How did its design reflect its main purpose?

4. Where does the writer say that "the true roots" of the motorcycle jacket lie (para. 11)? How and why did World War II veterans adapt the coats for their own use?

5. What does Farren mean when he says that the motorcycle jacket is "a symbol of raw and basic power" (para. 13)? What kinds of people wear the jacket in this symbolic way?

---

[21] **ESL yuppies:** Slang term for young, urban professionals.

6. Why did ABC's Department of Standards and Practices object to the Fonz's wearing of a bike jacket? How did ABC compromise?

7. Does Farren believe that the motorcycle jacket will become so widely accepted that it will become "conventional" (para. 18)? What example does he give to prove his argument?

CONSIDERING CRAFT

1. Which of Farren's examples of people who wear motorcycle jackets were already familiar to you? How did his use of examples that you did and did not already recognize affect your reading of the essay?

2. What does Farren's description of the bike jacket and discussion about its history add to your understanding of the essay's main point? Why do you think he waited several paragraphs to discuss the background of the jacket?

RESPONDING TO THE WRITER

What other kinds of clothing besides the motorcycle jacket cause such diverse reactions in people? What people in real life, television, or movies wear these "shocking" fashions? What message are these people trying to send?

For a quiz on this reading, go to www.bedfordstmartins.com/mirror.

The "Modern Primitives"

John Leo

Body modification, whether by piercing, tattooing, scarring, or stretching, has been practiced for centuries by diverse cultural groups around the world. Only in recent years, however, has this phenomenon provoked serious popular attention in the United States. Body modification, initially taken to extremes by certain groups, has become much more mainstream. Multiple ear piercings are common, and people no longer stop and stare at nose and belly rings. Even Barbie once sported a butterfly tattoo. What is behind this renewed popularity in body modification? What kind of message are its practitioners trying to send?

In this essay from the July 31, 1995, edition of *U.S. News & World Report*, cultural critic and celebrated columnist John Leo tries to answer just these questions. Leo, whose weekly column appears in 140 newspapers, has written for the *New York Times* and *Time* magazine and is the author of *Two Steps Ahead of the Thought Police* (1998) and *Incorrect Thoughts: Notes on Our Wayward Culture* (2000).

THINKING AHEAD

When you think of body modification like piercing or tattooing, who comes to mind? A friend? A movie star? A musician? A gang member? What image do you have of people with piercings or tattoos? Do you have a piercing or tattoo, or have you considered getting one? What was your motivation? What effect did you want to achieve? What reactions did your piercing or tattoo elicit from other people?

INCREASING VOCABULARY

coveted (adj.) (1)	bland (adj.) (7)
decry (v.) (2)	commodified (v.) (7)
deviancy (n.) (4)	faux (adj.) (7)
rationale (n.) (5)	mortified (v.) (9)
centered (adj.) (5)	repudiate (v.) (9)
reclaiming (v.) (5)	latent (adj.) (11)
pathological (adj.) (5)	welling (v.) (11)

The days when body piercers could draw stares by wearing multiple earrings and a nose stud are long gone. We are now in the late baroque phase[1] of self-penetration. Metal rings and bars hang from eyebrows, noses, nipples, lips, chins, cheeks, navels and (for that coveted neo-Frankenstein[2] look) from the side of the neck.

"If it sticks out, pierce it" is the motto, and so they do, with special attention to genitals. Some of the same middle-class folks who decry genital mutilation in Africa are paying to have needles driven through the scrotum, the labia, the clitoris, or the head or the shaft of the penis. Many genital piercings have their own names, such as the ampallang or the Prince Albert. (Don't ask.)

And, in most cases, the body heals without damage, though some women who have had their nipples pierced report damage to the breast's milk ducts, and some men who have been Prince Alberted no longer urinate in quite the same way.

What is going on here? Well, the mainstreaming-of-deviancy thesis naturally springs to mind. The piercings of nipples and genitals arose in the homosexual sadomasochistic[3] culture of the West Coast. The Gauntlet, founded in Los Angeles in 1975 mostly to do master and slave piercings, now has three shops around the country that are about as controversial as Elizabeth Arden[4] salons. Rumbling through the biker culture and punk, piercing gradually shed its outlaw image and was mass marketed to the impressionable by music videos, rock stars and models.

The nasty, aggressive edge of piercing is still there, but now it is coated in happy talk (it's just body decoration, like any other) and a New Age[5]-y rationale (we are becoming more centered, reclaiming our bodies in an anti-body culture). Various new pagans, witches and New Agers see piercing as symbolic of unspecified spiritual transformation. One way or another, as Guy Trebay writes in the *Village Voice,* "You will never find anyone on the piercing scene who thinks of what he's doing as pathological."

The yearning to irritate parents and shock the middle class seems to rank high as a motive for getting punctured repeatedly. Some ask for dramatic piercings to enhance sexual pleasure, to seem daring or fashionable, to express rage, or to forge a group identity. Some think of it as an ordeal that serves as a rite of passage, like ritual suspension of Indian males from hooks in their chests.

Piercing is part of the broader "body modification" movement, which includes tattooing, corsetry, branding and scarring by knife. It's a sign of the times that the more bizarre expressions of this movement keep push-

---

[1] **late baroque phase:** A period of ornate, richly ornamented decoration.
[2] **ESL Frankenstein:** Monster created from parts of dead bodies by Dr. Victor Frankenstein in Mary Shelley's 1818 novel *Frankenstein.*
[3] **sadomasochistic:** That which associates sexual pleasure with the infliction of pain on both others and on oneself.
[4] **Elizabeth Arden:** A company that specializes in beauty products.
[5] **ESL New Age:** A collective spiritual movement that stresses the unity and practice of all belief systems despite their differences.

ing into the mainstream. The current issue of *Spin* magazine features a hair-raising photo of a woman carving little rivers of blood into another woman's back. "Piercing is like toothbrushing now," one of the cutters told *Spin*. "It's why cutting is becoming popular." Slicing someone's back is a violent act. But one of the cutters has a bland justification: People want to be cut "for adornment, or as a test of endurance, or as a sacrifice toward a transformation." Later on we read that "women are reclaiming their bodies from a culture that has commodified starvation and faux sex." One cuttee says: "It creates intimacy. My scars are emotional centers, signs of a life lived."

But most of us achieve intimacy, or at least search for it, without a   8
knife in hand. The truth seems to be that the sadomasochistic instinct is being repositioned to look spiritually high-toned. Many people have found that S&M[6] play "is a way of opening up the body-spirit connection," the high priest of the body modification movement, Fakir Musafar, said in one interview.

Musafar, who has corseted his waist down to 19 inches and mortified   9
his flesh with all kinds of blades, hooks and pins, calls the mostly twenty-ish people in the body modification movement "the modern primitives." This is another side of the movement: the conscious attempt to repudiate Western norms and values by adopting the marks and rings of primitive cultures. In some cases this is expressed by tusks worn in the nose or by stretching and exaggerating holes in the earlobe or nipple.

Not everyone who pierces a nipple or wears a tongue stud is buying   10
into this, but something like a new primitivism seems to be emerging in body modification, as in other areas of American life. It plugs into a wider dissatisfaction with traditional Western rationality, logic and sexual norms, as well as anger at the impact of Western technology on the natural environment and anger at the state of American political and social life.

Two sympathetic analysts say: "Amidst an almost universal feeling of   11
powerlessness to 'change the world,' individuals are changing what they have power over: their own bodies. . . . By giving visible expression to un-known desires and latent obsessions welling up from within, individuals can provoke change."

Probably not. Cultural crisis can't really be dealt with by letting loose   12
our personal obsessions and marking up our bodies. But the rapid spread of this movement is yet another sign that the crisis is here.

EXERCISING VOCABULARY

1. In paragraph 1, Leo speaks of "that coveted neo-Frankenstein look." What does it mean to covet something? What then does *coveted* mean? What does *neo* mean? Describe the opposite of a "neo-Frankenstein" look.

---

[6] S&M: Sadomasochistic.

2. Paragraph 4 refers to "the mainstreaming-of-deviancy thesis." What does it mean to mainstream? How can you apply that meaning of *mainstream* to Leo's phrase?

PROBING CONTENT

1. In what cultures or among what groups of people did body piercing first become popular in the United States? What was its significance?

2. Explain the broader movement of which, according to Leo, body piercing is a part.

3. Before Leo explains what he means by the "new primitivism," he offers several other motives for body modification. What are these?

4. How effectively does the writer think body modification deals with "cultural crisis"? Why is this true?

CONSIDERING CRAFT

1. The title is an oxymoron, or a phrase made up of seeming opposites. Explain how people with tattoos or body piercings can be both modern and primitive.

2. Why does Leo mention several other motives for body modification and then dismiss them in favor of the idea that the "new primitivism" is the major motive?

3. What effect do Leo's many graphic examples of body modification have on you?

4. Describe the writer's attitude toward his subject. What is the tone of this essay? How difficult is the vocabulary? Based on this information, for what audience do you think Leo is writing?

RESPONDING TO THE WRITER

You probably know several people who have body piercings or tattoos or have them yourself. What were their or your motives for these body modifications? What images did they or you want to project? Did these body modifications produce the anticipated results?

For a quiz on this reading, go to www.bedfordstmartins.com/mirror.

Latino Style Is Cool. Oh, All Right: It's Hot.

RUTH LA FERLA

"'Hispanic is hip. Right now, it's the thing to be,'" says Lisa Forero, a student whom Ruth La Ferla interviewed for the following article. What is Latino style? How are some Latinos using fashion to embrace their cultural heritage, and why are people outside Latino culture borrowing it? How is the fashion industry responding to the current fascination with all things Latino? And as leading apparel makers such as Ralph Lauren, Nike, Tommy Hilfiger, and the Gap attempt to mass-market provocative Latino styles, will cultural stereotyping result?

La Ferla explores these questions in "Latino Style Is Cool," which first appeared in the *New York Times* on April 15, 2001. A fashion writer for the *New York Times*, La Ferla has also written about style for *Mirabella* magazine, where she formerly served as fashion director. La Ferla, along with Kim Johnson Gross and Jeff Stone, coauthored *Chic Simple: Scents* (1993), a guide to using, choosing, and mixing scents for candles, potpourris, and oils.

THINKING AHEAD

The influence of the growing Hispanic population in the United States is increasing steadily in every area, from music and dance to language, education, and politics. What indicators of this growing influence do you see in the world around you? What future indicators do you expect to see?

INCREASING VOCABULARY

fret (v.) (2)	ostentatiously (adv.) (8)
clout (n.) (4)	insignia (n.) (9)
bemused (adj.) (5)	appropriated (v.) (10)
allude (v.) (6)	enamored (adj.) (14)
aping (v.) (6)	sultry (adj.) (16)
flaunting (v.) (6)	emulated (v.) (17)
solidarity (n.) (6)	bristle (v.) (19)
iconography (n.) (7)	besotted (adj.) (23)

On a recent Friday afternoon, Lisa Forero, her dark, shoulder-length hair parted in the center, stalked the corridors of La Guardia High School of Performing Arts in Manhattan, perched on four-inch platform boots. Ms. Forero, a drama major, played up her curves in a form-fitting gray spandex dress and wore outsize gold hoops on her ears. Her fingertips were airbrushed in tints of pink and cream.

Did she fret that her image—that of a saucy bombshell—bordered   2
on self-parody? Not a bit. Dressing up as a familiar stereotype is Ms.
Forero's pointedly aggressive way of claiming her Latino heritage, she
says. Ms. Forero, seventeen, acknowledged that she had not always been
so bold. "Two or three years ago, I didn't usually wear gold," she said,
"and I usually wouldn't get my nails done. But as I've gotten older, I've
needed to identify more with my cultural background."

Her sandy-haired classmate Kenneth Lamadrid, seventeen, is just as   3
brash. "Because of the way I look and because my parents called me Ken,
a lot of people don't know that I'm Cuban," he said. But Mr. Lamadrid
takes pains to set them straight. That afternoon, he was wearing a sou-
venir from a recent family reunion, a snug T-shirt emblazoned with the
names of all of his relatives who have emigrated to the United States from
Cuba. "I'm wearing my family history," he said. "You have to be proud
of who you are."

Ms. Forero and Mr. Lamadrid are members of a population that, ac-   4
cording to the 2000 census, seems on the verge of becoming America's
largest minority group. Wildly heterogeneous,[1] its members come from
more than twenty countries and represent a mixture of races, backgrounds
and even religions. What Latinos share, as Ms. Forero well knows, is a
common language—Spanish—and rapidly expanding cultural clout.

"Hispanic is hip," she observed dryly. "Right now, it's the thing to   5
be." Indeed, in the last couple of years Latinos have been surprised and
flattered to find themselves courted as voters, consumers, workers and entertainers. And now many are bemused to discover that, like hip-hop-
influenced African Americans before them, they are admired as avatars[2] of
urban chic.

"There is an emerging Latino style, and I think it appeals to more than   6
just Latinos," said Clara Rodriguez, a professor of sociology at Fordham
University in Manhattan and the author of *Latin Looks: Images of Latinas
and Latinos in the U.S. Media* (Westview Press, 1997). Dr. Rodriguez made
a point of distinguishing between pervasive archetypes—the smoldering
vamp, the brilliantined Lothario[3]—and the fashion personas adopted by
young urban Hispanics, which allude to those types without aping them.
These Latin Gen X-ers[4] are rediscovering their roots and flaunting them,
she said, while communicating solidarity by the way they dress.

Rodrigo Salazar, the editor of *Urban Latino*, a general interest maga-   7
zine for young Hispanics, expressed a similar view. "As we stake our
claim in the culture, we are starting to take control of our own images,"
Mr. Salazar said. Young, trend-conscious Latinos do that in part, he said,
by experimenting with fashion and cultivating a street-smart style that is

---

[1] **heterogeneous:** Consisting of different kinds; varied.
[2] **avatars:** Embodiments in human form.
[3] **Lothario:** A man whose chief interest is in seducing women.
[4] **ESL Gen X-ers:** A generational term used by the media to apply to individuals in their late
   twenties or early thirties, who are marked by a cynical self-questioning worldview.

more overtly sensual than hip-hop and is at the same time heavily steeped in Hispanic iconography.

Flounces, ruffles and ear hoops are among the generic, ostentatiously Hispanic symbols being tossed into a pan-Latino blender these days. Even crosses are part of the mix, not as a symbol of faith but as a hip accessory. Mr. Salazar conceded that such items lend themselves to ethnic stereotyping but argued that perhaps that is all the more reason to flaunt them. For many young Hispanics, he said, they are a visual shorthand that signals their identity.   8

Latino style also incorporates the provocative cropped T-shirts, low-slung chinos, stacked heels and chains that are the fashion insignia of cholos, members of Latin street gangs. And it incorporates components of a style adopted by young Puerto Rican New Yorkers in the late 1970s: fitted shirts in phantasmagorial[5] patterns, hip-riding denims, cropped halters, blouses tied at the midriff, navel-baring T-shirts and platform shoes. Similar regalia survives as the style uniform of pop icons like Ricky Martin and Jennifer Lopez.   9

But the look is also indebted to the traditional garb favored by an earlier generation of Latino immigrants. On some days, for example, Mr. Lamadrid, the drama student, wears a guayabera, a loose multipocket shirt like the ones his Cuban grandfather used to wear. Nowadays, the shirts, worn by many young Hispanics as a badge of their heritage, have been appropriated by non-Hispanics as well.   10

"We take our lead from the things we've seen our parents wear and the things we've seen in movies," Mr. Salazar said, "but our style is evolving as our influence is growing. We're seeing ourselves in the street, and we're following the cues of our friends and celebrities who are Latino."   11

Mr. Salazar was describing a cultural pastiche[6] that has become increasingly identifiable—and some maintain, consummately marketable. Its potential mass appeal is surely not lost on Ms. Lopez, the singer and actress, who is negotiating with Andy Hilfiger, Tommy's younger brother, to market her own brand of Latina glam in a fashion line.   12

At the same time, Latina chic is being packaged for mass consumption by some leading apparel makers. In the last several months, Ralph Lauren, Nike, Tommy Hilfiger and the Gap have played to the current fascination with Latina exoticism in advertisements featuring variations on the full-lipped, south-of-the-border sexpot. Ralph Lauren's campaign showcases the Spanish film star Penélope Cruz in a snug top and a swirling skirt, performing what looks like flamenco. Both Guess and Sergio Valente display ads in which halter tops and rump-clutching denims encase Brazilian brunettes. And Vertigo, a midprice sportswear company, is showing its scarlet trouser suit on a raven-haired vamp, a ringer—it can't be coincidence—for a young Bianca Jagger.   13

[5] **phantasmagorial:** Relating to a shifting series of illusions.
[6] **pastiche:** A composition made up of several different parts.

"Our industry has become enamored with the dark, mysterious confi-　14
dence that these women portray," said Steven Miska, the president of Sergio Valente.

Magazine editors, too, find the Latin look compelling. The March　15
issue of Italian *Vogue,* the fashionista's bible, has a feature in which
young Latino-Americans model the season's key looks.

Is the industry trying to market Latinness as a commodity? "Defi-　16
nitely," said Sam Shahid, the president and creative director of Shahid, a
New York advertising agency with fashion clients. Mr. Shahid employed
Hispanic models for the latest Abercrombie & Fitch catalog. "No one
moves as freely," he said, then added: "Selling a Latin look doesn't mean
it has to be a Carmen Miranda,[7] cha-cha type thing. 'Latin' can simply be
a sultry sex appeal."

Should Mr. Hilfiger and Ms. Lopez reach an agreement, industry in-　17
siders speculate that the collection will draw heavily on Ms. Lopez's
Puerto Rican heritage. "Her flash look, the stacked heels, the low-rise
jeans—these things are already being emulated by people well outside the
Hispanic community," said Tom Julian, a trend analyst for Fallon Worldwide, a Minneapolis branding company.

Deliberately packaging an urban Hispanic look for mass consumption　18
makes sense to Mr. Julian. "Ethnicity is good in today's marketplace," he
said. "All of a sudden you are talking about hair, makeup, clothing and
accessories that are part of a lifestyle that is distinctive, that has a point of
view." Noting that so-called urban apparel—the streetwise casual wear
favored by young blacks and Hispanics—is a $5 billion-a-year business,
he ventured that a Latino subgenre could generate at least half that
amount.

Some Hispanics bristle at the reduction of their identity to a handful　19
of styling cues, which might then be peddled as Latin chic. They are un-
easy about being lumped by outsiders into an undifferentiated cultural
mass. "I think the world would often like to describe us as a bunch of hot
tamales," said Betty Cortina, the editorial director of *Latina,* a lifestyle
magazine for young women. "That happens to be the way many Latinas
see themselves," she conceded, "but if our cultural identity is all wrapped
up in a sexy sense of style, then we have a lot of work to do."

Others maintain that a degree of cultural stereotyping is inevitable　20
and may not be all bad. "It's important for people to understand that
within the Latin community there is range," said Elisa Jimenez, a New
York fashion designer and performance artist of part-Mexican descent. At
the same time, an attraction to certain cultural stereotypes can be positive,
she asserted, if "it inspires us to be happier, more expressive—any or all
of those things that we want to be more of."

---

[7]**Carmen Miranda (1909–1955):** A Portuguese dancer and singer and star of Brazilian and
　Hollywood musicals, remembered particularly for her elaborate costumes and head-
　dresses made from tropical fruit.

Latino-influenced apparel and grooming are seductive to many non-   21
Latins intent on borrowing elements of a culture that they perceive as
more authentic, spontaneous and alluring than their own. "Latin equals
sexy," said Kim Hastreiter, the editor of *Paper*, a magazine that features a
generous sampling of Latino artists, models, fashion, film and pop stars in
its April issue. "It's heat and a certain aliveness."

Ms. Hastreiter might have been describing Cindy Green, a New   22
York performance artist and the graphic design director of the DKNY
fashion house. Ms. Green flaunts acrylic-tipped nails airbrushed in hot
pink and silver, a hyperfeminine look copied from the young Latina
women she sees on her way to work. "I'm completely obsessed with my
nails," she said, adding that she is just as much taken with the tight
ponytails, dark lip liner and extreme makeup worn by many young Hispanic women. "I come from Ohio," she said, "and all this is very exotic
to me."

Danielle Levitt, a New York City fashion photographer, is equally be-   23
sotted. "I can't explain my attraction to things that are Latin," she said. "I
think it's the glamour." Ms. Levitt likes to pile on Latina-style gold ban-
gles and heart-shaped pendants. At her throat she wears an elaborate gold
nameplate, similar to those worn on the air by the stars of *Sex and the
City,* a show that is arguably influenced by Latina style.

Ms. Jimenez had never designed clothes that were identifiably Latin   24
until Kbond, a vanguard Los Angeles clothing store, asked her recently for
a look that was patently Hispanic. She responded by lopping the sleeves
off a series of ruffled men's tuxedo shirts — "tricking them out," as she
put it, into "sexy little halters" for women.

At the moment she is selling a line of sportswear steeped in Latin   25
kitsch[8] — "La Vida Loca" T-shirts, for example, printed with the charac-
teristically Mexican images of a rose, a pair of dice and a skull. "It's time
to get our heritage out there," Ms. Jimenez declared with mingled defiance and mirth. She envisions her designs teamed with uptight little hand-
bags and immaculate white jeans.

Who's going to wear them?   26

"Are you kidding?" she said. "They're going to be the height of Upper   27
East Side[9] chic."

EXERCISING VOCABULARY

1. What relation does a parody have to the real thing? Why would someone consciously engage in the kind of self-parody La Ferla describes in paragraphs 1 and 2?

---

[8] **kitsch:** Something that appeals to popular taste and is often of poor quality.
[9] **Upper East Side:** One of the most socially select sections of Manhattan in New York City,
it borders Central Park on the east and includes portions of Park and Fifth Avenues.

2. In paragraph 6, one of La Ferla's sources differentiates between young Hispanic trendsetters and "pervasive archetypes" of Hispanic culture. What is an archetype? How do the two archetypes mentioned in this paragraph fit this definition? What is significant about them?

3. In what sense are "flounces, ruffles and ear hoops" a type of "visual shorthand" (para. 8)? What do these accessories signify?

PROBING CONTENT

1. La Ferla compares young Latinos with "hip-hop-influenced African Americans before them" (para. 5). What similarities does she see?

2. What seems to account for the attraction of Hispanics and non-Hispanics alike to Latino style?

3. What evidence does La Ferla offer that "Latino chic" is significant enough to attract some serious interest from the business world?

4. What are the positive and negative aspects of the association of young Latinos with certain obvious stereotypes?

CONSIDERING CRAFT

1. Interesting mental images and apparent contradictions are part of the title La Ferla has chosen for this essay. Are the two parts of the title really contradictory? How does the title predict the content of the essay?

2. This selection includes a number of direct quotations from a variety of sources. How does the author's selection of sources and quotations enhance her assertions? What other methods of proof does La Ferla employ to convince her readers?

RESPONDING TO THE WRITER

Have you personally seen the Latino style that La Ferla discusses? List some specific examples you have seen of clothing and accessories that typify this style. Your examples may come from everyday life or from movies and television. If you have not seen anyone expressing this style, why do you think you have not?

For a quiz on this reading, go to www.bedfordstmartins.com/mirror.

Belly-Baring Fad Not Cute as a Button

Hayley Kaufman

"Navels, no longer novel, have been embraced by the American mainstream" writes Hayley Kaufman. Bellybuttons — for centuries, a private domain — are now being flaunted, pierced, and surgically altered to look more attractive. Have you embraced the bellybutton-baring fad? Have you noticed anyone with a less-than-perfect midsection wearing a midriff-baring outfit? What does the belly craze say about our culture? How far do you think the trend will go?

Kaufman has written for the *Boston Globe* for three years. "Belly-Baring Fad Not Cute as a Button" first appeared there on February 11, 2002. She has written for a variety of Boston-based newspapers since graduating from the University of California at Davis, including *Boston* magazine, the *Cambridge Chronicle*, the *Tab*, and *Stuff at Night*. She has won a New England Press Association award for environmental reporting.

THINKING AHEAD

They're pierced, peeking out from under short tops, and emerging over low-slung jeans. Should navels be functional or fun? Should everyone who wishes to do so be allowed to put his or hers on public display? Explain your response.

INCREASING VOCABULARY

obscured (adj.) (1)	feckless (adj.) (2)
whorled (adj.) (1)	ominously (adv.) (8)
perforate (v.) (2)	ubiquity (n.) (15)
oglers (n.) (2)	innovators (n.) (18)
taut (adj.) (2)	chagrin (n.) (22)

For centuries our collective navel was hidden from view, obscured first by animal pelts, later by togas[1] and Sans-a-Belt slacks.[2] The bellybutton — innie or outie, whorled or smooth — was a private domain, a shadowy vista to be meditated on by slack-jawed philosophers and prissy lint fiends. Like all good things, navel gazing was something best done alone.

The '90s changed all that, of course. No longer was the bellybutton something to cloak or conceal. Young, edgy, unwashed sorts — not content

---

[1] **ESL** **togas:** The loose outer garments worn in public by citizens of ancient Rome.
[2] **ESL** **Sans-a-Belt slacks:** A type of pants that require no belt, usually worn for sports.

merely to perforate their nostrils or eyebrows or tongues—began piercing their navels. Soon Britney Spears was cavorting through videos in skimpy hip-hugging ensembles, flaunting her flat belly for record execs and MTV oglers. The taut and the feckless (Jennifer Lopez, Sarah Jessica Parker, the Hilton sisters) followed suit. These days, you can't enter a mall without tripping over throngs of sixth-grade girls, their midriffs proudly bared.

Unfortunately, however, it's not just preteens. Navels, no longer novel, have been embraced by the American mainstream. They're protruding everywhere. Prime-time TV, general interest magazines, next to you in line at CVS.[3]

And the results, frankly, aren't pretty.

During the Super Bowl, AT&T Wireless shelled out millions on ads for its new mLife wireless service, one of which featured bellies and buttons of all shapes and sizes—blubbery, wrinkly, saggy, you name it. At least one New York plastic surgeon has begun practicing umbilicoplasty, fashioning prettier bellybuttons for the abdominally challenged—or those who think they are. The cost of the procedure? About $2,500 a pop.

Meanwhile, if you can't think of an instance when you've seen a midriff-baring outfit on someone who should have known better, you're not looking hard enough.

The belly craze "started out with crop tops and lowriders that you had to be young and fit to wear," said Sondra Grace, associate professor and head of fashion design at the Massachusetts College of Art. "Then, as the trend carried through and people started getting comfortable with it, some people thought you didn't have to be so young and fit."

She paused ominously. "It's an exposure that's not that flattering."

Indeed. But it is how real people look, said Mark Siegel, a spokesman for AT&T Wireless, when queried about the bellybutton ad, which aired during the third quarter of the Super Bowl. In it, wordless images of older people, overweight people, even newborns, their bellies bared, floated across the screen. The point? Our navels are evidence of our need to be connected and our need to be free.

"We wanted people to see themselves in these ads," Siegel said. "We wanted there to be recognizable human beings and not just fashion plates in them."

There's little chance the bellies popping up all over will be mistaken for the flat, artfully framed tummies of the models and starlets who launched the navel trend several years ago. But that's not stopping regular folks from trying to achieve a similar look.

New York plastic surgeon Bruce Nadler says requests for bellybutton-reshaping surgery have soared over the past couple of years. "With the latest trends in fashion, all of a sudden it's an area that's really come into focus," he said. Patients come in with pictures of navels they admire, "so they can look like their favorite pop star."

---

[3] **ESL** CVS: A popular East Coast pharmacy store chain.

Many umbilicoplasty patients are twenty- and thirty-somethings, says   13
Nadler, but not all.

"I'm 55, and I have a pierced navel," he said. "A lot of times older   14
women will come in with a pierced navel, and I'll ask them why they did
it. They say it's because their daughters look so well. They still have a
competitive thing going on. They've maintained themselves, and now they
get the final touch."

The clothing industry, meanwhile, has paved the way for belly ubiq-   15
uity. Skirts and pants have been cut to sit lower and lower, regardless of
whether the wearer can, or should, sport the hip-hugger look.

"You have people who normally would be wearing things to cover   16
their waist, but the clothes aren't made to do that anymore," said Jacque-
line Stathis, group exercise manager at Sports Club/LA in Boston's new
Ritz-Carlton hotel. "So sometimes, whether you want to expose yourself
or not, you have to."

There is some good news, trend watchers say. Now that middle Amer-   17
ica has warmed to the American middle, the belly trend is officially on its
way out.

"The fashion innovators, the people onstage, they introduce a trend,"   18
Grace said. "When it gets oversaturated and the wrong people are doing
it, that's what kills it."

Anyone who's seen the recent perplexing Levi's ad—the one that fea-   19
tures a gaggle of bellybuttons *singing* like little toothless mouths—can at-
test that it's time to return the bellybutton to its rightful place: out of
sight.

So what's the next hot body part—the one that teen queens will re-   20
veal years before the rest of the country would even consider it?

"The back and the leg," Grace said.   21

Those styles will be much to the chagrin of hip-hugger manufacturers   22
and crop-top wearers. But those of us who've seen one belly too many will
breathe a sigh of relief.

EXERCISING VOCABULARY

1. Kaufman says that models and starlets "launched the navel trend" (para. 11).
   What kinds of things are usually launched? How does another possible
   spelling of *navel* make this a play on words?

2. In paragraph 3, Kaufman writes that navels have been "embraced by the American mainstream." How is *embraced* usually used? What does it mean here?

PROBING CONTENT

1. According to the author, what is the problem with the belly-baring trend?
   What is a possible solution to this problem?

2. Why were navels chosen to play a large role in introducing mLife wireless service for AT&T? What purpose do mLife and navels share?

3. According to the New York plastic surgeon, why are many older women piercing their navels? How do his patients decide what their navels should look like?

4. What is "officially" ending the belly-baring trend? What body parts may take center stage next?

CONSIDERING CRAFT

1. After reading this essay, a reader has no doubt what the author thinks about the belly-baring trend, yet Kaufman never directly states her feelings. How then does she so clearly convey her opinion? Give some specific examples to support your answer.

2. How does the double meaning in the title prepare the reader for Kaufman's style in this essay? Find another place where the author plays with language to achieve a humorous effect and make a serious point at the same time.

3. The word choice in this essay helps us visualize some very clear images. Identify one spot in the text where Kaufman's choice of words creates a strong image.

RESPONDING TO THE WRITER

Do you agree that certain fashion trends should be restricted to those who have the right figure for them? Name another fashion trend or style that looks best on a particular body type. Who should decide which people are eligible to wear new styles or follow new trends? Why do people sometimes wear something trendy even when it is unflattering?

For a quiz on this reading, go to www.bedfordstmartins.com/mirror.

A New Day:
Fashion Contemplates Fresh Icons

KATE BETTS

How does clothing affect the way we feel about ourselves? Do fashion trends reflect the overall mood of consumers? In this essay, Kate Betts looks at the ways fashion has changed since September 11, 2001. She speaks with designers, buyers, fashion directors, and social figures about the direction in which they see fashion heading, and everyone seems to agree: "The unbelievably sexy look of recent seasons is over. Comfortable and grounded feels better."

Betts is a contributor to the *New York Times*, where "A New Day: Fashion Contemplates Fresh Icons" first appeared on October 28, 2001. Before she joined the staff of the *New York Times*, Betts worked for various prestigious fashion magazines. She was fashion news director of *Vogue* from 1991 to 1999 and then became the editor-in-chief of *Harper's Bazaar*. Betts has also held positions at *Women's Wear Daily*, *W*, *Metropolitan Home*, the *International Herald Tribune*, and *European Travel & Life*.

THINKING AHEAD

As much as we have all been affected by the events of September 11, 2001, you may never have envisioned that tragedy affecting clothing styles. Why might a disaster such as this cause Americans to rethink the way they dress? What changes might result? How might such changes affect our culture, either positively or negatively or both?

INCREASING VOCABULARY

canny (adj.) (1)	resilient (adj.) (9)
exhibitionism (n.) (4)	contrite (adj.) (15)
apogee (n.) (5)	potently (adv.) (16)
vagaries (n.) (7)	

There she is, appearing daily with her canny smile and oh-so-current outfit. Sometimes it's a Kelly green cardigan sweater over a persimmon shirt with a neat gleam from the gold hoop earrings. Sometimes it's a crisp cotton shirt in must-have mauve. Even with a burqa[1] draped over her head she still looks chic.

---

[1] **burqa:** A long garment worn by Muslim women that covers the entire body except the eyes.

And because every fashion icon needs a signature, she's never without   2
the sleek titanium glasses.

No, this is not a sun-kissed celebrity like Gwyneth Paltrow, or a newly   3
minted socialite with an enviable collection of Birkin bags. This is
Ashleigh Banfield, a TV journalist for MSNBC, who swapped her perky
blond bob for a brunet crop before heading off to report from Pakistan. In
fact, there is so much buzzing about Ms. Banfield—both her smart, self-
effacing delivery and her low-key stylish look—that she might be a contender for a new kind of fashion figurehead.

Goodbye to social minxes like Nicky and Paris Hilton.[2] Farewell to   4
belly-button-baring celebrities like Britney Spears. A mere seven weeks
ago, they paraded into premieres and black-tie benefits in a frenzy of exhibitionism. The more they flashed their diamonds and borrowed designer
dresses, the louder the applause.

It was the apogee of an American culture of conspicuous display. Its   5
demise is one more layer of the protective innocence seared away since
Sept. 11. Now fashion magazines, advertisers and consumers are looking
for new direction. What kind of style icons will emerge when the conspic-
uousness of style itself seems hazardous?

Being fashionable used to entail a kind of visibility. But when build-   6
ings are targeted for their symbolic might and bioterror is directed
at public figures, fame and the red carpet seem like liabilities. The Park
Avenue[3] princesses have beaten a hasty retreat to Bedford.[4] Celebrities are
hiding out in their Malibu dachas,[5] refusing to cross the country for
movie premieres.

But fashion never disappears entirely. Even when a display culture is   7
folding up its feathers, fashionable instincts are operating, and fashion itself becomes a barometer of the vagaries of life. It's a paradox: How
should women display themselves when display itself might be hazardous,
and at a minimum connotes a blinkered[6] return to business as usual?

"Yes, the idea of vulgarity and overt sexuality seems so inappropri-   8
ate," said Josh Patner, one of the designers for Tuleh. "And yes it's not
the time for disrespectful frivolity. But should everyone walk around in a
hair shirt?[7] I think people need authenticity now. A good suit, a beautiful
coat, but not anything too aggressive, too expensive or hard-edged."

Authenticity may be the theme that the resilient forces of fashion and   9
display embrace. Authenticity, or perhaps something familiar and safe, as
society retreats from the exposure of the cutting edge. For the moment,
the premium in fashion seems to be on safety, not sexuality.

---

[2] **Nicky and Paris Hilton:** Two young celebrity heiresses to the Hilton Hotel fortune.
[3] **Park Avenue:** An exclusive area of Manhattan, New York.
[4] **Bedford:** A neighborhood in Brooklyn, New York.
[5] **dachas:** Russian word for cottages or houses in the suburbs or countryside.
[6] **blinkered:** Narrow-minded.
[7] **hair shirt:** A shirt made from harsh, scratchy animal hair once worn next to the skin by
   members of some religious orders as a form of self-imposed punishment.

"We have sold out on all of our simple black dresses and tweed   10
suits," said Stephanie Greenfield, the owner of Scoop, the chain of
trendy stores in Manhattan and East Hampton that offers one-stop hipness for young women. "Our image has always been one of sexy, hard-
edged, street-inspired fashion, but for next spring I'm going softer.
People want warm, light comfort clothes. You see it and you hear it
everywhere. People are staying home, they're taking a more familiar approach to their lifestyle."

Nina Griscom, a contributor to *Food and Wine* magazine and an up-   11
town social figure, said: "We all have a feeling of nervousness. The unbelievably sexy look of recent seasons is over. Comfortable and grounded
feels better. I think people think about trousers and skip the heels."

At *Vanity Fair,* the fashion department has supplied every woman in   12
the office with a pair of bright red quilted neoprene Puma sneakers in case
of an emergency evacuation. Retailers from Madison Avenue to NoLIta
are reporting sales of more classical clothes. At Liz Lange Maternity in
Midtown, shoppers who used to purchase piles of brightly colored cash-
mere cardigans are now going for plain black and gray.

"The department store buyers are asking for safer-looking heels," said 13
Christian Louboutin, the shoe designer, who was in New York last week
catching up on spring buying appointments that never happened in Paris.
"They see a stiletto heel and they say, 'Oh, could you just make that a
little safer-looking? We don't want anything that looks vulnerable.'"

Even the image makers—photographers and art directors who create   14
ads and editorials that set the mood in fashion—are contemplating a
major swing. "It's much quieter," said Sam Shahid, the art director responsible for Abercrombie & Fitch's catalog and Wonderbra's full-frontal
cleavage ads. This month Abercrombie tore up its signature Christmas
catalog filled with brazenly sexual Bruce Weber photos of half-naked
young people.

"We want comfort and safety, not sex and aggression," said a contrite- 15
sounding Mr. Shahid. "I just see the word comfort everywhere now."

Who, then, will replace yesterday's style icons? Like Ms. Banfield,   16
Carolyn Murphy, the potently American blonde whom Estée Lauder has
just anointed as its million-dollar figurehead, strikes the appropriate note
for uncertain times: her fresh, forthright beauty is a relief from the busty
sexuality of her predecessor, Elizabeth Hurley.

Another contender is Laura Bush, the first lady, who, with her sooth-   17
ing colors and neat presentation, is the fashion equivalent of meatloaf and
rice pudding—comfort food. "Laura Bush looks pleasing and neat because she is pleasing and neat as a person," said Arnold Scaasi, who
dresses her. "That is not phony. Simple is appropriate now, but I don't
think people should look dowdy or unattractive, because the whole idea is
to keep our spirits up. Fashion plays an important role in making people
feel good about themselves."

Alexandra Lebenthal, president of Lebenthal & Company, whose of-   18
fice looks out on the rubble that once was the World Trade Center, said
that on her first day at work after Sept. 11 she wore jeans and sneakers,
but felt horrible. "The next day I wore red pants, a white shirt and a blue
blazer, and I felt so much better; I felt dressed and patriotic," she said.
"My attitude is, the more dressed up I am the better I feel. And I think
that's more appropriate than ever."

Judging from the recent collections shown in New York and Europe,   19
women might be forgoing both elegance and provocation for comfort
next spring. "I call it the Big Easy," said Joan Kaner, the fashion director
of Neiman Marcus, who did not attend the Milan and Paris shows "for
safety reasons" but who spent last week writing spring orders in show-
rooms around Manhattan. "There's an ease and a looseness. A lot of the
clothes are oversized."

For designers, the next six months will be telling. Some on Seventh   20
Avenue have already ordered their assistants to think about more uplifting
colors and a happier, brighter mood. Others have banished anything that
looks vaguely military or aggressive from their design studios.

"We need some time," said Helmut Lang, who chose to show his   21
spring collection on the Internet instead of on the runway. "But certainly
we are already reacting emotionally, and the first thing to respond to
those kinds of shifts is always fashion. Whatever it is, it's not going to be
all sweet and practical. Our emotions are raw, and we have been forced
into the present.

"The most modern thing of the last few years was this global connec-   22
tion we all felt. We knew there were risks, and now we have to learn how
to live with those risks and to dress for a global world."

EXERCISING VOCABULARY

1. In general, is it positive or negative to be considered conspicuous? In what
   ways has the American culture been "a display culture" (para. 7), even one of
   "conspicuous display" (para. 5)?

2. According to one designer quoted in this report, American women "'. . . don't
   want anything that looks vulnerable'" (para. 13). Why would women want to
   avoid such a look? What are the implications of looking vulnerable?

3. In the wake of September 11, the author states, "fame and the red carpet seem
   like liabilities" (para. 6). In this context, what does the red carpet represent?
   Why might association with it be a liability?

PROBING CONTENT

1. Before September 11, what brought the loudest applause when celebrities like
   Britney Spears appeared? Why are new fashion icons necessary?

2. What was different about the emphasis among fashion designers shortly after September 11? What words best express the new style? Cite several specific examples.

3. Why did Abercrombie & Fitch destroy its planned Christmas catalog for 2001? What did the art director think a replacement should reflect?

4. How did fashion designers Joan Kaner and Helmut Lang show their personal concern after the events of September 11?

CONSIDERING CRAFT

1. Most people who read this article when it was originally published in the *New York Times* will never wear clothes designed by the famous designers quoted here. Why, then, does Betts include so many quotations from these designers? Why does she think that her readers want to hear such opinions?

2. The author refers to First Lady Laura Bush as "the fashion equivalent of meatloaf and rice pudding" (para. 17). What images do these foods convey? What does Betts want to communicate when she chooses these words?

RESPONDING TO THE WRITER

In this essay Alexandra Lebenthal insists that "'. . . the more dressed up I am the better I feel'" (para. 18). However, others quoted in this piece put the new emphasis on comfort and casual clothing. What style makes you feel best about yourself? How does the clothing you wear influence how you feel about yourself and how you react to the world around you? How are you discovering your own personal style?

For a quiz on this reading, go to www.bedfordstmartins.com/mirror.

Champagne Taste, Beer Budget

DELIA CLEVELAND

Have you ever splurged on an outfit you knew you couldn't afford? In "Champagne Taste, Beer Budget," Delia Cleveland compares herself to a recovering junkie whose drug of choice was designer clothing. She looks at the financial and intellectual drain of keeping her wardrobe current and shows how her addiction made her miss out on more rewarding experiences. Today, Cleveland actively seeks the culture her designer clothing implied she had.

"Champagne Taste, Beer Budget" first appeared in the March 2001 issue of *Essence* magazine. Cleveland, currently attending New York University as a media studies major, has published her work in *Black Elegance* and *Spice* magazines. She is also the author of a novel entitled *Fallin' Out* (2002).

THINKING AHEAD

Have you ever been obsessed with owning something, going somewhere, or doing some particular thing? How did this obsession affect you? How did you achieve the object of your desire? To what extent did reaching your goal satisfy you?

INCREASING VOCABULARY

paltry (adj.) (2)	stagnation (n.) (8)
façade (n.) (2)	swaggering (v.) (10)

My name is Dee, and I'm a recovering junkie. Yeah, I was hooked on the strong stuff. Stuff that emptied my wallet and maxed out my credit card during a single trip to the mall. I was a fashion addict. I wore a designer emblem on my chest like a badge of honor and respect. But the unnatural high of sporting a pricey label distorted my understanding of what it really meant to have "arrived."

At first I just took pride in being the best-dressed female at my high school. Fellows adored my jiggy style; girls were insanely jealous. I became a fiend for the attention. In my mind, clothes made the woman and everything else was secondary. Who cared about geometry? Every Friday I spent all my paltry paycheck from my part-time job on designer clothes. Life as I knew it revolved around a classy façade. Then slowly my money started getting tight, so tight I even resorted to borrowing from my mother. Me, go out looking average? Hell no! I'd cut a class or wouldn't bother going to school at all, unable to bear the thought of friends saying that I had fallen off and was no longer in vogue.

Out of concern, my mother started snooping around my bedroom to   3
see where my paycheck was going. She found a telltale receipt I'd care-
lessly left in a shopping bag. Worse, she had set up a savings account for
me, and I secretly withdrew most of the money—$1,000—to satisfy my
jones.¹ Then I feverishly charged $600 for yet another quick fashion fix.

"Delia, you're turning into a lunatic, giving all your hard-earned   4
money to multimillionaires!" she screamed.

"Mama," I shrugged, "you're behind the times." I was looking fly,²   5
and that was all that mattered.

Until I got left back in the tenth grade.   6

The fact that I was an *A* student before I discovered labels put fire   7
under my mother's feet. In her eyes, I was letting brand names control my
life, and I needed help. Feeling she had no other choice, she got me transferred to another school. I had screwed up so badly that a change did
seem to be in order. Besides, I wanted to show her that labels couldn't
control me. So even though everyone, including me, knew I was "smart"
and an excellent student, I found myself at an alternative high school.

Meanwhile, I began looking at how other well-dressed addicts lived to   8
see where they were headed. The sobering reality: They weren't going
anywhere. In fact, the farthest they'd venture was the neighborhood corner or a party—all dressed up, nowhere to go. I watched them bop
around³ in $150 hiking boots—they'd never been hiking. They sported
$300 ski jackets—never went near a slope. I saw parents take three-hour
bus trips to buy their kids discount-price designer labels, yet these parents
wouldn't take a trip to make a bank deposit in their child's name. Watching them, I was forced to look at myself, at my own financial and intellectual stagnation, at the soaring interest on my overused credit card.

That's when it all became clear. At my new high school I attended   9
classes with adults—less emphasis on clothes, more emphasis on work.
Although the alternative school gave me invaluable work experience, I
never received the kind of high-school education I should have had—no
sports, no prom, no fun. I realized I had sacrificed an important part of
my life for material stuff that wasn't benefiting me at all.

That was twelve years ago. Today I'm enjoying a clean-and-sober   10
lifestyle. Armed with a new awareness, I've vowed to leave designer labels
to people who can truly afford them. I refuse to tote a $500 baguette until
I can fill it with an equal amount of cash. I'm not swaggering around in
overpriced Italian shoes till I can book a trip to Italy. On my road to recovery, I have continued to purchase clothing—sensibly priced. And every
now and then, the money I save goes toward a Broadway play or a vacation in the sun. I'm determined to seek the culture my designer clothes once
implied I had. I no longer look the part—because I'm too busy living it.

---

¹ **ESL** **jones:** A craving for something.
² **ESL** **fly:** Cool, fabulous.
³ **ESL** **bop around:** To go freely from place to place.

EXERCISING VOCABULARY

1. Examine the title. What does the phrase "champagne taste" imply? How would such taste be in conflict with a "beer budget"? How well does this title work for this essay?

2. The author comments that in high school she couldn't bear the thought of not being "in vogue" (para. 2). What does it mean to be in vogue? How could being in vogue in one area of the United States mean being hopelessly out of fashion in another area? Give several examples to illustrate your answer.

PROBING CONTENT

1. What was the author's obsession in high school? What effect did this have on her life?

2. How did Cleveland's mother find out about her daughter's problem? How did her mother's reaction to this discovery change Cleveland?

3. What event finally caught Cleveland's attention? What action did her mother take? Why was this an unexpected decision?

4. What important realizations did the author reach? How did she arrive at these conclusions?

5. What evidence does Cleveland offer to confirm that she has recovered from her addiction?

CONSIDERING CRAFT

1. When you begin reading this essay, you might think that Cleveland's obsession is going to be with drugs. What language does she use to encourage this misdirection? Cite several specific examples. Why does the author deliberately allow the reader to be misled in this way? How does her use of such language affect the way you read the essay?

2. Throughout her essay, the author sprinkles slang that may be unfamiliar to you. Cite several examples of such language. Why would the author include these expressions if many readers and dictionaries would not be familiar with them? What would be lost if they were to be omitted or replaced by standard English?

RESPONDING TO THE WRITER

To what extent do you identify with the author's willingness to invest most of her money in clothes? Does the fact that her decisions caused her to miss much of the fun of high school make you sympathize with her? Did you know people like Cleveland in high school, or do you know them now in college? What advice would you offer them?

For a quiz on this reading, go to www.bedfordstmartins.com/mirror.

The Tyranny of "Abercrappie"

DAMIEN CAVE

In the following essay, Damien Cave describes his horror upon learning that his younger brother has joined the millions of teenagers entranced by Abercrombie & Fitch's homogenized clothing. What is it about the brand that teenagers find so appealing? Are they drawn to A&F's sexually charged advertisements? Or is it the brand's "frat boy mentality" and image of freedom and excitement that have made the logo an essential part of today's teen uniform? Cave examines Abercrombie's marketing campaign and makes some interesting discoveries.

"The Tyranny of 'Abercrappie'" first appeared on *Salon.com*, where Cave is a senior writer who covers high-tech policy, economics, and international affairs. He has also written for the *Keene Sentinel*, *Takeoffs and Landings*, the *Bolivian Times*, and *Time Out New York*. Cave gratefully attributes his interest in fashion to his grandfather, the owner and primary designer of a men's outerwear company, and fondly remembers childhood excursions to department stores, where his grandfather lectured him on fabrics, styles, and changes in the industry.

THINKING AHEAD

Is there a particular store where you shop for clothes and accessories? Are there stores whose clothing you would never consider wearing? What has influenced you to make these decisions about what is right for you to wear?

INCREASING VOCABULARY

stumped (v.) (2)

banter (n.) (3)

manipulative (adj.) (4)

ogle (v.) (5)

irk (v.) (9)

self-deprecation (n.) (9)

staunching (v.) (10)

amplified (v.) (11)

trysts (n.) (11)

arbiter (n.) (11)

frugal (adj.) (12)

incensed (adj.) (12)

fervor (n.) (14)

brandishing (n.) (22)

incessant (adj.) (22)

smugness (n.) (24)

pedantic (adj.) (24)

trump (v.) (25)

savvy (adj.) (32)

"Abercrappie" is what my youngest brother called Abercrombie & Fitch after Ryan, our fifteen-year-old sibling, begged for the worn-looking, overpriced clothes du jour.

Shirts, pants, sweaters, socks—Ryan wanted Abercrombie everything and he stumped for the stuff like a wide-eyed activist. In the kitchen, tossing punches at Josh and me, he used the word "quality." When I walked away, he chased me with a speech about owning "just a few things that you love to wear." He even suggested that *I* pick up some Abercrombie—"It might help you get a girlfriend," he offered with very little tact.

Christmas was only a few days away and the smart-alecky banter—"I want X" vs. "So what, you can't have it"—rang typical, as much a part of our family's holiday tradition as egg nog. But a specific brand request: That was new.

I remembered longing for Air Jordans,[1] Champion sweatshirts, even Ralph Lauren Polo shirts. But my parents shamed me into either buying them myself or squeezing them out of relatives. On occasion, Mom or Dad gave in, but they always had a choice. Never, strong as my longing was, had one designer inspired the single-branded passion I heard in Ryan's voice. Somehow, Abercrombie was different: more manipulative and more coveted than both its past and present rivals.

That drug-like draw angered me. After watching packs of pimply teenage boys in Massachusetts malls ogle the boobs and brands of the opposite sex, I couldn't help but want Ryan to swim against the current in this sea of conformity.

I swore I would never buy him the Abercrombie clothing I saw his peers wearing like a uniform. In fact, I decided I would play with his repulsive desire by putting a "Just kidding!" note inside an Abercrombie gift-certificate envelope.

First, though, I tried to fight back with words.

"Why would you want to be a billboard?" I asked. "They're not paying you to advertise their name."

Ryan went for finely tuned sarcasm. "But it's just so *cool,*" he said, trying to irk me in the short term while offering the kind of self-deprecation that just might convince me to give him what he wanted later on.

By that time, my question was largely rhetorical. I already knew the real reason he was lusting after these clothes. Only two months earlier, Ryan had begun fusing himself to Nicole, a blond A student who won our family's favor by staunching Ryan's class-clown tendencies.

But while she kept his bragging to a minimum, Nicole also amplified Ryan's navel-, chest- and shoulder-gazing. When I picked her up on Christmas night, she wore a yellow Abercrombie T-shirt, and as I drove the magnetic couple back to our family's house, A&F earned at least as

---

[1] **ESL** **Air Jordans:** Brand of expensive sneakers named for famous basketball player Michael Jordan.

much air time as the latest gossip about teachers and other high school trysts. Nicole, like many women present and past, had become the arbiter of her man's taste. And in her court, Abercrombie was king.

"I think it's all she wears," said my mother that same afternoon, 12 chuckling. She had already decided that Nicole passed muster, so her criticism remained light. Still, as a frugal New Hampshire native who stocks her shelves with generic foods and her closets with closeouts, my mom became easily incensed when discussing Abercrombie's prices.

"Seventy dollars for pants! It's outrageous." 13

What's more, as a mother who objects to premarital sex with a puri- 14 tanical fervor, she also objected to the company's marketing campaign. Essentially, it sexualizes America's love of the aristocratic golden boy and girl—the blond, WASPish,[2] Ivy League[3] party animals most recently represented by Jude Law and Gwyneth Paltrow in "The Talented Mr. Ripley."

Ads for Ralph Lauren, Tommy Hilfiger and Nautica have played on 15 similar themes for years, but Abercrombie's models look younger, more collegiate. And Abercrombie plays closer to the frat-boy mentality, plastering naked male chests in most of its 205 store windows, while selling 300-page, quarterly catalogs that cost $6 and include interviews with porn stars and articles about drinking.

Indeed, women appear in the ads as well, but the boys rule. When 16 they're not baring their asses to clamber naked aboard a dock or laying prostrate in the grass, the models huddle, flex and pose in store foregrounds like ten-foot trophies, a fact that most teens couldn't help but notice and want to copy in their own lives.

My mother didn't much care about whether the bare butts were male 17 or female. She objected to what she perceived as the encouragement of sex. In so doing, she was in cahoots with[4] Illinois Lt. Gov. Corinne Wood, who called for a consumer boycott of Abercrombie because of the sexually explicit nature of its holiday "Naughty or Nice" catalog.

But as I tried to decide what to buy Ryan and my two other adoles- 18 cent siblings for Christmas, the sex didn't bother me. The brand's dominance did. That dominance, in my opinion, has less to do with skin than with the company's fusion of two settings: the city of hip-hop lore, and the college of the frat-inspired free-for-all. The former can be seen in the company's baggy, urban-inspired designs; clean-cut models on grassy fields embody the latter.

Sex is a mythical part of these settings, but parents often fail to realize 19 that these places—and thus Abercrombie—symbolize more than the longing to get naked. Ultimately, they represent freedom, excitement—a wide array of adventures that remain off-limits to the teenage children of today's SUV-driving parents.

---

[2] **ESL** **WASPish:** Characteristic of a White Anglo-Saxon Protestant.
[3] **ESL** **Ivy League:** A group of prestigious universities located in the eastern United States.
[4] **ESL** **in cahoots with:** Cooperating with.

The Reynoldsburg, Ohio, company has posted twenty-nine consecu- 20
tive quarters of record sales and earnings, making it one of the world's
best-performing retail brands. Surveyed teenagers repeatedly rank it near
the top in terms of "coolness." To see that success only in terms of sex implies that teenagers are nothing more than their hormones, and that they
are the company's only customers.

Neither implication is correct. I know adults who wear Abercrombie 21
clothing, if only the shirts that carry the company name on the inside
label. And as for sex: Yes, many teenagers' bodies insist that the subject
come up, and often. But hormones affect more than sexual desire. As
adults, in our own lives, we know this. But when we eye our sons and
brothers, amnesia[5] strikes.

Somehow we have forgotten — probably because of our fears — that 22
the hormone-inspired energy of youth leads most often to neither sex nor
violence. The brandishing of bare chests by teenage boys and their incessant raunchy[6] chatter represent a healthy desire to learn, to push against
adult boundaries, to discover the art of living. It's the same force that can
be heard on the first Beck[7] album, completed before he was old enough to
vote.

Even though Abercrombie taps into this pent-up energy with contro- 23
versial content, the images don't matter. The company is "cool" not because of the sex or the beer, but because these subjects signify a much wider
idea, namely the freedom to live as the kid — not the parent — sees fit.

Opining on Abercrombie's appeal, however, didn't much change my 24
decision to boycott the store. I still wanted Ryan to be above it all. But
after putting my note in the gift certificate envelope, my smugness stung
me. I already had bought books and movie passes. I feared the trick certificate placed me at risk of becoming the pedantic big brother.

So I gave in. On Christmas eve, I bought Ryan a fleece jacket, marked 25
down from $49.99 to $29.99. I justified it by remarking that the name
"Abercrombie" only appeared on the inside tag and on the zipper. Ryan
had been getting good grades, so I figured he deserved it. I figured my love
should trump my politics. I figured his tastes mattered more than mine.

Much to my surprise, my parents did the same thing. On Christmas 26
morning, Ryan opened not just my Abercrombie box, but several others.
We had resisted the call of the $70 pants, but ultimately we had given in.
We had conformed, accepting Ryan's argument for "quality" and
"clothes worth loving." And we all knew it. Mom, Dad and I glanced at
Ryan as he stripped to try on each jersey, then stared guiltily back at each
other.

"I can't believe it," Dad said. 27

---

[5] **ESL** **amnesia:** Loss of memory.
[6] **ESL** **raunchy:** Sexually explicit or obscene.
[7] **ESL** **Beck:** Contemporary rock star who blends folk, electronic, punk rock, and rap influences.

"The little twit got what he wanted," I added. "And Abercrappie   28
won. They got us."

Then and now, I continue to fight back. I explain to Ryan how he's   29
been made a pawn, a cookie-cutter version of youth. I'm hoping that he'll
learn to dress and live for himself, not his peers or his girlfriends. I'm hoping he'll rebel against Abercrombie and his peers.

If and when he does, we'll still have other battles to fight. Joshua, my   30
thirteen-year-old brother, coiner of the term "Abercrappie," didn't get
any of the company's clothing for Christmas. But when he opened the surf
sweatshirt I got him, his first question was: "Where did you get it?" And
as he watched Ryan open box after box from Abercrombie, Josh's eyes
opened wide with yearning. Later, he dropped hints that maybe Abercrombie wasn't so bad.

Ultimately, I'm not surprised. When Hannibal Lecter asked, "What   31
do we covet?" he couldn't have been more right in answering, "We covet
what we see."

My only wish is that suburban, teenaged style looked less like a dress   32
code. I wish Abercrombie had stiffer competition; that kids would demand
more from their merchants. But most of all, I wish Ryan, Nicole and so
many other teenagers would act as smart and savvy as I know they are.

Until then, I'll buy them what they want — then try and convince   33
them to hate it.

EXERCISING VOCABULARY

1. Restaurants often offer a "soup du jour," or soup of the day. In the first paragraph, the author refers to Abercrombie & Fitch's offerings as "clothes du
   jour." What does this usage imply?

2. In paragraph 14, Cave states that Abercrombie & Fitch's advertising campaign
   "sexualizes America's love of the aristocratic golden boy and girl." Since America has no aristocracy, what does Cave mean by this? In what sense are such
   young people "golden"?

PROBING CONTENT

1. What had happened in the past when the author wanted specific name-brand
   clothing? How was Ryan's desire different?

2. What are Cave's objections to Ryan's wearing Abercrombie & Fitch clothing?
   What started Ryan's obsession and kept it going?

3. What are the main objections of the author's mother to Abercrombie & Fitch?
   How valid are her objections?

4. What does the author find objectionable about Abercrombie & Fitch's marketing campaign? What does he think is the message behind the ads that
   makes A&F a "cool" company?

5. How does Cave justify his Christmas gift for his brother Ryan? What does Christmas morning lead Cave to conclude?

CONSIDERING CRAFT

1. Cave uses an extended example from his own family to argue a much larger point in this essay. Why is this personalized method more effective than simply developing more objective steps in a logical argument?

2. Near the end of this essay, the author quotes Hannibal Lecter, the gruesome murderer in the films *Silence of the Lambs*, *Hannibal*, and *Red Dragon*. Lecter's desires were certainly far more at odds with society than wanting a particular clothing brand. Why does Cave choose this quotation from this character? What point is Cave making?

RESPONDING TO THE WRITER

Damien Cave wants teenagers to take more individual control of their lives, to have higher expectations, and to overcome the status quo. How is his desire at odds with current teenage culture?

For a quiz on this reading, go to www.bedfordstmartins.com/mirror.

DRAWING CONNECTIONS

1. Compare the reactions of Cleveland's and Cave's mothers to their children's obsession with what they wear. What circumstances might account for the differences in their reactions?

2. Do you think that Ryan Cave will become a "junkie" like Delia Cleveland? Offer evidence from these two essays to support your position.

FOCUSING ON YESTERDAY, FOCUSING ON TODAY
Score in the Schoolyard

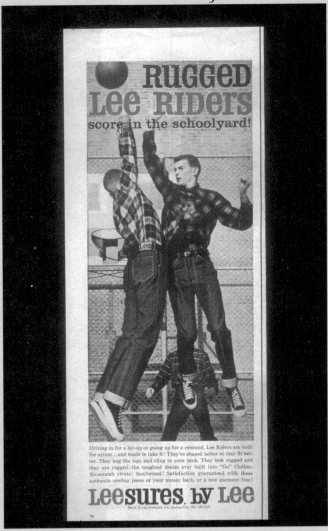

Blue jeans are assuredly a fashion classic, but does this ad make you want to rush out to buy Lee Riders? The ad worked in the 1950s, back before Ralph Lauren and Gap were household words. Its appeal is very macho, rugged, and competitive. Now examine the contemporary ad for an Austin, Texas, "piercing, branding, and scarification" center located inside a tattoo parlor. For some, to express oneself today requires more than wardrobe enhancement; it requires body modification.

Body Rites

What changes in our culture explain the differences in these two ads? Note the closed fist in the Lee Jeans ad and the head-on stare in the tattoo parlor ad. How do the facial features and stances of the individuals in these two images differ? What function does the text in the Lee Jeans ad serve? What function does the split image serve in the ad for the tattoo parlor? Why are so many people today exploring fashion trends beyond clothing, like piercing or tattooing? Do these two ads represent a way of "fitting in" or a way of standing out?

REFLECTING ON THE WRITING

1. Write an essay in which you examine the role shopping for clothes plays in your life and in the lives of your peers.

2. Pick a popular fashion trend, as La Ferla, Leo, Farren, and Kaufman did in their essays, and write an essay in which you trace its popularity. Explain the reasons behind that popularity. You may wish to use magazine articles, the Web, and interviews for source material.

3. As La Ferla does in her essay, choose one group within our larger culture and write an essay in which you examine fashion trends or styles that can be directly linked to that group. Be sure to select a trend or style that has permeated our culture. Include an explanation of why that trend or style has become popular among many people.

4. Design an advertising campaign for an imaginary fashion product such as a piece of clothing or an accessory. Devise a logo and write advertising copy for your product. Present your campaign to a hypothetical fashion buyer who is looking for a new advertising agency. Include visuals and talk about such items as your target audience, best-selling features, and price.

CONNECTING TO THE CULTURE

1. Pick a popular fashion trend like body piercing, nail art, or baseball caps and write an essay in which you examine the reasons, both direct and indirect, behind the trend's popularity. You may consult magazine articles and the Web and conduct interviews to gather material for your essay. Make sure that you properly document your sources.

2. Think about what kind of fashion consumer you are. What do you spend your money on and why? Do you feel pressured to buy certain brands? Write an essay in which you examine your consumer habits and what they say about you and the culture in which you live.

3. Study the different fashions on your campus. Divide the students into groups according to the clothes and accessories they wear. In an essay, give names to each of these groups, describe their individual fashion statements, and speculate on what messages they are trying to send by their unique styles.

4. Choose one brand of clothing and examine its advertising campaign. Be sure to look at print ads and ads on television and billboards, if they are available. What consumers do the ads target? What message lies behind the advertising? How successful is the advertising strategy? Consider these questions in an essay in which you analyze the ad campaign for your brand of clothing.

CHAPTER 6

Fantasies for Sale
Marketing American Culture

If the day ever comes when each of us looks in the mirror and smiles, delighted with the image we see, advertising companies will be out of business. Think about what makes an ad campaign successful. Study this unusual anti-ad from *Adbusters Magazine*, a "watchdog" publication whose goal is to reveal the ways the advertising industry markets fantasy to consumers in the guise of truth.

- Describe the figure in the ad. What do you think he is feeling?
- How does the model's posture reflect the message of the ad?
- Notice the use of the word *GAP* in the square on the right. What is that symbol suppose to suggest?
- What is the effect of the use of white space in this ad?
- Why is the message "Is there a gap in your life?" so central to advertising?

Research this topic with TopLinks at www.bedfordstmartins.com/toplinks.

GEARING UP

Make a list of all the brand-name products you have used, worn, or eaten since you got up this morning. Briefly describe commercials or advertisements for some of these products. Was the advertising an influence on your decision to buy or use them? Try to honestly evaluate why you made these choices. How much are your habits as a consumer influenced by advertising?

I remember the exact day. I was thirteen, and I saw this big billboard on Decatur Street, not far from my house, had this big, lean black guy, really good-looking, with his jeans rolled up, splashing water on a beach, cigarette in one hand and a slinky black chick on his back. All smiles. All perfect teeth. Salem menthols. What great fun. I thought to myself, Now there's the good life. I'd like to have some of that. So I went home, went to my drawer, got my money, walked down the street, and bought a pack of Salem menthols.

The speaker is Angel Weese, a young character in John Grisham's best-selling novel *The Runaway Jury*. Our own encounters with advertising may not cause such immediate and direct responses, but we do respond. Most of us want what Angel wants—some of the good life. And if those jeans, that cologne, that car, that deodorant, or those sneakers help get us to the good life, we're there. Advertising is so much a part of our lives that we may not notice its pervasive, subtle effect. How are ads created? What messages are ads sending? Why do some ad mascots like Tony the Tiger, the Energizer Bunny, the Snuggle Bear, the Budweiser Frogs, and the AFLAC duck become our friends? Why do some jingles or famous ad phrases—like "Pepsi: For Those Who Think Young," "Whassup?," "Make 7-Up Yours," "Just Do It," and "Dude, you're gettin' a Dell"—stay in our heads? How do ad agencies find the perfect pitch, the best "hook," the winning slogan?

What do the ads that get our attention and send us to the stores say about us as consumers? We are advertising targets not just as individual consumers but also collectively. Of the groups you belong to—college students, men or women, groups based on race or ethnicity—which ones seem to have been targeted by manufacturers' ad campaigns? "One size never fits all" in strategic advertising. When we move beyond asking what product an ad is selling and demand to know instead what the ad is really saying about our culture and ourselves, we may be quite surprised at the insights we gain and the savvy consumers we become.

COLLABORATING

In groups of three or four students, list five phrases, symbols, jingles, or slogans associated with widely advertised products. Collect these lists and play an "Advertising IQ" game based on the *Jeopardy* model. Choose a host to read the clues aloud and to call on teams guessing the product. For example, if the answer read aloud is "We love to see you smile," the correct question would be "What is an advertising slogan for McDonald's?" (Naturally, teams may not respond when their own cues are used.)

After the game, discuss why you can so easily supply questions for these advertising answers when it's so difficult to remember other things like dates in history or the Periodic Table of the Elements.

Mad Ave.

JOHN FOLLIS

Ever wonder if advertising people have a conscience? How can they do their best to convince us we must have things we can't afford, don't really need, and may even suffer for having used? Based on John Follis's assertion — "I can't imagine how anyone could be part of a campaign like Joe Camel, even if they smoke. It utterly amazes me that anyone can say with a straight face that a campaign featuring a cartoon camel is not directed at kids." — at least one person in the advertising business has given this some serious thought. And his conclusions have put him at odds with many others in his profession. An insider in the "mad" world of advertising for over twenty years, Follis writes about advertising from a quite different perspective. He has won over eighty awards, including nine CLIOs for excellence in advertising. His book, *Mad Ave.*, has been called "a collection of Seinfeldesque vignettes from Madison Avenue." Follis's unique insight brings an entirely different picture of the glib world of slogans and jingles. The following essay appeared in the Winter 1998 issue of *Adbusters*.

In addition to his work in ad agencies, Follis has shared advertising secrets with students in his classes at The School of Visual Arts and Parson's School of Design in New York City. Away from magazine shoots and television spots, Follis participates in Outward Bound Wilderness Survival courses — where he sees very few ads.

THINKING AHEAD

What one product would you absolutely hate to develop a credible advertising campaign to sell? Why? How would you get started?

INCREASING VOCABULARY

erudite (adj.) (1)   provocative (adj.) (18)
vindication (n.) (11)

I remember a day, early in my career, when I was young and naive and   1
on staff at a large agency. On this particular day management had gathered the troops to screen the agency reel for one of those "Aren't-We-Great" morale boosting meetings. As the lights dimmed the hushed crowd gazed at beautifully shot images of puppies and children and Kraft marshmallows seductively blended with seamless editing and incredibly com-

posed music. The lights came back up and, after a rousing hand, the erudite CEO,[1] pipe in hand, took the stage and opened the floor for questions.

After listening to him answer inquiries like, "Gee, how'd you get that puppy to lick the little girl's face," I decided to take advantage of this unexpected opportunity to "Ask the Cheese." Eventually, The Cheese nods in my direction and I spit it out:

"Do you have any reservations about advertising a product like marshmallows — which is almost 100 percent sugar with zero nutritional value — and targeting mothers and young children?"

As if a party guest had just knocked over the host's best crystal vase, a sudden uncomfortable silence filled the room. A few heads turned to see which of their co-workers was so bold, or stupid, to put the agency CEO on the spot in front of his entire staff. The CEO calmly paused, took a few slow puffs on his pipe, and with carefully measured words, responded:

"It is my belief that it's the government's role to decide which products should or shouldn't be advertised. And as long as the product is legal, it's the agency's responsibility to do the best job possible to advertise its clients' products." I suddenly had visions of the corporate Gestapo[2] quickly escorting me out of the room and beating me senseless.

As the days passed, I never second-guessed the legitimacy of my question. I just began to second-guess the timing of it. I also began to wonder how much it affected my termination several months later.

I can't imagine how anyone could be part of a campaign like Joe Camel, even if they smoke. It utterly amazes me that anyone can say with a straight face that a campaign featuring a cartoon camel is not directed at kids.

Obviously, some people just see it as a job they're paid (very well, no doubt) to do. Maybe it's no different than being a criminal lawyer:

> Judge: We have 14 witnesses that claim they saw your client shoot the
> woman. His fingerprints are on the gun and we have it on videotape.
> How does your client plead?
> Defense attorney: Not guilty.

A copywriter buddy of mine is one of the most talented writers in the business. The guy's amazing. After moving around a bit he settled into a high-level, well-paying job at a huge agency. He's got a couple of young kids and a nice home in a fancy neighborhood. I called him the other day just to catch up. When I asked about his job, I sensed a slight tone of resignation. He told me he's working on a battery account which features a fictitious family called "The Puttermans."

The Puttermans can only be described as a plastic-coated, alien-looking, TV family-from-hell, with giant batteries fused to their spines.

---

[1] **CEO:** Chief executive officer, highest officer in a business or corporation.
[2] **ESL** **Gestapo:** Nazi Germany's secret police.

The spots consist of bad sitcom-like shenanigans.[3] By the time you read this The Puttermans will probably have been put to rest with the other ill-fated ad characters.

It doesn't seem so long ago that my writer buddy and I sat around   11
talking about the advertising hacks who sell out for the money to do the dreck we both hated. Now, with a family and mortgage, my friend has new priorities. Before our chat concluded, he shared what seemed like an attempt at vindication. The five-year-olds at his daughter's birthday party wanted his autograph when they heard he was the guy who did the Putterman commercials.

During my career I've had to work on some challenging assignments (in-   12
fant anal thermometers comes to mind) but never anything that I've really had a problem with—like Spam[4] or Barney.[5] I have, however, been in-volved with a few products that seemed a bit, shall we say, questionable.

I had to struggle to keep a straight face when a marketing consultant   13
started going into a little too much detail about a high-tech toilet seat called the "Santi-Seat."

Apparently, I'm not alone. I've heard similar tales of woe from other   14
agency owners. In one such case, the agency was approached by a company called Burial at Sea. Apparently, if your dearly departed was so inclined, a burial at sea could be arranged. When the company was asked how they used their boats when business was slow, we were told, "porno movies."

For every advertisable product on the market there's a hidden army of   15
trade salespeople. Everyday, these people pack their suitcases with pencil erasers or GI Joe Battle Action accessories or whatever it is they're selling and take off on the road to places like Wilmington and Boise and Greenville trying to make quota to keep their jobs so they can do the same thing for another year. In the Great Sales War these men and women are the infantry, the front-line grunts. Compared to them, ad people are the air force, the glamorous flyboys who get the credit. The ad agency, equipped with the latest high-tech weaponry, goes in for the kill with a blitzkrieg[6] campaign. But even if it's a stupid product, most ad people don't have to devote too big a part of their lifetime trying to sell it.

One of my clients was an umbrella company. They made good quality   16
umbrellas—they didn't break with the first gust of wind. The guy I dealt with was the sales director. Nice guy. Smart guy. But basically, the guy was an umbrella salesman. He'd travel around the country with a bag full of umbrellas: the standard, the mini, the micro-mini, the full-size, the golf,

---

[3] shenanigans: Tricky or mischievous behavior.
[4] ESL Spam: A processed meat product packaged in a can.
[5] ESL Barney: A popular children's television program featuring a large purple dinosaur named Barney.
[6] blitzkrieg: German for *lightning war;* an attack waged with great speed and force.

the automatic, the semi-automatic, the designer line, the cane-style, the water-resistant.

This guy spent about 80 percent of his waking hours dealing with umbrellas. Don't get me wrong. Umbrellas are certainly an important and necessary part of society. I just wouldn't want to devote my life to selling them. 17

Thirteen years after the "Marshmallow Incident," I find myself having lunch with the very man to whom I addressed my provocative question. When I bring up the incident he confesses to a lack of recollection. Prefacing it with how young and naive I was, I recall the scene. 18

"Hmmm . . . so what did I answer?" he asks curiously. 19

"You said that it's the government's role to determine which products should or shouldn't be advertised and that as long as a product is legal it's the agency's responsibility to do the very best job possible to advertise its clients' products." 20

With hardly a pause the ex-CEO speaks in a soft but certain manner, "I think my answer would be different today." 21

He goes on to say how we all must be willing to accept more social responsibility for the decisions we make in business. I feel vindicated. 22

A year later, I notice a blurb in the trades about my converted CEO pal. He has just passed away. 23

In the agency business there's always pressure. The creatives feel it to get great work produced. The account people feel it to keep their clients happy and spending their money. The president feels it to be winning new business. The chairman feels it to be making a profit and keeping his Board happy. And the Board feels it to keep its stockholders happy. If you work in an agency, there's the additional pressure of never-ending deadlines, demanding bosses, and corporate politics. And if the agency loses a client, which happens all the time, you could be out of a job. 24

When people are subjected to that kind of pressure they can do some strange things. I once knew an art director who physically attacked an account exec with a metal T-square just for being asked to make the logo bigger. 25

There's a saying, "It's only advertising." It's true. It's not like finding a cure for AIDS. However, if you're serious about the business, and most are, it can feel like mortal combat. I've worked with many whose philosophies are *Survival of the Fittest,* and *The End Justifies the Means.* 26

Somewhere there was some kind of survey done about which careers the public respected most. I'm not sure which ranked the highest, but I know "Advertising Executive" ranked somewhere at the bottom. I think it was between "Lawyer" and "Used Car Salesman." I guess the American public figures that being saved from ring-around-the-collar isn't like being saved from cancer or nuclear war. 27

How soon they forget about those cute little Dancing Raisins. And   28
Clara Peller and her "Where's the beef?" Don't tell me that didn't have
some socially redeeming value. Even President Bush used that line. And
does anyone actually watch the Superbowl for the game?

But I have to admit, it does seem a bit weird when some woman   29
working on a cure for AIDS is in some lab cubicle somewhere making
25K while the guy who came up with "It's Bubblicious!" is sitting in some
corner office making a half mil.

Hey, welcome to Mad Ave.   30

EXERCISING VOCABULARY

1. In paragraph 1, Follis describes a former CEO as "erudite." With what kind of person might you associate the word *erudite*? Does Follis mean this sincerely? What makes the CEO appear to be erudite?

2. If people feel a need to vindicate themselves (para. 11), what might you conclude about their previous behavior? How is this true of Follis's friend's explanation for his "new priorities"?

PROBING CONTENT

1. What reaction does the writer's question to the CEO receive? Why is this so? What does the question indicate about the writer?

2. Follis's copywriting friend once felt as Follis does about ethics in advertising. What changed his friend's priorities? How does Follis make it clear that his friend feels some guilt about changing his attitude?

3. Follis asks, "And does anyone actually watch the Superbowl for the game?" (para. 28). What does he mean? How appropriate is this question?

CONSIDERING CRAFT

1. Identify some of the military words and images Follis uses in paragraph 15 to create an extended metaphor that compares a life in marketing to one spent fighting a war. How effective is this comparison? What does it say about Follis's attitude toward his subject?

2. The title is a deliberate play on words, since many ad agencies in New York City have Madison Avenue addresses. What does Follis's shortening this address to "Mad Ave." in his title allow the reader to predict about his essay's theme?

RESPONDING TO THE WRITER

People in many professions sometimes have to do things that make them uncomfortable. Lawyers sometimes must defend people they would like to see behind bars; military personnel sometimes must carry out orders they do not support. Advertisers sometimes must design effective sales campaigns for unnecessary or poorly made products or even products that are potentially harmful (like alcohol or cigarettes). How sympathetic are you toward these advertisers, who may just be "doing their jobs"? Should advertisers be held accountable for the effects of their clients' products? Why? In what ways?

For a quiz on this reading, go to www.bedfordstmartins.com/mirror.

Custom-Made

Tara Parker-Pope

"I'll take a beer and a Big Mac, please."
"Make that pizza a large with pickled herring and reindeer."
"I'll have a double scoop of vanilla on a cone with corn sprinkles."

McDonald's and Pizza Huts may now serve diners in many major cities outside of the United States, but if you are ever in one of these restaurants, you will notice that the menu may not be what you're used to. We may marvel at these unusual variations on some of the most popular foods in the American diet, but businesspeople responsible for international marketing cannot afford the luxury of being surprised when it comes to pleasing local tastebuds. It's their job to study the preferences of the target population and then to market what people in India or England or Russia will buy.

Tara Parker-Pope takes us on a fascinating trip around the world and behind the scenes where marketing decisions are made to see what's hot and what's not about American favorites. Parker-Pope has been a *Wall Street Journal* reporter since 1993 and writes a weekly health journal column. She is the author of a book titled *Cigarettes: Anatomy of an Industry from Seed to Smoke* (2001). This essay was first published in *Wall Street Journal Europe* on September 30, 1996.

THINKING AHEAD

What's the strangest thing or combination of things you have ever tasted? Why were you eating this? Where were you? What did you learn from the experience? What unusual foods would you like to try?

INCREASING VOCABULARY

sequentially (adv.) (2)	quintessential (adj.) (28)
tweaked (v.) (5)	quirky (adj.) (29)
globalizing (v.) (8)	laconic (adj.) (30)
ubiquitous (adj.) (24)	slew (n.) (31)
concoct (v.) (28)	

P ity the poor Domino's Pizza Inc. delivery man. 1
    In Britain, customers don't like the idea of him knocking on their 2
doors—they think it's rude. In Japan, houses aren't numbered sequentially—finding an address means searching among rows of houses numbered willy-nilly. And in Kuwait, pizza is more likely to be delivered to a waiting limousine than to someone's front door.

"We honestly believe we have the best pizza delivery system in the world," says Gary McCausland, managing director of Domino's international division. "But delivering pizza isn't the same all over the world."

And neither is making cars, selling soap, or packaging toilet paper. International marketers have found that just because a product plays in Peoria, that doesn't mean it will be a hit in Helsinki.

To satisfy local tastes, products ranging from Heinz ketchup to Cheetos chips are tweaked, reformulated, and reflavored. Fast-food companies such as McDonald's Corp., popular for the "sameness" they offer all over the world, have discovered that to succeed, they also need to offer some local appeal—like selling beer in Germany and adding British Cadbury chocolate sticks to their ice-cream cones in England.

The result is a delicate balancing act for international marketers: How does a company exploit the economies of scale that can be gained by global marketing while at the same time making its products appeal to local tastes?

The answer: Be flexible, even when it means changing a tried-and-true recipe, even when consumer preferences, like Haagen-Dazs green tea ice cream, sound awful to the Western palate.

"It's a dilemma we all live with every day," says Nick Harding, H. J. Heinz Co.'s managing director for Northern Europe. Heinz varies the recipe of its famous ketchup in different markets, selling a less-sweet version in Belgium and Holland, for instance, because consumers there use ketchup as a pasta sauce (and mayonnaise on french fries). "We're looking for the economies from globalizing our ideas, but we want to maintain the differences necessary for local markets," says Mr. Harding.

For those who don't heed such advice, the costs are high. U.S. auto makers, for instance, have done poorly in Japan, at least in part because they failed to adapt. Until recently, most didn't bother even to put steering wheels on the right, as is the standard in Japan. While some American makers are beginning to conform, European companies such as Volkswagen AG, Daimler-Benz AG, and Bayerische Motoren Werke AG did it much sooner, and have done far better in the Japanese market as a result.

For Domino's, the balancing act has meant maintaining the same basic pizza delivery system world-wide—and then teaming up with local franchisers[1] to tailor the system to each country's needs. In Japan, detailed wall maps, three times larger than those used in its stores elsewhere, help delivery people find the proper address despite the odd street numbering system.

In Iceland, where much of the population doesn't have phone service, Domino's has teamed with a Reykjavik drive-in movie theater to gain access to consumers. Customers craving a reindeer-sausage pizza (a popular flavor there) flash their turn signal, and a theater employee brings them a cellular phone to order a pizza, which is then delivered to the car.

---

[1] **franchisers:** People who pay for the right to use a company's name and market the company's products.

Local Domino's managers have developed new pizza flavors, including   12
mayo jaga (mayonnaise and potato) in Tokyo and pickled ginger in India.
The company, which now has 1,160 stores in 46 countries, is currently trying to develop a nonbeef pepperoni topping for its stores in India.

When Pillsbury Co., a unit of Britain's Grand Metropolitan PLC,   13
wanted to begin marketing its Green Giant brand vegetables outside the
United States, it decided to start with canned sweet corn, a basic product
unlikely to require any flavor changes across international markets. But to
Pillsbury's surprise, the product still was subject to local influences. Instead of being eaten as a hot side dish, the French add it to salad and eat it
cold. In Britain, corn is used as a sandwich and pizza topping. In Japan,
school children gobble down canned corn as an after-school treat. And in
Korea, the sweet corn is sprinkled over ice cream.

So Green Giant tailored its advertising to different markets. Spots   14
show corn kernels falling off a cob into salads and pastas, or topping an
ice-cream sundae.

"Initially we thought it would be used the same as in the United   15
States," says Stephen Moss, vice president, strategy and development, for
Green Giant. "But we've found there are very different uses for corn all
over the world."

And Green Giant has faced some cultural hurdles in its race to foreign   16
markets. Although vegetables are a significant part of the Asian diet,
Green Giant discovered that Japanese mothers, in particular, take pride in
the time they take to prepare a family meal and saw frozen vegetables as
an unwelcome shortcut. "Along with the convenience comes a little bit of
guilt," says Mr. Moss.

The solution? Convince moms that using frozen vegetables gives them   17
the opportunity to prepare their families' favorite foods more often. To
that end, Green Giant focused on a frozen mixture of julienned[2] carrots
and burdock root, a traditional favorite root vegetable that requires several hours of tedious preparation.

The company also has introduced individual seasoned vegetable serv-   18
ings for school lunch boxes, with such flavors as sesame-seasoned lotus
root. Although fresh vegetables still dominate the market, Green Giant
says its strategy is starting to show results, and frozen varieties now account for half the vegetable company's sales in Japan.

The drive for localization has been taken to extremes in some cases: 19
Cheetos, the bright orange and cheesy-tasting chip brand of PepsiCo Inc.'s
Frito-Lay unit, are cheeseless in China. The reason? Chinese consumers
generally don't like cheese, in part because many of them are lactose-
intolerant.[3] So Cheetos tested such flavors as Peking duck, fried egg, and
even dog to tempt the palates of Chinese.

---

[2]**julienned:** Sliced into very thin strips.
[3]**lactose-intolerant:** Unable to properly digest lactose, the sugar in milk and certain other
dairy products.

Ultimately, says Tom Kuthy, vice president of marketing for PepsiCo 20
Foods International's Asia-Pacific operations, the company picked a but-
ter flavor, called American cream, and an Asianized barbecue flavor
called Japanese steak. Last year, Frito rolled out its third flavor, seafood.

In addition to changing the taste, the company also packaged Cheetos 21
in a 15-gram size priced at one yuan, about 12 cents, so that even kids
with little spending money can afford them.

The bottom line: These efforts to adapt to the local market have paid 22
off. Mr. Kuthy estimates that close to 300 million packages of Cheetos
have been sold since they were introduced two years ago in Guangzhou.
Cheetos are now available in Shanghai and Beijing as well.

Frito isn't through trying to adapt. Now the company is introducing a 23
33-gram pack for two yuan. Mr. Kuthy also is considering more flavors,
but dog won't be one of them. "Yes, we tested the concept, but it was
never made into a product," he says. "Its performance was mediocre."

Other PepsiCo units have followed with their own flavor variations. 24
In Thailand, Pizza Hut has a *tom yam*-flavored pizza based on the spices
of the traditional Thai soup. In Singapore, you can get a KFC Zinger
chicken burger that is hot and spicy with Asia's ubiquitous chili. The Sin-
gaporean pizza at Pizza Hut comes with ground beef, green peppers and
chili. Elsewhere in Asia, pizzas come in flavors such as Mongolian, with
pork, chili, and garlic; salmon, with a creamy lobster sauce; and Satay,
with grilled chicken and beef.

Coming up with the right flavor combinations for international con- 25
sumers isn't easy. Part of the challenge is building relationships with customers in far-flung markets. For years, the founders of Ben & Jerry's
Homemade Inc. had relied on friends, co-workers, and their own taste
buds to concoct such unusual ice-cream flavors as Chunky Monkey and
Cherry Garcia.

But introducing their ice cream abroad, by definition, meant losing 26
that close connection with their customers that made them successful.
"For Ben and me, since we've grown up in the United States, our customers were people like us, and the flavors we made appealed to us," says
co-founder Jerry Greenfield, scooping ice cream at a media event in the
Royal Albert Hall in London. "I don't think we have the same seat-of-the-
pants feel for places like England. It's a different culture."

As a result, one of the company's most popular flavors in the United 27
States, Chocolate Chip Cookie Dough, flopped in Britain. The nostalgia
quotient of the ice cream, vanilla-flavored with chunks of raw cookie
dough, was simply lost on the Brits, who historically haven't eaten
chocolate-chip cookies. "People didn't grow up in this country sneaking
raw cookie-dough batter from Mom," says Mr. Greenfield.

The solution? Hold a contest to concoct a quintessential British ice 28
cream. After reviewing hundreds of entries, including Choc Ness Monster
and Cream Victoria, the company in July introduced Cool Britannia, a
combination of vanilla ice cream, strawberries, and chocolate-covered

Scottish shortbread. (The company plans to sell Cool Britannia in the United States eventually.)

And in a stab at building a quirky relationship with Brits, the duo   29
opted for a publicity stunt when Britain's beef crisis meant farmers were left with herds of cattle that couldn't be sold at market. Ben & Jerry's creative solution: Use the cows to advertise. The company's logo was draped across the backs of grazing cattle, and the stunt made the front page of major London newspapers.

The company has just begun selling ice cream in France but isn't sure   30
whether the company will try contests for a French flavor in that market. One reason: It's unclear whether Ben & Jerry's wry humor, amusing to the Brits, will be understood by the laconic French. "We're going to try to get more in touch, more comfortable with the feel of the French market first," says Mr. Greenfield.

But for every success story, there have been a slew of global market-   31
ing mistakes. In Japan, consumer-products marketer Procter & Gamble Co. made several stumbles when it first entered the market in the early 1970s.

The company thought its thicker, more-absorbent Pampers diapers in   32
big packs like those favored in America would be big sellers in Japan. But Japanese women change their babies twice as often as Americans and prefer thin diapers. Moreover, they often have tiny apartments and no room to store huge diaper packs.

The company adapted by making thinner diapers packaged in smaller   33
bags. Because the company shifted gears quickly, Procter & Gamble is now one of the largest and most successful consumer-goods companies in Japan, with more than $1 billion in annual sales and market leadership in several categories.

EXERCISING VOCABULARY

1. According to the article, Ben & Jerry's Chocolate Chip Cookie Dough ice cream failed to appeal to the British because in England that flavor has no "nostalgia quotient" (para. 27). What does *nostalgia* mean? What other foods have a high nostalgia value for Americans?

2. What does the verb *opted* mean in paragraph 29? In answering, consider what the noun *option* means.

PROBING CONTENT

1. According to Parker-Pope, why must companies custom-market American products to better suit the tastes of international consumers?

2. Choose one of the author's examples and discuss the changes made to market that product in another country. Explain why the effort failed or succeeded.

3. Not only are ingredients often varied, but sometimes whole products are put to entirely different uses outside the United States. What examples does Parker-Pope give of such products?

4. What kind of pizza is Domino's trying to develop for its Indian market? Why would Domino's choose such a product in India?

CONSIDERING CRAFT

1. This essay first appeared in the *Wall Street Journal Europe*'s section called "World Business." Knowing this, how might you characterize Parker-Pope's audience? Why would this essay also appeal to readers outside that audience?

2. Why is it important to this essay that its examples of marketing campaigns or custom-made products be very specific? How do you think Parker-Pope determined how many specific examples to use?

3. How does the writer use the example in the final paragraph to create a satisfying conclusion? How else might the author have ended this essay?

RESPONDING TO THE WRITER

Think about the essay's content from the other direction. What foods that originated in other countries are popular in the United States? How have those foods been adapted to look or taste better to Americans?

For a quiz on this reading, go to www.bedfordstmartins.com/mirror.

Flagging Enthusiasm

Quinn Eli

Have you seen the ad in which General Motors urges us to "keep America rolling"? Since September 11, 2001, television ads have been portraying a love of America not seen in many years — indeed, perhaps not in the lifetime of the average twenty-year-old. As Quinn Eli points out in this essay, advertisers are increasingly using the Stars and Stripes in newspaper and magazine ads, television commercials, and Web site banners, suggesting that "purchasing a certain car or salad dressing is a patriotic gesture." This nationalistic and overbearing manipulation is bound to become stale and uninspiring, according to Eli. Do you agree with the author that "in their rush to seem at one with America, these companies have oversimplified the national mood"? How do you feel about the use of patriotism as a marketing tool?

Eli is a columnist for the *Philadelphia Weekly*, where this essay first appeared on October 17, 2001, and a frequent commentator on National Public Radio. His most recent book, *Homecoming: The Story of African-American Farmers* (2000), is a companion volume to the PBS film of the same name. He has also published two anthologies of quotations and proverbs, *African-American Wisdom* (1996) and *Many Strong and Beautiful Voices* (1997). In addition to his books, Eli has written fiction and essays for *Essence, Emerge, Working Woman*, and the *Philadelphia Inquirer Magazine*. He currently teaches English and creative writing at the Community College of Philadelphia.

THINKING AHEAD

Did you notice the many advertisements with patriotic themes in magazines and on television after the September 11, 2001, tragedy? How did you react to these ads? Had you noticed patriotic ads prior to this date? What do you think of patriotism as a marketing strategy?

INCREASING VOCABULARY

hail (n.) (1)

profusely (adv.) (3)

inconsequential (adj.) (3)

implicit (adj.) (4)

mortar (n.) (5)

cynical (adj.) (6)

embellishing (v.) (7)

desecration (n.) (7)

aversion (n.) (8)

veritable (adj.) (8)

iconic (adj.) (11)

obsolete (adj.) (11)

irony (n.) (12)

abstraction (n.) (13)

volatile (adj.) (13)

retaliation (n.) (14)

These days, when telemarketers[1] call, as they so often do while I'm eating my dinner in front of the evening news, I turn up the TV so they can hear the dour tone of Dan Rather[2] describing the hail of bombs over Afghanistan, and I say to the person on the other end of the phone, "Does this really seem to you like an appropriate time to be discussing vacation resorts in Florida?"

I swear, it works like a charm.[3]

Invariably the telemarketer apologizes profusely, acknowledging that, yes, these are grim times and all things recreational seem remote and inconsequential. The steak knives, the magazine subscriptions, the discounts on long-distance phone service—who has the time to consider such material concepts when the world, for all intents and purposes, is at war?

This is the implicit question I put to the telemarketers, which they can never sufficiently answer. So instead they hang up, leaving me in peace.

I'm not just being mean-spirited. Like a lot of Americans, I suffer from a rampant case of commercial schizophrenia: On the one hand I'd like to spend a little more money to do my bit for the national economy, but at the same time I don't have much interest in purchasing any new tchotchkes[4] while unclaimed bodies from New York to Kabul lie buried under mortar and dust.

Also, I've lately become more cynical than usual about the world of capitalist commerce. Since the attacks on the World Trade Center and the Pentagon, many marketers and advertisers have started to wrap their products in the American flag, as if purchasing a certain car or salad dressing is a patriotic gesture, no less heroic than joining your fellow passengers to subdue a terrorist hijacker.

For this reason, the flag now appears regularly in TV commercials, website banners and newspaper ads. And networks such as NBC insist on embellishing their promotional logos with glimmering red, white and blue graphics—which, according to *New York Times* columnist Frank Rich, is perhaps the best evidence that a constitutional amendment banning flag desecration might not be such a bad thing.

It's not that I have an aversion to being manipulated. If the editors of *Maxim* insist to me that reading their magazine will make me a sexier guy, a veritable chick magnet,[5] I'm willing to go along with the ploy, at least until it's time to renew my subscription. But I get a little touchy when that manipulation starts to sound nationalistic and overbearing.

For example, every time I see the latest ads for General Motors, the ones that command me to "keep America rolling"[6] by purchasing a GM

1

2

3

4

5

6

7

8

9

---

[1] **ESL telemarketers:** People who sell goods and services over the phone.
[2] **ESL Dan Rather:** Anchor of the *CBS Evening News.*
[3] **ESL works like a charm:** Functions effectively.
[4] tchotchkes: A Yiddish word meaning trinkets.
[5] **ESL chick magnet:** A slang term denoting a man who is popular with women.
[6] **ESL "Keep America Rolling":** Ad campaign suggesting the last words of Todd Beamer "Let's roll" to his fellow passengers urging them to overtake the September 11 hijackers.

car, I always get a little afraid that we're all supposed to jump into our brand new Chevy Blazers and minivans and *roll* over anyone who gets in our way, like the Nazis driving tanks into Poland.

Other ads just strike me as bizarre. eBay, for instance, is currently running some promotional gimmick called "Auction for America," and its ads feature an American flag billowing proudly over a post-disaster Manhattan skyline. But if you look at the ad quickly, as it crawls atop your computer screen while you're shopping online for gas masks, you're likely to think that America itself is for sale and that eBay is auctioning away the country as though it were some dust-covered doodad[7] on *Antiques Roadshow.*[8]   10

Like all fads, this habit of using patriotism to sell products is destined to come to an end. If you, like me, had the pleasure of living through the 1970s, you've learned that everything in the commercial world has an expiration date—from bellbottoms to pet rocks[9] to power ballads by Foreigner.[10] Before long the red, white and blue will disappear from our TV and computer screens, if only because the image of the flag will begin to seem stale and uninspiring, its iconic value made obsolete from sheer overexposure.   11

Such is the twisted irony of being an American. The thing that makes us the object of so much international scorn—we're perceived as a country of godless hedonists[11] who consume everything in sight—is the very quality that'll eventually redeem us. All the patriotic chest-thumping we're doing now will start to bore us soon, and on our way to finding some new diversion to feed our relentless appetites, we're likely to abandon all the bloated nationalism and offensive jingoism[12] that is currently in vogue.   12

Happily, the marketers and advertisers who have wrapped their products in the flag will have no choice but to follow suit. In their rush to seem at one with America, these companies have oversimplified the national mood. They've reduced patriotism to an abstract concept—using it to sell jeans and furniture—and forgotten that the brand of patriotism a lot of Americans are experiencing right now isn't an abstraction. Instead, it's a very real and volatile emotion inspired by the deaths of thousands of people.   13

If the death toll continues to climb—if we lose soldiers in Afghanistan or there's retaliation on American soil—then nothing any company can sell us will help heal our grief, and no amount of flag-waving will comfort us in the end.   14

---

[7] **ESL** **doodad:** Trinket.
[8] **ESL** *Antiques Roadshow:* A prime-time PBS series that features the appraisal of antiques and collectibles.
[9] **ESL** **pet rocks:** A 1970s novelty gift item consisting of a rock in a box.
[10] **ESL** **Foreigner:** A rock band popular in the 1970s and early 1980s.
[11] **hedonists:** Pleasure seekers.
[12] **jingoism:** Zealous patriotism expressed especially in hostility toward other countries.

EXERCISING VOCABULARY

1. Study the essay's title. What does the word *flagging* mean? How does this adjective announce the subject of Eli's essay? What word is he playing on in the title? How effective is this word play?

2. In paragraphs 6 and 13, Eli mentions advertisers who wrap their products in the American flag. What does this phrase mean? Is the author using language literally or figuratively here or both? Explain your response.

3. In paragraph 5, Eli says that he suffers from "a rampant case of commercial schizophrenia." What is schizophrenia? How is the author using the word here? What does the word *rampant* mean in this context?

PROBING CONTENT

1. How does the author handle telemarketers? Why does he do this? How effective is his strategy?

2. How has marketing changed since September 11, 2001? Give some specific examples. What is the author's reaction to this change?

3. Does Eli think this change will be permanent? Why or why not?

CONSIDERING CRAFT

1. Why does Eli begin his essay with an anecdote, or short narrative? How effective is this strategy? Explain your response.

2. The author mentions the word *flag* several times in his essay. Find some examples and discuss the effectiveness of this repetition. How does it reinforce Eli's thesis?

3. The author concludes his essay by looking toward the future. Why does he choose to end this way? To what extent does this provide a satisfactory conclusion? Explain your response.

RESPONDING TO THE WRITER

In paragraph 11, Eli states that "Like all fads, this habit of using patriotism to sell products is destined to come to an end." Do you agree with his conclusion? Why or why not?

For a quiz on this reading, go to www.bedfordstmartins.com/mirror.

Illusions Are Forever

JAY CHIAT

Do you think advertisements often show products that seem too good to be true? According to marketing executive Jay Chiat, ads are indeed full of lies — but not the lies you might expect. Although the facts about a product are almost always true, it's the "situations, values, beliefs, and cultural norms" that constitute "the real lie in advertising," creating false reality, telling us how we should look, feel, and act. Should we accept the version of truth offered by media-makers, or can we find our own truth? Do you buy into the vision of the world created for you by ad executives?

When Chiat died in 2002, he was remembered as a creative genius who revolutionized the advertising industry. In 1967, he founded the Chiat/Day advertising agency, which quickly grew into one of the industry's most prestigious companies. Chiat was the mastermind behind many ground-breaking advertising campaigns, including the battery ads featuring the Famous Energizer Bunny and the original Apple computer ads launched in 1984, featuring striking images from George Orwell's novel *1984*. He was also responsible for making the Super Bowl into the advertising showcase that it is today. In 1997, Chiat left the marketing industry to lead ScreamingMedia, a provider of information management services. "Illusions Are Forever" was first published in the October 2, 2000, issue of *Forbes* magazine.

THINKING AHEAD

What image of the world does advertising present to us as consumers? How can this image affect us? How attainable is this world for most of us?

INCREASING VOCABULARY

sobriety (n.) (1)

piety (n.) (1)

transgressor (n.) (1)

unrelenting (adj.) (5)

pervasiveness (n.) (5)

acculturated (adj.) (5)

arbitrary (adj.) (6)

preposterous (adj.) (6)

infinitely (adv.) (7)

patently (adv.) (8)

pernicious (adj.) (8)

culprit (n.) (9)

obscuring (v.) (9)

plausible (adj.) (9)

inviolable (adj.) (11)

I know what you're thinking: That's rich,[1] asking an adman to define truth. Advertising people aren't known either for their wisdom or their morals, so it's hard to see why an adman is the right person for this assignment. Well, it's just common sense—like asking an alcoholic about sobriety, or a sinner about piety. Who is likely to be more obsessively attentive to a subject than the transgressor?

Everyone thinks that advertising is full of lies, but it's not what you think. The facts presented in advertising are almost always accurate, not because advertising people are sticklers[2] but because their ads are very closely regulated. If you make a false claim in a commercial on network television, the FTC[3] will catch it. Someone always blows the whistle.[4]

The real lie in advertising—some would call it the "art" of advertising—is harder to detect. What's false in advertising lies in the presentation of situations, values, beliefs, and cultural norms that form a backdrop for the selling message.

Advertising—including movies, TV, and music videos—presents to us a world that is not our world but rather a collection of images and ideas created for the purpose of selling. These images paint a picture of the ideal family life, the perfect home. What a beautiful woman is, and is not. A prescription for being a good parent and a good citizen.

The power of these messages lies in their unrelenting pervasiveness, the twenty-four-hour-a-day drumbeat that leaves no room for an alternative view. We've become acculturated to the way advertisers and other media-makers look at things, so much so that we have trouble seeing things in our own natural way. Advertising robs us of the most intimate moments in our lives because it substitutes an advertiser's idea of what ought to be—What should a romantic moment be like?

You know the De Beers diamond advertising campaign? A clever strategy, persuading insecure young men that two months' salary is the appropriate sum to pay for an engagement ring. The arbitrary algorithm[5] is preposterous, of course, but imagine the fiancée who receives a ring costing only half a month's salary? The advertising-induced insult is grounds for calling off the engagement, I imagine. That's marketing telling the fiancée what to feel and what's real.

Unmediated is a great word: It means "without media," without the in-between layer that makes direct experience almost impossible. Media interferes with our capacity to experience naturally, spontaneously, and genuinely, and thereby spoils our capacity for some important kinds of

[1] **ESL** **That's rich:** Sarcastic expression remarking on an event or story that is particularly amusing and ironic.
[2] **ESL** **sticklers:** People who respect and enforce discipline and order.
[3] **FTC:** Federal Trade Commission, an organization that regulates trade between the United States and foreign countries.
[4] **ESL** **blows the whistle:** Reports unfavorable information or alerts authorities.
[5] **algorithm:** A procedure for solving a mathematical problem in a finite number of steps, often involving repetition of the same basic operation.

personal "truth." Although media opens our horizons infinitely, it costs us. We have very little direct personal knowledge of anything in the world that is not filtered by media.

Truth seems to be in a particular state of crisis now. When what we watch is patently fictional, like most movies and commercials, it's worrisome enough. But it's absolutely pernicious when it's packaged as reality. Nothing represents a bigger threat to truth than reality-based television, in both its lowbrow and highbrow versions—from *Survivor*[6] to A&E's *Biography*.[7] The lies are sometimes intentional, sometimes errors, often innocent, but in all cases they are the "truth" of a media-maker who claims to be representing reality.   8

The Internet is also a culprit, obscuring the author, the figure behind the curtain, even more completely. Chat rooms, which sponsor intimate conversation, also allow the participants to misrepresent themselves in every way possible. The creation of authoritative-looking Web sites is within the grasp of any reasonably talented twelve-year-old, creating the appearance of professionalism and expertise where no expert is present. And any mischief-maker can write a totally plausible-looking, totally fake stock analyst's report and post it on the Internet. When the traditional signals of authority are so misleading, how can we know what's for real?   9

But I believe technology, for all its weaknesses, will be our savior. The Internet is our only hope for true democratization,[8] a truly populist[9] publishing form, a mass communication tool completely accessible to individuals. The Internet puts CNN on the same plane with the freelance journalist and the lady down the street with a conspiracy theory,[10] allowing cultural and ideological pluralism[11] that never previously existed.   10

This is good for the cause of truth, because it underscores what is otherwise often forgotten—truth's instability. Truth is not absolute: It is presented, represented, and re-presented by the individuals who have the floor,[12] whether they're powerful or powerless. The more we hear from powerless ones, the less we are in the grasp of powerful ones—and the less we believe that "truth" is inviolable, given, and closed to interpretation. We also come closer to seeking our own truth.   11

That's the choice we're given every day. We can accept the very com-   12

---

[6] **ESL** *Survivor:* Popular prime-time television program on which participants use survival skills to compete for a $1 million prize.

[7] **ESL** **A&E's** *Biography:* A documentary program on the Arts and Entertainment cable channel that profiles celebrities and historical figures.

[8] democratization: The process of placing a country under the control of its citizens by allowing them to participate in government or decision-making processes in a free and equal way.

[9] populist: Advocating the rights and interests of ordinary people, for example, in politics or the arts.

[10] **ESL** conspiracy theory: A belief that a particular event is the result of a secret plot rather than chance or the actions of an individual.

[11] pluralism: The existence of groups with different ethnic, religious, or political backgrounds within one society.

[12] **ESL** have the floor: To have the attention of a group of people and permission to speak.

pelling, very seductive version of "truth" offered to us daily by media-makers, or we can tune out its influence for a shot at finding our own individual, confusing, messy version of it. After all, isn't personal truth the ultimate truth?

EXERCISING VOCABULARY

1. Chiat states that advertising gives us "a prescription for being a good parent and a good citizen" (para. 4). Who usually gives us a prescription? For what reason? Explain how advertising can give us a prescription.

2. Chiat tells us that most of our knowledge of the world is "filtered by the media" (para. 7). What does it mean to filter something? What can you think of that is filtered? How then can the media filter our knowledge of the world?

3. In paragraph 8, Chiat speaks of "lowbrow" and "highbrow" versions of reality-based television. Examine his examples and think of some of your own. What is the difference between lowbrow and highbrow?

PROBING CONTENT

1. What did Jay Chiat do for a living? Why is this important to know when reading this essay?

2. According to Chiat, what is the "real lie" in advertising? What "truth" does advertising represent? Explain your response.

3. Why is advertising so effective, according to Chiat? In what ways is this either beneficial or harmful for consumers?

4. According to Chiat, what will be "our savior" (para. 10)? From what will it save us? How will this be accomplished?

CONSIDERING CRAFT

1. Chiat addresses the reader directly in the first sentence of his essay. Why does he do this? How do you respond to his introduction? Is this an effective opening strategy? Why or why not?

2. Chiat ends his essay with a rhetorical question. Explain what a rhetorical question is and how one might be used. Find one of the other rhetorical questions Chiat uses. How effective is his use of this writing strategy throughout the essay, including in the conclusion?

3. Chiat uses an extended example in paragraph 6. Describe this example. Why did the author choose this particular example to support his argument? How effective is his choice? Defend your response.

RESPONDING TO THE WRITER

In his concluding paragraph, Chiat suggests that we "tune out" the influence of media in order to find our own version of "truth." To what extent is this possible? Explain your conclusion.

For a quiz on this reading, go to www.bedfordstmartins.com/mirror.

The Selling of Rebellion

JOHN LEO

According to the adage "sex sells," sex is supposedly the sure-fire way to sell any product from alcohol to automobiles. But John Leo identifies another common "hook" for advertising — the idea of rebellion against the dominant culture. According to Leo, "The message is everywhere — 'the rules are for breaking.'" Is this merely the latest advertising approach, or is there a much more serious issue involved here? If there are truly "no rules," then what governs actions and responses? Is this selling or selling out? Leo exposes a wave of advertising that may inadvertently do much more than influence our decisions about which restaurant to choose or which jeans to wear.

John Leo wrote this essay for the "On Society" column in the October 12, 1998, issue of *U.S. News & World Report*. Leo, whose weekly column appears in 140 newspapers, has written for the *New York Times* and *Time* magazine and is the author of *Two Steps Ahead of the Thought Police* (1998) and *Incorrect Thoughts: Notes on Our Wayward Culture* (2000).

THINKING AHEAD

List as many products as you can that have advertising associated with breaking rules, dissolving boundaries, ignoring typical culturally accepted behavior, or reaching beyond the ordinary. Why do these ads seem dangerous to some people? What messages do these ads deliver?

INCREASING VOCABULARY

satirical (adj.) (3)	mantra (n.) (6)
drivel (n.) (3)	decorum (n.) (7)
repressive (adj.) (4)	motif (n.) (8)

Most TV viewers turn off their brains when the commercials come on. But they're worth paying attention to. Some of the worst cultural propaganda is jammed into those sixty-second and thirty-second spots.   1

Consider the recent ad for the Isuzu Rodeo. A grotesque giant in a business suit stomps into a beautiful field, startling a deer and jamming skyscrapers, factories, and signs into the ground. (I get it: Nature is good; civilization and business are bad.) One of the giant's signs says "Obey," but the narrator says, "The world has boundaries. Ignore them." Trying to trample the Rodeo, the hapless giant trips over his own fence. The Isuzu zips past him toppling a huge sign that says "Rules."   2

Presumably we are meant to react to this ad with a wink and a 　3
nudge, because the message is unusually flat-footed and self-satirical.
After all, Isuzus are not manufactured in serene fields by adorable lower
mammals. The maddened giant makes them in his factories. He also hires
hip ad writers and stuffs them in his skyscrapers, forcing them to write
drivel all day, when they really should be working on novels and frolicking with deer.

But the central message here is very serious and strongly antisocial: 　4
We should all rebel against authority, social order, propriety, and rules of
any kind. "Obey" and "Rules" are bad. Breaking rules, with or without
your Isuzu, is good. Auto makers have been pushing this idea in various
ways since "The Dodge Rebellion" of the mid-1960s. Isuzu has worked
the theme especially hard, including a TV ad showing a bald and repres-
sive grade-school teacher barking at kids to "stay within the lines" while
coloring pictures, because "the lines are our friends."

A great many advertisers now routinely appeal to the so-called post- 　5
modern sensibility, which is heavy on irony (wink, nudge) and attuned to
the message that rules, boundaries, standards, and authorities are either
gone or should be gone. Foster Grant sunglasses has used the "no limits"
refrain. So have Prince Matchabelli perfume ("Life without limits"), Show-
time TV (its "No Limits" campaign) and AT&T's Olympics ads in 1996
("Imagine a world without limits"). No Limits is an outdoor-adventure
company, and No Limit is the name of a successful rap record label. Even
the U.S. Army used the theme in a TV recruitment ad. "When I'm in this
uniform I know no limits," says a soldier—a scary thought if you remember Lt. William Calley[1] in Vietnam or the Serbian Army today.

Among the ads that have used "no boundaries" almost as a mantra 　6
are Ralph Lauren's Safari cologne, Johnnie Walker scotch ("It's not tres-
passing when you cross your own boundaries"), Merrill Lynch ("Know
no boundaries"), and the movie *The English Patient* ("In love, there are
no boundaries").

Some "no boundaries" ads are legitimate—the Internet and financial 　7
markets, after all, aim at crossing or erasing old boundaries. The antisocial message is clearer in most of the "no rules" and "antirules" ads, starting with Burger King's "Sometimes, you gotta break the rules." These include Outback steakhouses ("No rules. Just right"), Don Q rum ("Break
all the rules"), the theatrical troupe De La Guarda ("No rules"), Neiman
Marcus ("No rules here"), Columbia House Music Club ("We broke the
rules"), Comedy Central ("See comedy that breaks rules"), Red Kamel
cigarettes ("This baby don't play by the rules"), and even Woolite (wool
used to be associated with decorum, but now "All the rules have
changed," an ad says under a photo of a young woman groping or being
groped by two guys). "No rules" also turns up as the name of a book and

---

[1]**Lt. William Calley:** American army officer held responsible for the massacre of civilians
during the Vietnam War.

a CD and a tag line for an NFL video game ("no refs, no rules, no mercy"). The message is everywhere—"the rules are for breaking," says a Spice Girls lyric.

What is this all about? Why is the ad industry working so hard to use   8
rule-breaking as a way of selling cars, steaks, and Woolite? In his book *The Conquest of Cool*, Thomas Frank points to the Sixties counterculture. He says it has become "a more or less permanent part of the American scene, a symbolic and musical language for the endless cycles of rebellion and transgression that make up so much of our mass culture . . . rebellion is both the high- and mass-cultural motif of the age; order is its great bogeyman."

The pollster-analysts at Yankelovich Partners Inc. have a different   9
view. In their book *Rocking the Ages: The Yankelovich Report on Generational Marketing*, J. Walker Smith and Ann Clurman say rule-breaking is simply a hallmark of the baby boom generation: "Boomers always have broken the rules. . . . The drugs, sex, and rock 'n roll of the '60s and '70s only foreshadowed the really radical rule-breaking to come in the consumer marketplace of the '80s and '90s."

This may pass—Smith says the post-boomers[2] of generation X[3] are   10
much more likely to embrace traditional standards than boomers were at the same age. On the other hand, maybe it won't. Pop culture is dominated by in-your-face transgression now and the damage is severe. The peculiar thing is that so much of the rule-breaking propaganda is largely funded by businessmen who say they hate it, but can't resist promoting it in ads as a way of pushing their products. Isuzu, please come to your senses.

EXERCISING VOCABULARY

1. What is satire? How is the Isuzu ad "self-satirical" (para. 3)?

2. In what sense has the expression *no boundaries* become a mantra for advertisers? With what groups are mantras usually associated? Why are mantras usually repeated?

PROBING CONTENT

1. According to Leo, what is the central message in the Isuzu ad using the giant? What is the probable intent of the Isuzu company?

2. Which automaker does the essay say introduced the "breaking rules" ad approach? When was this? Why is the timing significant?

---

[2] **ESL** **post-boomers:** Referring to members of Generation X.
[3] **ESL** **Generation X:** A generational term used by the media to apply to individuals in their late twenties or early thirties, who are marked by a cynical and self-questioning world view.

3. Name three products besides Isuzu that Leo says have been marketed under the banner of rebellion. If the "no boundaries" hook is so widely used in advertising, it must work. Why does the idea of "no limits" appeal to many people?

4. According to Thomas Frank, author of *The Conquest of Cool*, what is the "great bogeyman" of this age in history (para. 8)? How did the 1960s promote this idea?

CONSIDERING CRAFT

1. Explain this essay's title. Why is it so appropriate?

2. What is the writer's own opinion about the use of "no boundaries, no rules" advertising? Cite specific references from the essay to support your answer. Does the writer expect most of his audience to agree or disagree? Why?

3. What does Leo return to in the final paragraph to bring his essay to a satisfying conclusion? Why is this method of ending an essay generally so successful?

RESPONDING TO THE WRITER

In the last paragraph, Leo refers to a book whose authors believe that "the post-boomers of generation X are much more likely to embrace traditional standards than boomers were at the same age." Do you agree or disagree with this assertion? Why? Based on your position, describe the future of "no rules" advertising campaigns.

For a quiz on this reading, go to www.bedfordstmartins.com/mirror.

Swoosh!

READ MERCER SCHUCHARDT

Our culture lives by symbols; in fact, every day more and more symbols replace the words they represent. Look at traffic signs. The word *stop* isn't
needed to understand what that octagonal red sign means. And railroad
tracks on a sign speak clearly for themselves. Computer screens are home to
endless icons, as are designer clothes. No one needs to explain to you what
the H on Hilfiger clothing represents.

Read Mercer Schuchardt calls our world "postliterate." He doesn't mean
we can no longer read and write — we can and we do. He does mean we do
so with less and less frequency because we are required to less and less
often. As the introduction to this essay outlines, using symbols or icons isn't
new, but the motivation is different, and the movement is gaining strength.
Schuchardt examines one of modern America's most successful icons, the
Nike Swoosh, in this essay originally published in *Re: Generation Quarterly*
and reprinted in *The Utne Reader,* Summer 1997. Schuchardt is currently at
work on a Ph.D. in Media Ecology at New York University. Having lived as a
child outside the United States in the practically media-free West Indies, the
writer has stated that he needs his work toward this degree "to overcome
the culture shock" that he has never quite shaken off.

THINKING AHEAD

Think about some product symbols or icons that are so successful that the
product's actual name need not be used. How did these symbols become so
familiar to us? Why do we understand their meaning without the help of
words? How do they work to unite us in a common understanding?

INCREASING VOCABULARY

transected (v.) (1)	innovative (adj.) (4)
emulate (v.) (3)	equity (n.) (4)

The early followers of Christ created a symbol to represent their be-   1
liefs and communicate with one another in times of persecution.
The well-known Ichthus, or "Christian fish," consisted of two
curved lines that transected each other to form the abstract outline of fish
and tail. The word for fish also happened to be a Greek acronym wherein:

- Iota = Iesous = Jesus
- Chi = Christos = Christ

- Theta = Theos = God
- Upsilon = Huios = Son
- Sigma = Soter = Savior

Combining symbol and word, the fish provided believers with an integrated media package that could be easily explained and understood. When the threat of being fed to the lions forced Christians to be less explicit, they dropped the text. Without the acronym to define the symbol's significance, the fish could mean anything or nothing, an obvious advantage in a culture hostile to certain beliefs. But to Christians the textless symbol still signified silent rebellion against the ruling authorities. Within three centuries, the faith signified by the fish had transformed Rome into a Christian empire.

Today, in an electronically accelerated culture, a symbol can change the face of society in about one-sixteenth that time. Enter the Nike Swoosh, the most ubiquitous icon in the country, and one that many other corporations have sought to emulate. In a world where technology, entertainment, and design are converging, the story of the Swoosh is by far the most fascinating case study of a systematic, integrated, and insanely successful formula for icon-driven marketing.

The simple version of the story is that a young Oregon design student named Caroline Davidson got $35 in 1971 to create a logo for then-professor (now Nike CEO) Phil Knight's idea of importing and selling improved Japanese running shoes. Nike's innovative product line, combined with aggressive marketing and brand positioning, eventually created an unbreakable mental link between the Swoosh image and the company's name. As Nike put it, there was so much equity in the brand that they knew it wouldn't hurt to drop the word *Nike* and go with the Swoosh alone. Nike went to the textless format for U.S. advertising in March 1996 and expanded it globally later that year. While the Nike name and symbol appear together in ads today, the textless campaign set a new standard. In the modern global market, the truly successful icon must be able to stand by itself, evoking all the manufactured associations that form a corporation's public identity.

In the past, it would have been unthinkable to create an ad campaign stripped of the company's name. Given what was at stake—Nike's advertising budget totals more than $100 million per year—what made them think they could pull it off?

First, consider the strength of the Swoosh as an icon. The Swoosh is a simple shape that reproduces well at any size, in any color, and on almost any surface—three critical elements for a corporate logo that will be reproduced at sizes from a quarter of an inch to 500 feet. It most frequently appears in one of three arresting colors: black, red, or white. A textless icon, it nevertheless "reads" left to right, like most languages. Now consider the sound of the word Swoosh. According to various Nike ads, it's the last sound you hear before coming in second place, the sound of a basketball hitting nothing but net. It's also the onomatopoeic analogue of the icon's visual stroke. Reading it left to right, the symbol itself actually seems to say "swoosh" as you look at it.

However it may read, the Swoosh transcends language, making it the perfect corporate icon for the postliterate global village. 7

With the invention of the printing press, according to Italian semiotician[1] Umberto Eco, the alphabet triumphed over the icon. But in an overstimulated electronic culture, the chief problem is what advertisers call "clutter" or "chatter" — too many words, too much redundancy, too many competing messages. Add the rise of illiteracy and an increasingly multicultural world and you have a real communications problem. A hyperlinked global economy requires a single global communications medium, and it's simply easier to teach everyone a few common symbols than to teach the majority of non-English speakers a new language. 8

The unfortunate result is that language is being replaced by icons. From the rock star formerly known as Prince to e-mail "smileys" to the NAFTA[2]-induced symbolic laundry labels, the names and words we use to describe the world are being replaced by a set of universal hieroglyphs.[3] Leading the charge, as one would expect, are the organizations that stand to make the most money in a less text-dependent world: multinational corporations. With the decline of words, they now can fill in the blank of the consumer's associative mind with whatever images they deem appropriate. 9

After watching Nike do it, several companies have decided to go textless themselves, including Mercedes-Benz, whose icon is easily confused with the peace sign (an association that can only help). According to one of their print ads, "right behind every powerful icon lies a powerful idea," which is precisely the definition of a global communications medium for an accelerated culture. Pepsi's new textless symbol does not need any verbal justification because it so clearly imitates the yin-yang[4] symbol. In fact, a close look reveals it to be almost identical to the Korean national flag, which is itself a stylized yin-yang symbol in red, white, and blue. 10

Never underestimate the power of symbols. Textless corporate symbols operate at a level beneath the radar of rational language, and the power they wield can be corrupting. Advertising that relies on propaganda methods can grab you and take you somewhere whether you want to go or not; and as history tells us, it matters where you're going. 11

Language is the mediator between our minds and the world, and the thing that defines us as rational creatures. By going textless, Nike and other corporations have succeeded in performing partial lobotomies[5] on our brains, conveying their messages without engaging our rational 12

[1] semiotician: One who studies signs and symbols and how they operate in everyday life.
[2] NAFTA: North American Free Trade Agreement.
[3] hieroglyphs: Characters in a system of picture writing.
[4] yin-yang: Chinese symbol that represents completeness by combining both halves of the universe.
[5] lobotomies: Surgical procedures that sever nerves in the brain, once used to control unruly psychiatric patients.

minds. Like Pavlov's bell, the Swoosh has become a stimulus that elicits a conditioned response. The problem is not that we buy Nike shoes, but that we've been led to do so by the same methods used to train Pavlov's dogs.[6] It's ironic, of course, that this reflex is triggered by a stylized check mark—the standard reward for academic achievement and ultimate symbol for the rational, linguistically agile mind.

If sport is the religion of the modern age, then Nike has successfully   13 become the official church. It is a church whose icon is a window between this world and the other, between your existing self (you overweight slob) and your Nike self (you god of fitness), where salvation lies in achieving the athletic Nietzschean[7] ideal: no fear, no mercy, no second place. Like the Christian fish, the Swoosh is a true religious icon in that it both symbolizes the believer's reality and actually participates in it. After all, you do have to wear something to attain this special salvation, so why not something emblazoned with the Swoosh?

EXERCISING VOCABULARY

1. This essay begins with the history of an acronym. What is an *acronym?* Why are acronyms used? Give an example of an acronym that means something to you and explain what the letters mean, for example, scuba for self-contained underwater breathing apparatus or C.E.O. for Chief Executive Officer.

2. The author refers to the Nike Swoosh as *ubiquitous* in paragraph 3. How accurate is this word in describing the popularity of the Nike symbol? Name at least five different places where the Swoosh appears.

PROBING CONTENT

1. Why does this essay say the early Christians adopted the Ichthus symbol? What significance did it hold for them?

2. Why, according to Schuchardt, must a successful advertising icon be clearly understood by a wide range of people without supporting language? How do you determine whether an icon is successful as a marketing tool?

3. What examples does the writer provide to support his position stated in paragraph 9 that "language is being replaced by icons"? What motive do companies have for replacing language with symbols?

4. What does this essay describe as the conditioned or predictable response to the stimulus of the Nike Swoosh? How effective is the Swoosh in generating this response?

---

[6] **Pavlov's dogs:** Russian scientist Ivan Pavlov (1849–1936), whose experiments with dogs showed their reactions to be predictable under certain circumstances.

[7] **Nietzschean:** Friedrich Nietzsche (1844–1900), a German philosopher and author of *Man and Superman.*

CONSIDERING CRAFT

1. The writer chooses a complicated introduction. How well does the Christian fish symbol work as an introduction to this topic? Why do you think Schuchardt chose this symbol to introduce his essay?

2. This essay contains a number of unfamiliar references. If the writer knew that some readers would not understand these references, why did he include them? How do they improve or weaken the essay?

3. What does the final paragraph have in common with the introduction? What does the author want to accomplish by using this strategy? To what extent is he successful?

RESPONDING TO THE WRITER

Reread paragraph 11. What threat does the writer find in the growth of "textless corporate symbols"? Do you agree that his fear is justified? When you think about it carefully, to what extent do you feel surrounded by less language and more symbols? At what point might you become concerned?

For a quiz on this reading, go to www.bedfordstmartins.com/mirror.

The Brand Expands

NAOMI KLEIN

How did brand logos, once hidden on the inside tags of our clothing, suddenly grab center stage? In "The Brand Expands," Naomi Klein traces the history of branding, which began as a way to let others know what you were willing to pay for style. In the past decade, though, companies have started branding more than just their products. Companies now sponsor cultural events, hoping that certain ideas and values associated with the event will reflect back on their brand. But the reverse also happens — the company's own ideas and values color the event. In essence, this "advanced branding" doesn't sponsor culture but *is* the culture. Have you ever attended a concert or an event that was sponsored by a corporation? How was your experience of the event affected by the product ads surrounding you? Did you even notice you were being sold a product?

For the past six years, Klein has traveled throughout North America, Asia, Latin America, and Europe, tracking the rise of anticorporate activism. She is an award-winning journalist and the author of *No Logo: Taking Aim at the Brand Bullies* (2000), which received several awards and has been translated into twenty-two languages. "The Brand Expands" is an excerpt from this book. Klein currently writes an internationally syndicated column for the *Toronto Globe and Mail* and the *Guardian* in Great Britain, and her articles have also appeared in the *Nation*, the *New Statesman*, *Newsweek International*, the *New York Times*, the *Village Voice*, and *Ms.* magazine.

THINKING AHEAD

Think about how pervasive logos are today. Where do you see logos? Give some specific examples. Why do we see so many logos today? To what extent are logos replacing written language? What effect do they have on you as a consumer?

INCREASING VOCABULARY

ubiquitous (adj.) (2)

intrusive (adj.) (2)

flamboyance (n.) (3)

ostentatious (adj.) (3)

affectation (n.) (3)

ballooning (v.) (3)

adherents (n.) (3)

outposts (n.) (5)

iconography (n.) (5)

transcends (v.) (7)

conflation (n.) (8)

supplanted (v.) (8)

238

I was in Grade 4 when skintight designer jeans were the be-all and end-all,[1] and my friends and I spent a lot of time checking out each other's butt for logos. "Nothing comes between me and my Calvins," Brooke Shields assured us, and as we lay back on our beds Ophelia-style[2] and yanked up the zippers on our Jordache jeans with the wire hangers, we knew she was telling no word of a lie. At around the same time, Romi, our school's own pint-sized Farrah Fawcett,[3] used to make her rounds up and down the rows of desks turning back the collars on our sweaters and polo shirts. It wasn't enough for her to see an alligator or a leaping horseman—it could have been a knockoff.[4] She wanted to see the label behind the logo. We were only eight years old but the reign of logo terror had begun.

About nine years later, I had a job folding sweaters at an Esprit clothing store in Montreal. Mothers would come in with their six-year-old daughters and ask to see only the shirts that said "Esprit" in the company's trademark bold block lettering. "She won't wear anything without a name," the moms would confide apologetically as we chatted by the change rooms. It's no secret that branding has become far more ubiquitous and intrusive by now. Labels like Baby Gap and Gap Newborn imprint brand awareness on toddlers and turn babies into mini-billboards. My friend Monica tells me that her seven-year-old son marks his homework not with check marks but with little red Nike swooshes.

Until the early seventies, logos on clothes were generally hidden from view, discreetly placed on the inside of the collar. Small designer emblems did appear on the outside of shirts in the first half of the century, but such sporty attire was pretty much restricted to the golf courses and tennis courts of the rich. In the late seventies, when the fashion world rebelled against Aquarian[5] flamboyance, the country-club wear of the fifties became mass style for newly conservative parents and their preppy[6] kids. Ralph Lauren's Polo horseman and Izod Lacoste's alligator escaped from the golf course and scurried into the streets, dragging the logo decisively onto the outside of the shirt. These logos served the same social function as keeping the clothing's price tag on: everyone knew precisely what premium the wearer was willing to pay for style. By the mid-eighties, Lacoste and Ralph Lauren were joined by Calvin Klein, Esprit, and, in Canada, Roots; gradually, the logo was transformed from an ostentatious affecta-

---

[1] **ESL** **be-all and end-all:** Final, most desirable, or most popular.
[2] **ESL** **Ophelia:** Character in Shakespeare's *Hamlet* who goes mad and commits suicide by drowning.
[3] **ESL** **Farrah Fawcett:** Popular 1970s sex symbol and actress who played a featured role in *Charlie's Angels*.
[4] **ESL** **knockoff:** A cheaper version of the original.
[5] **ESL** **Aquarian:** Relating to Aquarius, an astrological sign.
[6] **ESL** **preppy:** Slang term referring to well-educated, fairly affluent young people who are known for their neat, traditional, often expensive clothing style.

tion to an active fashion accessory. Most significantly, the logo itself was growing in size, ballooning from a three-quarter-inch emblem into a chest-sized marquee.[7] This process of logo inflation is still progressing, and none is more bloated than Tommy Hilfiger, who has managed to pioneer a clothing style that transforms its faithful adherents into walking, talking, life-sized Tommy dolls, mummified in fully branded Tommy worlds.

This scaling-up of the logo's role has been so dramatic that it has become a change in substance. Over the past decade and a half, logos have grown so dominant that they have essentially transformed the clothing on which they appear into empty carriers for the brands they represent. The metaphorical alligator, in other words, has risen up and swallowed the literal shirt. . . .   4

By the mid-nineties, companies like Nike, Polo, and Tommy Hilfiger were ready to take branding to the next level: no longer simply branding their own products, but branding the outside culture as well — by sponsoring cultural events, they could go out into the world and claim bits of it as brand-name outposts. For these companies, branding was not just a matter of adding value to a product. It was about thirstily soaking up cultural ideas and iconography that their brands could reflect by projecting these ideas and images back on the culture as "extensions" of their brands. Culture, in other words, would add value to their brands. For example, Onute Miller, senior brand manager for Tequila Sauza, explains that her company sponsored a risqué photography exhibit by George Holz because "art was a natural synergy[8] with our product."   5

Branding's current state of cultural expansionism is about much more than traditional corporate sponsorships: the classic arrangement in which a company donates money to an event in exchange for seeing its logo on a banner or in a program. Rather, this is the Tommy Hilfiger approach of full-frontal branding, applied now to cityscapes, music, art, films, community events, magazines, sports and schools. This ambitious project makes the logo the central focus of everything it touches — not an add-on or a happy association, but the main attraction.   6

Advertising and sponsorship have always been about using imagery to equate products with positive cultural or social experiences. What makes nineties-style branding different is that it increasingly seeks to take these associations out of the representational realm and make them a lived reality. So the goal is not merely to have child actors drinking Coke in a TV commercial, but for students to brainstorm[9] concepts for Coke's next ad   7

---

[7]**marquee:** A canopy projecting out over the entrance to a large building such as a hotel or theater.

[8]**synergy:** The working together of two or more things, people, or organizations, especially when the result is greater than the sum of their individual capabilities.

[9]**ESL brainstorm:** To generate creative ideas spontaneously.

campaign in English class. It transcends logo-festooned[10] Roots clothing designed to conjure memories of summer camp and reaches out to build an actual Roots country lodge that becomes a 3-D manifestation of the Roots brand concept. Disney transcends its sports network ESPN, a channel for guys who like to sit around in sports bars screaming at the TV, and launches a line of ESPN Sports Bars, complete with giant-screen TVs. The branding process reaches beyond heavily marketed Swatch watches and launches "Internet time," a new venture for the Swatch Group, which divides the day into one thousand "Swatch beats." The Swiss company is now attempting to convince the on-line world to abandon the traditional clock and switch to its time-zone-free, branded time.

The effect, if not always the original intent, of advanced branding is to   8
nudge the hosting culture into the background and make the brand the star. It is not to sponsor culture but to *be* the culture. And why shouldn't it be? If brands are not products but ideas, attitudes, values and experiences, why can't they be culture too? . . . [T]his project has been so successful that the lines between corporate sponsors and sponsored culture have entirely disappeared. But this conflation has not been a one-way process, with passive artists allowing themselves to be shoved into the background by aggressive multinational corporations. Rather, many artists, media personalities, film directors and sports stars have been racing to meet the corporations halfway in the branding game. Michael Jordan, Puff Daddy, Martha Stewart, Austin Powers, Brandy and *Star Wars* now mirror the corporate structure of corporations like Nike and the Gap, and they are just as captivated by the prospect of developing and leveraging[11] their own branding potential as the product-based manufacturers. So what was once a process of selling culture to a sponsor for a price has been supplanted by the logic of "co-branding" — a fluid partnership between celebrity people and celebrity brands.

EXERCISING VOCABULARY

1. In paragraph 3, Klein describes some fans of Tommy Hilfiger as "walking, talking, life-sized Tommy dolls, mummified in fully branded Tommy worlds." Why does the author describe them as "mummified"? What does it mean to "mummify" someone? With what culture do we normally associate the word "mummy"? Do you think that Klein believes that a "fully branded Tommy world" is a good or a bad environment? Why or why not?

2. In paragraph 6, Klein describes Tommy Hilfiger's marketing approach as "full-frontal branding." When you hear the term "full-frontal," what do you usually think of? Why does the author use this term in this context? What are the implications of her word choice?

---

[10] **ESL** **festooned:** Covered with decorations.
[11] **leveraging:** Building one's advantage or power over other people.

PROBING CONTENT

1. Where were logos generally located before the early seventies? How has this changed?

2. What does Klein mean when she says that the change in the role of the logo has become "a change in substance" (para. 4)? How have logos changed the clothing itself?

3. What happened in the mid-nineties to "take branding to the next level" (para. 5)? Explain what some companies have done to accomplish this.

4. What is advanced branding? Which celebrities have been eager to participate? Describe their relation to the product they are advertising.

CONSIDERING CRAFT

1. Why does Klein begin her essay with an anecdote from her past? Describe what happened to her in fourth grade. How does this narrative forecast the rest of the essay? How effective is this opening strategy?

2. Klein mentions many brand names and celebrity endorsers in her essay. How important is this specificity? How would her writing be different for you as a reader without all these specific details and examples?

3. Klein gives a historical perspective on the development of the logo in her essay. How does this help you understand her argument?

4. In paragraph 4, what does Klein mean when she says "The metaphorical alligator . . . has risen up and swallowed the literal shirt"? How effective is her use of figurative language here? Why?

RESPONDING TO THE WRITER

Do you think that "co-branding," described by the author as "a fluid partnership between celebrity people and celebrity brands" (para. 8), is desirable? Do you "buy into" co-branding? Why or why not?

For a quiz on this reading, go to www.bedfordstmartins.com/mirror.

DRAWING CONNECTIONS

1. In paragraph 2 of "The Brand Expands," Klein recounts the story of a friend's young son who "marks his homework not with check marks but with little red Nike swooshes." She then uses Nike as an example of "branding the outside culture" (para. 5). Compare Klein's thoughts about the logo's role in contemporary advertising with Schuchardt's in "Swoosh!"

2. How might Klein use the idea of the Swoosh logo as "the perfect corporate icon for the postliterate global village" in Schuchardt's essay (para. 7)? Consider whether Klein would see the use of "textless" advertising campaigns as positive or negative.

Wrapping Up Chapter 6

REFLECTING ON THE WRITING

1. Using materials from any of the essays in this chapter, write an essay explaining the extent to which you believe advertisers and corporations should be held accountable for the results of the use of their products.

2. Write an essay drawing specific connections between the self-image and cultural image of one group of people (distinguished by age, gender, or cultural identity) and the way they are portrayed in advertising. Research your paper by finding specific ads that support your argument. Refer back to the essays in Chapters 2, 3, and 4 on gender identity, body image, and cultural identity to generate some starting ideas.

3. As a consumer advocate, one who acts to protect consumers' rights, write an essay to other consumers alerting them to the different kinds of advertising manipulation mentioned in this chapter. Illustrate your argument with detailed descriptions of ads from some specific advertising campaigns.

CONNECTING TO THE CULTURE

1. Write an essay in which you detail how advertising has changed in light of the tragic events of September 11, 2001, and how you feel about these changes. You may write about television, print, or Internet advertising. Be sure to use specific examples in your essay to support your thesis.

2. Locate ads for at least five different products that use the same hook to sell a product (consider sex, celebrities, unusual art, shock value, children, or animals as possible hooks). Analyze each ad, explaining how the same advertising angle is used differently to sell each product. Explore the real message each ad sends to consumers.

3. Choose one group of people (for example, the elderly, teenagers, parents, African Americans) and develop a hypothesis about how they are portrayed in advertising. Then go to magazines, television, or the Internet to locate ads featuring that group. If the evidence you find supports your hypothesis, you have a thesis. If the evidence contradicts your hypothesis, develop a new thesis based on the evidence. Write an essay using your examples to fully support your thesis.

4. Invent a product and create an advertising campaign for it. Include all the details, such as how print and Web ads will look, where the print ads will be placed, how a short script for a television ad will read, which famous persons will star in the commercials, what background music will play in the ads, who the target audience will be, and other specifics.

FOCUSING ON YESTERDAY, FOCUSING ON TODAY

Dressing Well for God and Country

These two advertisements from the beginning and the end of the twentieth century showcase patriotism as an effective marketing tool. The American flag has been used to sell a wide variety of merchandise—and not just in times of war. Notice how prominently the flag is displayed in these ads. Think about how it is used in each and, more important, *why*. The original ads are both in vibrant color with red, white, and blue predominating.

Why did the Kuppenheimer Clothing Company use an overtly patriotic painting to sell its clothing in the 1910s? Why does the word *good* appear twice in the advertisement? Why is the attention of the man and the Boy Scout directed at the flag? What American values does Kuppenheimer want to bring to the consumer's mind?

Marketing Wrapped in the Flag

Now study the 1990s ad for Tommy Hilfiger's *Freedom* perfume. You know that Hilfiger has capitalized on the consumer's symbolic associations with red, white, and blue for years. What other selling strategy is used in this ad? How does a photo of a young man and woman wrapped in what looks like oversized beach towels bearing the stars and stripes sell perfume? Why are the man and woman each wearing only stars or stripes?

CHAPTER 7

Flickering Illusions

Television and Movie Messages

"I SAID SHE COULD GROW UP TO BE WHATEVER SHE WANTED. SHE'S NARROWED IT DOWN TO 'WARRIOR PRINCESS' OR 'VAMPIRE SLAYER.'"

©1999 Wm. Hoest Enterprises, Inc.

Television and movies today showcase a wide range of career options for female viewers. Now that women have won the right to be whoever they wish, they may still face problems fulfilling society's expectations of what it means to be a woman. This cartoon offers a humorous look at the effect some of television's empowered female role models may have on young women.

- Why do you think the little girl has made the career choices she has?
- How realistic are her choices?
- How do the parents appear to be reacting to their daughter's choices?
- How might this cartoon's message relate to the idea that a woman today is expected to be Superwoman, one who can "have it all" at home and in the workplace?

Research this topic with TopLinks at www.bedfordstmartins.com/toplinks.

GEARING UP

If you could assume the life of any character in a weekly television show, whose life would you choose? What would be the advantages and disadvantages of being this character?

What do the messages bouncing off our satellite dishes say about us? If the only available evidence of our existence were our movies and television shows, what could an outsider assume about our culture? Are we projecting the best and the brightest our society has to offer? Do our television and movie screens simply reflect our popular culture, or do they go beyond mirroring and actually cause us to behave in certain ways?

Even while they are sending mixed messages, the people, places, and situations presented in television shows and movies provide us with a common bond. No matter how diverse the group in a classroom, on a plane, or at a party, most of the people there can connect through a conversation about a sitcom episode or a film. Phrases from television and movies are a large part of shared discourse: "E.T. phone home," "I see dead people," "Hasta la vista, baby," "You are the weakest link," and "Is that your final answer?" But just how diverse are the faces and families we watch? Do the stereotypes we fail to question divide us even as they give us a common ground for conversation?

Children to adults, we are all influenced by the moving images we see in television shows and films. Even the most independent-minded of us have to admit that in some areas, movies and television shows influence who we are and who we feel we should be. Did you ever choose a hairstyle because of a TV character? Declare you would stick to your workout after seeing an episode of *Sex and the City* or *Friends*? Consider the law as a profession after watching a John Grisham movie or resolve to stay away from dogs, cars, birds, or motels after biting your nails through a horror film? Some of these seem like rather inconsequential influences. But our notions of beauty, self-worth, and justice are all bombarded by the bright images flashing before our eyes. To what extent are you influenced by movies and television shows?

COLLABORATING

Working in small groups of three or four, brainstorm a list of fads or trends that you can trace back to a movie or television show. Be sure you can recall the specific movie or TV show. Consider such things as hairstyles, clothing, jewelry, words or expressions, food fads, and habits or mannerisms.

Brave New Girls

DEBBIE STOLLER

Buffy, Xena, Mulan—television rankings and movie attendance testify to the popularity of these strong, in-charge, take-no-prisoners women. What impact are these dynamic female characters having on young women? Where are the boundaries when gender identity no longer seems harnessed to traditionally feminine values? What do men think about these in-control women who regularly kung-fu not only villains but also fixed notions about gender roles and female self-esteem? Tackling these questions, Debbie Stoller offers these powerful female role models as the antidote to the crisis some say society inflicts on adolescent girls. Stoller, who holds a Ph.D. from Yale University in the psychology of women, is coeditor of *Bust*, the feminist "Voice of the New Girl Order." She has written for *MTV Online* and *New York Newsday* and first published this essay in the Fall 1998 edition of *On the Issues*.

THINKING AHEAD

Make a list of the female characters from television shows or movies whom you most admire. What characteristics do they share? Are these traits generally considered "male" or "female"? What would it mean if our culture accepted a shift of traditionally male values onto female characters and vice versa? How would you feel about it?

INCREASING VOCABULARY

withering (adj.) (4)	vindicated (v.) (10)
mundane (adj.) (7)	bastion (n.) (16)
genre (n.) (8)	touted (v.) (16)
pretext (n.) (10)	sphere (n.) (17)

M ove over Spice Girls—there's a new breed of girl in town, and when she says "power," she means business. In the last few seasons, television shows like *Buffy the Vampire Slayer, Xena: Warrior Princess, Sabrina the Teenage Witch,* and *The Secret World of Alex Mack* have brought us heroines who give real meaning to the words "girl power." Whether they're chucking spears faster than a speeding bullet, kung-fu kicking unruly vampires into kingdom come, or simply breaking the laws of physics, these characters all share a common strength: the ability to leap over sexist stereotypes in a single bound.

Buffy, Xena, Alex, and Sabrina arrived on the cultural landscape just as adults were realizing that the world of teenage girls wasn't all pajama parties and pimple cream. Carol Gilligan, professor of gender studies, sounded the alarm in 1991 when she and her team of Harvard University researchers reported that girls undergo a "crisis in self-esteem" in adolescence from which they never fully recover.

Whereas young girls of nine or ten are self-confident, happy, and assertive—made of more piss and vinegar than sugar and spice—at puberty, a majority of them claim to be "unhappy with the way they are," an effect which is more pronounced among white girls than it is among Black and Hispanic girls. As a result of this loss of self-esteem, many girls become withdrawn and demure, starving their bodies and suppressing their talents in an effort to fit in.   3

Then, in 1994, Mary Pipher's book *Reviving Ophelia: Saving the Selves of Adolescent Girls* became a best-seller among parents concerned with how to keep their bratty, outgoing young girls from becoming anorexic, self-mutilating teens. In the book, Pipher, a Ph.D. and practicing therapist, describes how, at puberty, "girls become 'female impersonators' who fit their whole selves into small, crowded spaces. Girls stop thinking, 'Who am I? What do I want?' and start thinking, 'What must I do to please others?'" She lays a good portion of the blame for girls' withering sense of self flatly at the feet of the media, calling to task a "girl-hostile culture" and its ability to crush their self-esteem. "American culture has always smacked girls on the head in early-adolescence," she writes.   4

Seen from this angle, presenting girls in the larger-than-life roles of vampire slayers, teenage witches, and warrior princesses may be just what Dr. Pipher ordered. And, judging from their popularity, these shows have been hitting a nerve among girls of all ages.   5

First on the scene was Nickelodeon's *The Secret World of Alex Mack*, a show about a teenage girl who gets into an accident with a chemical truck that leaves her with bizarre powers—like the ability to shoot electricity out of her finger and float things around the room, *à la* Uri Geller, and the even stranger capacity to transform herself into a puddle of liquid. Alex uses these skills to help herself through the day-to-day difficulties of being a teenage girl, but there's one complication: she needs to keep her powers secret, not only because she doesn't want the other kids to think she's a freak, but also because the chemical company responsible for her misfortune is out to get her. (Not insignificant is the fact that the company, which is presented as being 100 percent evil, is in the business of making diet drugs.) It's this plot twist that makes Alex's situation a neat metaphor for the circumstances that most teenage girls find themselves in. As Pipher points out, girls at this age "are expected to sacrifice the parts of themselves that our culture considers masculine on the altar of social acceptability and shrink their souls down to a petite size." In other words, teenage girls can easily identify with the character of Alex Mack because, like her, they too have far more power than they are willing to let on.   6

Sabrina, of *Sabrina the Teenage Witch*, is another female character who has magical powers that she is trying to keep secret from the kids at   7 school. And, like Alex, Sabrina basically uses her powers to help herself through the more mundane challenges of teenagerhood. When, for example, Sabrina decides to hold a Halloween party at her house, she begs her aunts, who are also witches, to promise they won't do any magic stuff during the party. The friends come, the aunts work at maintaining appearances, and everyone's bored. It's only when the magical powers can no longer be kept under wraps—the furniture starts yacking away, monstrous looking houseguests arrive from "The Other Realm," and a river of candy corn pours from the kitchen—that the party really comes alive. "Cool!" says the cute boy, at which point Sabrina decides to pull out all the stops and conjures up a live band in the middle of the living room. The message to young girls? Stop trying to cover up who you are. Revealing your true self might even get you the boy.

But it is *Buffy the Vampire Slayer* that is far and away the most successful show in the average-teenage-girl-with-extraordinary-powers genre. Buffy is quite different from either Sabrina or Alex Mack. For one thing, her skills are more physical than magical in nature—she accomplishes her slaying through what seems to be a combination of kung-fu and gymnastics. And Buffy's powers serve as more than party tricks; in fact, her survival and the survival of her closest and dearest friends and family members depend on them.

8

Buffy is the kind of heroine most girls can relate to: She's neither the most popular nor the most nerdy at school, neither the prettiest nor the ugliest. She doesn't come from a perfect home: She lives alone with her mother; in fact, the only male authority figure in the show is the softly sexy British librarian who serves as Buffy's mentor.

9

The pretext of the show is that it is Buffy's destiny to fight the undead. But, as is suggested by each episode's subplot, what she's really doing is fighting back against the run-of-the-mill sorts of sexism faced by all teenage girls. When her boyfriend suddenly goes cold-shoulder on her after they've finally slept together ("Lighten up—we had a great time, let's not make a big deal out of it."), Buffy doesn't just get mad—she gets even. Of course, her drop-kicking outburst is actually inspired by the fact that the boyfriend is also a vampire, but still, it's satisfying to watch Buffy avenge her pain and frustration in such a direct manner. Other objects of her wrath have been a domestic abuser ("You just went O. J. on your girlfriend!"), and anyone who threatens the safety of her best friend, the sweet and nerdy Willow. The brilliance of *Buffy the Vampire Slayer* is not just that it shows us life from a teenage girl's point of view, but that this point of view is vindicated. Sure, maybe you're not a teenage vampire slayer, the series tells its viewers, but we understand that your daily battles can be just as trying.

10

And then there's Xena. In many ways, she doesn't fit with the others: For one thing, she's certainly no high school student—in fact, she doesn't even live in the present. She's also not hiding anything about herself from anyone. Xena is powerful with a capital P, and she kicks plenty of butt.

11

No one would ever make the mistake of calling large-and-in-charge Xena "petite." But Xena is not simply a male superhero in drag. She's all girl, and with her blue eyes, long dark hair, and severe bangs, she resembles no one so much as legendary pin-up queen Bettie Page. In her costume—a molded breast-plate contraption that would make Madonna's mouth water—she is an interesting combination of curves and combat. She's also a woman who indulges her hungers—for food, for fighting, and for men. When Xena sees a rival female make a play for one of her gorgeous, full-lipped, long-haired male conquests, she doesn't bother mincing words, or actions. Flinging a knife at her opponent, she hisses, "That's my piece of meat you're reaching for!" Xena is the farthest thing from a "Rules" girl; she is a girl who rules.

Xena's best friend is the ultra-feminine Gabrielle. While Xena is from 12 Mars, Gabrielle is from Venus. Gabrielle is the voice of peace-loving, female maternal wisdom, playing the role of the long-suffering wife to Xena's aggressive, bull-dyke husband. When Gabrielle tries to prevent Xena from going on yet another violent rampage, Xena just pushes her aside, saying, "Gabrielle, this is something I have to do."

For girls who are getting socialized to think of their bodies as the re- 13 ward they give to others, it's great to see Xena's re-working of the female body as an active and aggressive subject. After Xena punches out some mealy-mouthed enemy guys, she has the chutzpah[1] to raise her arm, sniff her pit, and sigh, "I love the smell of warrior sweat in the morning!" And while we almost always think of a naked female body as vulnerable, Xena never seems more powerful than when she is armed in nothing but her flesh and muscle, slinking like a cat across enemy territory. It's a fantasy we women rarely have access to, and it's a particularly empowering one.

Sabrina, Alex, Buffy, and Xena are all representatives of a new kind of 14 pop-culture heroine, one that is at once powerful and undeniably girly. This idea—that girlyness and strength aren't mutually exclusive—was first brought to light by a loosely-formed movement of young women who called themselves "Riot Grrls." In the early '90s, they gathered in latter-day consciousness raising groups in Washington, D.C., and Olympia, Washington. With their roots in punk-rock music, and their motto, "Grrls need guitars," the Riot Grrls resurrected old feminist themes for a new generation, and also reclaimed the word "girl" itself by injecting a ferocious, double-r growl into its center. Riot Grrls celebrated the fierce, tantrum-throwing little girl as one of the last examples of socially-acceptable female aggressiveness, before girls are taught to be "perfect little ladies" and instructed to suppress any display of anger.

In the Riot Grrls' wake, numerous all-girl rock bands were born, and 15 the slogan "girl power" began to be bandied about. T-shirts with pro-girl sentiments like "Girls Rule" and "Girls Kick Ass" started to show up at malls across the country, and slowly but surely, the idea of a mass girl-

---

[1] **chutzpah:** A yiddish term meaning extreme self-confidence, nerve.

power movement—one that could instill a sense of pride in girls and allow them to embrace their own power—has been taking shape. And the media, finally, have taken notice. "What female teens want is empowered female teen characters, which is something that has been missing for a long time on television," said Jamie Kellner, CEO of WB Broadcasting, in a *New York Times* article on the growing economic power of teenage girls.

Today, even Disney, that bastion ad nauseum of traditional male and female roles (Beauty and the Beast, Sleeping Beauty and Prince Charming, and so on), is jumping on the girl-power bandwagon with their latest animated film, *Mulan*. The story of a Chinese girl who breaks with tradition and poses as a boy to become a respected warrior, *Mulan* is being touted as projecting Disney's first really powerful role model for girls. But the claim is, at the very least, problematic: Mulan only gains access to power when she's disguised as a boy—she's a heroine who relies on that old strategy, if you can't beat 'em, join 'em. As important as it is to encourage girls to get in touch with the "masculine" part of their nature, and to be comfortable with the role of tomboy, we must be careful of the message that is on the opposite side of that coin. When *Mulan* suggests, as it does, that the best way to be a girl is to act like a boy, it supports the sexist notion that to be truly girly is to be a whiny, helpless sissy.

In her book *Where the Girls Are: Growing Up Female with the Mass Media,* feminist scholar Susan J. Douglas points out that the TV shows *Bewitched* and *I Dream of Jeannie* hit the airwaves just as women were beginning to realize that there was more to happiness than housework. While *The Feminine Mystique*[2] was making its way up the best-seller lists, both these shows were suggesting that if the little lady at home was ever allowed to actually unleash her powers, she could probably destroy the world, or at least do some serious damage to the male sphere.

So it is probably no coincidence that today, as teenage girls are beginning to come into their own as both a social and an economic force to be reckoned with (the financial success of the box-office hit *Titanic* has been attributed to the power of their purses), shows like *Buffy the Vampire Slayer, Xena: Warrior Princess, Sabrina the Teenage Witch,* and *The Secret World of Alex Mack* are hinting that there's a wellspring of untapped girl power out there, with the potential to change the world if it could only be released. You go, girls.

EXERCISING VOCABULARY

1. According to Dr. Mary Pipher, how does society force young girls to become "'female impersonators'" (para. 4)? To whom is that term usually applied? How does it apply in this context?

---

[2] *The Feminine Mystique:* Betty Friedan's 1963 book, considered important in the feminist movement for its suggestion that women do not find fulfillment only in childbearing and homemaking.

2. Stoller refers to Disney as a "bastion ad nauseum of traditional male and female roles" (para. 16). What does the word *ad nauseum* mean? What message about Disney's movies is Stoller conveying here?

PROBING CONTENT

1. What does Stoller say that characters like Buffy and Xena have been able to "leap over . . . in a single bound" (para. 1)? With whom is this phrase usually associated? What's ironic about Stoller's use of it here?

2. How, according to the writer, are television shows like *Sabrina* and *Buffy* "just what Dr. Pipher ordered" (para. 5)? To what extent are young women accepting the new role models?

3. According to Stoller, why do teenage girls identify with Alex Mack? What does Stoller say is the message teenage girls learn from Sabrina?

4. How is Xena noticeably different from the other heroines in this article? What message does this send to teenage girls?

5. Explain how female rock groups furthered the evolution of girl power. What is the significance of the name *Riot Grrls*?

6. With *Mulan*, Disney seemed to recognize the growing strength of girl power. What about *Mulan* earns criticism from this author?

CONSIDERING CRAFT

1. This essay uses a series of very specific examples. What effect do these examples have? Which examples work especially well? Why?

2. How does Stoller communicate successfully with readers who are not familiar with these shows? How does she compensate for readers who don't know these characters?

3. Reread the final paragraph. How does Stoller ensure that her essay feels finished? Explain why she chooses to end with the slang phrase "You go, girls."

RESPONDING TO THE WRITER

Lucy Lawless, the actor who plays Xena, graced the cover and a number of pages in the April 1999 *Maxim* magazine for men. Posed and dressed provocatively, Lawless seems to contradict her character's on-screen messages. Can the same female character fuel men's sexual fantasies while appealing to women to remove themselves from men's control? What is confusing about these signals to both men and women? What might Stoller's comments be about Lawless's portrayal in *Maxim*? How might Mary Pipher evaluate the impact on teenage girls?

For a quiz on this reading, go to www.bedfordstmartins.com/mirror.

Tuning in Trouble

JEANNE ALBRONDA HEATON AND NONA LEIGH WILSON

Leeza Gibbons, herself a TV talk show host, said in a *McCall's* interview in August 1998, "I believe talk shows are the therapy of the '90s." If therapy involves dumping into the nation's lap heartache, backstabbing, lying, and deceit, then the writers of this next essay agree with her.

Today's talk shows seem to thrive on conflict and controversy, often dragging out under the bright studio lights things long left in dark and private closets. While they may make for arresting viewing, these revelations have consequences. Sometimes the consequences are immediate and visible to all—chairs fly, and blows are exchanged. Sometimes the consequences may unfold later. Remember the case of the *Jenny Jones* episode about secret crushes that resulted in the murder of a gay man by the unwilling male object of his affection? Jenny Jones and her staff, while deploring the violence, failed to see how they could in any way be held responsible. A Michigan jury disagreed, finding the show negligent and awarding $25 million to the slain man's family. That decision is being appealed.

Jeanne Albronda Heaton and Nona Leigh Wilson, authors of *Tuning in Trouble: Talk TV's Destructive Impact on Mental Health* (1995), clearly express their feelings in their book's title. Heaton, a practicing psychologist, also teaches psychology at Ohio University. Wilson teaches counseling and human resource development at South Dakota State University. Together they have written a severe indictment of talk TV. The following adaptation from their book appeared in the September/October 1995 issue of *Ms.* magazine.

THINKING AHEAD

Which talk shows have you watched recently? What were the shows about? Why did you watch? Who do you think sits in talk show audiences?

INCREASING VOCABULARY

perpetual (adj.) (6)

predatory (adj.) (6)

cajole (v.) (7)

flamboyant (adj.) (11)

skewed (adj.) (12)

myriad (adj.) (13)

embellish (v.) (13)

incessant (adj.) (14)

gratuitously (adv.) (14)

postmortem (n.) (17)

archaic (adj.) (17)

cognitive (adj.) (18)

platitudes (n.) (18)

disseminating (v.) (20)

In 1967, *The Phil Donahue Show* aired in Dayton, Ohio, as a new day-   1
time talk alternative. Donahue did not offer the customary "women's
fare." On Monday of his first week he interviewed atheist Madalyn
Murray O'Hair. Tuesday he featured single men talking about what they
looked for in women. Wednesday he showed a film of a baby being born
from the obstetrician's point of view. Thursday he sat in a coffin and interviewed a funeral director. And on Friday he held up "Little Brother,"
an anatomically correct doll without his diaper. When Donahue asked
viewers to call in response, phone lines jammed.

For eighteen years daytime talk *was* Donahue. His early guests re-   2
flected the issues of the time and included Ralph Nader[1] on consumer
rights, Bella Abzug[2] on feminism, and Jerry Rubin[3] on free speech. Never
before had such socially and personally relevant issues been discussed in
such a democratic way with daytime women viewers. But his most revolutionary contribution was in making the audience an integral part of the
show's format. The women watching Donahue finally had a place in the
conversation, and they were determined to be heard. The show provided
useful information and dialogue that had largely been unavailable to
housebound women, affording them the opportunity to voice their opinions about everything from politics to sex—and even the politics of sex.

No real competition emerged until 1985, when *The Oprah Winfrey*   3
Show went national. Her appeal for more intimacy was a ratings winner.
She did the same topics Donahue had done but with a more therapeutic
tone. Donahue seemed driven to uncover and explore. Winfrey came to
share and understand. In 1987, Winfrey's show surpassed Donahue's by
being ranked among the top twenty syndicated shows. Phil and Oprah
made it easier for those who followed; their successors were able to move
much more quickly to the top.

At their best, the shows "treated the opinions of women of all classes,   4
races, and educational levels as if they mattered," says Naomi Wolf in her
book *Fire with Fire:* "That daily act of listening, whatever its shortcom-
ings, made for a revolution in what women were willing to ask for; the
shows daily conditioned otherwise unheard women into the belief that
they were entitled to a voice." Both Donahue and Winfrey deserve enormous credit for providing a platform for the voices of so many who
needed to be heard, and for raising the nation's consciousness on many
important topics, including domestic violence, child abuse, and other crucial problems. But those pioneering days are over. As the number of
shows increased and the ratings wars intensified, the manner in which issues are presented has changed. Shows now encourage conflict, name-

---

[1] **Ralph Nader:** Well-known American consumer advocate.
[2] **Bella Abzug:** Well-known feminist and human rights advocate and former U.S. Represen-
tative from New York.
[3] **Jerry Rubin:** Author of *Do It;* defendant in 1969 Chicago conspiracy trial for participation in 1968 riots at the Democratic National Convention.

calling, and fights. Producers set up underhanded tricks and secret revelations. Hosts instruct guests to reveal all. The more dramatic and bizarre the problems the better.

While more air time is given to the problems that women face, the topics are presented in ways that are not likely to yield change. The very same stereotypes that have plagued both women and men for centuries are in full force. Instead of encouraging changes in sex roles, the shows actually solidify them. Women viewers are given a constant supply of the worst images of men, all the way from garden-variety liars, cheats, and con artists to rapists and murderers.

If there is a man for every offense, there is certainly a woman for every trauma. Most women on talk TV are perpetual victims presented as having so little power that not only do they have to contend with real dangers such as sexual or physical abuse, but they are also overcome by bad hair, big thighs, and beautiful but predatory "other" women. The women of talk are almost always upset and in need. The bonding that occurs invariably centers around complaints about men or the worst stereotypes about women. In order to be a part of the "sisterhood," women are required to be angry with men and dissatisfied with themselves. We need look no further than at some of the program titles to recognize the message. Shows about men bring us a steady stream of stalkers, adulterers, chauvinistic sons, abusive fathers, and men who won't commit to women.

The shows provide a forum for women to complain, confront, and cajole, but because there is never any change as a result of the letting loose, this supports the mistaken notion that women's complaints have "no weight," that the only power women have is to complain, and that they cannot effect real changes. By bringing on offensive male guests who do nothing but verify the grounds for complaint, the shows are reinforcing some self-defeating propositions. The idea that women should direct their energies toward men rather than look for solutions in themselves is portrayed daily. And even when the audience chastises such behavior, nothing changes, because only arguments and justifications follow.

On *The Jenny Jones Show* a woman was introduced as someone who no longer had sex with her husband because she saw him with a stripper. Viewers got to hear how the stripper "put her boobs in his face" and then kissed him. The husband predictably defended his actions: "At least I didn't tongue her." The next few minutes proceeded with insult upon insult, to which the audience "oohed" and "aahed" and applauded. To top it all off, viewers were informed that the offense in question occurred at the husband's birthday party, which his wife arranged, *stripper and all.* Then in the last few minutes a psychologist pointed out the couple weren't wearing rings and didn't seem committed. She suggested that their fighting might be related to some other problem. Her comments seemed reasonable enough until she suggested that the wife might really be trying to get her husband to rape her. That comment called up some of the most absurd and destructive ideas imaginable about male and female relationships—yet there was no explanation or discussion.

It is not that women and men don't find lots of ways to disappoint each other, or that some women and some men don't act and think like the women and men on the shows. The problem is talk TV's fixation on gender war, with endless portrayals of vicious acts, overboard retaliations, and outrageous justifications. As a result, viewers are pumped full of the ugliest, nastiest news from the front.

When issues affecting people of color are dealt with, the stereotypes about gender are layered on top of the stereotypes about race. Since most of the shows revolve around issues related to sex, violence, and relationships, they tend to feature people of color who reflect stereotypical images—in a steady stream of guests who have children out of wedlock, live on welfare, fight viciously, and have complicated unsolvable problems. While there are less than flattering depictions of white people on these shows, white viewers have the luxury of belonging to the dominant group, and therefore are more often presented in the media in positive ways.

On a *Ricki Lake* show about women who sleep with their friends' boyfriends, the majority of the guests were African American and Hispanic women who put on a flamboyant display of screaming and fighting. The profanity was so bad that many of the words had to be deleted. The segment had to be stopped because one guest yanked another's wig off. For many white viewers these are the images that form their beliefs about "minority" populations.

The shows set themselves up as reliable sources of information about what's really going on in the nation. And they often cover what sounds like common problems with work, love, and sex, but the information presented is skewed and confusing. Work problems become "fatal office feuds" and "back-stabbing coworkers." Problems concerning love, sex, or romance become "marriage with a fourteen-year-old," "women in love with the men who shoot them," or "man-stealing sisters." TV talk shows suggest that "marrying a rapist" or having a "defiant teen" are catastrophes about to happen to everyone.

Day in and day out, the shows parade all the myriad traumas, betrayals, and afflictions that could possibly befall us. They suggest that certain issues are more common than they actually are, and embellish the symptoms and outcomes. In actuality, relatively few people are likely to be abducted as children, join a Satanic cult in adolescence, fall in love with serial rapists, marry their cousins, hate their own race, or get sex changes in midlife, but when presented over and over again the suggestion is that they are quite likely to occur.

With their incessant focus on individual problems, television talk shows are a major contributor to the recent trend of elevating personal concerns to the level of personal rights and then affording those "rights" more attention than their accompanying responsibilities. Guests are brought on who have committed villainous acts (most often against other guests). The host and audience gratuitously "confront" the offenders about their wrongdoing and responsibilities. The alleged offenders almost always refute their accountability with revelations that they too were "victimized." On *Sally Jessy Raphael,* a man appeared with roses for the daughter he had sexually molested. He then revealed that he had been molested when he was five, and summed it up with "I'm on this show too! I need help, I'll go through therapy."

His sudden turnabout was not unusual. Viewers rarely see guests   15 admit error early in the show, but a reversal often occurs with just a few minutes remaining. This works well for the shows because they need the conflict to move steadily to a crescendo before the final "go to therapy" resolution. But before that viewers are treated to lots of conflict and a heavy dose of pseudo-psychological explanations that are really nothing more than excuses, and often lame ones at that. The guests present their problems, the hosts encourage them to do so with concerned questions and occasional self-disclosures, and the audience frequently get in on the act with their own testimonies. Anything and everything goes.

The reigning motto is "Secrets keep you sick." On a *Jerry Springer*   16 show about confronting secrets, a husband revealed to his wife that he had been having an affair. Not only was the unsuspecting wife humiliated and speechless, but Springer upped the ante by bringing out the mistress, who kissed the husband and informed the wife that she loved them both. Conflict predictably ensued, and viewers were told this was a good idea because now the problem was out in the open. When Ricki Lake did a similar show, a man explained to his very surprised roommate that he had "finally" informed the roommate's mother that her son was gay, a secret the roommate had been hiding from his family.

Referring to these premeditated catastrophes as simply "disclosures"   17 softens their edges and affords them a kind of legitimacy they do not deserve. On a program about bigamy, Sally Jessy Raphael invited two women who had been married to the same man at the same time to appear on the show. The man was also on, via satellite and in disguise. His nineteen-year-old daughter by one of the wives sat on the stage while these women and her father tore each other apart. Sally and the audience encouraged the fight with "oohs" and "aahs" and rounds of applause at the ever-increasing accusations. A "relationship therapist" was brought on to do the postmortem. Her most notable warning was that all this turmoil could turn the daughter "to women," presumably meaning that she could become a lesbian. The scenario was almost too absurd for words, but it was just one more show like so many others: founded on stereotypes and capped off with clichés. From the "catfight" to the "no-good father" to archaic explanations of homosexuality—cheap thrills and bad advice are dressed up like information and expertise.

These scenarios are often legitimized by the use of pseudo-psychological explanations, otherwise known as psychobabble. This is regularly used   18 as a "disclaimer," or as a prelude to nasty revelations, or as a new and more sophisticated way of reinforcing old stereotypes: "men are cognitive, not emotional," or "abused women draw abusive men to them." This not only leaves viewers with nothing more than platitudes to explain problems and clichés to resolve them, but it fails to offer guests with enormous conflicts and long histories of resentment and betrayals practical methods for changing their circumstances. The "four steps to get rid of your anger" may sound easy enough to implement, but what this kind of ready-made solution fails to acknowledge is that not all anger is the same, and certainly not everyone's anger needs the same treatment. Sometimes anger is a signal to people that they are being hurt, exploited, or taken advantage of, and it can motivate change.

Rather than encouraging discussion, exploration, or further under- 19
standing, psychobabble shuts it off. With only a phrase or two, we can believe that we understand all the related "issues." Guests confess that they are "codependents" or "enablers." Hosts encourage "healing," "empowerment," and "reclaiming of the inner spirit." In turn, viewers can nod knowingly without really knowing at all.

Talk TV initially had great potential as a vehicle for disseminating ac- 20
curate information and as a forum for public debate, although it would be hard to know it from what currently remains. Because most of these talk shows have come to rely on sensational entertainment as the means of increasing ratings, their potential has been lost. We are left with cheap shots, cheap thrills, and sound-bite stereotypes. Taken on its own, this combination is troubling enough, but when considered against the original opportunity for positive outcomes, what talk TV delivers is truly disturbing.

EXERCISING VOCABULARY

1. In paragraph 5, the writers charge talk TV with solidifying gender stereotypes instead of working to change them. How does knowing the adjective *solid* help you to explain the verb *solidify*? In what sense do talk shows solidify gender stereotypes?

2. Reread paragraph 18. Explain the term *psychobabble*. How do the writers relate this term to talk TV?

PROBING CONTENT

1. According to the writers, what valuable function did early talk shows serve? What do the writers feel modern talk shows encourage?

2. According to the writers, how are men frequently represented on talk shows? How are minorities represented? What effect do the writers believe this has on audiences?

3. In the opinion of these writers, what must women do to join the talk show "sisterhood"? Why might women choose to do this?

4. Explain the writers' statement in paragraph 17 that "cheap thrills and bad advice are dressed up like information and expertise." What is the danger in this deception?

5. Compare the writers' view of the original potential of talk shows with what they have become. What has fueled this transition?

CONSIDERING CRAFT

1. This article was reprinted in *Ms.* magazine. Describe that magazine's primary audience. How well do Heaton and Wilson relate to that audience?

2. Is this a balanced look at talk shows today? How is the opinion of the writers made clear?

3. Heaton and Wilson put many of the terms associated with TV talk shows in quotes: "sisterhood," "rights," "relationship," "therapist," "disclaimer," and "issues." How is the reader's response to these words affected by the quotation marks?

RESPONDING TO THE WRITER

How do you explain the popularity of today's talk shows? What age groups are most attracted to them? One essay by Nichols Fox, "Gawk Shows," suggests that talk shows have replaced the freak shows that used to attract people at fairs and circuses. To what extent is this unflattering comparison accurate? What comment does it make about talk show audiences? Explain any redeeming social value that you find in talk shows.

For a quiz on this reading, go to www.bedfordstmartins.com/mirror.

Why We Crave Horror Movies

STEPHEN KING

This traditional old English prayer — "From ghoulies and ghosties, long-leggedy beasties, and things that go bump in the night, Lord God protect us" — makes it obvious that people have worried about "things that go bump in the night" for a long time. If ghouls and ghosts frighten us so, why do so many of us love to be scared to death at the movies? Fantastic otherworldly monsters, knife-wielding psychopaths, lunatics with pitchforks or chain saws — the scarier, the better. What kind of civilization are we that we are secretly thrilled by all kinds of on-screen murder, torture, and gruesome evil?

A fairly normal and fun-loving one, insists the famous author of this essay who needs no introduction to either readers or movie buffs around the world. Stephen King is the creator of such frightening tales as *Carrie* (1973), *The Shining* (1977), *Misery* (1987), *The Eyes of the Dragon* (1987), *Bag of Bones* (1998), *Hearts in Atlantis* (1999), and *Riding the Bullet* (2000), an e-book available only on the Internet. King repopularized the serial novel with *The Green Mile*, published in six installments from March through August 1996. He has also authored many short stories and screenplays and has played cameo roles in several films based on his works. The king of horror's prolific writing career nearly came to an end in 1999, when he was struck by a van and critically injured while walking near his summer home in western Maine. The author chronicles this painful period of both his personal and professional life in *On Writing: A Memoir of the Craft* (2000). The classic essay "Why We Crave Horror Movies," King's attempt to explain why we love it when he scares us to nightmares, was first published in *Playboy* in December 1981.

THINKING AHEAD

Do you like horror movies? Which ones really terrify you? Why? If they frighten you, why do you go to see them?

INCREASING VOCABULARY

grimaces (n.) (1)
depleted (v.) (3)
innately (adv.) (4)
voyeur (n.) (6)
penchant (n.) (7)

status quo (n.) (9)
sanctions (n.) (10)
remonstrance (n.) (10)
recoil (v.) (11)

I think that we're all mentally ill; those of us outside the asylums only   1
hide it a little better—and maybe not all that much better, after all.
We've all known people who talk to themselves, people who sometimes squinch their faces into horrible grimaces when they believe no one
is watching, people who have some hysterical fear—of snakes, the dark,
the tight place, the long drop . . . and, of course, those final worms and
grubs that are waiting so patiently underground.

When we pay our four or five bucks and seat ourselves at tenth-row   2
center in a theater showing a horror movie, we are daring the nightmare.

Why? Some of the reasons are simple and obvious. To show that we   3
can, that we are not afraid, that we can ride this roller coaster. Which is
not to say that a really good horror movie may not surprise a scream out
of us at some point, the way we may scream when the roller coaster twists
through a complete 360 or plows through a lake at the bottom of the
drop. And horror movies, like roller coasters, have always been the special
province of the young; by the time one turns forty or fifty, one's appetite
for double twists or 360-degree loops may be considerably depleted.

We also go to reestablish our feelings of essential normality; the hor-   4
ror movie is innately conservative, even reactionary. Freda Jackson as the
horrible melting woman in *Die, Monster, Die!* confirms for us that no
matter how far we may be removed from the beauty of a Robert Redford
or a Diana Ross, we are still light-years from true ugliness.

And we go to have fun.   5

Ah, but this is where the ground starts to slope away, isn't it? Because   6
this is a very peculiar sort of fun indeed. The fun comes from seeing others
menaced—sometimes killed. One critic suggested that if pro football has
become the voyeur's version of combat, then the horror film has become
the modern version of the public lynching.

It is true that the mythic, "fairy-tale" horror film intends to take away   7
the shades of gray. . . . It urges us to put away our more civilized and
adult penchant for analysis and to become children again, seeing things in
pure blacks and whites. It may be that horror movies provide psychic relief on this level because this invitation to lapse into simplicity, irrational-
ity, and even outright madness is extended so rarely. We are told we may
allow our emotions a free rein . . . or no rein at all.

If we are all insane, then sanity becomes a matter of degree. If your in-   8
sanity leads you to carve up women like Jack the Ripper or the Cleveland
Torso Murderer, we clap you away in the funny farm (but neither of those
two amateur-night surgeons was ever caught, heh-heh-heh); if, on the
other hand, your insanity leads you only to talk to yourself when you're
under stress or to pick your nose on your morning bus, then you are left
alone to go about your business . . . though it is doubtful that you will
ever be invited to the best parties.

The potential lyncher is in almost all of us (excluding saints, past and   9
present; but then, most saints have been crazy in their own ways), and
every now and then, he has to be let loose to scream and roll around in

the grass. Our emotions and our fears form their own body, and we recognize that it demands its own exercise to maintain proper muscle tone. Certain of these emotional muscles are accepted—even exalted—in civilized society; they are, of course, the emotions that tend to maintain the status quo of civilization itself. Love, friendship, loyalty, kindness—these are all the emotions that we applaud, emotions that have been immortalized in the couplets of Hallmark cards and in the verses (I don't dare call it poetry) of Leonard Nimoy.[1]

When we exhibit these emotions, society showers us with positive reinforcement; we learn this even before we get out of diapers. When, as children, we hug our rotten little puke of a sister and give her a kiss, all the aunts and uncles smile and twit and cry, "Isn't he the sweetest little thing?" Such coveted treats as chocolate-covered graham crackers often follow. But if we deliberately slam the rotten little puke of a sister's fingers in the door, sanctions follow—angry remonstrance from parents, aunts, and uncles; instead of a chocolate-covered graham cracker, a spanking.   10

But anticivilization emotions don't go away, and they demand periodic exercise. We have such "sick" jokes as "What's the difference between a truckload of bowling balls and a truckload of dead babies?" (You can't unload the truckload of bowling balls with a pitchfork . . . a joke, by the way, that I heard originally from a ten-year-old.) Such a joke may surprise a laugh or a grin out of us even as we recoil, a possibility that confirms the thesis: If we share a brotherhood of man, then we also share an insanity of man. None of which is intended as a defense of either the sick joke or insanity but merely as an explanation of the best horror films, like the best fairy tales, manage to be reactionary, anarchistic, and revolutionary all at the same time.   11

The mythic horror movie, like the sick joke, has a dirty job to do. It deliberately appeals to all that is worst in us. It is morbidity unchained, our most base instincts let free, our nastiest fantasies realized . . . and it all happens, fittingly enough in the dark. For those reasons, good liberals often shy way from horror films. For myself, I like to see the most aggressive of them—*Dawn of the Dead,* for instance—as lifting a trapdoor in the civilized forebrain and throwing a basket of raw meat to the hungry alligators swimming around in that subterranean river beneath.   12

Why bother? Because it keeps them from getting out, man, it keeps them down there and me up here. It was Lennon and McCartney who said that all you need is love, and I would agree with that.   13

As long as you keep the gators fed.   14

EXERCISING VOCABULARY

I. At the end of paragraph II, King asserts that really good horror movies "manage to be reactionary, anarchistic, and revolutionary all at the same time."

---

[1] **Leonard Nimoy:** Actor who played Mr. Spock in television's original *Star Trek* series.

Define these three words. Usually these words have a political meaning and are used with reference to governments. Explain their meaning when King applies them to horror movies.

2. In paragraph 12, King describes the "mythic horror movie" as "morbidity unchained." Define *morbidity* and explain King's use of it here.

PROBING CONTENT

1. To what is King referring when he mentions "those final worms and grubs that are waiting so patiently underground" (para. 1)? How does this reference contribute to the main point of this essay?

2. How is watching a horror movie "daring the nightmare" (para. 2)? Why, according to King, do we do this?

3. In what sense, according to the essay, do horror movies encourage us to think like children? Why might adults want an opportunity to think like children again?

4. Which emotions does the writer say "tend to maintain the status quo of civilization itself" (para. 9)? Why are these emotions so important to society?

5. What "dirty job" does King think horror movies perform for us? Why is it important that something assume this job?

6. What do "the hungry alligators" in paragraph 12 represent? How do horror movies feed the alligators?

CONSIDERING CRAFT

1. Does King literally "think that we're all mentally ill" as he says in paragraph 1? How does such a statement add to King's essay?

2. Describe the effect of the single-sentence paragraphs 5 and 14. How does this effect aid the overall impact of each point? How does it aid the essay's main idea?

3. Some of the language and references deliberately chosen by King are not polite — "to pick your nose" (para. 8), "rotten little puke of a sister" (para. 10), and the joke about dead babies in paragraph 11. What do you expect audience reaction to these references to be? What is your own reaction? Why does King include these?

RESPONDING TO THE WRITER

From your own experience, evaluate King's explanation of why we like horror movies. How accurate is it to assume that there is a dark side in each of us lurking just beneath our civilized skins? What difference does it make in your relationships with other people if you accept or reject this notion?

For a quiz on this reading, go to www.bedfordstmartins.com/mirror.

Soldiers on the Screen

RICHARD SCHICKEL

"*Black Hawk Down* makes [its] point without preachment, in precise and pitiless imagery. And for that reason alone it takes its place on the very short list of the unforgettable movies about war," writes Richard Schickel in *Time* magazine's December 17, 2001, issue. His review of the film casts it as an unsparing portrait of men under fire, a movie that stresses the anarchy of war. "You can see *Black Hawk Down* as antiwar if you're so inclined," Schickel writes, "but you cannot possibly see it as antisoldier. It is precisely that ambiguity that makes this picture a compelling experience." Other recent films in the genre, most notably *Saving Private Ryan*, have also depicted horrific warfare, but *Black Hawk Down* doesn't contain their "good war" rationale — these soldiers aren't fighting to rid the world of Nazis. The only principle they end up fighting for is their own survival. Is the public ready for a film that is relentless in showing the horrors of a war that, in the end, accomplishes nothing?

Schickel is a film critic, author, and documentary filmmaker whose work reflects his fascination with Hollywood. The author of more than thirty books, Schickel has chronicled the lives of numerous celebrities in biographies that include *The Disney Version* (1968), *Cary Grant: A Celebration* (1983), *Brando: A Life in Our Times* (1991), and *Clint Eastwood: A Biography* (1996). Among his documentaries are three television programs about the making of the *Star Wars* trilogy. Since 1972, Schickel has been reviewing films for *Time* magazine.

THINKING AHEAD

Which combat films have you seen? Which were your favorites? Which were your least favorite? Why? What was the message these films were trying to convey to the audience?

INCREASING VOCABULARY

accrues (v.) (1)

repercussions (n.) (2)

inferentially (adv.) (2)

expletives (n.) (3)

relentless (adj.) (3)

impotent (adj.) (4)

extraction (n.) (6)

foreground (n.) (8)

presumptive (adj.) (10)

ambiguity (n.) (11)

compelling (adj.) (11)

analogies (n.) (13)

belies (v.) (13)

ineradicable (adj.) (14)

They're just kids—late teens, early twenties. They mainly believe in   1
God, country and kicking ass. About religion and patriotism they
are straightforward and uncomplicated, pretty typically American.
Kicking ass is a different matter. At that, a Ranger or a Delta Force soldier
is a world-class expert—superbly trained, heedlessly brave, a figure set
very much apart from the rest of us. In large measure, that's because his
élite military status has given him something he didn't find in school or on
the streets back home—that fierce pride in self, unit and mission that accrues when you are volunteering your life to be, as the recruiting slogan
would have it, all that you can be.

This much is made vividly clear in Mark Bowden's powerful best-   2
seller, *Black Hawk Down,* which is virtually minute-by-minute reconstruction of the helicopter and humvee[1] incursion into Mogadishu, Somalia, in
October 1993, that resulted in unacceptable American casualties and
geopolitical[2] repercussions still rumbling today. Director Ridley Scott's
terrific movie adaptation is only inferentially concerned with the motives
and back story Bowden provided. It also lacks a movie-star hero—a Tom
Cruise or a Mel Gibson—reassuring us, simply by showing up, that everything will come out O.K. in the end.

What the film, which was written largely in cries, whispers and exple-   3
tives by Ken Nolan and Steven Zaillian, stresses instead is the sheer anarchy of war: bloody, terrifying, tragic and meaningless except as a test of a
fighting man's virtue. Like every other great war movie, *Black Hawk
Down* succeeds because it becomes, almost unintentionally, an antiwar
movie—or at least one that can be read that way by anyone so inclined—
a relentless catalog of the many absurd and accidental ways you can die
when you are ordered into harm's way.

That was especially true in Somalia in the fall of 1993. At that point,   4
the 25,000 U.S. Marines who had brought order to the distribution of
food in a starving land had been withdrawn. The U.N. peacekeeping force
on the ground was essentially impotent to intervene in the clan warfare
that had brought the country well over the edge of chaos. The most powerful of the clans was the Habr Gadir, led by Mohammed Farrah Aidid. It
became American policy to arrest him and the clan's other leaders and
subdue its "militia."

Major General William F. Garrison (played in the movie by play-   5
wright Sam Shepard) was three weeks past the deadline Washington had
set for completing that task when he got solid intelligence that two Habr
Gadir "Tier One Personalities" and a raft of smaller fry were meeting near
the Bakhara Market in "Mog." He ordered a midafternoon assault—
Delta Force troops roping down out of helicopters to make the grab,
Rangers securing a perimeter around the building. The captives would

[1] **ESL** **humvee:** A large extended Jeep.
[2] **geopolitical:** Having to do with the relation between a country's politics and its geogra-
    phy and population distribution.

then be loaded into an armored convoy and taken back to the airfield headquarters.

The U.S. troops, too long cooped up, were spoiling for this fight. Most had not been under fire, but no matter. They knew they were good—superbly equipped and well led. And, indeed, the Delta Force quickly and painlessly accomplished the extraction. Subsequently, everything that could go wrong did. One of the first Rangers out of the helicopter missed the rope and free-fell 60 ft. to the ground. The ground convoy got hopelessly lost in the debris-strewn streets of the city. Pinned down, the American soldiers began to attract vast crowds of armed clansmen, often advancing behind human shields of women and children. One Black Hawk helicopter was shot from the sky, then another. The Ranger creed holds that no fallen comrade, even a dead one, can be left behind. The Americans stood by that oath.

The fire fight would extend for an astonishing fifteen hours, virtually without a break. Eighteen Americans would die, seventy-three more would be wounded—well over half our troops on the scene. But you cannot imagine the hot chaos those chilling figures contain.

Ridley Scott, however, could. A bluff, down-to-earth Brit who started out to be a painter (he still does some of his own production sketches), he has become a master of all kinds of moviemaking—the visionary (*Blade Runner*), the intimate (*Thelma & Louise*) and the spectacular (*Gladiator*). He has not, however, done anything quite as grimly realistic as *Black Hawk Down*. Like most of his subjects here, Scott is from a working-class background, and he says that what he liked about this film was the simplicity of his characters—"they're like highly trained athletes, really." He is also something of an old-fashioned British traveler, the kind of man who relishes harsh conditions in odd corners of the world. Art director Arthur Max's brilliant re-creation of battered Mogadishu (built in Morocco) concentrated Scott's mind, eye and energies most wonderfully. More than anything else, he says, he wanted "to create an anatomy of a war that could be any war," and to that end he stripped away all talk, all thought, of this fight's larger geopolitical implications. Real soldiers don't think much about such matters, and neither do Scott's. Why, he wonders, "do we need such background when we have such a strong foreground?"

Good question, though not one that's comfortably answered by a brutal film that requires us to embrace the same deadly chaos our soldiers encountered eight years ago—a battle without visible turning points, a battle no one could map, a battle in which the hero is the group whose members become so grime smeared and blood spattered that audiences will have trouble identifying the players.

There are powerful incidents—a downed chopper pilot captured by a raging mob, the bloody struggle to save the life of a soldier whose artery has been severed. There's even a presumptive hero, Josh Hartnett's Sergeant Matt Eversmann, leading a Ranger "chalk" (small unit) into combat for the first time. He's a guy who thinks maybe they can eventually "make a difference" in Somalia. But his unit catches much of the movie's hard luck, and by its end he sadly realizes what every soldier finally learns—that the only principle anyone fights for is existential: your own survival and that of your buddies.

That does not mean, however, that the troops in Mogadishu fought   11
badly. On the contrary, they took everything the enemy threw at them, improvising their own deadly responses on the run. Under fire, they were, indeed, all that they could be. Afterward, Garrison pointed out that they carried out their mission successfully (he got his "personalities") and killed at least 300 of the enemy. It merely took more time and American blood than they ever imagined it would. In other words, you can see *Black Hawk Down* as antiwar if you're so inclined, but you cannot possibly see it as antisoldier. It is precisely that ambiguity that makes this picture such a compelling experience.

But that still raises the big question: Will people go to see it in num-   12
bers large enough to repay its estimated $90 million cost? It was, of course, shot and largely edited before Sept. 11. The only changes made since then, both Scott and producer Jerry Bruckheimer insist, were to ensure it's action and geography are understandable to audiences.

Still, there is less distance between the event *Black Hawk Down* recounts   13
and the events that most of the other great war movies relate. You have to wonder if the movie's immediacy, its obvious analogies to Afghanistan, will frighten audiences away. This is a matter of some moment to Bruckheimer. His soft-spoken intelligence belies his fame as producer of big-scale action films (*Top Gun, Armageddon*). At fifty-six, he has reached an age at which he wants to move beyond popcorn movies, and he observes that in *Black Hawk Down* he and Scott were trying very soberly to make an entire two-and-a-half-hour movie in the spirit of *Saving Private Ryan*'s unforgettably horrific D-day[3] sequence—and without its "good war" rationale. No such glory attaches to Somalia. The country is today, as Bruckheimer notes, "exactly as we left it," still starving, still sunk in hopeless anarchy. Worse were the implications that the world's only superpower was unwilling to fight in defense of hard-to-explain principles. Osama bin Laden has specifically cited our Somalian retreat as an inspiration for his depredations.[4]

But *Black Hawk Down* begins with a quotation from T.S. Eliot: "All   14
our ignorance brings us closer to death." By the light of its flash-bang grenades, this movie seeks to banish some of that darkness. It offers a paradigm[5] of what war in the twenty-first century is going to be—modernism run amuck[6] as it defends itself against primitivism, innocence savagely fragmented in incomprehensible combat. *Black Hawk Down* makes that point without preachment, in precise and pitiless imagery. And for that reason alone it takes its place on the very short list of the unforgettable movies about war and its ineradicable and immeasurable costs.

---

[3] **D-day:** June 6, 1944, day of World War II invasion of Western Europe by Allied Forces.
[4] **depredations:** Acts involving plunder and pillage.
[5] **paradigm:** An example.
[6] **ESL run amuck:** To rush about madly, out of control.

EXERCISING VOCABULARY

1. In paragraphs 3 and 13, Schickel refers to "the sheer anarchy of war" and to Somalia as "still sunk in hopeless anarchy." What does the word *anarchy* mean? How does the author's use of the word in these two phrases reflect his view of the movie's message?

2. In paragraph 10, Schickel writes that the "only principle anyone fights for is existential." What does the word *existential* mean? What is existential philosophy, or existentialism? How does the author use the word in this sentence?

3. In paragraph 13, Schickel writes that Jerry Bruckheimer, the movie's producer, wants to move beyond "popcorn movies" with *Black Hawk Down*. What does the author mean by "popcorn movie"? Name some movies that would fall into that category. How are they different from a movie like *Black Hawk Down*?

PROBING CONTENT

1. Which military action does the film *Black Hawk Down* depict? What was the outcome of this battle?

2. What message about war does the film deliver? What did the director purposely decide *not* to stress in this movie? Why is there no "movie-star hero"?

3. How can a viewer see this film as "antiwar" but not "antisoldier" (para. 11)? What does this add to the audience's viewing experience?

4. According to Schickel, how does *Black Hawk Down* compare to other combat films? Why does he believe this?

CONSIDERING CRAFT

1. Richard Schickel is a film critic. In what ways is this movie review similar to others you have read or heard on television? How does it differ?

2. Schickel refers to a recruitment motto in paragraphs 1 and 11. Reread each paragraph. Why does the author use this phrase twice in his essay? How does its use affect you as a reader?

3. In paragraph 14, Schickel repeats the T.S. Eliot quotation used in the movie and then writes, "By the light of its flash-bang grenades, this movie seeks to banish some of that darkness." Reread the Eliot quotation. What does Schickel mean by his comment? How effective is Schickel's metaphor?

RESPONDING TO THE WRITER

If you have seen *Black Hawk Down*, how does your assessment of it compare with Schickel's? If you have not seen this film, has this review made you want to see it? Why or why not?

For a quiz on this reading, go to www.bedfordstmartins.com/mirror.

Reality's Fight

NINA WILLDORF

Are sitcoms and drama shows becoming "'endangered species' in the wake of the reality-TV boom?" Will reality television become another enduring genre, like the cop show or family sitcom? Or are programs like *Survivor* and *Fear Factor* merely a passing fad? Nina Willdorf explores these questions in "Reality's Fight" and finds that the lure of reality TV is in voyeurism and exhibitionism. But in the wake of September 11, have viewers grown tired of reality TV? Do audiences long to be transported out of reality and into the fictional worlds of sitcoms and dramas?

A staff writer at the *Boston Phoenix*, Willdorf has won two awards from the New England Press Association for religious reporting and human interest feature writing. She has previously held jobs at the *Chronicle of Higher Education*, *Health* magazine, and the *New York Observer*. "Reality's Fight" first appeared in the *Boston Phoenix* on January 11, 2002.

THINKING AHEAD

Which reality television shows have you watched? What is your opinion of them? Why do they appeal to so many people? Who should watch these shows? Who should not?

INCREASING VOCABULARY

genre (n.) (1)	predominant (adj.) (12)
heralded (v.) (2)	maudlin (adj.) (12)
catapulted (v.) (3)	elegy (n.) (12)
saturated (adj.) (5)	niche (n.) (13)
blasé (adj.) (5)	premise (n.) (14)
titillating (adj.) (5)	taboo (adj.) (14)
voyeurism (n.) (5)	degenerated (v.) (14)
glut (n.) (6)	exhibitionism (n.) (16)
pillaging (n.) (10)	eschewed (v.) (16)
appropriating (n.) (10)	adherence (n.) (16)
debacle (n.) (11)	audibly (adv.) (17)

L ast month, the Associated Press exuberantly reported that the Miss 1
America Pageant is looking to incorporate elements of the so-called
reality-television genre into its competition. If the changes are approved by the individual states, the pageant, which will air next month on ABC, could loosely follow the format of CBS's phenomenally successful

Survivor, with losing contestants logging votes for the woman they think should win the crown.

Some consider this news yet another sign of the genre's success. During the past year, endless reports have shrilly heralded the arrival of the latest Fabulous New Reality Show—each more over-the-top than the last. *The BBC re-creates life in the trenches of World War I! MTV is casting for* Kidnapped! *Matt and Ben[1] want YOU to participate in their new reality-TV show,* The Runner! (All true.)

And the Nielsen ratings have fed the storm. This past season, *Survivor* beat long-standing favorite *Friends* in its Thursday-night slot. The gross-out[2] fest *Fear Factor* catapulted itself into first place in its time slot for a number of weeks. As Tom Shales at the *Washington Post* recently fretted, both the sit-com[3] and the quality drama are becoming "endangered species" in the wake of the reality-TV boom.

But other critics aren't too concerned. Despite a full roster of shows in the pipeline, scads of reality-inspired books and movies, and rah-rah back-patting in networks' high-rise boardrooms, many critics believe the reality-TV phenomenon of 2001 is like the teen-pop-star trend of 2000 or the Internet craze of 1999: bloated, self-congratulatory, out of touch, and on the fast track to a very necessary shake-out.

Says Mark Crispin Miller, professor of media studies at New York University and the author of *The Bush Dyslexicon* (Norton, 2001): "As the culture has become more saturated by TV, and as the audience has become more blasé, and as the industry has come to be dominated by a few giant, heavily debt-ridden players who have to compete with each other ever more frantically for the high ball, the content of TV has become more titillating." He pauses. "The kind of voyeurism that appeals today tends to be quite naked."

But he's not surprised. "This *always* happens," he says. "[The networks] all try to repeat what succeeded 10 minutes ago. There's a glut and then a number of them fail."

Cultural critic Douglas Rushkoff, author of several books, including the online open-source novel *Exit Strategy,* agrees: "It's over."

But if that's the case, where does television go next?

If you've been listening to the TV hype over the past two years, you might think that what's called reality television is innovative and fresh. But ask your parents: the truth is, the stuff's been around for decades. You can find its roots in shows like *Candid Camera, The National Lampoon Radio Hour,* and *Cops.*

Although the groundwork was laid as far back as the 1950s, today's reality shows seem more like bastard children of MTV, which aired the

---

[1] **ESL** **Matt and Ben:** Ben Affleck and Matt Damon, two popular movie actors.
[2] **ESL** **gross-out:** Inspiring repulsion.
[3] **ESL** **sit-com:** Television situation comedy usually dealing with everyday life.

first glorious episode of *The Real World* in 1992. Seven strangers were picked to live in a house, have their lives taped, and start getting *real*—and Americans were glued to their sets. The formula of intrigue, sexual tension, confession, angry confrontation, and coming-of-age—all on camera—was a winner. But European stations caught on faster than American ones. It wasn't until the honchos[4] at CBS picked up their binoculars, spotted a hit overseas, and created *Who Wants To Be a Millionaire?*—their own version of the British game show *Millionaire*—that the precedent was set for pillaging and appropriating European television shows.

After *Millionaire*, CBS followed by grabbing up and retooling the 11 Dutch show *Big Brother,* and then the Swedish program *Survivor.* Then, in the final hour, perhaps to save face after the failed debacle of the XFL[5], NBC—under the new direction of TV wunderkind[6] Jeff Zucker—stepped in with grosser, flashier, *realer* programming. In the past year, the network—which Salon.com's Joyce Millman dubbed "Nothing But Cruelty"—has raced to compete, offering reality shows including *Fear Factor* and *Spy TV.*

The predominant theory about the lure of reality TV can be summed 12 up in one word: voyeurism. The problem is, as with anything addictive—sugar, cigarettes, drugs—it's possible to have too much of a good (or, in this case, popular) thing. The tide already seems to be turning. Three weeks after Tom Shales's maudlin elegy for dramas and sit-coms, Nielsen spit out a whole new set of ratings showing that prime time was losing viewers across the board. Just two weeks later, noted *The Hollywood Reporter,* the spoils for all shows, including reality TV, were "meager." UPN's flop of a reality-TV show, *Manhunt,* couldn't even win a respectable number of viewers with a real scandal, when a contestant accused producers of rigging the show's final result and reshooting footage, and filed a complaint with the FCC. Must-see TV? More like who-cares TV.

Viewers weeping into their TV dinners can blame it on the Web. In 13 many ways, reality is the necessary new niche for television in the wake of the Internet. Before the dot-com days, television provided an immediacy that countered film's heavily edited, stylized form. But with its faster headlines, news reports, and up-to-the-minute services, the Net elbowed in on TV's territory, and the tube was forced to redefine itself. So-called reality television—which is in fact a heavily edited, pseudo-documentary[7] format—is the result.

The genre's whole premise is more, more, more. And not surprisingly, 14 what once seemed novel—the delivery of titillating and taboo inside dope[8]—has degenerated. It's like watching someone do a striptease: it

---

[4] **ESL** **honchos:** Leaders.
[5] **ESL** **XFL:** Extreme Football League.
[6] **ESL** **wunderkind:** Person who is extremely successful at a young age.
[7] **ESL** **pseudo-documentary:** A staged reenactment that mimics a real event.
[8] **ESL** **inside dope:** Insider information.

starts out sexy, but soon you become as blasé as a gynecologist. *Yeah, she's naked. So what?*

Douglas Rushkoff believes that all the behind-the-scenes access given   15
to viewers of shows like *Big Brother, The Real World,* and *Temptation Island* — the bathroom cam,[9] the bedroom cam, the watch-me-floss cam — has led the genre to its death cam.

"It's not as much voyeurism as it is about exhibitionism," Rushkoff   16
says. Sure enough, just look at the folks populating the programs: most are media whores hoping to find fame by logging face time[10] on prime time. Many are actors, musicians, or wanna-bes.[11] One of reality TV's biggest stars, *Survivor* host Jeff Probst, recently eschewed any adherence to "reality" by launching a career as a film director, with an upcoming indie flick,[12] *Finder's Fee.* "Most [people on reality programs] aren't behaving, they're auditioning for work," Rushkoff adds. "It's gotten so boring."

So what's next? Rushkoff, sighing audibly into the phone when asked   17
for his thoughts on the future of reality TV, wearily dismisses the genre. "By the time networks pick up on this stuff, it's already over," he says. "After O.J.[13] and Monica,[14] [viewers] are basically just passing the time until the next big scandal."

But despite the deathwatch, the genre isn't without its merits, or with-   18
out a future, argues Robert Thompson, director of Syracuse University's Center for the Study of Popular Television, who admits he's "countin' down the days" till upcoming reality program *Love Cruise* starts. A show like *Survivor* synthesizes "the unpredictability from sports" and "the catty[15] sexuality from soap operas," yet "ends with narrative steamrollers of voting out," Thompson says. "It's not another doctor, lawyer, detective show."

Thompson believes that shows like *Survivor,* the genre's best, will   19
eventually take their place in TV's ranks without pushing out other forms. "Reality TV of the kind we're seeing now is going to join the sit-com and the drama," he says. "There won't be as much of it on. It will be less exciting. It'll just become . . . just one of the other genres."

Thompson guesses that a show like *Big Brother,* which mixes the Web   20
(live shots are available 24 hours a day), the TV, and the mighty dollar (a show-themed board game, baseball caps, and T-shirts are all available), is paving the way for the future profitability of reality TV. "You can literally

---

[9] **ESL** **cam:** Abbreviation for "camera."
[10] **ESL** **face time:** Time someone is on camera.
[11] **ESL** **wanna-bes:** Persons who "want to be" like someone else.
[12] **ESL** **indie flick:** An independent movie, not associated with a major studio.
[13] **ESL** **O.J.:** O. J. Simpson, former football superstar who became the chief suspect in the murder of his wife, Nicole Simpson.
[14] **ESL** **Monica:** Monica Lewinsky, a White House intern famous for her affair with former president Bill Clinton.
[15] **ESL** **catty:** Vicious, conniving, spiteful.

stalk these characters," he says. "If I could have followed Farrah Fawcett around 24 hours a day after watching *Charlie's Angels*, that's how money could be made."

Obsessive in its access and not edited *enough*, *Big Brother* has a long   21 way to go before it can be expected to carry the Future of Television. Even Thompson doesn't think the show is "any good yet." But he believes it has the potential to "clear the real estate for TV and the Internet to become bosom buddies." He pauses. "The history of *that* is still to be written."

EXERCISING VOCABULARY

1. In paragraph 3, the author quotes Tom Shales, who described quality television shows as " 'endangered species.' " When you hear the term "endangered species," what do you usually think of? How can the term be applied to television shows?

2. In paragraph 4, Willdorf employs personification to describe the reality television trend as "bloated, self-congratulatory, [and] out of touch." What is personification? How does the author use personification in this sentence? How effective is its use in this context?

3. In paragraph 18, Willdorf, quoting Robert Thompson, says "A show like *Survivor* synthesizes 'the unpredictability from sports' and 'the catty sexuality from soap operas.'" What does the word *synthesize* mean? How does this definition apply to reality television? What is the noun form of this verb? What other things can be synthesized?

PROBING CONTENT

1. What does the author see as the future of reality television? Why?

2. According to the author, what is the primary reason that people watch reality television? Do you agree with this assessment?

3. According to Willdorf, is reality television a new idea? Explain your answer.

4. What is the relation between reality television and the Internet? Explain your response.

CONSIDERING CRAFT

1. Willdorf begins her essay with several examples of new scenarios for reality television shows. Describe some and explain why she opens her essay in this manner. How effective is this opening?

2. Reread paragraphs 18–20. Whose viewpoint does the author provide in these paragraphs? Why does she include this viewpoint in her essay? What message is she sending to her readers?

3. Willdorf quotes numerous other writers in her essay. Find several examples. Why does she use this strategy? How does her use of multiple sources affect your reaction to her argument?

RESPONDING TO THE WRITER

What do you believe the future will hold for reality television? What forces will determine its future? What other kinds of reality shows do you believe we will see in the near future?

For a quiz on this reading, go to www.bedfordstmartins.com/mirror.

Soaking Up Attention

James Poniewozik

Today's cartoons are smarter than the knock-offs of the 1970s and 1980s, when cartoons were largely created to sell toys. (Remember the *Smurfs*? *The Care Bears*?) Shows like *SpongeBob SquarePants* are a good example of how cartoons are changing, and Nickelodeon's squeaky-voiced sponge is getting a lot of attention — from both kids and adults. According to James Poniewozik, this dual appeal is a positive change for the world of cartoons. Do you agree? What do you think lies behind SpongeBob's appeal, and what might explain the narrowing gap between children's and adults' entertainment? Can you think of other cartoons that have become "not just hits but cultural icons" for people of all ages?

"Soaking Up Attention" first appeared in the December 17, 2001, issue of *Time* magazine, where Poniewozik is a staff writer. He previously wrote for Salon.com and has published his work in magazines including *Fortune, Rolling Stone, New York,* the *New York Times Book Review,* and *Talk.* Poniewozik also contributes radio commentary to WNYC and National Public Radio's "On the Media."

THINKING AHEAD

What were your favorite cartoons as a child? Why? Do you watch any cartoons now? If so, which ones do you watch? Why? If you no longer watch cartoons, why don't you? Explain your response.

INCREASING VOCABULARY

surrealistic (adj.) (2)	churned (v.) (5)
temperamentally (adv.) (4)	renaissance (n.) (5)
unruly (adj.) (4)	idiosyncratic (adj.) (5)
slump (n.) (5)	

I n America, if you want to be successful, you go to college, study hard and pack your head full of arcane[1] knowledge. Then you head for Hollywood and learn to tell plankton[2] jokes. That, anyway, was the route to fame and fortune for Stephen Hillenburg, an avid surfer, scuba diver and marine-biology teacher fascinated with tide-pool life. After he later went to art school and became an animator, he decided to base his debut

---

[1] arcane: Difficult or impossible to understand.
[2] plankton: A mass of tiny animals and plants found in the sea or in lakes and eaten by fish and other aquatic animals.

cartoon, loosely, on the creatures that he had made his life's study. *Very loosely.* His star: a talking sponge who wears a tie, flips Krabbie Patties at a submarine fast-food joint and resembles a slice of Swiss cheese more than his real-water counterparts.

Hail SpongeBob SquarePants: delightfully biologically incorrect and the new invertebrate king of children's television. Launched in 1999, his sweet, surrealistic, self-titled Nickelodeon cartoon recently unseated the long-reigning *Rugrats* as the most popular kids' show on TV, attracting an average of 10 million kids ages two to eleven (and more than 5 million adults) each week.

Not bad for a complete nerd. Hillenburg says he conceived SpongeBob as an offbeat, dweeby[3] child-man in the mold of Pee-wee Herman.[4] (Hillenburg, who wears a funky[5] surfer haircut at age forty and hangs sea-life mobiles outside his office, fits the offbeat, dweeby child-man profile a bit himself.) Like Pee-wee, the squeaky-voiced sponge lives in a colorful, goofy wonderland—inside an undersea pineapple in the town of Bikini Bottom. "I wanted to create a small town underwater where the characters were more like us than like fish," Hillenburg says. "They have fire. They take walks. They drive. They have pets and holidays." Of course, there are a few differences. In Bikini Bottom, no one thinks it's strange that the town villain, the megalomaniacal[6] Plankton, is a one-celled organism, or that SpongeBob's boss, a crab, has a daughter who's a whale (literally).

Like Pee-wee's appeal, SpongeBob's lies in his innocence. He's the anti–Bart Simpson,[7] temperamentally and physically: his head is as squared-off and neat as Bart's is unruly, and he has a personality to match—conscientious, optimistic and blind to the faults in the world and those around him. He never seems to notice that his cynical neighbor and co-worker Squidward (an octopus) drips contempt toward everything SpongeBob does, or that his best friend Patrick Starfish is a certified nitwit.[8] Kids are drawn by the show's loopy[9] slapstick, grownups by its dry (so to speak) wit: "I order the food, and you cook the food," Squidward tells SpongeBob, describing their jobs at the restaurant. "We do that for 40 years, and then we die."

That dual appeal is a sign of a welcome change in animation. Cartoons have bridged kids' and adult entertainment since the heyday of Walt Disney and Chuck Jones,[10] but the field went through a long creative slump in

---

[3] **ESL** dweeby: Unpopular and weak.
[4] **ESL** Pee-wee Herman: Star of a popular children's show from the 1980s that featured a grown man acting like a child.
[5] **ESL** funky: Strange, neat, or cool.
[6] megalomaniacal: Enjoying having power over other people and craving more of it.
[7] Bart Simpson: The precocious main character of Fox's popular animated television program, *The Simpsons*.
[8] **ESL** nitwit: Someone with limited intelligence.
[9] **ESL** loopy: Crazy or out-of-control.
[10] Chuck Jones: American motion-picture animator, writer, director, and producer, known for his work on Looney Tunes cartoons.

the '70s and '80s, as programmers churned out Saturday-morning knock-
offs made mainly to shill[11] toys (*My Little Pony*) or repurpose sitcom characters (*The Fonz and the Happy Days Gang*). Today cartoons have under-
gone a renaissance, as kids' channels such as Nickelodeon and Cartoon
Network have given their animators the freedom of auteurs.[12] Smarter and
more idiosyncratic, these animators have created shows like Cartoon Network's *The Powerpuff Girls* that have become not just hits but cultural
icons. "It harkens back to the old days at Warner Bros., when guys were
creating Daffy Duck and Bugs Bunny, and they had free rein,"[13] says *Powerpuff* creator Craig McCracken. There's still plenty of toy-driven junk,
particularly in the animé-action[14] category, but cartoons have also become
more diverse (with new entries like Disney Channel's African-American
The Proud Family) and ambitious (Cartoon Network's epic *Samurai Jack*).

Of course, there's still cashing in to be done—SpongeBob has lent his   6
image to Target, Burger King and Nabisco Cheese Nips, and a SpongeBob
movie is in the works. But Hillenburg says, the art comes first. "I could
get more money from a [broadcast] network," he says, but "I was interested in doing the show the way I wanted." Now that creators like him
can do that, it is, in the world of cartoons at least, a great time to be a kid,
a grownup or—best of all—a little of each.

EXERCISING VOCABULARY

1. In paragraph 4, Poniewozik writes that "Kids are drawn by the show's loopy
   slapstick, grownups by its dry (so to speak) wit." What is slapstick comedy?
   How does the word itself reflect the content of old slapstick routines? What
   is dry wit? Why does the author add the phrase in parentheses between *dry*
   and *wit*?

2. In paragraph 5, Poniewozik argues that "Cartoons have bridged kids' and
   adult entertainment since the heyday of Walt Disney and Chuck Jones." What
   is the purpose of a bridge? How does the author use this term here? How effective is his word choice? What other term could he have used?

PROBING CONTENT

1. Who is the creator of *SpongeBob SquarePants*? How did his lifestyle and
   schooling influence the subject matter of the show?

2. What kind of character did Hillenburg wish to create with SpongeBob? After
   which real-life television and movie actor did Hillenburg model SpongeBob?

---

[11] **shill:** To promote a product for reasons of self-interest.
[12] **auteurs:** Authors or originators.
[13] ESL **free rein:** Freedom or liberty to do what one pleases.
[14] ESL **animé-action:** A type of Japanese cartoon.

3. Where does SpongeBob live? What kind of a place is this? Describe some of his neighbors.

4. How have cartoons changed since the 1970s and 1980s? How has the audience changed? How does Poniewozik view this change?

CONSIDERING CRAFT

1. Examine the title of the essay. What play on words do you notice? Explain how this phrase works as a clever introduction to the essay.

2. Reread the first two sentences of the essay. What did you expect the second sentence to say? How does the second sentence relate to the first? Why does Poniewozik open his essay in this manner?

3. Poniewozik alludes to other cartoon shows and their characters by name. Find and study several examples. Why do you think the author employs this strategy? How does it affect your reading of the essay?

4. In paragraph 5, Poniewozik says that some of the new cartoon characters like *The Powerpuff Girls* have become "not just hits but cultural icons." Explain how something or someone becomes a cultural icon. What effect does the author's comparison of animated characters to icons have on your reading? Why does he reserve this comparison for late in the essay?

RESPONDING TO THE WRITER

Poniewozik mentions in the final paragraph that "there's still cashing in to be done." In what ways does the co-branding or merchandising of *SpongeBob SquarePants* affect its appeal for adults and children? How then will this show ultimately differ from the cartoons of the 1970s and 1980s that the author terms "Saturday-morning knock-offs made mainly to shill toys" (para. 5)?

For a quiz on this reading, go to www.bedfordstmartins.com/mirror.

Barrier Between Adults' and Children's Entertainment Is Breaking Down

Louise Kennedy

Is there a way to create art that speaks to both children and adults? Is the line between what's made for kids and what's made for adults becoming harder to define today? In this essay, Louise Kennedy examines several recent films that are popular with viewers of all ages. Are *Harry Potter and the Sorcerer's Stone, Shrek,* and *Monsters, Inc.* really as "family friendly" as marketers make them out to be? In Kennedy's opinion, they're not: "[It's] not about what will satisfy or enlighten children and their parents; it's about what will open their wallets." This kind of marketing, she argues, harms both children and adults. Do you agree with the author's assessment, or do you feel more positively about this line-blurring? Could it bring parents and children together?

Kennedy began working as an editor for the *Boston Globe* in 1988 and is now a columnist for the *Boston Globe Magazine,* where this essay first appeared on January 13, 2002. She has also worked as a freelance reporter for both the *New Haven Register* and the *New Haven Advocate* and has published in *New England Monthly.* She is currently at work on *Roar into Reading,* a guide to help parents teach their children to read.

THINKING AHEAD

What is the difference between adults' and children's entertainment? In what ways can "children's" television shows, movies, games, or books appeal to adults? In what ways can "adult" entertainment appeal to children? Give specific examples.

INCREASING VOCABULARY

allusions (n.) (5)

incisive (adj.) (5)

provoke (v.) (5)

panders (v.) (7)

cynical (adj.) (7)

freighted (adj.) (7)

mainstream (adj.) (8)

ceded (v.) (8)

graphic (adj.) (8)

succumbing (v.) (8)

consign (v.) (8)

L et's imagine two people. One loves *Harry Potter,* collects *Scooby-Doo* action figures, spends hours every week playing computer games, and couldn't wait to see *The Lord of the Rings.* 1

The other trades stocks online, watches *The Sopranos,* wouldn't be caught dead at any movie rated G, and is thinking of starting his own 2

Web-based business. Now, let's say one of these people is forty-nine, and the other is twelve.

Which one is which?   3

And what does it mean that we can't tell? Clearly, something is happening to the line between children and adults. Adults play children's games, read children's books, and watch children's movies more than ever before; children, meanwhile, surf freely through the adult world online and on TV, encountering images and ideas that only fifty years ago would have been strictly off-limits. Adults try to look younger and children try to look older; sometimes it feels as if the whole world wants to be sixteen.   4

Meanwhile, the distinction between items created for adults and those intended for kids seems harder and harder to make. Is *SpongeBob SquarePants* really a cartoon for kids, and is *Fear Factor* really aimed at grown men and women? Who's meant to watch professional wrestling? And if Daniel Handler is writing his Lemony Snicket books strictly for children, why do they include allusions to Sunny von Bulow[1] and Albert Camus?[2] Sometimes, as in Lemony Snicket's case, the blurring of boundaries results in a delightful entertainment for all ages; sometimes it even goes on to create powerful art. The first installment of *The Lord of the Rings,* to the surprise of those of us who had lumped it in with Dungeons & Dragons,[3] combines sweeping action and grand themes to reach all but the youngest audiences. *The Simpsons* remains fresh and incisive, still managing to provoke both adult thinking and childlike glee. And, in my house at least, everybody loves the big heart and big laughs of *Malcolm in the Middle.*   5

But let's consider the three top-grossing movies of 2001: *Harry Potter and the Sorcerer's Stone, Shrek,* and *Monsters, Inc.* Are they for children or for adults? The industry skirts that question by calling them "family films," a term that marketers love because it means they can sell to everybody. And, given the success of *Harry Potter* and *The Fellowship of the Ring,* Hollywood is already racing to work on a whole new crop of family-friendly flicks, based on such old favorites as *Curious George, The Cat in the Hat,* and *Where the Wild Things Are.*   6

The hype would have you believe that this is a golden age for children's movies, but the bottom line is the bottom line: These familiar titles make it easy to cross-market and cross-promote the books, movies, and action figures all at once. It's not about what will satisfy or enlighten children and their parents; it's about what will open their wallets. Just look at, say, *Shrek,* with its weird mix of gross-out potty humor and nasty Hollywood in-jokes. This isn't art that appeals simultaneously to the deepest   7

---

[1] **Sunny von Bulow:** The diabetic wife of Claus von Bulow. She has been in a coma since her husband allegedly tried to kill her with an overdose of insulin.

[2] **Albert Camus (1913–1960):** Algerian-born French existential novelist, essayist, and dramatist.

[3] **Dungeons & Dragons:** Famous role-playing game invented in the 1970s.

longings of children and adults; it's a marketing vehicle that panders to adults' lowest impulses and at the same time asks of children a cynical knowingness that they'd be better off waiting years to acquire. *Monsters, Inc.*, though it's lighter and less freighted with insider baggage, also contains too much winking at adults to make real sense to young kids, and too little thematic depth or sophistication to hold lasting meaning for adults. No wonder everyone's wild about *Harry*—even though it's far too frightening for any child under eight.

If it sounds old-fashioned or overprotective to make that kind of blanket statement, maybe that's an indication of where we are. The mainstream culture has ceded to conservatives the idea that some things are too graphic, too frightening, or just too much for young children; to draw the line is to mark ourselves as squares. But isn't it possible to say that we want children to be children, and adults to be adults, without succumbing to a sugarcoated fantasy of childish innocence on the one hand and a wisecracking dystopia[4] of aging cynics on the other? For one of the strangest things about the current blurring of childhood and adulthood is that it presents, as the sole alternative, a rigid and oversimplified division of the world. Either take your child to a movie that's too adolescent for either of you, or consign him to the pastel paradise of *Dragon Tales* while you dive into *Hannibal,* with its soullessly jokey gore. But surely there's a way to make art that speaks to both children and adults—that enriches our sense of what it means to be human, no matter how old a human we happen to be.

"There is a category of brilliance which is neither stupid and innocent nor winking and blinking," says the artist and author Maurice Sendak. "It's very hard to walk that line." . . .

Crossing a line

Even as children move into the adult realm, adults drift back into the entertainments of their childhood. They collect toys, watch cartoons, play games. That's a shift that goes back at least to the 1950s, says Henry Jenkins, who directs comparative media studies at MIT and is the editor of *The Children's Culture Reader.* After World War II, fathers were encouraged to come home and play with their kids—not just for the kids' sake, but because it was good for the dads, too. And the kids who grew up with more playful dads, Jenkins says, "have become a generation of adults who want to hold on to play even later, and even if they have no children." Can you say "baby boomers"? The generation that began by refusing to trust anyone over 30, with all its members now past that milestone, still insists on acting forever young. "A lot of the crossover happened in the '60s, early '70s," says Michael Patrick Hearn, because teen

8

9

10

---

[4] dystopia: An invented society with lower values and quality of life.

culture became infantilized. "They didn't want to grow up," says Hearn, whose *Annotated Wizard of Oz* and *Annotated Huckleberry Finn* appeal as much to adults as to children, "so you stay within the child's culture." Young adults then read *The Velveteen Rabbit* and *The Little Prince,* J.R.R. Tolkien and *Alice in Wonderland;* on the radio, they listened to "White Rabbit" or *House at Pooh Corner.*

Now, "there's a lot of crossover" again, Hearn says. These same   11
people are returning to Tolkien, rediscovering picture books, picking up comics and buying tickets to *Scooby-Doo in Stage Fright*—playing downtown right now. While he thinks some adult interest in children's literature arises from the universal desire for compelling narratives and vivid characters, which modern adult literature has often *scanted,* he's blunt about another cause for the blur: "I think it's a marketing tool," he says. "They're trying to get as many markets as they can."

Film writer David Thomson agrees that the influence of marketing is   12
pervasive. "It constantly amazes me," he says, "how much television has advertising aimed at children," with the result that the "purchasing ambition" of children "has just been building steadily through the 20th century." Thomson also cites the growing tendency to market movies to teenagers. And beyond that, he says, "'Teenager' is a thing that seems to me to be reaching back into childhood. I have a twelve-year-old; he's been a teenager since he was ten. Children are sort of getting into that act earlier. Teenism, or whatever you want to call it, is extending forward and backward."

Culture medium?

So will we all, in fact, end up acting sixteen forever? And if we do, what   13
happens to the genuinely free spirit of child's play and the genuinely complex pleasures of adult seriousness? It might sound like a marketer's dream to have everyone going back to see *Shrek* twelve times, then marching in *lockstep* to the next big thing, but surely it's possible to create a culture that's deeper, richer, and wilder than that. . . .

EXERCISING VOCABULARY

1. In paragraph 7, Kennedy states that *Monsters, Inc.* is "lighter" and less "freighted with insider baggage" than *Shrek.* How can one movie be "lighter" than another? What is "insider baggage"? What does the author imply about these two movies by using this phrase?

2. In paragraph 8, Kennedy mentions a "sugarcoated fantasy of childish innocence." What does it mean to sugarcoat something? How can childish innocence be described as a sugarcoated fantasy?

PROBING CONTENT

1. According to Kennedy, what is happening to adults' and children's entertainment? What evidence does she provide to support her argument?

2. What does Kennedy think of popular children's movies today? What two major examples does she use to drive her point home? What does she say about these two movies?

3. According to the essay, what have adults desired since the 1950s? What part has marketing played in capitalizing on these desires?

4. How has marketing influenced children? What does Kennedy think of the "crossover" between adults' and children's entertainment?

CONSIDERING CRAFT

1. Reread the first three paragraphs. What is unusual about the way the author begins her essay? How does her opening writing strategy affect your reading?

2. Kennedy asks many questions in her essay. Find several examples, beginning with the fourth paragraph. Why does she include so many questions? Does she expect answers? What part do these questions play in the development of her argument?

3. Kennedy uses many specific examples of movies, television shows, books, and games in her essay. Locate several of these examples. How do they function in the essay? From your perspective as a reader, how well do these examples serve the author's purpose?

RESPONDING TO THE WRITER

Do you consider the crossover between adults' and children's entertainment to be beneficial, problematic, or a combination of the two? Answer the question posed in this essay by considering your own experiences and those of your friends and family.

For a quiz on this reading, go to www.bedfordstmartins.com/mirror.

DRAWING CONNECTIONS

1. Louise Kennedy asks, "Is *SpongeBob SquarePants* really a cartoon for kids, and is *Fear Factor* really aimed at grown men and women?" (para. 5). What is her implied answer to these rhetorical questions? How do you think her opinion of these shows would compare to Poniewozik's opinion?

2. Poniewozik ends his essay "Soaking Up Attention" by saying that "it is, in the world of cartoons at least, a great time to be a kid, a grownup or — best of all — a little of each." How would Louise Kennedy respond to that statement? What is your response?

Wrapping Up Chapter 7

REFLECTING ON THE WRITING

1. "The 'Fragile American Girl' Myth" from Chapter 2 and "Brave New Girls" from this chapter both refer to Dr. Mary Pipher's book *Reviving Ophelia: Saving the Selves of Adolescent Girls* (1994). Using information from the essays as well as your own observations and experiences, write an essay in which you argue either for or against Dr. Pipher's thesis that our society destroys the self-esteem and potential of adolescent girls.

2. Read the essays by Louise Kennedy ("Barrier Between Adults' and Children's Entertainment Is Breaking Down") and George Felton ("Wrestling with Myself," Chapter 9). Then write an essay in which you answer the question posed by Kennedy: "Who's meant to watch professional wrestling?" (para. 5). Refer to both essays in your paper.

3. Using the essays in this chapter as well as your own observations and experiences, write an essay in which you discuss how the self-image of men or women is handled or mishandled in movies or on television shows. Include several specific examples from movies or television. You may also refer to other essays in this book, such as those in Chapters 2, 3, and 4.

4. Watch several episodes of *Sabrina the Teenage Witch, Charmed, Buffy the Vampire Slayer, Xena, Alias, Dark Angel,* or any other television show that features a strong female hero. Write an essay in which you analyze the roles of men in the episodes you watched. How are the men portrayed? What similarities and differences do you observe among the male characters? Be sure to discuss their relationships with the main female characters.

CONNECTING TO THE CULTURE

1. Watch several different reality television shows during one week. Use specific examples from what you watch to prove or disprove the idea that reality television is "bloated, self-congratulatory, out of touch, and on the fast track to a very necessary shake-out" as Nina Willdorf asserts in "Reality's Fight" (para. 4).

2. Watch several different talk shows during one week. Use specific examples from what you watch to prove or disprove the idea that talk television offers "cheap thrills and bad advice," as the authors of "Tuning in Trouble" assert (para. 17).

3. Reread Stephen King's "Why We Crave Horror Movies." Write an essay in which you agree or disagree with his argument that horror films allow a safe release for what would otherwise be expressed as insane or even criminal behavior. You may extend your argument to include other forms of "dangerous" leisure-time activities like playing violent video or computer games, watching violent television shows, reading violent novels, or listening to violent music. George Felton's essay in Chapter 9, "Wrestling with Myself," may prove useful as you develop your ideas.

FOCUSING ON YESTERDAY, FOCUSING ON TODAY

PSYCHO *Scream*

Screams, from both the actors and the audience, have always been associated with horror movies. Two of the most famous film screams are shown here: Janet Leigh's in the Alfred Hitchcock classic *Psycho* (1960) and Drew Barrymore's in the first movie in Wes Craven's wildly popular *Scream* series (1996). *Psycho* is the tale of Norman, a nice young man turned serial killer who runs the Bates motel, where guests check in and then check out permanently. This photo from the movie shows Janet Leigh's character Marion Crane as she encounters her killer in the infamous shower scene. The *Scream* photo shows a terrified Drew Barrymore listening to the person who has just murdered her boyfriend in the backyard and will murder her momentarily.

What exactly do these two images convey? What part of each woman's face is featured most prominently? Based on these two images alone, how do you think horror films have changed since the 1960s? Do the same elements frighten us today? How has the depiction of women changed from classic horror movies to contemporary ones?

SCREAM *Scream*

CHAPTER 8

What's That Sound?
How Music and Culture Mix It Up

This car advertisement, which appeared in a music magazine, highlights a significant moment from a rock concert. The ad capitalizes on the power of music, morphing what could be a pure musical experience into a selling tool.

- Why did the ad designer choose this unusual setting for a car ad?
- What is significant about the bracelet on the arm shown in this ad?
- What is the association between going to a rock concert and wanting to buy a car?
- Have you ever been to a concert where people have held up their lighters? What kind of song is usually playing when this happens? Why is this significant?

Research this topic with TopLinks at www.bedfordstmartins.com/toplinks.

GEARING UP

What kinds of music do you listen to? When do you listen? Where? What effect does listening have on you? What songs do you associate with special occasions, events, or memories? Who are your favorite musical performers? What would influence you to listen to a kind of music you haven't heard or liked before?

What medium other than music is as completely bound up in the culture that creates it? The sounds change as the instruments do, the lyrics and language keep pace with our fears and our ambitions, and rhythm and meaning continue to be created. Music, like other forms of communication, is both personal and communal. Our powerful response to music comes from deep within us and may sometimes surprise us with its intensity. Like smells or photographs, songs have the power to recreate significant events and even entire periods of our lives. The kinds of music we like and the songs that reside in our heads, refusing to go away, are as indicative of who and what we are as the clothes we wear, the books we read, and the causes we support.

We react to a song individually, but when many of us react positively to the same songs, musical success happens. Of course, it's not all magic — our musical tastes, like our tastes in fast food or jeans, are always being bombarded by the media. And just as fashions recycle themselves, so do musical trends. What's old suddenly becomes hot again; what was hot yesterday is cold today. Recycled musical trends are a little different from their sources. They are impacted by new instruments, new voices, new rhythms, and new times. But it's worth a glance backward to see where the sounds have been heard before.

COLLABORATING

In small groups of three or four, discuss why music is important to each of you. Find out everyone's favorite kind of music. See if you can explain why some music maintains its popularity from one generation to the next, but other musical groups and songs fail to last from one Grammy season to another.

I Hate World Music

DAVID BYRNE

What do you think of when you hear the term *world music?* Do you think of music that is exotic but has nothing to do with your life? If so, you're among the majority of pop music listeners. But David Byrne, whose band Talking Heads helped shape popular music today, disagrees: "To restrict your listening to English-language pop is like deciding to eat the same meal for the rest of your life." To Byrne, the term "world music" is a way of dismissing artists; it places musicians into "us" and "them" categories. And if we ignore music because it's not familiar to us, we will likely miss out on rewarding experiences. As Byrne writes, "There are times when you want to be transported, to get your mind around some stuff it never encountered before. And what if the thing transporting you doesn't come from your neighborhood?"

Byrne is an accomplished musician, photographer, writer, and actor. He played with the band Talking Heads from 1980 until its demise in 1991. Since then, he has formed the pop label Luaka Bop and has co-produced many of its albums. Byrne's solo efforts include *In Spite of Wishing and Wanting, Rei Momo,* and his latest, *Look into the Eyeball.* He has also written many books, including *Strange Ritual* (1995), *Your Action World* (1999), and *New Sins* (2001). This selection is an excerpt from "I Hate World Music" which was originally published in the *New York Times,* October 3, 1999.

THINKING AHEAD

How popular is the music of foreign countries in the United States? Do you hear it on the radio? Buy the CDs? From which foreign countries? Which artists? How familiar are you and your friends with music from beyond our borders? Name several musical artists who record in a language other than English.

INCREASING VOCABULARY

perverse (adj) (1)

blatantly (adv.) (1)

surreal (adj.) (1)

relegating (v.) (2)

exotic (adj.) (2)

hegemony (n.) (2)

audacious (adj.) (2)

subversive (adj.) (5)

cathartic (adj.) (7)

contaminated (adj.) (9)

I hate world music. That's probably one of the perverse reasons I have been asked to write about it. The term is a catchall[1] that commonly refers to non-Western music of any and all sorts, popular music, traditional music and even classical music. It's a marketing as well as a pseudo-musical term—and a name for a bin in the record store signifying stuff that doesn't belong anywhere else in the store. What's in that bin ranges from the most blatantly commercial music produced by a country, like Hindi film music (the singer Asha Bhosle being the best well-known example), to the ultra-sophisticated, super-cosmopolitan art-pop of Brazil (Caetano Veloso, Tom Zé, Carlinhos Brown); from the somewhat bizarre and surreal concept of a former Bulgarian state-run folkloric choir being arranged by classically trained, Soviet-era composers (Le Mystère des Voix Bulgares) to Norteño songs from Texas and northern Mexico glorifying the exploits of drug dealers (Los Tigres del Norte). Albums by Selena, Ricky Martin and Los Del Rio (the Macarena kings), artists who sell millions of records in the United States alone, are racked next to field recordings of Thai hill tribes. Equating apples and oranges[2] indeed. So, from a purely democratic standpoint, one in which all music is equal, regardless of sales and slickness of production, this is a musical utopia.

In my experience, the use of the term *world music* is a way of dismissing artists or their music as irrelevant to one's own life. It's a way of relegating this "thing" into the realm of something exotic and therefore cute, weird but safe, because exotica is beautiful but irrelevant; they are, by definition, not like us. Maybe that's why I hate the term. It groups everything and anything that isn't "us" into "them." This grouping is a convenient way of not seeing a band or artist as a creative individual, albeit from a culture somewhat different from that seen on American television. It's a label for anything at all that is not sung in English or anything that doesn't fit into the Anglo-Western pop universe this year. (So Ricky Martin is allowed out of the world music ghetto—for a while, anyway. Next year, who knows? If he makes a plena[3] record, he might have to go back to the salsa[4] bins and the Latin mom and pop record stores.) It's a none too subtle way of reasserting the hegemony of Western pop culture. It ghettoizes most of the world's music. A bold and audacious move, White Man!

There is some terrific music being made all over the world. In fact, there is more music, in sheer quantity, currently defined as world music than any other kind. Not just kinds of music, but volume of recordings as well. When we talk about world music we find ourselves talking about 99 percent of the music on this planet. It would be strange to imagine, as

---

[1] **catchall:** A place to collect dissimilar things.

[2] **ESL equating apples and oranges:** Attributing likeness to two completely different things.

[3] **plena:** A style of Puerto Rican folk music with West African influences.

[4] **salsa:** Popular music of Latin American origin that has absorbed characteristics of rhythm and blues, jazz, and rock.

many multinational corporations seem to, that Western pop holds the copyright on musical creativity.

No, the fact is, Western pop is the fast food of music, and there is more exciting creative music making going on outside the Western pop tradition than inside it. There is so much incredible noise happening that we'll never exhaust it. For example, there are guitar bands in Africa that can be, if you let them, as inspiring and transporting as any kind of rock, pop, soul, funk or disco you grew up with. And what is exciting for me is that they have taken elements of global (Western?) music apart, examined the pieces to see what might be of use and then re-invented and reassembled the parts to their own ends. Thus creating something entirely new. (Femi Kuti gave a great show the other night that was part Coltrane, part James Brown and all African, just like his daddy, Fela Kuti, the great Nigerian musical mastermind.)

To restrict your listening to English-language pop is like deciding to eat the same meal for the rest of your life. The "no-surprise surprise," as the Holiday Inn advertisement claims, is reassuring, I guess, but lacks kick. As ridiculous as they often sound, the conservative critics of rock-and-roll, and more recently of techno[5] and rave,[6] are not far off the mark. For at its best, music truly is subversive and dangerous. Thank the gods.

Hearing the right piece of music at the right time of your life can inspire a radical change, destructive personal behavior or even fascist[7] politics. Sometimes all at the same time.

On the other hand, music can inspire love, religious ecstasy, cathartic release, social bonding and a glimpse of another dimension. A sense that there is another time, another space and another, better universe. It can heal a broken heart, offer a shoulder to cry on and a friend when no one else understands. There are times when you want to be transported, to get your mind around[8] some stuff it never encountered before. And what if the thing transporting you doesn't come from your neighborhood?

This interest in music not like that made in our own little villages (Dumbarton, Scotland, and Arbutus, Md., in my own case) is not, as it's often claimed, cultural tourism, because once you've let something in, let it grab hold of you, you're forever changed. Of course, you can also listen and remain completely unaffected and unmoved—like a tourist. Your loss. The fact is, after listening to some of this music for a while, it probably won't seem exotic any more, even if you still don't understand all the words. Thinking of things as exotic is only cool when it's your sister, your co-worker or wife; it's sometimes beneficial to exoticize that which has

---

[5] **techno:** A type of rhythmic electronic dance music.

[6] **rave:** A type of electronic dance music.

[7] **fascist:** Having a tendency toward or actually exercising strong autocratic or dictatorial control.

[8] **ESL** **to get your mind around:** To understand.

become overly familiar. But in other circumstances, viewing people and cultures as exotic is a distancing mechanism that too often allows for exploitation and racism.

Maybe it's naive, but I would love to believe that once you grow to   9
love some aspect of a culture—its music, for instance—you can never again think of the people of that culture as less than yourself. I would like to believe that if I am deeply moved by a song originating from someplace other than my own hometown, then I have in some way shared an experience with the people of that culture. I have been pleasantly contaminated. I can identify in some small way with it and its people. Not that I will ever experience music exactly the same way as those who make it. I am not Hank Williams, or even Hank Jr., but I can still love his music and be moved by it. Doesn't mean I have to live like him. Or take as many drugs as he did, or, for that matter, as much as the great flamenco[9] singer Cameron de la Isla did.

That's what art does; it communicates the vibe,[10] the feeling, the atti-   10
tude toward our lives, in a way that is personal and universal at the same time. And we don't have to go through all the personal torment that the artist went through to get it. I would like to think that if you love a piece of music, how can you help but love, or at least respect, the producers of it? On the other hand, I know plenty of racists who love "soul" music, rap and rhythm-and-blues, so dream on, Dave.

EXERCISING VOCABULARY

1. Byrne refers to world music as both a marketing and a "pseudomusical" term (para. 1). What does the prefix "pseudo" mean? What denotative and connotative meanings does the term pseudomusical have? What attitude about the subject of world music does the term imply?

2. What kind of place is a utopia? To what extent would a music store that featured music from all over the world fit this definition?

3. What relationship usually exists between tourists and the places they visit? Why does Byrne state that a genuine interest in music from a different part of the world must be more than "cultural tourism" (para. 8)? What might happen to a musical adventurer who decides to move beyond cultural tourism?

PROBING CONTENT

1. How does Byrne define world music? Why is he so irritated by this term? In what sense does the use of this term "ghettoize" the music of other cultures?

---

[9] **flamenco:** A vigorous rhythmic dance style of the Andalusian Gypsies and the music that accompanies such dance.
[10] **ESL** **vibe:** A sense or a feeling.

2. How does Byrne describe English-language pop music in paragraphs 4 and 5? What is his opinion of this music?

3. What are some of the effects, both positive and negative, that music may have on a listener? Use several specific examples from this essay.

4. What does the author hope may be the broader effect of listening to another culture's music? How optimistic is he about such an occurrence? Support your answer with material from the text.

CONSIDERING CRAFT

1. David Byrne's unique perspective on the subject of popular music certainly influences this essay's point of view. Who is Byrne? Why is he particularly qualified to offer his opinion on this topic?

2. Examine the author's tone throughout this essay. Look at paragraphs 5 and 10, for example. How and when does his tone vary? How well does his tone help to convey his message?

3. In this relatively brief essay, Byrne often uses words in an unfamiliar way ("ghettoizes" in para. 2) or combines terms not usually joined together ("pleasantly contaminated" in para. 9). Does this unusual word choice hamper or enhance his writing? Explain your answer.

RESPONDING TO THE WRITER

Do you accept Byrne's argument that music from other countries has not been given an equal opportunity in the United States? Should such music get as much shelf space and air time on the radio as American music? Why or why not?

For a quiz on this reading, go to www.bedfordstmartins.com/mirror.

Same Old Song

Lorraine Ali

In "Same Old Song," first published in *Newsweek* on October 9, 2000, Lorraine Ali writes that pop music essentially stays the same, despite changing. And whichever decade you consider, its music is often designed to make elders angry. Music's shock value, however, gets turned up a notch with every generation, and today, lyrics with themes of sex and violence are increasingly dominating the charts. The new frontier in music is a rebellion against political correctness: women are debased and degraded, "excess and greed are extolled as worthy attributes." The result? Pop is as predictable as an action movie. Is shock value being used as a selling tool — a substitute for musical innovation and originality?

Ali is a general editor at *Newsweek* who primarily covers music for the magazine's Arts and Entertainment section. She has written about everything from Christian alternative rock to Latino Lone Star rap and has interviewed musicians from Dolly Parton to Marilyn Manson. Ali has contributed stories to the *New York Times, GQ,* and *Rolling Stone,* and her piece on Palestinian rappers ("West Bank Hardcore") was recently included in *DaCapo's Best Music Writing 2001.* She is currently working on a book about growing up Arab American.

THINKING AHEAD

Why is some of today's music offensive to some adults? Are they upset in the same way and for the same reasons that adults in the past were upset by Elvis Presley and with groups like the Beatles? Which elements are the same? Which elements are different?

INCREASING VOCABULARY

avid (adj.) (1)
esthetic (adj.) (2)
irk (v.) (2)
saturated (adj.) (5)
proliferate (v.) (5)
precursor (n.) (6)
induced (v.) (6)
debased (v.) (6)
retool (v.) (6)

vilest (adj.) (6)
revitalized (v.) (7)
misogyny (n.) (7)
homophobia (n.) (7)
jaded (adj.) (8)
desensitized (adj.) (8)
vacuous (adj.) (9)
withers (v.) (9)

All the controversy, criticism and praise surrounding Eminem's recent release *The Marshall Mathers LP* finally caused a fiftyish coworker of mine to go out and buy the album to see what all the commotion was about. It's not as if he was treading on totally foreign terrain—he did, after all, love N.W.A.'s *Straight Outta Compton* when it came out a dozen years ago, and has avid interest in most anything that rubs people the wrong way. He just needed to know what the newest source of outrage was all about. He locked himself in his office and came out an hour later. "Wow," he said. "This sure isn't for adults."

He was right. And that's the point: pop music is an esthetic and consumer product targeted at kids between grade school and grad school, and often designed to irk their elders. It's been that way since young Frank Sinatra crooned[1] to screaming girls in the 1940s, Little Richard camped and gyrated in the '50s, the Beatles championed free love in the '60s, the Sex Pistols spat on fans in the '70s and Public Enemy instilled fear of a black planet in 1990. Throughout each trend and era, parents have been deeply concerned and kids have done their best to keep them that way.

Things get ratcheted up a notch with every generation. You're not rebelling if you're listening to the same stuff your parents did; you're embarrassing yourself. Remember Jim Morrison's hammy Oedipal[2] psychodrama[3] in the Doors' "The End" (1967): "Father, I want to kill you! Mother, I want to . . . arrgh!" Eminem's cartoonish "Kill You" moves the ball forward by collapsing both parents into a single Bad Mommy to be raped and murdered. Those parental warning stickers may really be for parents, as if to say, "Hey, there's stuff in here your kid will understand and you won't."

There's a hitch. As every book about raising kids will tell you, children need limits—in part to protect them, and in part to give them boundaries to smash and trample. Generation after generation of iconoclasts,[4] from Joyce and Picasso to Elvis and Marilyn to punks and gangstas, have gradually pushed the limits a little further. When N.W.A. dropped "F—k Tha Police" in 1988, it was a shocking moment. When DMX conveys essentially the same sentiments, who really notices? Even N.W.A.'s raps about killing rivals "like it ain't no thang" weren't so far from Johnny Cash's in "Folsom Prison Blues," where he sang of shooting a man in Reno "just to watch him die."

But in some ways, it is different. Johnny may have sung about doing hard time—and other things you wouldn't want your mama to know about—but his fantasy seems tame compared with the sex-and-violence-saturated lyrics that proliferate and dominate the *Billboard*[5] charts today.

[1] **crooned:** Sang in a gentle, murmuring manner.
[2] **Oedipal:** Characterized by sexual attraction of a son toward his mother and hostile or jealous feelings toward his father.
[3] **psychodrama:** A dramatic narrative or event characterized by psychological overtones.
[4] **iconoclasts:** People who attack settled beliefs or institutions.
[5] **ESL** *Billboard:* A music magazine featuring top sales listings on contemporary artists.

It's a change that hasn't gone unnoticed. With hip-hop's current debate over whether rap has gone too far, insiders are once again trying to decipher what the dividing line is between true artistic value and provocative schlock.[6] The answers will come in retrospect, but in order for the genre to continue growing, it's an important debate that needs to start now.

At the moment, the new frontier of rebellion seems to be against political correctness — the well-intentioned fear of offending any person or "group." In the 1960s and '70s, the fashionably rebellious attitude was to celebrate differences, to elevate the condition of women, minorities and gays ("Come on people now, smile on your brother"). That precursor to the P.C.[7] ethos has now become the cultural mainstream; this election year, Democrats with their many-colors-of-Benetton constituency and Republicans with their many-colors-of-Benetton convention are eagerly trying to top each other in their respect for each and every group that might be induced to vote for them. But in popular entertainment, and especially music, women are being debased in ever more degrading ways, excess and greed are extolled as worthy attributes and gay-bashing serves as a mark of deep-down daring. To be a counterculture rebel now, all you have to do is retool the vilest prejudices of your grandparents' day in the vilest language of your own. What's being promoted as the slaughter of sacred cows is McBigotry, with a state-of-the-art beat and no beef at all.

The result? Mainstream rap and hard rock, addicted to ever-escalating doses of defiance, can now feel as predictable as bad Hollywood action flicks. Part of the problem is that no really new style or scene has busted out of the gate since gangsta rap revolutionized hip-hop in the late '80s and grunge revitalized rock back in the early '90s. If there was anything out there in whatever today's equivalents might be of Compton, Calif., or Seattle, the entertainment corporations would have ferreted it out by now, exploited it and stamped it with their own trademarks. True, the Internet offers the promise of an under-the-radar musical bohemia[8] where an alternative sound might lie low long enough to flourish — the trouble is, most stuff on the Web is so far under the radar that a potentially supportive fan base can't find it. So pop music has fallen back on the tried-and-true attention-getters — sex, violence, sex, consumerist excess and sex — and added the latest kinks in the Zeitgeist:[9] misogyny and homophobia as expressions of free-floating countercultural rage and anxiety.

Another part of the problem is that we risk becoming jaded and desensitized. When — as rappers and deliberately obnoxious bands like Limp Bizkit are proving every day — you can say absolutely anything you want, what's the point of saying anything? And how can you be outrageous enough to get anybody's attention when everybody is shouting at the same volume?

6

7

8

---

[6] **schlock:** Something of low quality or value.
[7] **ESL P.C.:** Abbreviation for "politically correct."
[8] **bohemia:** A community of people such as writers or artists living an unconventional life.
[9] **Zeitgeist:** The general intellectual, moral, and cultural climate of an era.

Of course, today's most vacuous pop—from bling-bling[10] to Britney   9
to Blink-182—will pass away, either because it collapses under the
weight of its own decadence like disco of the '70s and the hair bands of
the '80s, or because it withers from sheer neglect. This happens to the vacuous pop of most every generation: the musical equivalents of Chia Pets
give way to the musical equivalents of Razor scooters. The kids to whom
these fads are marketed outgrow them and are replaced by new ranks of
kids, snickering at yesterday's amusements and suckered in by tomorrow's. The great hope of pop music has always been that in these ruthless
revolutions and counter-revolutions a terrible beauty will be born. It was
with Public Enemy, with Nirvana—and with Elvis, too. We can only
hope we'll get lucky again.

EXERCISING VOCABULARY

1. What is an icon? What is an iconoclast (para. 4)? What role have iconoclasts
   played in the development of popular music?

2. What are some of the characteristics and habits of a ferret? Why has the word
   ferret become a verb, as in "ferreted it out" (para. 7)? What does this verb imply?

3. In paragraph 6, Ali refers to "the slaughter of sacred cows" and "McBigotry."
   What famous company does this language call to mind? What about today's
   rock music does Ali consider bigotry? Why?

PROBING CONTENT

1. Why did Ali's coworker buy an Eminem album? What was the coworker's reaction after listening to the album? Who is the target audience for pop music?

2. What twofold purpose do boundaries serve for children? What has traditionally been the relation of music to those boundaries? How is today's music
   both similar to and different from the traditional relationship?

3. In the 1960s and 1970s, what marked rebellious attitudes? What is necessary
   for an artist to be referred to as "a counterculture rebel" (para. 6) today?
   What has resulted from this difference?

4. According to the author, what will happen to "today's most vacuous" pop
   music (para. 9)? Why is she so certain about this eventual outcome?

CONSIDERING CRAFT

1. In paragraph 9, Ali labels the insignificant pop music of yesterday and today
   "the musical equivalents of Chia Pets" and "Razor scooters." Describe these

---

[10] **bling-bling:** A rap term for lots of money.

two objects. What do they have in common? What is the author saying about pop music by using this unusual analogy?

2. There is an element of hope and positive thinking in the last paragraph of Ali's essay that is lacking earlier. Why does she choose to end this way? Is this ending out of character with the rest of her essay? Why or why not?

RESPONDING TO THE WRITER

Ali asserts that the real attention grabbers in music have always been the same, no matter how musical styles change. Chief among these attractors are sex and violence. To what extent do you agree with her evaluation? What other factors in music are equally important to its popularity and success? Give some specific examples to support your ideas.

For a quiz on this reading, go to www.bedfordstmartins.com/mirror.

A Voice for the Lonely

Stephen Corey

Can you recall a memorable song from a certain time in your life—a song that meant everything to you during the beginning or the ending of a relationship, for instance? Did you apply the lyrics of the song to your own emotional state? In the following personal account, Stephen Corey examines the link between music and memory, thinking back to a time when he learned that much of music is about "love—lost, found, hoped for, and despaired of." He discovered this in Roy Orbison's song "Pretty Woman." When Corey learns of Orbison's death, he reflects on how music, at times, cannot be distinguished from feeling. What do you think he means by this? What is it about music that can transport us back to emotions we experienced years earlier?

Corey is a widely published poet and essayist. He is currently an editor of the *Georgia Review* and has written eight collections of poetry, including *Stephen Corey: Greatest Hits 1980–2000* (2000) and *All These Lands You Call One Country* (1992). His poems and essays have appeared in *American Poetry Review*, *Kenyon Review*, *Republic*, and *Shenandoah*, and his work has also been widely anthologized. He has twice been named Georgia Author of the Year by the Georgia Council of Writers and Journalists. This piece was published in *In Short: A Collection of Brief Creative Nonfiction* (1996).

THINKING AHEAD

Think of a time in your life when one special song seemed to exactly capture your feelings. What made that song so appealing? How did you react when you heard the song? Were you more moved by the lyrics or the music? How does hearing this song affect you today?

INCREASING VOCABULARY

jolt (v.) (4)

flurry (n.) (5)

ranting (adj.) (11)

implications (n.) (11)

roused (v.) (12)

modulations (n.) (13)

camaraderie (n.) (15)

errant (adj.) (16)

commendable (adj.) (18)

erratic (adj.) (18)

The right silence can be a savior, especially in these days of motorcy- 1
cles, leaf blowers, and malls that thrum with a thousand voices and
dozens of sundry[1] machines. Five or six days a week, I get up pretty
early—generally around 4 A.M.—and one of the things I like most about
those last hours of darkness is their stillness. The house is quiet, the streets
are quiet, and (except on weekends, when some of the serious drunks are
hanging on) the all-night restaurants are quiet. Reading and writing and
thinking come more easily when you know you won't be interrupted, and
over the past twenty years I've never found a better mental bodyguard
than the hours before dawn.

I got my first serious training as an early riser when I acquired a news- 2
paper delivery route in seventh grade: three miles of widely scattered
houses on the edge of Jamestown, New York, and beyond—just me, the
moon, darkness, and the various faces of silence. I recall stopping my
brisk walk sometimes, especially in winter when every step squeaked and
crunched on the snow that nearly always covered the ground, and mar-
veling at how there were no sounds except those of my own making. But
just as often, that quiet made me nervous, even though my hometown was
awfully safe in those days. I learned to offset the urge to look over my
shoulder by carrying a pocket-sized transistor radio.

The music helped me to cope with more than just the empty morning 3
streets—I was, as I said, in seventh (and then eighth, and finally ninth)
grade during those lone marches. In short, I was just learning something
of what much of that music was about: love—lost, found, hoped for, and
despaired of.

Most habits die hard, and old ones can seem immortal. Last week, I 4
was up as usual at 4 A.M., and I headed out in the car toward the nearest
newspaper box. As always during these quick runs, I flipped on the radio
for some wake-up rhythms to jolt my system for the solitary work time
soon to come back at the house.

Instead of music, I caught the voice of the all-night deejay[2] just as she 5
was saying, "We have tragic news in over the wire: singer Roy Orbison is
dead . . ." She gave a quick flurry of details (heart attack, Hendersonville,
North Carolina, hospital), repeated the central fact—"Roy Orbison, dead
at fifty-two"—and then (my heart applauds her still for this) said not a
word but cut straight into "Only the Lonely."

There I was, cruising down the abandoned city street with the radio 6
now up as loud as I could stand it, mouthing the rising and falling words,
rocking side to side as I held the wheel, and riding Orbison's waiting,
nearly-cracking voice back twenty-four years to the passenger seat of Jon
Cresanti's Volkswagen Beetle.[3]

---

[1] **sundry:** Various.
[2] **ESL** **deejay:** Slang for disc jockey, one who plays recorded music for the public.
[3] **ESL** **Volkswagen Beetle:** A type of car popular in the 1960s, so named because of its
   unique rounded shape.

We're told these days that the hottest and fastest wire into memory is   7
our sense of smell, but music must run a close second. Some songs carry
us into a certain mood, some to a general region of our past lives, and
some to a very particular moment and situation in time. Jon and I were
brought together by chance and loneliness for a couple of months during
our sophomore year in high school. The alphabetical seating in our home-
room put us next to each other in the back row, and Jon was a talker. We
hadn't known each other before: we came from different parts of town,
had different friends, and moved through different sequences of classes.
But for a while we found a bond: my girlfriend had recently dropped me
after more than a year of going steady, and Jon had eyes for a girl who
had none for him.

I had time—all the time I was no longer spending with my girl. Jon   8
had a car and was old enough to drive it, having failed a grade and
thereby become a crucial year older than the typical sophomore. I signed
on board, and we cruised day after day, weekend after weekend, killing
time and eating at the wondrous new "fast food restaurant" that had just
opened. We sat in his car eating fifteen-cent hamburgers and twelve-cent
french fries near the real golden arches, the kind that curved up and over
the entire little structure (no inside seating, no bathrooms)—and, naturally, listening to the radio. The Four Seasons were with us, as were The
Beach Boys, Nat King Cole, The Supremes.

But in those two desperate months of shotgunning for Jon, there was   9
only one song that really mattered, one song we waited for, hoped for,
and even called the radio station and asked for: Roy Orbison's "Pretty
Woman."

That opening handful of heavy guitar notes (a lovesick teenager's   10
equivalent of Beethoven's Fifth) carried us into a world of possibility, a
world where a moment's fancy could generate love, where losers could be
winners just by wishing for success. The pretty woman walks on by, and
another failure has occurred—but suddenly, the downward sweep of the
wheel is reversed as the woman turns to walk back, and there is nothing
in the world but fulfillment of one's dreams.

Pop songs are full of such stuff, of course, and have been for as long   11
as the phonograph record and the radio have been with us; we get all
kinds of talk about the importance of television in modern life, but I think
we need more examination of the ways we have been encompassed by
music. I'm not talking about ranting "discussions" of the immorality of
certain strains of pop music, but some real studies of the much wider and
deeper implications of growing up in a world awash with radio waves.

Needless to say, I wasn't concerned about such matters there in the   12
McDonald's parking lot. I wouldn't even have thought about what it was
in Orbison's singing that made him so important to me. I took the words
of the song's story for their relevance to my own emotional state, and I
floated with those words inside a musical accompaniment that both
soothed and roused my fifteen-year-old body.

When I heard of Orbison's death, I found myself wanting to figure out 13
just what it was in that strange voice that might have been so compelling
for me and others across the years. I think it might be in the way the voice
itself often seems about to fail: in Orbison's strange and constant modulations, from gravelly bass-like sounds to strong tenor-like passages to
piercing falsetto[4] cries, there is the feeling for the listener that the singer is
always about to lose control, about to break down under the weight of
what he is trying to sing. Never mind that this is not true, that Orbison's
style was one carefully achieved; what we are talking about here is emotional effect, the true stuff of pop and country music.

If Roy could make it, we could make it. And if Roy could stand fail- 14
ing, so could we.

This feeling of camaraderie with the faraway record star increased for 15
me, I think, the first time I saw him. He was so ordinary-looking—no, he
was so *homely,* so very contrary to what one expects romantic musical heroes to look like. He was *us.*

The right singer, the right sadness, the right silence. The way I heard 16
the story of the death of Orbison's wife in 1966 (and the way I'll keep believing it) was that the two of them were out motorcycling when an errant
car or truck hit them from an angle. She was riding just a few feet to the
side of and behind him, so the other vehicle clipped the back of his cycle
but caught hers full force. I've never gotten over this chilling illustration of
the forces of circumstance and the fate of inches, so much so that over the
years I have regularly found the story called to mind for retelling in classrooms or at parties.

I graduated from high school the year of the accident, and Orbison 17
disappeared from the national music scene. (It wasn't until recently that I
heard how the death of two sons by fire in 1967 compounded Orbison's
private tragedies.) Oddly, there is a way in which the disappearance or the
death of a singer these days doesn't really matter to his or her listeners,
since that person is still present in exactly the same way as before. All the
songs take on a slightly new cast, but the singer still lives in a way that
one's own deceased relatives and friends cannot.

When my girl wanted me back, I dropped Jon's friendship and never 18
tried to regain it—a not-very-commendable way to be. But we were glued
for a while by those banging Orbison notes and those erratic vocals, and
maybe that was enough, or at least all that one could hope for.

Music can block out silence, on dark scary roads and in moments of 19
loneliness. But there's also a sense or two in which a song can create silence: when we're "lost in a song" the rest of the world around us makes,
for all practical purposes, no sound. And in an even more strange way, a
song we love goes silent as we "listen" to it, leaving us in that rather primitive place where all the sounds are interior ones—sounds which can't be

---

[4] **falsetto:** An artificially high voice used by singers.

distinguished from feelings, from pulsings and shiverings, from that gut need to make life stronger than death for at least a few moments.

When "Only the Lonely" faded, that wonderful deejay still knew   20 enough not to say a word. She threw us straight forward, 4:15 A.M., into "Pretty Woman."

EXERCISING VOCABULARY

1. What responsibilities does a bodyguard have? Why does the author refer to the predawn stillness as a "mental bodyguard" (para. 1)? What does the stillness guard against?

2. It's easy to understand how "music can block out silence" (para. 19). But how is it possible, as Corey continues, for music to "create silence," when *silence* means "the absence of sound"?

PROBING CONTENT

1. How and where did Corey first learn of Roy Orbison's death? What did the author admire about the way the message was delivered? What was the immediate effect of the news on Corey?

2. What circumstances brought Corey and Jon Cresanti together? What further circumstances solidified their relationship? What part did music in general and Roy Orbison's music in particular play in their friendship?

3. According to the author, what was at the core of Orbison's musical appeal? What message did his music transmit? Why was this message so important?

4. What does Corey mean when he writes that "the death of a singer these days doesn't really matter" (para. 17)? How is this a change from Corey's youth?

CONSIDERING CRAFT

1. As a reader, you may strongly identify with the author's feelings in this essay even though you may be unfamiliar with or not attracted to the music of Roy Orbison. How does Corey accomplish this? How does his writing give a sense of universality to this piece about his personal connection with one artist's music?

2. In the last paragraph of the essay, Corey returns the reader to the time when Corey first learned of Orbison's death. How does this recalling of the past function in the structure of the essay? What might be accomplished by modeling this technique in your own writing?

RESPONDING TO THE WRITER

Do you agree with Corey that music may open a direct channel into our memory (para. 7)? Choose one song that always moves you backwards in time and causes you to refocus on a particular person, place, or event. Explain why this song has such a powerful effect on you.

For a quiz on this reading, go to www.bedfordstmartins.com/mirror.

Rock of Ages

RICHARD LACAYO

"Pop music is no longer mostly a way that one generation defines itself against its elders," writes Richard Lacayo in "Rock of Ages," first published in the February 26, 2001, issue of *Time*. In fact, Lacayo says, music can bring generations together by encouraging communication between parents and children. Conversations about music allow parents to discuss pop culture with their kids and give children the opportunity to let parents into their world. But how can parents be "cool" with the music their kids listen to without explicitly endorsing lyrics that glorify sex, drugs, and profanity?

A senior writer for the Nation section of *Time* magazine, Lacayo often covers controversial topics including abortion, gun control, and the right to privacy. His work has been published in the *New York Times*, and he is the coauthor of *Eyewitness: 150 Years of Photojournalism* (1990).

THINKING AHEAD

What kinds of music do your older friends or your parents listen to? Do you like some of it? Do they listen to the music you like? What similarities and differences do you hear between the music they listen to and the music you choose?

INCREASING VOCABULARY

fevered (adj.) (1)	gouging (v.) (5)
toddling (adj.) (2)	decrepitude (n.) (7)
bonding (n.) (2)	endorse (v.) (8)
incest (n.) (2)	pun (n.) (8)
taboo (n.) (2)	splintered (v.) (10)
collaborate (v.) (3)	unflinching (adj.) (11)
supplanted (v.) (5)	

> *Let's all get up*
> *And dance to a song*
> *That was a hit before*
> *Your mother was born —* The Beatles

Remember when that song was about your mother? You do? Too bad. In that case, now it's about you. The very thought is enough to send a chill down the spines of most baby boomers,[1] who already have plenty of reasons to wonder if they haven't started looking as old as Paul McCartney. (And remember, he was the Cute Beatle.) At one time it probably seemed that rock music was entirely yours, a thing that you

---

[1] **ESL** **baby boomers:** The generation born in the United States immediately after World War II, named for its high birth rate.

306

could imagine grew out of your own fevered brain. Now a good slice of it apparently belongs to somebody else, somebody who likes gangsta rap and tinny kid pop and fight songs from WWF Smackdown![2] It doesn't help that this week the Grammy for album of the year may go to Eminem, the white rapper who wants to rape his mother, or at least he says he does on the album that may get the Grammy. Hey, you're probably old enough to be his mother. For that matter, so is Elton John, who is taking the risk of performing a duet with him at the Grammys.

To make things worse, pop music is otherwise going through one of   2
those moments when the general run of things is so toddling — Britney Spears, Backstreet Boys — that skinny white boys who talk a little tough, meaning Eminem, get to seem like a big deal. So if you happen to be a parent in, say, your forties or fifties, nobody would blame you if you just turned away from pop music altogether. And if you happen to be a teenager, of course, you might not mind if they did. But the funny thing is, at the same time that the hard edge of pop gets harder and the soft edge gets softer, it's plain that rock has also become one of those things, like pets and baseball, that lets parents and kids find a shared passion. It may be that Eminem doesn't provide much opportunity for parent-child bonding, unless you're trying to explain why the incest taboo is not just some stupid rule that Mom invented to be mean. But a lot of baby boomers have figured out that it's a short trip from the Pink Floyd they once loved to the Radiohead their kids love now. And a lot of their kids have likewise found their way back to the music of their parents.

This explains Emily Curtin, twenty-two, who now plays guitar in a   3
New York City rock band. When she was in her late teens in Worcester, Mass., Emily used to collaborate with her twin younger brothers to make rock-music-compilation tapes — they called them Kids' Pix — for her parents. The idea was to educate the folks, who already understood the rock music of their own warmly remembered youth, about newer stuff. "They listened to the tapes all the time," she says. "My mom got into the Magnetic Fields. Dad got into My Bloody Valentine."

In Marshfield, Wis., John Spellman and his wife Jeanne are fiftysome-   4
things who reawoke to rock music as the older ones among their four kids discovered the Beatles, the Grateful Dead and Pink Floyd. "Now we spend time talking about things like how the Dead are not really a rock band," says John. "How they come out of a tradition of classic American blues, from Appalachia and the South." In return, he has picked up from his kids a taste for the Dave Matthews Band and U2, a group he finds "inspirational." Spellman's children even introduced him to music from his youth that he had missed the first time it came along. Through them he discovered Bob Marley, the reggae[3] star whose supreme moment was in the 1970s.

---

[2] **ESL** **WWF Smackdown!:** A type of World Wrestling Federation championship competition.
[3] **ESL** **reggae:** Popular music of Jamaican origin that combines native styles with elements of rock and soul music.

Even if guitar-band rock is a niche market now, supplanted by hip- 5
hop as the reigning format of pop music, it still qualifies as the lingua
franca[4] of pop culture. Roughly a half-century after Elvis recorded
"Heartbreak Hotel," nearly everybody under seventy has some emotional
attachment to electrified music with a beat. As a consequence, pop music
is no longer mostly a way that one generation defines itself against its elders. The baby boomers' own parents grew up with Frank Sinatra, Rose-
mary Clooney and Nat "King" Cole. Rock was such an unmistakable
break with that creamy tradition that teenagers of the 1960s and '70s understood it right away as music to fight Mom and Dad to, especially since
their parents usually hated the stuff. Now kids have to accept that most of
their own music is not so different from what their parents had, parents
who grew up on Lou Reed, to say nothing of Iggy Pop, a guy who was
gouging his skin with broken glass when Marilyn Manson was still stick-
ing thumbtacks in his tricycle tires.

But that also makes it easier for them to comprehend the music their 6
parents used to love. This helps explain the watershed[5] success of the
Beatles 1 album, which topped *Billboard*'s album charts for eight weeks
and has sold more than 20 million copies worldwide. You don't score numbers like that just from the middle-aged Beatlemaniacs still shaking their
imaginary moptops.[6] It requires massive sales to the teenagers and twen-
tysomethings who buy most records. The phenomenon of that album followed the success of Santana's *Supernatural,* which paired a survivor of the
'60s with up-to-the-minute acts like Lauryn Hill, Everlast and Rob Thomas
from Matchbox 20. And before Santana, there was Aerosmith and Eric
Clapton, Neil Young and Tina Turner, Sting and Cher, David Bowie and
Bruce Springsteen. All of them sustained long careers by adding younger
fans to the ones who remember them from before they got reading glasses.

What all this means is, simply by pointing out to your children that 7
you understand that Phish owes a lot to the Grateful Dead, you can dis-
tract them briefly from your otherwise evident decrepitude. There are already institutions that have positioned themselves to benefit from that
fact, adapting rock to the family-theme-park phenomenon. The Experience Music Project in Seattle, which opened last year, aims to be a place
where parents can explain to their kids that James Brown is the old guy
who sounds like Mystikal, and kids can tell their parents that Mystikal is
the young guy who sounds like James Brown. The Rock 'n' Roll Hall of
Fame in Cleveland, Ohio, even offers guidance to local high school teachers on how to work rock history into their lesson plans. This will make it
easier for parents to talk to their kids about the music of their own youth,
though it also opens the way to a day when sophomores will get detention
for not turning in their term papers on Frank Zappa.

---

[4] **ESL** **lingua franca:** Common or shared language.
[5] **watershed:** Indicating a significant change.
[6] **ESL** **moptops:** Mop-like haircuts that were popularized by the Beatles.

All the same, as a means to reach kids, rock is more complicated than   8
pets and baseball. It has never been completely domesticated by age and
commercial calculation. One way that rock bands keep their distance
from respectability these days is by shouting "F—" a few dozen times on
every album. (Or even "I wanna f— you like an animal," as Trent Reznor
famously offered on one of his Nine Inch Nails albums.) Rock is still all
tied up with sex and drugs, and it's a supremely subtle parent who can
share all kinds of music with her kids without also seeming to endorse the
troubling stuff. On this past New Year's Eve, the Experience Music Project sponsored a sold-out dance party that attracted 1,200 people, including parents, teenagers and even younger children. The aim was to provide
something with the feel of a rave[7] party but without the drug scene that
goes with it. Then again, the main stage attraction was the band Crystal
Method, whose name is an obvious pun on crystal meth, the ampheta-
mine-based party drug. "A band can call itself what it wants to call itself,"
says Robert Santelli, deputy director of public programs at EMP. Which is
true, of course. But the adults who offer the band to kids are inescapably
complicit in any message the band conveys. It all gets complicated.

The skanky[8] side of pop music is something that Sheila Brown turns   9
to her advantage. Brown is an executive secretary at Tribune Interactive,
part of the Tribune Co., the Chicago-based media empire. Her daughters
Nnyla, twenty-three, and Rayna, thirteen, love some kinds of rap. So does
she. And the parts she doesn't love—the trash talk, the relentless treatment of women as nothing more than walking booties[9]—give her a
chance to discuss with her daughters just why she doesn't love them. "We
discuss things openly about sex and relationships," says Brown. "What's
tacky[10] and what's not tacky. Sometimes the kids are more embarrassed
by things they see in music videos than I am." Nnyla agrees that music
provides a way for her and her mother "to talk about sex more than we
might otherwise. Mom will say she doesn't like a song because it makes
women look like sex objects, that rap music and rap videos take women
back twenty to thirty years. I thought about it, and I can see that."

Even when you like the music you hear them listening to, there are   10
reasons why it takes hard work to share music with kids. Pop-music
turnover is faster than ever. The group that gets two or three successful albums in a row is harder to find. No sooner do you figure out who Blink-
182 is, than Blink-183 takes its place. And music is more splintered into
niche markets and tribal followings. It can be tricky to navigate the by-
ways of postpunk and trip-hop, ambient techno and speed metal. But remember, there was a time when you had no trouble telling the difference
between surf music and Merseybeat.

---

[7] **ESL** **rave:** A type of party or dance in a warehouse, usually featuring electronic music.
[8] **ESL** **skanky:** Slang word for "disgusting."
[9] **ESL** **booties:** Slang word referring to the buttocks.
[10] **ESL** **tacky:** Tasteless or of low quality.

And what do you do when your kids find their way back to the very   11
music you always hated as a kid? You try to steer them to the iconoclastic[11] New York Dolls; they stumble into the cheesy pyrotechnics[12] of Kiss.
You send them off to discover early Chicago; they come back with Kansas.
And what if, after all your careful guidance, they still love Limp Bizkit and
Papa Roach? What if they still go out and buy that stuff by Eminem? At
that point only the wisdom of age will do. Go back and take an unflinch-
ing look at your old record collection. There's probably a Black Sabbath
album in there somewhere.

EXERCISING VOCABULARY

1. In paragraph 5, Lacayo suggests that guitar-band rock is now only a "niche
   market." In paragraph 10, the author states that music is now more divided
   into "niche markets." What is a niche? How significant is something in a
   niche? If certain types of music are confined to niches, what does this say
   about their popularity and visibility?

2. The author argues that popular music "has never been completely domesticated" (para. 8). What does it mean to domesticate something? To what or
   whom is the term usually applied? What are its implications? What does this
   mean with regard to rock music?

PROBING CONTENT

1. What is it about today's music that is opening up conversations between
   parents and children? Why is this surprising?

2. According to the authors, what kind of music dominates today's popular
   music? What kind of music still forms the most common basis for popular culture? Why is there a difference?

3. How have the older musicians and groups retained their audiences? Why is
   the ability to do this essential? What evidence do the authors offer to prove
   that this is happening?

4. What was ironic about the dance sponsored by the Experience Music Project?
   What dilemma did that present for the adult sponsors of the event?

CONSIDERING CRAFT

1. When the author refers to the example of Sheila Brown and her two daughters in paragraph 9, why does he suddenly shift language patterns to use
   words like "skanky," "trash talk," and "walking booties"? What effect does this

---

[11] iconoclastic: Attacking beliefs or institutions.
[12] pyrotechnics: A fireworks display.

shift in language have on you? How does it affect the impact of his example? What would be lost if the writer had just continued with standard English?

2. This essay is filled with the names of musicians and music groups. You probably are not familiar with every one of them. Do you think that the author expects every reader to be? Why are so many of these references included? What effect does their inclusion have on your reading?

RESPONDING TO THE WRITER

In your experience, do people of different generations seem to be drawn to the same musical styles and performers? Cite specific examples to reinforce your answer. How tolerant are people of music they may not appreciate or approve of? Why do you think this is true?

For a quiz on this reading, go to www.bedfordstmartins.com/mirror.

Crossing Pop Lines

ALISA VALDES-RODRIGUEZ

When was the last time you heard the name of a Latino singer without the word *hot* attached to it? Are you insulted by the media's obsession with these singers' body parts? In "Crossing Pop Lines," Alisa Valdes-Rodriguez examines the media's portrayal of Latino singers, which often focuses on their sexuality rather than their talent. Furthermore, Valdes-Rodriguez argues, the media has a tendency to lump all Latinos together, ignoring the singers' individual cultures, nationalities, and backgrounds. For example, did you know that both Ricky Martin and Jennifer Lopez were born in the United States? Why, then, are they often referred to as "crossover" artists? Why do you think this label may be insulting to many Latino musicians?

Valdes-Rodriguez is currently the Arts and Entertainment editor for the *Albuquerque Tribune.* She has previously worked as a staff writer for the *Boston Globe* and the *Los Angeles Times,* and her work has also appeared in numerous other publications, including the *Village Voice, Latina, Newsday,* and *Mother Jones.* Although Valdes-Rodriguez covers mainly pop music, she is particularly interested in writing about body image issues. She has been a professional aerobics instructor for ten years.

THINKING AHEAD

Name three musical artists who are classified as Latino pop singers. Are they classified this way because of the country where they were born, because of the type of music they sing, or because of the language in which they sing? Who sings salsa music? In what country is the merengue the national dance? If you can answer these questions, how did you learn this information?

INCREASING VOCABULARY

phenomenal (adj.) (1)
vying (v.) (1)
pervasive (adj.) (3)
genre (n.) (3)
posited (v.) (4)
afforded (v.) (5)
irrelevant (adj.) (7)
abysmal (adj.) (8)
nascent (adj.) (10)
oblivious (adj.) (10)
clichéd (adj.) (12)

connotation (n.) (12)
propensity (n.) (13)
indigenous (adj.) (13)
incendiary (adj.) (15)
immune (adj.) (15)
innuendo (n.) (16)
amorphous (adj.) (18)
palatable (adj.) (26)
whittled (v.) (26)
ostensibly (adv.) (28)

First, the well-known facts: Puerto Rican pop star Ricky Martin is en- 1
joying phenomenal success with his first English-language album,
and more Latino pop artists, such as Enrique Iglesias, are vying to do
the same. This has led the U.S. media—including a *Time* magazine cover
story—to trumpet a new "Latin crossover phenomenon."

Now, the lesser-known facts. 2

One: Many of the so-called crossover artists are American by birth, 3
including Martin. But the pervasive impression in the media and in the
culture at large is that these artists are exotic foreigners. Example? *USA
Today* calling Martin's sounds "south-of-the-border," even though residents of his native Puerto Rico have been United States citizens since
1917, and the island's signature musical genre, salsa,[1] was invented in the
1960s in a city south of the Connecticut border: New York.

Two: Even though in the pop music business "crossover" generally 4
means switching genres, Martin's music—pop by any standards—has
not changed, only the language he sings in. He is not, as some publications have posited, a salsa singer.

For Martin and others, the only real "crossover" is their language; it's 5
an unusual category, and one that French-speaking Canadian Celine Dion
managed to avoid. Latinos, even those U.S.-born like Martin, are not afforded the same leeway.[2]

Shakira, for example, is a Colombian rock singer whose style has been 6
compared to Alanis Morissette; her "crossover" album will consist of
translations of rock songs she has recorded in Spanish. Enrique Iglesias
sings syrupy ballads in the tradition of Air Supply; it's a formula that will
likely work as well for him in English. And Martin's music, while injected
occasionally with percussive[3] instruments, is no more or less "Latin" than
that of, say, Puff Daddy, who also uses Spanish phrases.

All of this has led East Harlem's Marc Anthony, who records salsa in 7
Spanish and R&B dance music in English, to declare "crossover" irrelevant, venturing to say the term has only been applied to these artists because they are Latinos on the mainstream charts, not because they perform Latin music on the mainstream charts.

While no one denies that focusing the mainstream media spotlight on 8
Latino musicians and singers is overdue, the recent storm of coverage has
exposed an abysmal ignorance about the complexity, diversity and reality
of Latinos and Latin music.

Lost in the frenzy to cover "crossover" artists have been two simple 9
facts: Latino artists do not necessarily perform in Latin music genres; and
Latin music is not always performed by Latinos.

In the case of Jennifer Lopez, who is often lumped into this nascent 10

---

[1] **salsa:** Popular music of Latin American origin that has absorbed characteristics of rhythm
and blues, jazz, and rock.
[2] **leeway:** An allowable margin of freedom or variation.
[3] **percussive:** Of or relating to percussion instruments or drums.

category, the only "crossover" is in the minds of a media establishment oblivious to the fact that she is a Bronx native who has recorded her debut album of commercial pop songs in her "native tongue": English. Yes, Lopez has two Spanish-language pop songs on the album, but artists from Madonna to Bon Jovi have been recording in Spanish for release in Latin America for years, and yet no one has called them crossover artists.

Beyond the assumptions about Latino Americans seeming somehow   11
foreign, there is another, more unsettling bit of stereotyping being done in the media about the new "crossover" stars.

Clichéd adjectives are used over and over in the mainstream press in   12
general but take on a different connotation when used to describe artists such as Martin, Lopez, Anthony and others. Words such as "hot," "spicy" and "passionate" are taken, one assumes, from the flavors of Mexican cuisine and outdated stereotypes of the "Latin lover."

Particularly upsetting is the media propensity to comment on certain   13
body parts when writing about Latino artists, namely hips and rear ends. *Entertainment Weekly* labeled Martin "hot hips." And the vast majority of stories on Lopez refer to her hind side. This is no mere coincidence; several academics have shown direct links between the view European settlers took of the American land and indigenous peoples, both of which were seen as wild, sexual and, in their view, in need of taming.

Speaking of hot: According to *Billboard* magazine, Ricky Martin is a   14
"hot tamale."[4] This phrase appears several times, and is ridiculous because Martin hails from Puerto Rico, where the local cuisine includes neither chili peppers nor tamales, both of which come from Mexico. The recent *TV Guide* cover story on Martin made it only three paragraphs before calling the singer "spicy," and a few paragraphs later made reference to his wiggling hips.

According to the *New York Daily News*, Martin is "red hot," while   15
the *Atlanta Constitution* calls him "hot stuff." The *Seattle Times* says Martin is "incendiary" (gives them credit for consulting a thesaurus, at least). The list goes on and on. Even the *New York Times* has not been immune to the stereotyping; the headline of its recent concert review of Chayanne — a singer who appeared in the film *Dance with Me* alongside Vanessa Williams and who has plans to release an English-only album soon — read: Amor (Those Hips!) Pasion: (Those Lips!).

When it comes to Lopez, the coverage is even more troubling, tainted   16
with sexism and sexual innuendo in addition to ignorance. Lopez was called "salsa-hot" by the *Hartford Courant*. Like Martin, Lopez is Puerto Rican; once more, on that island, salsa is to be danced, not eaten. The *New York Daily News* calls Lopez a "hot tamale." Even in Canada the stereotypes, and mistakes, persist: The *Ottawa Citizen* called Lopez "a hot-blooded Cuban."

---

[4] **tamale:** A Mexican food made of cornmeal dough rolled up and filled with ground meat or beans.

Marc Anthony is so disgusted with the "heated" coverage he and others are getting in the mainstream press—he has been called "red-hot" by the *Boston Herald* and "white-hot" by the *New York Daily News*—that he has started refusing to do some interviews. He jokingly told his publicist that he will "jump off a bridge" if he is called "hot" or "spicy" by one more publication.   17

To understand why this type of writing is so offensive, one must be familiar with the complex reality of Latinos and the dozens of musical genres that have been lumped into the amorphous "Latin music" category.   18

Most of the 30 million Latinos in the U.S. speak English as their primary language. Beyond that, they are as racially and economically diverse as the entire U.S. population. While many people continue to believe that all Latinos are "brown," this is simply not true.   19

In fact, the history of the U.S. is parallel to that of Latin America: The Native American inhabitants were "conquered" by Europeans; many Native Americans were killed in the process, and Africans were "imported" to replace them as slaves. Documents from slave ships show that fully 95 percent of the Africans brought to the Americas as slaves went to Latin America, according to historians.   20

Brazil is home to the largest African American population on Earth, and five of every six Dominicans is of African descent. My father's birth was dedicated to the Yoruba god Obatala, as were those of most other white kids in his neighborhood in Cuba; he has often said that to be a Caribbean Latino is to be African, regardless of color.   21

At this moment, there are plenty of black Latinos succeeding in mainstream American pop music, but few, if any, ever get mentioned in the Latin crossover write-ups. In some instances, this is due to the artist's decision not to make his or her background known. But in other cases, as in the exclusion of R&B crooner Maxwell, who is half Puerto Rican, it's due mostly to reluctance on the part of both the English and Spanish media to include blacks in the discussion at all.   22

Pop singer Usher is half Panamanian. Other Puerto Ricans include TLC rapper Lisa "Left Eye" Lopes, "Ghetto Superstar" singer Mya—who has recorded in Spanish—and rappers Fat Joe and Big Pun. And Mariah Carey, who describes her father as a black Venezuelan and who routinely includes Spanish singles on her albums for import to Latin America, is also absent from the crossover discussion.   23

With one notable exception in the *New York Times* last month, merengue[5] singer Elvis Crespo has been left out of the crossover equation too, even though he is probably the only Latin artist who currently qualifies in the traditional sense of the term. Crespo currently has two Spanish-language albums on the *Billboard* 200 mainstream chart.   24

---

[5] **merengue:** A ballroom dance of Haitian and Dominican origin; also, the music for such a dance.

Some music executives, including Sony Music Chairman and CEO   25
Thomas D. Mottola, have said outright that they are excited about Martin and other crossover candidates because these artists fill the role of the
white male pop star that has been vacant since the glory days of George
Michael.

While a white Latino is just as Latino as a brown or black one, it un-   26
fortunately seems that in the world of American pop culture, Latinos are
still only palatable as long as they appeal to a mainstream, Caucasian
standard of beauty. Jennifer Lopez seems to have figured this one out: Her
naturally wavy, dark brown hair has been lightened and straightened, and
her once-fuller body has been whittled down by a fitness guru to something virtually indistinguishable from the lean, muscular Madonna.

All of this brings us to the ungainly truth no one seems to want to em-   27
brace in this country: Simply, there is no such thing as a singular
"Latino," and efforts, no matter how well-intentioned, to classify 30 million racially, economically and educationally diverse individuals as one
unit is ignorant—and irresponsible.

The term "Hispanic" was invented by the U.S. Census Bureau in the   28
1970s in order to classify a group of Americans ostensibly linked through
a common language—Spanish. Hispanics, or Latinos, don't exist in Latin
America where people identify themselves by nationality, class and race—
just like here. "Latinos" have been invented in the U.S. for the convenience of politics and marketing, overlooking considerable cultural differences and complexity that can make your head spin.

Think about this: Much of what we call "Mexican food" today is re-   29
ally Native American food; the unifying "Latino" language, Spanish, is a
European import, just like English; the backbone of salsa music, the clave
rhythm, comes from West Africa, as does merengue's two-headed tam-
bora drum; Mexican norteno and banda music is rooted in Germany and
Poland . . . but Cajuns in Louisiana who play essentially the same stuff in
French are not Latinos. Got that?

Complexity! It is anathema[6] to good capitalist marketing plans, which   30
promise big bucks to whomever can lasso[7] the elusive buyers of the world.
And yet history is complex—all of ours—and journalists owe it to everyone to accurately chronicle the history of our world and one of its most
powerful cultural forces: music.

We leave you with a sadly typical example of the comedy and tragedy   31
of simplification of Latinos and Latin music. It happened, of all places, at
a recent Los Angeles Dodgers game. As each Dodger goes to bat, the
scoreboard lists personal facts, including the player's favorite band. A

---

[6] **anathema:** A ban or a curse.
[7] **lasso:** To pull in or grab.

snippet[8] from said band is then played over the loudspeakers. Two Dominican players both listed the New Jersey–based merengue group Oro Solido as their favorite. Yet when one came up to the plate, the folks in charge of the public address system chose instead to play . . . Ricky Martin!

To many a Dominican, the exchange of Martin for Oro Solido could be seen as a slap in the face; first, merengue is the official national dance of the Dominican Republic. Secondly, there is a long history of tension between Puerto Ricans and Dominicans over class and citizenship issues. In this context, replacing Oro Solido with Martin was not only ignorant, but possibly even insulting. But to know this means to study history. It means entertaining complex thought. And that, in a trend-driven pop culture obsessed with simple marketing categories and the almighty dollar, is apparently too much work. 32

EXERCISING VOCABULARY

1. When *Time* magazine announced a "'Latin crossover phenomenon'" (para. 1), who or what had "crossed over"? What did they cross over? What has to happen for something to be considered phenomenal?

PROBING CONTENT

1. What two important facts have been overshadowed by the rush to popularize the music of crossover artists? Why are these facts significant?

2. Why is Jennifer Lopez a good example of the author's point about the confusion about "Latino" artists?

3. What is unbalanced in the media's coverage of Latino artists? Give specific examples.

4. How much of a factor have black Latinos been in the new interest surrounding Latino music? According to the author, why has this happened?

CONSIDERING CRAFT

1. Valdes-Rodriguez incorporates several mini-history lessons into her essay, notably in paragraphs 20 and 28. How do these lessons contribute to the development of her thesis? What would be lost if they were omitted?

2. The author obviously has strong feelings about the injustices that she believes have been done to Latino artists. Where in this essay does she let her feelings show? What steps does she take to ensure that her essay remains factual and her argument logically developed? How well does she succeed?

---

[8] **snippet:** A small part.

RESPONDING TO THE WRITER

Valdes-Rodriguez speculates that the media's lack of attention to the truth about Latino artists stems from "a trend-driven pop culture obsessed with simple marketing categories and the almighty dollar" (para. 32). To what extent do you believe this is true? Is this the only reason why some Latino artists have been misrepresented? What other reasons may also be factors?

For a quiz on this reading, go to www.bedfordstmartins.com/mirror.

Value of Life Lost in Gangsta Rap's Refrain

LEONARD PITTS

In the following essay, Leonard Pitts claims that "rap music has proved poisonous to the spirit and aspirations of African American men." He traces gangsta rap's beginnings to the 1980s, when urban American life was falling apart. Social crises of the time included a dramatic rise in drug use (particularly crack cocaine), the advent of the AIDS epidemic, and the widespread desertion of inner cities. Pitts doesn't blame rap music for these problems, but he does question why some artists would want to romanticize the sense of hopelessness that prevailed in many people at that time. Do you agree with Pitts that "rap is largely a music of thug values, celebrating that which deserves no celebration"? Or do you think his criticism is overly harsh? What about rap music that is concerned with more positive subjects, such as faith, feminism, or personal relationships?

Pitts is a columnist for the *Miami Herald*, where "Value of Life Lost in Gangsta Rap's Refrain" first appeared on November 14, 1999. He has also written about music for *Musician, Spin, Billboard*, and Casey Kasem's *American Top 40* radio program. Though he started working at the *Miami Herald* in 1991 as a music columnist, Pitts began covering race, politics, relationships, and other topics when he felt he had become "too old for pop music." He has also published a book about fatherhood, *Becoming Dad* (1999).

THINKING AHEAD

What are the major themes of gangsta rap? What accounts for the popularity of this kind of rap among blacks and nonblacks alike? To what extent do you think gangsta rap represents the black experience in America?

INCREASING VOCABULARY

commemorating (adj.) (2)

crystallize (v.) (2)

concede (v.) (3)

defiant (adj.) (3)

explicitness (n.) (4)

coarse (adj.) (4)

portends (v.) (5)

resonates (v.) (6)

genre (n.) (7)

exploited (v.) (8)

reek (v.) (8)

barrenness (n.) (11)

oblivion (n.) (12)

On Tuesday night, right before they executed him for murdering   1
police officer Kenny Wallace in 1994, Virginia officials asked
Thomas Lee Royal Jr. if he had anything to say. He did. Royal, a
thirty-two-year-old black man, asked them: "How you're going to kill a
man when a man is willing to die?"

I came across that story as I was preparing to write this column com-   2
memorating the twentieth anniversary of the hip-hop revolution. It struck
me because it seemed to crystallize the ways in which rap music has
proved poisonous to the spirit and aspirations of African American men.

This is not, I realize, an entirely fair thing to say. In the first place, I   3
haven't a clue whether Royal was a fan of rap. In the second, I concede
that, since a song called "Rapper's Delight" brought it to national attention in November 1979, rap has concerned itself with a variety of subjects: Christian faith, defiant feminism, adolescent rebellion, black nationalism, party fun, and cheating hearts.

My problem is that rap is largely a music of thug[1] values, celebrating   4
that which deserves no celebration: drug-dealing, dream-stealing, woman-
pimping,[2] man-killing. I refer, of course, to so-called gangsta rap, a death-
affirming music of explicitness and coarse joys.

The violence it portends is not implied or merely pretend. It has be-   5
come common for rappers and their hangers-on to die by gunfire. Arenas
are reluctant to book rap concerts because of security concerns and high
insurance premiums.

It's worth noting that the biggest sin in the world of these men is to be   6
"soft"—to be caught feeling something. So Thomas Royal's doomed
bravado resonates. "How you're going to kill a man when a man is willing to die?" It could be a rap record refrain.

It's no coincidence that the gangsta genre was born in the '80s, just at   7
the moment when everything was going to hell in urban America, the moment when something ugly crept into the heart of the city, when mama
became a crack addict and daddy the invisible man, when nobody knew,
nobody saw, and nobody cared.

Gangsta rap didn't cause this, but it did—and does—represent the   8
attempt to romanticize it, to turn life in hell into a badge of awful honor.
It did—and does—represent the triumph of a cynical, values-free vision
exploited and mass-marketed so effectively that it becomes possible for a
sheltered suburban kid who couldn't find the inner city with a road map
to adopt its hopelessness as his own. It did—and does—reek to high
heaven.

"How you're going to kill a man when a man is willing to die?"   9

One wonders what he wished us to conclude from that. That the man   10
who holds to life with both hands is weak, but the one who has nothing
to lose is strong?

---

[1] thug: A brutal ruffian or gangster.
[2] pimping: Soliciting clients for a prostitute.

Better to recognize the statement for the lie it is: a man's desperate at-   11
tempt to assert control over the barrenness of his own existence.

And you struggle to make that man hear you over the beat of a song   12
that romanticizes death, that rewards it with that badge of awful honor.
Struggle to make him know that when he leaps from oblivion's cliff, he
takes us with him. Struggle to make him reject a limiting vision of who he
is and what he might be.

We already know young black men are not afraid to die. We must chal-   13
lenge them to prove a more difficult thing: that they're not afraid to live.

EXERCISING VOCABULARY

1. In paragraph 6, Pitts refers to Thomas Royal Jr.'s last words as "doomed bravado." What does it mean if something is doomed? How is bravado different from bravery? How do Royal's words and circumstances fit the meaning of this phrase?

2. Pitts accuses rap of "celebrating that which deserves no celebration" (para. 4). What does he mean by this variation on one word? How does he justify this assertion?

3. In paragraph 8 the author accuses gangsta rap of "romanticizing" ugliness, of turning "life in hell into a badge of awful honor." In paragraph 12 he repeats this idea using the same words. What is a badge of honor? How is one usually earned? What is ironic about his use of this phrase, especially with the word "awful" added?

PROBING CONTENT

1. What propelled Pitts to write this article? How did his purpose change? What does he dislike about gangsta rap?

2. How are rappers living out their lyrics? How might Royal's words illustrate this?

3. How did the creation of gangsta rap represent what was taking place in America at the time?

CONSIDERING CRAFT

1. Pitts begins with a narrative about a man who was not a rapper and whom Pitts doesn't even attempt to prove listened to rap. Why does he choose such an apparently unrelated opening? How does he make it an integral part of his essay? How well does it eventually fit his thesis?

2. Throughout the essay, Pitts repeats Thomas Royal Jr.'s last words, almost like the refrain he mentions in his title. What function does a refrain serve in a piece of music? What function does the refrain serve in the essay? How effective is this technique?

RESPONDING TO THE WRITER

To what extent do you agree with Pitts that gangsta rap "reek[s] to high heaven" (para. 8) and encourages young black men to accept "a limiting vision" of their futures (para. 12)? Do you see positive values in rap and gangsta rap that Pitts largely ignores? Explain your response.

For a quiz on this reading, go to www.bedfordstmartins.com/mirror.

To the Academy with Love, from a Hip-Hop Fan

JAMILAH EVELYN

Whatever your stance on hip-hop, you cannot deny that it has shaped the lives of many college students. Do professors therefore have a responsibility to better understand this music and the culture that has formed around it? Jamilah Evelyn thinks they do, and in "To the Academy with Love, from a Hip-Hop Fan," she encourages professors to see the positive side of hip-hop — "its poetic, solicitous, and uplifting facets." What do you find positive about hip-hop?

Evelyn was formerly the editor of *Black Issues in Higher Education*, where this essay first appeared on December 7, 2001. She has also served as editor of *Community College Week* and has written about minority issues for several other education trade publications. Evelyn is currently an assistant editor at the *Chronicle of Higher Education*, a weekly newspaper that covers important issues at colleges and universities across the country.

THINKING AHEAD

To what extent do you think college professors are obligated to be aware of the major influences on the lives of their students? What would those major cultural influences be? What is their relevance to the classroom?

INCREASING VOCABULARY

empathetic (adj.) (2)
rapport (n.) (2)
enhanced (v.) (2)
hue (n.) (4)
vulgarities (n.) (4)
incarnation (n.) (4)
demoralizing (n.) (6)
facet (n.) (6)

confounds (v.) (7)
inclusive (adj.) (8)
introspective (adj.) (8)
prolific (adj.) (8)
revelry (n.) (9)
sanctioning (n.) (11)
solicitous (adj.) (12)
disengaged (adj.) (13)

While putting together the cover story for this edition, a source asked me if I thought it was the academy's[1] responsibility to get to know and understand hip-hop—the music and its accompanying culture.

Pausing first, I replied: It may not be a professor's job to run out and buy the latest Jay-Z CD in order to better identify with her students. But the extent to which academe[2] can develop an empathetic rapport with the devotees[3] of this cultural phenomenon is partly the extent to which academe's reach will be further enhanced. And yes, I do think it's the academy's responsibility to find new ways to extend its reach.

Too many potential students, potential dropouts and potential great black (and other) leaders are at stake.

For better or worse, hip-hop has molded several generations of college students—black, white and every hue in between. With its vulgarities, its black political consciousness, its misogyny[4] and its soulful nourishment, this latest incarnation of black expression has quite simply taken the world by storm.

So love it or hate it. But do attempt to understand it.

As a member of the "hip-hop generation," and an admitted hip-hop fan, I too am distressed by any celebration of black sadism,[5] ho-ism[6] and the effect such money-making demoralizing has on our youth. But the fact that violence sells is indicative more of American pop culture in general than of this one particular facet. The recipe for that disaster is easy to explain.

Perhaps what disappoints and confounds me more is seeing a cadre[7] of scholars—often clever enough to be unmoved by the media's misplaced stereotypes—dismiss a whole genre of black music and its fans.

Where else besides higher education's forgiving, reflective and ideally inclusive sphere should we expect introspective exchanges on the music and the society that shapes it? Who else besides a professor, conscious of the thoughtful and intellectual side of kids otherwise cast as degenerates,[8] should we expect to give a ringing endorsement of hip-hop's prolific proteges?[9]

Hip-hop is so much more than the rump-shaking, "ice"-flossing,[10] gangster revelry that fuels the record industry's multibillion dollar sales every year.

That said, let us all keep in mind that even the dark and demoralized

---

[1] **the academy:** A general term used to refer to the world of academia.
[2] **academe:** The academic world.
[3] **devotees:** Followers or supporters.
[4] **misogyny:** A hatred of women.
[5] **sadism:** A delight in cruelty.
[6] **ho-ism:** Acting like a prostitute or amoral person.
[7] **cadre:** A nucleus or core group.
[8] **degenerates:** People who do not act in ways that are normally accepted.
[9] **proteges:** People whose careers are furthered by a person of experience or influence.
[10] **"ice"-flossing:** Flaunting expensive jewelry (ice).

side of hip-hop is no more than a byproduct of the capitalist mindset that higher education often endorses.

So before we collectively disregard what the student on this edition's cover dubbed "the soundtrack of our lives," it would perhaps be a better strategy to show some understanding. We can accept and reach out to our students—the b-boys,[11] the hoochie mamas[12] and the thugged out[13] among them—without sanctioning the more destructive ethos[14] that unfortunately defines so much of the music today.

Truth be told, I was pleasantly surprised at the number of scholars I talked to who see hip-hop's redemptive aspects. Many even encourage their students to draw on its poetic, solicitous and uplifting facets to prepare their papers, understand current events, indeed to change the world.

But I would encourage more of their colleagues to recognize that hip-hop's fruitage[15] includes the disengaged learner as well as the Rhodes Scholar.[16] It includes the kid who never even made it to college and the one who exceeded everyone's expectations.

It also includes the editor of a magazine devoted to making sure that higher education opens more doors, expands more minds and reaches out to ever more students who traditionally have been left out of the equation. Anyone committed to that mission has got to keep it real.

EXERCISING VOCABULARY

1. Evelyn encourages other professors to try to see "hip-hop's redemptive aspects" (para. 12). What kinds of activities are usually referred to as redemptive? What aspects of hip-hop fit the definition of something redemptive? How do they fit?

2. The author insists that anyone who wants to keep education's doors open to a wide range of students "has got to keep it real" (para. 14). Keep what real? What does she mean by *real* here? How can this be accomplished?

PROBING CONTENT

1. What should a professor's obligation to hip-hop be? Why? What would this accomplish?

2. Why is a university environment the ideal place to evaluate hip-hop? What should a professor be able to see in hip-hop's listeners that others might miss?

---

[11]**b-boys:** Gang of men or boys, originally a basketball term.
[12]**hoochie mamas:** Amoral women.
[13]**thugged out:** Gangster-like.
[14]**ethos:** The distinguishing character or guiding belief of a person, group, or institution.
[15]**fruitage:** The product or result.
[16]**Rhodes Scholar:** A recipient of one of numerous scholarships founded by Cecil J. Rhodes to allow gifted students to study at Oxford University in England.

CONSIDERING CRAFT

1. This article was published in an academic journal called *Black Issues in Education*. Who likely reads this journal? How are Evelyn's writing style and vocabulary indicative of her awareness of this reading audience? Use examples to discuss how this essay might be different if it had been written for a university student publication.

2. Evelyn admits in paragraph 6 that she is a hip-hop fan. How does having this information early in the article influence your reading of her essay? Why did she feel it necessary to let her readers know her position?

RESPONDING TO THE WRITER

To what extent do you agree with Jamilah Evelyn that the university is a good environment in which to study hip-hop music? Explain what you think might be gained by such discussions. How receptive would most of the college faculty you know be to the inclusion of rap's merits or lack thereof in classroom discussions?

For a quiz on this reading, go to www.bedfordstmartins.com/mirror.

DRAWING CONNECTIONS

1. Leonard Pitts reveals that the original intent of the essay that became "Value of Life Lost in Gangsta Rap's Refrain" was to commemorate "the twentieth anniversary of the hip-hop revolution." How would a commemoration of hip-hop have been different if Jamilah Evelyn had been asked to write it?

2. Would Evelyn agree with Pitts that hip-hop and rap have chosen unfortunate aspects of the black experience in America to "celebrate"? To what extent do they agree on the reasons behind the popularity of these harsh themes? What arguments might Evelyn use to convince Pitts that rap does have redemptive value?

3. Evelyn writes that hip-hop's dark side is "a byproduct of the capitalist mind-set" (para. 10). Use examples from Pitts's essay to prove whether he would agree or disagree with her statement.

Wrapping Up Chapter 8

REFLECTING ON THE WRITING

1. In "Crossing Pop Lines," Valdes-Rodriguez writes that music is one of our society's "most powerful cultural forces." Write an essay in which you agree with this assertion, supporting your position with specific examples of music that has strongly influenced our history and cultural development as well as your own taste. Or, if you disagree, choose another powerful cultural force and prove its influence.

2. Following Stephen Corey's model, choose a recently deceased musical artist and write an essay about the impact of his or her life and death on you. Be sure to identify songs that were special to you (you may wish to include some lyrics) and such details as when you first became aware of the artist's music, to what extent you became a fan, and how you first learned of the artist's death.

3. Using essays from this chapter and your own experience, write an essay in which you agree or disagree with David Byrne's assertion that there "is more exciting creative music making going on outside the Western pop tradition than inside it" (para. 4). Be sure to use specific examples to reinforce your position.

4. Following Jamilah Evelyn's example, choose a style of music and write an essay in which you describe the benefits to our culture of that type of music. Be sure to defend the music you choose against the most obvious criticisms and also include specific references to artists and songs that illustrate your points.

CONNECTING TO THE CULTURE

1. Choose a genre of music with which you are not familiar. Do some research on the origins of the music, the prominent artists involved, and the popularity of the music. Listen to as much of this music as you can find, including CDs and videos, if possible, over a period of at least several days. Then write an essay in which you detail your new experience. Be sure to discuss how easy or difficult it was for you to spend time with this new music and describe its effects on you, both as you listened and as you reflect on the experience.

2. Select one style of music that you would not normally listen to and write an essay in which you explore its history, its current popularity, the way its artists are treated by the media, and what you predict will be its future. Be sure to refer to specific artists and especially well-known songs that best represent the type of music you have chosen.

3. Write an essay in which you explore the role of music in movies, in television shows, or in commercials. Choose specific examples to illustrate the degree to which music influences, enhances, or detracts from your chosen medium.

4. In an essay, explore the idea that listening to each other's music may be able to bring people of various cultures to a better understanding of each other. How would this exchange take place? How willing would people be to undertake such an experiment? What factors might hinder the success of such a project? What changes in our world might result? How lasting would the effects be?

FOCUSING ON YESTERDAY, FOCUSING ON TODAY

When Elvis Presley first gyrated his swiveling hips onto the American stage, parents were appalled. Predictions that Elvis and rock 'n' roll would be the downfall of American culture were rampant. But we call Elvis "The King," and rock 'n' roll has proven that it's "here to stay." Today the music scene offers Britney Spears, whose outfits are no less eye-catching and whose hips are no less swiveling.

How does Britney compare with Elvis as a force on the American music scene? Why might Britney have modeled her costume on one worn by Elvis? What message may she have wanted to send by wearing it for her Las Vegas tour? How do these two photographs reflect the stature of each singer? What are their similarities and differences as icons of popular culture?

Britney Spears

CHAPTER 9

Are We Having Fun Yet?

Sports and Leisure in Contemporary Culture

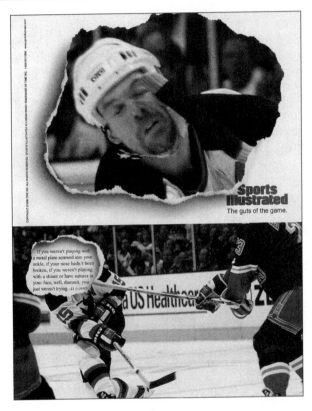

This advertisement for *Sports Illustrated* appeared in *People* magazine. It seems to reinforce the argument that our sports are sometimes more about violence than about sports. Notice the small type beneath the words *Sports Illustrated* in the top photo: "The guts of the game." Are sports all about guts and glory?

- Why would *Sports Illustrated* choose this set of photos for its advertising?
- Which readers of *People* were probably the intended target audience? How do you know this?
- Read the words in the cutout in the lower photo. What is your reaction to these words? What reaction were the advertisers hoping to generate?
- What message does this ad send about hockey players? What message does it send about sports in America in general? Is that message accurate?

Research this topic with TopLinks at www.bedfordstmartins.com/toplinks.

GEARING UP

If you suddenly had a free day to do whatever you wanted to, how would you choose to spend that time? What does "leisure time" mean to you? What role do sports play in your life? To what extent has playing sports video games replaced playing sports "for real"? Is there any harm in someone spending all his or her leisure time on the computer? Why or why not?

Do you ever think about what role leisure time play in your life? Maybe you just think you don't have any. But in those off minutes—or hours—what do you choose to do? Do you kick around a soccer ball? Read? Check email or surf the Web? Hang out at the mall? Does it even matter if you have any personal time in your life? Does it matter how you invest it? Are there harmful ways to spend leisure time? This chapter offers a wide range of experiences and opinions on the options available to fill our leisure moments. From the gaudy glitter of Las Vegas to playing and watching sports to cruising the local mall, the choices we make as we work to relax speak volumes about our lives, our values, and our culture. As you read, think about which activities attract you and why. Then think about the consequences of investing your hard-earned free time in those pursuits.

COLLABORATING

In groups of three or four, talk about how you spend your free time. Discuss the relative merits of the ways you invest these valuable moments and evaluate what you gain by spending time in these activities. Compare your list of activities with the list of one other group. Do the people who invest their time in the same way do so for the same reasons or feel that they gain the same benefits?

Wrestling with Myself

GEORGE FELTON

"Why do I love wrestling?" George Felton asks himself in the following essay. He knows that he's not "supposed" to like it, because it's fake and silly, but these are some of the very qualities that draw him to professional wrestling. "The great redemption of pro wrestling," writes Felton, "[is] the way it delivers me from civilization and its discontents." He finds himself interested in both the themes of wrestling ("warrior kings doing battle to see who is worthy") and its pop-culture novelty. As you read this amusing portrait of pro wrestling, consider your own opinion. If you're a fan, what do you find appealing about it? If you never tune in to WWF matches, does Felton's analysis of pro wrestling's appeal make you want to see what you might have been missing?

Felton is a professor of English at the Columbus College of Art and Design in Ohio, where he teaches writing and ad copywriting. He is the author of the textbook *Advertising: Concept and Copy* (1993), and his essays on pop culture, the media, and his own perplexities have appeared in the *New York Times, Newsweek, Brandweek, Advertising Age,* the *Chronicle of Higher Education,* and the *Wall Street Journal.* "Wrestling with Myself" originally appeared in the *Baltimore Sun Magazine* on November 11, 1990.

THINKING AHEAD

Are you a wrestling fan? Why or why not? Do you believe that televised matches represent true violence, or are they merely staged for profit, the winner identified before the first contestant even enters the ring? How do you explain the appeal of this sport?

INCREASING VOCABULARY

emote (v.) (1)
blithely (adv.) (1)
demographics (n.) (4)
mayhem (n.) (4)
passé (adj.) (5)

annihilations (n.) (6)
surfeit (n.) (6)
hybrid (adj.) (7)
ventricles (n.) (8)
temper (v.) (10)

It's Saturday morning, 11 AM, right after the cartoons: time for "The NWA Main Event." As I watch the ringside announcer set up today's card, a huge wrestler—topless and sweating, wearing leather chaps and a cowboy hat, carrying a lariat with a cowbell on it—bursts into frame, grabs the announcer by his lapels, and, chunks of tobacco spraying out of his mouth, begins to emote: "Well lookee here, this is just what eats in my craw. . . . I don't care if you're the president or the chief of police, it don't matter, I'm gonna do what I wanna do," and what he mostly wants to do is wrassle somebody good for once—enough nobodies in the ring, enough wimps running the schedule. As quickly as he spills into camera, he veers out, having delivered exactly the twenty-second sound bite required. Our announcer blithely sends us to commercial, and another Saturday's wrestling hour has begun. I feel better already.

I soon find out this cowboy's name is Stan Hanson, he's from Border, Texas, and lately he's been getting disqualified in all his matches for trying to kill his opponents and then "hogtying" them with his lariat. We get to watch a recent match in which he kicks some poor guy's stomach furiously with his pointed-toe cowboy boots and drop-slams his elbow into his neck and, after getting him down, hits him over the head with the cowbell, and first whips, then strangles him with his lariat. It's great stuff, with the bell ringing madly and the referee waving his arms, but Stan's already yanked the guy outside the ring onto the apron and he's still on top, trying to kill him.

Why do I love this? Why am I crazy about Stan Hanson, who's old and fat and a man the announcer warns us "ought to be in a straitjacket and chains"? Because he personifies the great redemption of pro wrestling, the way it delivers me from civilization and its discontents. Not only is Stan Hanson mad as hell and not taking it anymore, but he's doing it all for me—getting himself disqualified so that I won't run the risk myself, but inviting me to grab one end of the rope and pull. He is my own id[1]— the hairy beast itself—given a Texas identity and a push from behind, propelled out there into the "squared circle" where I can get a good look at it: sweat-soaked, mean, kicking at the slats, looking for an exposed neck. My heart leaps up, my cup runneth over.

Obviously I can't tell my friends about too much of this. If I even mention pro wrestling, they just stare at me and change the subject. They think I'm kidding. I am not supposed to like pro wrestling—its demographics are too downscale, its Dumb Show too transparent. They complain that it's fake and silly, which to me are two of its great charms. If it were real, like boxing, it'd be too painful to watch, too sad. I like knowing it's choreographed: the staged mayhem lets me know someone has studied me and will toss out just the meat the dark, reptilian centers of my brain require to stay fed and stay put. Sadomasochism?[2] Homoeroticism?[3] I am treated to the spectacle of Ric "The Nature Boy" Flair, astride the corner ropes and his opponent. His fist may be in the air, triumphant, but his groin is in the other guy's face, and he keeps it there. For once the ringside announcers are speechless as we all stare, transfixed, at this clearest of symbolic postures. Consciously I am squirming, but my reptilian center feels the sun on its back.

---

[1] **id:** Part of the psyche ruled by pleasure-seeking instinct.

[2] **sadomasochism:** The derivation of pleasure from the infliction of physical or mental pain either on others or on oneself.

[3] **homoeroticism:** Being aroused sexually by a member of the same sex.

Racism? Ethnocentrism?[4] Am I unsettled about Japanese hegemony?[5]   5
No problem. There is, in the World Wrestling Federation, a tag team of
scowling, unnervingly business-oriented Japanese toughs—the Orient Express, managed by Mr. Fuji—who invite me to hate them, and of course I
do. Their failure is my success, and I don't even have to leave the living
room. Two oversized, red-trunked Boris types used to parade around the
ring under a red flag and insist, to our booing, on singing the Russian national anthem before wrestling. Since the Cold War has become passé,
however, I've noticed matches pitting Russians *against each other,* and
that, as my newspaper tells me, is not passé. I hear groans of delight from
below, as this reprise of Cain and Abel[6] croons its libidinal[7] tune.

I mean, where else can I take my id out for a walk, how else to let it   6
smell the sweaty air, root its nose through the wet leaves? Cartoons? No
amount of Wile E. Coyote spring-loaded bounces, no pancakings of Roger
Rabbit, none of the whimsical annihilations of Cartoonville can approxi-
mate the satisfactions of a real boot in a real belly, a man's head twisted
up in the ropes, the merry surfeit of flying drop kicks, suplexes, sleeper
holds, and heart punches, all landed somewhere near real bodies. Pro
sports? I get more, not less, neurotic rooting for my teams—my neck
muscles ache, my stomach burns with coffee, after enduring another four-
hour Cleveland Browns loss on TV. The Indians? Don't even get me
started. The violence of movies like *The Last Action Hero* and
Cliffhanger? Needlessly complicated by storyline.

No, give it to me straight. Wrestling may be a hybrid genre—the epic   7
poem[8] meets Marvel Comics[9] via the soap opera—but its themes, with
their medieval tone, could hardly be simpler: warrior kings doing battle
after battle to see who is worthy, women pushed almost to the very edges
of the landscape, *Beowulf*'s[10] heroic ideal expressed in the language of an
after-school brawl: "I wanna do what I wanna do. You gonna try to stop
me?"

I also appreciate the pop-culture novelty of pro wrestling, its endear-   8
ing way of creating, a little smudged and thick-fingered, but with a great
earnest smile ("Here, look at this!") new *bêtes noires*[11] for our consumption. One of the newest is something called Big Van Vader, a guy in a
total upper torso headgear that looks like *Star Wars*[12] Meets a Mayan
Temple. He carries a stake topped with a skull and can shoot steam out of
ventricles on his shoulders, but it looks like all he can do to keep from

---

[4] ethnocentrism: The attitude that one's own group is superior.
[5] hegemony: Domination over others.
[6] Cain and Abel: Biblical sons of Adam and Eve; Cain murdered Abel in a jealous rage.
[7] libidinal: Of or relating to the sex drive.
[8] epic poem: A long narrative poem, often dealing with legendary or historical events.
[9] **ESL** Marvel Comics: A leading comic book, toy, and entertainment company.
[10] *Beowulf:* A long Anglo-Saxon epic poem; the most important work of Old English litera-
    ture.
[11] *bêtes noires:* A person or thing to be strongly avoided.
[12] **ESL** *Star Wars:* A science-fiction motion picture series directed by George Lucas.

toppling over. He's horrifying and silly all at once, an atavistic[13] night-dream wearing a "Kick Me" sign.

Such low rent Show Biz, this admixture of the asylum and the circus, is central to wrestling's double-tracked pleasure. Its emotional *reductio ad absurdum*[14] taps my anger like a release valve, but its silliness allows me to feel superior to it as I watch. I can be dumb and intelligent, angry and amused, on all fours yet ironically detached, all at the same moment.

It's a very satisfying mix, especially since my life between Saturdays is such an exercise in self-control, modesty, and late twentieth century angst.[15] To my students I am the helpful Mr. Felton. To my chairman I am the responsible Mr. Felton. To virtually everybody and everything else I'm the confused and conflicted Mr. F. My violence amounts to giving people the finger, usually in traffic. When I swear I mutter. To insults I quickly add the disclaimer, "just kidding," a move I learned from watching David Letterman[16] temper his nastiness. I never yell at people, threaten them, twist my heel into their ears, batter their heads into ring posts, or catch them flush with folding chairs. I don't wear robes and crowns and have bosomy women carry them around for me, either. In short, I never reduce my life to the satisfying oversimplification I think it deserves.

I'm a wimp. Just the sort of guy Cactus Jack or old Stan himself would love to sink his elbows into, a sentiment with which I couldn't agree more. And that brings us to the deepest appeal of pro wrestling: It invites me to imagine the annihilation of my own civilized self. When Ric Flair jabs his finger into the camera and menaces his next opponent with, "I guarantee you one thing—Junkyard Dog or no Junkyard Dog, you're going to the hospital," when another of the Four Horsemen growls, "I'm gonna take you apart on national television," the real thrill is that they're coming for me. And when Stan offers me one end of the rope, we both know just whose neck we're pulling on. Ah, redemption.

EXERCISING VOCABULARY

1. Felton refers to wrestling as "a hybrid genre" (para. 7). Define *genre*. What are the characteristics of a hybrid? To what extent are these definitions true of wrestling?

2. The wrestler Stan Hanson, Felton claims, "personifies the great redemption of pro wrestling" (para. 3). What is personification? What does Hanson personify for Felton? With what is the term *redemption* usually associated? For Felton, how is wrestling a form of redemption?

---

[13] **atavistic:** Reverting to a past style, manner, outlook, or approach.
[14] *reductio ad absurdum:* An argument that states a thesis must be accepted because its rejection would be illogical.
[15] **angst:** A feeling of anxiety, apprehension, or insecurity.
[16] **ESL** **David Letterman:** Host of a popular late-night talk show.

PROBING CONTENT

1. Why does George Felton watch pro wrestling? Why does this attraction seem an unusual one for this man?

2. According to the author's friends, what's wrong with pro wrestling? How does Felton view their objections?

3. In what sense is the failure of wrestlers who represent foreign cultures a success for Felton? How do these wrestlers "invite" the author to hate them (para. 5)?

4. What is there about watching pro wrestling that satisfies Felton more than watching other pro sports? What lessens his enjoyment of action movies?

CONSIDERING CRAFT

1. The author repeatedly uses vivid imagery to describe the part of himself to which pro wrestling appeals. For example, he mentions "my own id — the hairy beast itself" (para. 3). Find at least one other example of this imagery. What does Felton seem to be describing? Why does he choose such imagery? What does this imagery symbolize?

2. Felton ends paragraph 3 with a quotation from a William Wordsworth poem — "My heart leaps up when I behold / A rainbow in the sky" — followed by a quotation from Psalm 23 in the Bible. Such images of peace and contentment seem to be at odds with the violence of pro wrestling. Why then does Felton choose this language and these sources? What point is he attempting to make?

RESPONDING TO THE WRITER

To what extent do you accept Felton's inference that each of us has a dark, primitive core that longs for violent expression? If Sigmund Freud was correct and such a primal nature does exist in each of us, what keeps it suppressed? What do you see around you to support or deny Freud's — and Felton's — assertion?

For a quiz on this reading, go to www.bedfordstmartins.com/mirror.

Loving Las Vegas

Dan DeLuca

From a mecca of gambling and prostitution, Las Vegas has recently reinvented itself into what Dan DeLuca calls "a Disneyland for adults." Some promoters have gone so far as to claim that Las Vegas is now the perfect family vacation destination with its fantasy hotels, big-name entertainers, and overloaded buffet tables. Whatever Vegas was, or is becoming, captures the American imagination. Even if you can't travel to Nevada, you can experience a little bit of the Strip from the comfort of your local movie theater, Vegas theme restaurant, or casino. In this essay, which first appeared in the May 18, 1997, edition of the *Philadelphia Inquirer*, DeLuca explores the potentially dangerous appeal of this city in the desert, this truly American place. DeLuca has been a writer for the *Philadelphia Inquirer* since 1989. A lover of pop music, he has also written articles for *Billboard, Rolling Stone,* and *Request.* Of his first visit to Las Vegas in 1997, DeLuca says, "It was a monument to Mammon.[1] It was incredible, mind-blowing."

THINKING AHEAD

In what ways can Las Vegas be seen as "the pop-culture center of America"? Describe Las Vegas from what you have seen or heard about it and reflect on what the city represents.

INCREASING VOCABULARY

mecca (n.) (7)	doldrums (n.) (22)
swashbuckling (adj.) (7)	conjures (v.) (24)
replicate (v.) (8)	inhibition (n.) (24)
trilogy (n.) (10)	nostalgic (adj.) (24)
metamorphosis (n.) (19)	cliché (n.) (34)
decadence (n.) (21)	surreality (n.) (34)

In *Mars Attacks,* the aliens went there to blow Jack Nicholson—and his UFO-themed casino—to smithereens. 1

In *Showgirls,* Elizabeth Berkley went there to become a professional dancer, and got sidetracked into lap-dancing. 2

In *Honeymoon in Vegas,* Nicolas Cage went to the Mojave Desert's neon oasis to get married. In *Leaving Las Vegas,* he returned to drink himself to death. And in *Con Air,* out next month, he's back, crashlanding a transport plane in the middle of the Strip. 3

[1] **Mammon:** Material wealth.

Irish rockers U2 descended on Sin City last month to launch their   4
flashy, state-of-the-art "Popmart" tour, which hits Philadelphia on June 7
and 8.

And in September, Tupac Shakur went to the largest hotel in the   5
world, Vegas' 5,005-room MGM Grand, for a Mike Tyson fight, and,
hours later, was hit with a fatal barrage of gunfire while riding to Suge
Knight's hip-hop nightclub.

Las Vegas isn't only the fastest-growing city in the nation: It's where   6
American pop culture has gone to play out the end of the century.

The gambling mecca in the middle of nowhere has grown bigger than   7
visionary mobster Bugsy Siegel could have imagined when he opened the
Flamingo Hotel in 1946. With casinos from the Luxor (a black glass pyramid bigger than the Great Pyramid in Egypt) and New York–New York
(with its quarterscale replica of the Manhattan skyline), to the swashbuck-
ling Treasure Island and rock-and-roll Hard Rock, Vegas retains its reputation as a Disneyland for adults.

But Vegas doesn't just replicate culture. In the '90s, it has *become* cul-   8
ture, its influence reaching coast to coast and beyond.

The first in a national chain of Vegas-themed eateries will open in   9
Times Square next year. (Developers hope to follow with a Philadelphia
location in '99.) Filmmakers use the city as a metaphor for sex, greed and
the American dream of making the big score. Casinos are turning up on
riverboats and Indian reservations nationwide. Strip clubs like Delilah's
Den[2] have gone mainstream. And a new generation has embraced the
martini-swilling lounge culture epitomized by swingin' Vegas icons Frank
Sinatra, Dean Martin and Sammy Davis Jr.

"It's the place where the action is," says Michael Ventura, a long-   10
time Las Vegas resident whose latest novel, *The Death of Frank Sinatra*,
is the first of a Vegas trilogy. "What other symbol do we have that
says 'America, 1997'? Not New York City. Not the Grand Canyon.
It's Vegas."

What Nevadans insist on calling "gaming" is still what makes Vegas   11
run: Twenty-nine million visitors dropped $5.5 billion gambling there last
year. The industry is at the core of an economy that each month attracts
3,000 new residents to the town whose Spanish name translates as "the
meadows."

(Despite a growing number of visitors, gambling revenue on the Strip   12
was actually down slightly in 1996. Insiders attribute the drop to the family vacationers the city began cultivating a few years back and predict that
the department of tourism will soon return to its senses.)

But since the Hard Rock Hotel and Casino opened in 1995, Las   13
Vegas—once equated with the fat Elvis and has-been pop artists—has
gone hip. The image of Elvis has been unofficially banned from the Strip,

---

[2]**Delilah's Den:** Philadelphia nightclub known for its strippers.

and bands such as No Doubt, Live and Marilyn Manson have all played the Joint, the Hard Rock's concert venue.

U2's decision to open its intentionally sleazy Popmart spectacular in   14
Vegas made perfect sense. "I slept under a pyramid, looked outside my window and saw the New York skyline," Bono said from the stage of Sam Boyd Stadium. "This is the only town on the planet where nobody's going to notice a 40-foot lemon [on stage]."

Camera crews are crawling all over the town. Twenty-nine feature   15
films were at least partially shot in Vegas last year, according to Bob Hirsch, director of the Nevada Motion Picture Division. Never mind the music videos and TV shows and commercials.

In the last three months alone, the city has starred in Chevy Chase's   16
Vegas Vacation and the Matthew Perry–Salma Hayek romantic comedy *Fools Rush In,* and had a featured role in Mike Myers' hipster comedy *Austin Powers.* After *Con Air* in June, its next big part will come in the film adaptation of Hunter Thompson's hallucinogenic memoir *Fear and Loathing in Las Vegas,* which begins shooting in July with Johnny Depp playing the gonzo[3] journalist.

"We reinvent ourselves every six months, so there's always something   17
new for people to shoot" says Hirsch. "Next week, we're shooting a commercial for a chewing gum company in Finland and another with a company that makes stoves in Brazil."

"Vegas has become a required course in pop-cultural literacy," says   18
Hirsch. "It's a place that you're supposed to go."

Steve Saeta, associate producer of *Fools Rush In*—one of the few   19
flicks to acknowledge, in Hayek's Mexican American character, the existence of Vegas' swelling minority population—agrees that the city's constant metamorphosis is a draw.

"There are scenes we shot a year ago we couldn't get today," says   20
Saeta, who was an assistant director on Robert Urich's *Vega$* TV series in the '70s. Plus, he says, Vegas has "a collection of landmarks as identifiable as the Eiffel Tower. The bigger and the gaudier the better."

In last year's Gen X[4] lounge movie *Swingers,* director Doug Liman   21
sends two of his Los Angeleno characters to Vegas in quest of decadence.

"One of the guys hasn't been out of his apartment for six months,"   22
says Liman. "And there's only one cure for those kind of doldrums: Vegas."

But Vegas is more than a locale, Liman says. It's a state of mind.   23

"One of the things Vegas represents is the Rat Pack, and all the emo-   24
tions and images the Rat Pack[5] conjures up," says the director. It's about

---

[3] **gonzo:** Slang for bizarre, unconventional.
[4] **ESL Gen X:** (Generation X) People born between the years 1961–1981 who are thought to share a cynical view of the world.
[5] **ESL Rat Pack:** A social group of actors and entertainers from the late 1950s and 1960s, including Frank Sinatra, Dean Martin, Sammy Davis Jr., Peter Lawford, and Joey Bishop.

a lack of inhibition, and time "when smoking wasn't bad for you and drinking wasn't bad for you and it was fine to whistle at a woman. The characters in the movie have a nostalgic view of what dating was like in the '50s, before the age of the answering machine."

Kitschy[6] appreciation of the finger-snappin' Vegas of old is what de-   25
fines the Cocktail Nation, represented by new bands such as Combustible Edison and Love Jones, and cheesy '60s artists like Esquivel and Martin Denny.

"The MTV generation is looking back at people like Tony Bennett   26
and Frank Sinatra and thinking, 'Wow, that's really cool,'" says James Austin, producer of the Rhino Records anthology *Jackpot! The Las Vegas Story,* which includes Wayne Newton, Engelbert Humperdinck and Liber-ace. "Vegas used to have a real stigma attached to it, but now they look at the glitz and glitter as being fun."

Las Vegas native Susan Berman, who coproduced a four-hour docu-   27
mentary on the city for the Arts & Entertainment channel, is the daughter of Davie Berman, a Bugsy Siegel lieutenant who ran the Flamingo after Siegel's death. She says she isn't surprised by Vegas' growth spurt. (In ad-dition to the recently opened $460 million New York-New York, Vegas impresario Steve Wynn is building the $1.25 billion Italianate Bellagio, and there are Paris- and Venice-themed casinos under construction.)

"It's a town of second chances," says Berman, who's developing a   28
Vegas-based TV series with the producers of *Baywatch*. "Fantasy never quits," not even—or perhaps, especially—when the economy falls on hard times.

But for all its orchestrated unreality, Las Vegas is very much American.   29

"People act as if it's this weird place where you go that doesn't have   30
anything to do with America," says David Shields, author of the pop-culture memoir *Remote*. "But it's America multiplied—all concentrated on a 10-mile-by-10-mile plot of land in the desert. Good and bad, vital and comical . . . Las Vegas is like a pornographic movie of the American imagination."

"Las Vegas is the Rorschach test[7] of popular culture," says Andrew   31
Raines, chairman of Creative Cafes, the Los Angeles company that, in the next five years, plans to open twenty-five Vegas! restaurants in the United States and abroad. "It's the place where people take the idea of what fun and pleasure should be and create it.

"One of the exportable elements of American culture, besides music   32
and movies, is Las Vegas," says Raines, whose cafes will feature show-girls, marquee lounge entertainment and a "safe" gaming area where people can wager without losing money. "As the world becomes homoge-nized and American culture becomes dominant, people want to come to

---

[6] kitschy: In bad taste, trashy, especially referring to art or artwork.
[7] Rorschach test: Diagnostic test used by psychologists in which patients are asked to inter-pret ink blots.

Mecca. Vegas is one of the key icons, and people want to see it. I'm taking it around the world."

So even as the rest of the country goes lap-dancing and considers le-   33
galizing gambling, by remaking itself bigger and more outrageous than ever, Vegas has managed to preserve its unique identity.

"The cliché is that America has caught up to Vegas—that all the   34
things that used to be considered criminal aren't anymore," says Ventura. "But Vegas is still a place where you can go and be bad legally. And everywhere you go, there's a level of surreality that only means Vegas."

EXERCISING VOCABULARY

1. DeLuca writes, "But for all its orchestrated unreality, Las Vegas is very much American" (para. 29). Think about what an orchestra conductor does to get the musicians to play together. What then does it mean to *orchestrate* something?

2. DeLuca writes, "As the world becomes homogenized and American culture becomes dominant, people want to come to Mecca" (para. 32). What happens when you homogenize milk? What does it mean for many different cultures to be *homogenized?* Why does DeLuca refer to Las Vegas as "Mecca"?

3. DeLuca describes mobster Bugsy Siegel as "visionary" (para. 7). What visions do you think Siegel had for Las Vegas in 1946 when he opened the Flamingo Hotel? In what ways is being a visionary a good thing?

PROBING CONTENT

1. Why, according to the essay, is Las Vegas "a Disneyland for adults" (para. 7)? What are adults who go there looking for?

2. How, according to the writer, has Las Vegas "*become* culture" (para. 8)? How is its influence seen outside its city limits?

3. How does DeLuca describe Las Vegas in its early days of the Rat Pack and Bugsy Siegel? What stigma was once attached to it?

4. What does it mean when the author says that Las Vegas has "gone hip" (para. 13)? Whom do the MTV generation now consider "cool"? What does this say about their opinion of Las Vegas?

5. Why, according to the writer, are there so many movies filmed in Las Vegas? What kind of movies are they? What message are they trying to send to their viewers?

CONSIDERING CRAFT

1. The title, "Loving Las Vegas," sounds very similar to the movie title *Leaving Las Vegas* mentioned in paragraph 3. Keeping in mind what the author tells you about the basic storyline of the movie, why do you think DeLuca deliberately calls it to mind in his essay title? What two faces of Las Vegas is he trying to bring to mind?

2. Why does DeLuca begin his essay by mentioning several movie scenes that were shot in Las Vegas? What point is he trying to get across?

3. The original newspaper article had two large boldfaced headings that read, "Is gaudy, greedy Vegas a national symbol?" and "The pop-culture center of America is Las Vegas." Does the second heading answer the question posed in the first one? Discuss what is meant by both the question and the answer.

RESPONDING TO THE WRITER

DeLuca implies that Las Vegas is the pop culture center of America. Pick another possible city for this title and discuss why it is a better choice than Las Vegas.

For a quiz on this reading, go to www.bedfordstmartins.com/mirror.

The Only Game Not in Town

FRED BALDWIN

In online gaming, real players—who often have never met in person—face off against each other over the Internet. It's an activity that's quickly gaining popularity—one currently popular game, EverQuest, boasts a subscriber base of more than 300,000. Would you call games like this "antisocial"? What happens to the normal social dynamics of game play when participants aren't face-to-face? In the following essay, Fred Baldwin answers these questions by examining the virtual environment of online gaming. Baldwin finds that just as in face-to-face games, manners matter in virtual communities, too; you must know the social rules for each game and abide by them.

Baldwin is a full-time freelance writer, the author of four hundred articles and several books, including *The Camelot Contract* (1997) and *Infomedicine: A Consumer's Guide to the Latest Medical Research* (1996). Most of his articles have appeared in magazines that focus on health, technology, business, or regional topics. "The Only Game *Not* in Town" was first published in the June 2001 issue of U.S. Airways *Attaché* magazine. Baldwin's favorite online game is Go, a three-thousand-year-old Japanese game of strategy.

THINKING AHEAD

Do you enjoy computer games or have friends who do? What is the great attraction of these games? What effect has the fascination with computer and video games had on some people's ability to relate well to others?

INCREASING VOCABULARY

anonymity (n.) (1)	formidable (adj.) (14)
intricately (adv.) (3)	vendors (n.) (14)
simulated (v.) (4)	dynamics (n.) (16)
impeccably (adv.) (6)	lair (n.) (19)
etiquette (n.) (6)	taboo (n.) (20)
saga (n.) (11)	

When you play competitive games on the Internet—games with people you may never meet face-to-face—first impressions can be misleading. A poker player whose online alias is Bamabadboy may be a grandmother from Vermont; Princess Mithra, an elf maiden in a role-playing adventure game, may be a sixteen-year-old male. Over time, however, for all of the hi-tech wizardry that makes online gaming possible and despite a considerable degree of anonymity, the so-

1

cial aspects of online play are not all that different from those you learn playing kickball at elementary school, poker at a small-town firehouse, or bridge at a local club. Cyberspace or face-to-face, manners matter.

We're talking here about play with real people, of course, not play 2 against the computer programs that drive arcade games and gambling simulations. Because the Internet is such an immense playground, unless you do all your online play by pre-arrangement with friends, you'll meet lots of strangers. One major search engine lists over seventeen thousand Web sites for games and game-related material.

You can find traditional board and card games like backgammon, 3 chess, and bridge, as well as popular commercial games like Monopoly, Scrabble, and Risk. You can also find adventure-game sites whose intricately imagined playing environments are created by computers, but where other human players may become adversaries or allies.

Because the Internet spans the world's time zones, you can play the 4 more popular games whenever the mood strikes. I recently played online bridge on a spur-of-the-moment impulse. Three of us at the simulated table were physically located in different states of the United States; the fourth player was in Belgium, where the time would have been around midnight.

To find board games and card games that are popular enough to at- 5 tract thousands of players, your best places to start are multigame sites operated by Yahoo!, Microsoft, and other commercial companies. After choosing your game, you'll download free software that simulates a physical playing environment on your screen (for example, a chess board and chess pieces).

Less familiar games can be found at specialized sites maintained by 6 fans. My personal game of choice is the Asian board game Go, a two-person contest of strategy, which I find at NNGS, which stands for "No-Name Go Server." Most Americans have scarcely heard of Go, much less played it, but at NNGS and elsewhere I can challenge opponents from all around the United States, Europe, and Asia. A game developed in the impeccably polite culture of Japan, Go requires good manners. I always request a game respectfully and when playing against a much stronger player, I resign as etiquette dictates, rather than fight a hopelessly lost game to the bitter end. Win or lose, I am obligated to thank my opponent for the encounter.

Socially speaking, various sites for the same game differ from each 7 other, and if you visit the same places often, you'll get to know the regulars. Most game settings provide space for real-time chat during play — so you, Dustbunny, Goofball, and No-trump911 may show up for chitchat and wisecracks as much as for bridge. At other tables, the response to a joke will be "So play, already!" Similarly, some chess and checkers sites attract only serious players; others provide online hangouts for trash-talking teenagers (or maybe people practicing their impersonations of trash-talking teenagers). Mistake one culture for the other, and you'll be corrected in no uncertain terms.

"You have two different levels of community," says Stephen Jacobs,   8
assistant professor of information technology at Rochester Institute of
Technology in upstate New York. "There are relationships that come
about because of the virtual environment. I can track down guys I haven't
seen for years and say, 'Why don't we meet online to kill dragons or play
chess or whatever?'"

If you think that killing dragons does not require much in the way of   9
social skills, think again. It's true that some online action games differ
only in the sophistication of their graphics from the arcade-type action
games that teen-aged boys play in malls. These are known as "shooter" or
"twitch" games because they make demands only on the players' reflexes.

There are, however, other types of nontraditional games online — hy-   10
brids that combine aspects of twitch games, strategy games, and improv
theater. To play them, you buy CD-ROMs whose software creates playing
environments for battles in interstellar space or in magical kingdoms inspired by J. R. R. Tolkien's *The Lord of the Rings* fantasies. You get a li-
cense to play online for a monthly fee at a designated server (the host
computer). The current market leader is a game called EverQuest ("EQ"
to its fans). There is now a worldwide subscriber base of more than three
hundred thousand, according to a recent press release, with "over seventy-
two thousand adventurers and dragon slayers" online at peak periods.

"These things work by creating a world," explains Jacobs, whose aca-   11
demic training is in media theory. "They're an ongoing saga, comparable
to the Norse mythologies — short stories within the larger series of tales.
There's always a new campaign or a new quest to save people or acquire
magical devices."

You begin by choosing among a wide range of options for creating   12
your online persona, known as an *avatar*. Warrior or wizard? Human,
dwarf, or elf? Male or female?

Then you explore a computer-simulated environment — a field or a   13
forest, for example, or a castle or a cavern. As you explore, you see
through the eyes of your avatar.

As with the twitch games, you're forced to fight progressively more   14
formidable monsters generated by the computer program. Victory earns
you loot and weapons. (There's an over-the-counter market, discouraged
by game vendors, for characters that have fought their way to advanced
levels. My quick check of eBay auctions showed early bids in excess of
$300 for a "level-54 wizard" and a near-closing bid of $615 for a "level-51
druid" with a "16th-level shadow knight" thrown in.)

In these games, you'll meet not only computer-generated monsters, but   15
other people's avatars moving through the same space at the same time.
These encounters require quick decisions about whether a stranger's reaction to your online presence will be indifference, helpfulness, or hostility.

"Because there are so many people involved and the game is so so-   16
cial," says Douglas Davis, a professor of psychology at Haverford College
in Pennsylvania, who is fascinated by the social dynamics of online games,

"you very quickly get into relationships with other characters. That, to a psychologist, is part of what makes this so interesting.

"If I'm a warrior," Davis continues, "and you're a spell-caster and someone else is a healer, we're much stronger together than we are separately. So we start teaming up, and that means we have to get to know each other. We have to have some trust and decide how to divvy[1] the loot. And do we start exchanging regular email? And, if we do, do we tell the truth about each other?"   17

One of Davis' students, Nick Yee, has done extensive surveys of gamers. Yee has found, for example, that because male players outnumber female players by roughly four to one, the chances are nearly 50/50 that a female avatar will be fronting for a male human. (A commonly offered explanation is that players tend to be more willing to cooperate with female characters, even knowing that they may be fronts for guys.)   18

Sometimes acting on instinct, sometimes by pre-arrangement, players join forces to punish cheap shots and greed. The screen images may show a dragon's lair or a city on a faraway planet, but the dynamics of play will be understandable to the kids on any playground or the guys at the fire station.   19

For example, a young friend who's been involved with role-playing games since he was fourteen recently explained his site's taboo against "kill-stealing." Because the computer gives the spoils of victory to whichever player finally kills a monster, finishing off one that someone else has weakened is frowned upon.   20

I had watched a lot of apparently random hacking and slashing, and I'd begun to think that I was seeing a world where anything goes. But then my friend's avatar stood by doing nothing while a member of his own "guild"—a good buddy, he'd told me—whacked away with a broadsword at a troll. At one point the troll seemed about to win. Should not we, I asked, go to your friend's rescue?   21

"Oh, no!" he replied, sounding a bit shocked by my ignorance. "That would be impolite."   22

EXERCISING VOCABULARY

1. What are "shooter" or "twitch" games (para. 9)? Explain how these words relate to what such games require of a player.

2. What is an avatar? What possible avatars might be chosen in a role-playing game? Why is choosing such a role preferable to simply playing as oneself? What relationships might avatars develop among themselves? Why would such relationships develop?

---

[1] **ESL** divvy: To distribute equally.

PROBING CONTENT

1. How is it possible for online gaming to teach social skills? What social skills might be learned?

2. What games can be played online? When? With whom?

3. In what country did the game Go originate? In what ways does the game reflect the culture of its native country? What appeal does the game have for Baldwin?

4. True gamers understand that a code of ethics governs online gaming. Cite and explain one of Baldwin's examples of such a code of conduct.

CONSIDERING CRAFT

1. Is Fred Baldwin an insider in the world of online gaming? Support your answer with material from Baldwin's essay. How does his relationship to the subject affect the authenticity of his essay?

2. Why does Baldwin use more quotations from academic authority figures like Stephen Jacobs and Douglas Davis than from ordinary people who regularly play online games? How does this choice of sources work to support or deny his thesis?

RESPONDING TO THE WRITER

If you are not a player, explain why this essay has or has not motivated you to explore the world of online gaming. If you already play, discuss whether you agree with Baldwin's assertion that these games teach manners and require knowledge of the games' cultural rules.

For a quiz on this reading, go to www.bedfordstmartins.com/mirror.

My Farewell to Fandom

BOB KATZ

In "My Farewell to Fandom," Bob Katz examines what it means to be a sports fan. It's a harmless enough hobby, isn't it? Not necessarily. Although sports served as a bond between Katz and his father, he wonders whether the thousands of hours he's spent in front of the television could have been used more productively. Katz's amusing account of his struggle to say farewell to fandom raises some questions about our culture's obsession with sports. What role do sports play in our lives and our relationships? Can a love of sports become an addiction? Should parents encourage their children to take an interest in sports?

"My Farewell to Fandom" was originally published in the January 25, 1999, issue of *Newsweek*. Katz, who runs a speakers' agency in Massachusetts, has also authored a novel titled *Hot Air* (1990).

THINKING AHEAD

Are you a sports fan? What sports do you watch? To which sports are you dedicated? How is watching a sport as a spectator at the game different from watching that same sport on television? Would you describe yourself or anyone you know as a sports addict? What are the attributes of a sports addict?

INCREASING VOCABULARY

aptitude (n.) (1)	knack (n.) (6)
prances (v.) (2)	expenditure (n.) (7)
distraught (adj.) (3)	benignly (adv.) (8)
perceived (adj.) (3)	latent (adj.) (9)
verged (v.) (4)	gritty (adj.) (9)
prickly (adv.) (5)	banter (v.) (9)

Not to brag, but my eight-year-old son might be one of the most prodigiously talented sports fans to come out of this region in quite some time. His natural aptitude for fandom, I'm proud to say—or at least I have been until recently—is off the charts.   1

Exhausted after a workweek, I'll be on autopilot, watching some basketball game between two college squads. My son prances into the room and immediately wants to know who's winning. At his insistence, I explain that gold and black is Purdue, green and white is Michigan State. Based simply on color preference, he begins cheering wildly for the Boilermakers.   2

Within minutes, he is utterly distraught at some perceived bad break   3
for his newly chosen team. He slams his small fist on the top of the coffee
table. His eyes redden in anger. In no time flat, he has gone from blessed
ignorance to total despair. Is this a fan, or is this a *fan?*

He's a chip off the old block, and you'd think I'd feel good about that.   4
But I don't. I'm becoming afraid my son will grow into a sports addict like
his old man. Don't get me wrong. I know all the arguments in favor of fandom. In my relationship to my own father, who's not always been the easiest person to talk to, sports have served as a vital pathway of communication. Our discussions about various living athletes—Ernie Banks, Bill
Bradley—were thinly veiled tutorials on striving and achievement, while
conversations involving the honored dead—Gehrig, Thorpe—verged on
religion, providing an early primer on my father's complicated value system.

I was a young boy in Chicago when Ted Williams in his final season   5
came to town to play the White Sox. My father, who is a tall, slender, left-
handed and sometimes prickly high achiever, took my brother and me to
this farewell game. There was something about Williams—a determination, an obsessiveness—that our father wanted us to understand. The
Splendid Splinter came through, lining two crisp doubles to the gap in
right. You can look it up.

My prodigy of a son can look it up. He has already got the knack.   6
Mornings, he studies the local sports page as if it were the tattered map to
buried treasure. "Dad," he says, glancing up in puzzlement, "what's an
Average Yards Per Carry?" I'm only too tickled to explain. Last summer I
told him about passed balls on third strikes and tagging up. This winter
it's three-second violations and what's an assist. Apparently I have a
nearly limitless store of wisdom to impart. That's a nice thing to have
tucked near the heart of a relationship to a son.

Much misty-eyed sentimentality gets spent on the subject of dads   7
passing their love of sports on to sons. That is to say, dads instructing
their sons in the rituals of being a fan. Basically it's wonderful—unless
you pause to consider the expenditure of time.

Ah, yes, the massive amounts of time consumed, the accumulated   8
hours spent viewing televised games, flipping channels for the day's dramatic replays, lured into that thickening quicksand known so benignly as
"sports trivia." Dare we even calculate how much this amounts to over
the course of a lifetime? Could some of this time be better spent practicing
on a musical instrument, chiseling away at a craft, volunteering at a com-
munity-service project? Those are skills that you don't hear much about.
Unless you are a parent to young children.

Pondering this, I can't help wondering what latent traits I never tested,   9
never discovered. Who knows, but I might have mastered something gritty
and basic and useful, like my boyhood chum Billy, who learned the intricate internal logic of a V-6 engine by actually reassembling one. A fair
athlete, Billy had absolutely no interest in ever watching sports. Now he's
probably helpless as a chimpanzee when the hood's raised on a modern

computerized auto, while I can still banter authoritatively about who played infield on the '75 Redlegs.

On the other hand, knowing so darn much about the '75 Redlegs has   10 not exactly been a major asset. The larger lessons my dad hoped I'd learn from Ted Williams (and himself) cannot derive from so passive an act as plopping down to watch a telecast.

All this comes to mind as we approach Super Bowl Sunday. I'm think-   11 ing that this might be the place to make my stand. Like always, I'll be itching to switch on the tube and call for my son to come join me. As my father did unto me. I loved that feeling of sitting beside Dad and rooting. I loved it all.

But that's what addicts always say. Kicking the habit won't be easy.   12 But I'm doing it for my boy. I'm determined to save him. Being a sports fan is fine, but I cannot allow it to consume him. There are any number of options. We might visit friends, if any can be found not hunkered down by the tube. We could go bowling if Lanes & Games is open on this na- tional holiday. There's Monopoly, chess, hiking. I'll think of something. I have to. Because the stakes are high.

Big game's fast approaching. Now I'm getting psyched. Pressure's   13 mounting. Clock's ticking down. Crunch time for Dad!

EXERCISING VOCABULARY

1. In paragraph 1, Katz refers to his son as "prodigiously talented," and in para- graph 6, Katz refers to his "prodigy of a son." What is a *prodigy?* In what sense does Katz think his son fits this definition? Given Katz's thesis in this essay, how desirable is it to be a sports prodigy?

2. Examine the expression "a chip off the old block" (para. 4). What kind of block is Katz referring to? What does this expression mean literally? What figurative meaning is implied by this often-used expression?

3. What does it mean to get "psyched" about something (para. 13)? What asso- ciated words come to mind that originate from the same root word? Is this word association positive or negative?

PROBING CONTENT

1. What has convinced Katz that his son is a true sports fan? How does the au- thor feel about this development?

2. Why were sports important in Katz's relationship with his father? What did Katz's father hope Katz would learn from sports? Does Katz believe that he learned the lessons his father intended? Why or why not?

3. Who is Billy? Why does remembering Billy cause Katz to question his devotion to watching sports?

CONSIDERING CRAFT

1. At the end of paragraph 3, Katz asks a rhetorical question: "Is this a fan, or is this a *fan?*" What is a rhetorical question? What objective does he achieve by using *fan* in italics the second time? What effect do rhetorical questions have on a reader?

2. Katz refers to himself as an addict in paragraph 12. Explain to what extent Katz's dedication to sports fits the definition of an addiction. Why would Katz choose such connotatively negative language? Why has Katz vowed to kick his habit?

RESPONDING TO THE WRITER

How successful do you think Katz will be with his "farewell to fandom"? Explain your position, using material from this essay to support your ideas. Should Katz abandon his love for sports watching? Why or why not?

For a quiz on this reading, go to www.bedfordstmartins.com/mirror.

Mall Culture

STEVEN L. SHEPHERD

The mall has become the favorite social gathering place of many young Americans. But why the mall? There are plenty of other places where teenagers could congregate. In the following essay, Steven L. Shepherd examines the suburban shopping mall and what he sees as the basis of American culture: unsatisfied want. What would happen if we did away with the barrage of commercials that create our need to consume? "Life as we know it would end," Shepherd writes. He claims that malls are children's initiation into a life of "material desires that will never be satisfied" and that they prevent children from learning to provide for themselves. Do you agree with Shepherd, or do you see malls as harmless places for young people to gather? What positive social functions might malls serve?

Shepherd is a former writer and editor for *Executive Health Report*. "Mall Culture" was first published in the November 1998 issue of the *Humanist*, a publication of the American Humanist Association.

THINKING AHEAD

When you were in high school, where did your group hang out? How much time did you spend at this location? Why did you go there? What did you do? What was the real purpose of being there? How big a part did the local mall play in your social life?

INCREASING VOCABULARY

torrent (n.) (2)	tyranny (n.) (9)
converge (v.) (7)	benign (adj.) (9)
convening (adj.) (7)	myriad (adj.) (10)
gawk (v.) (7)	venues (n.) (10)
emissary (n.) (7)	visceral (adj.) (11)
surge (v.) (7)	innocuous (adj.) (12)
curfew (n.) (8)	sated (v.) (13)
hordes (n.) (8)	

S ome time ago I had one of those thoughts so simple as to be embarrassing. Still, though it has stuck with me.   1

It occurred to me while driving through Los Angeles in summertime, through mile after mile of store after store. Sign after sign, mall after mall. Perhaps it was the heat, or perhaps the idleness of mind wrought by the relentless assault, but somewhere along the way I thought: "What if   2 you could do magic? What if you could suddenly give everyone everything they wanted? What, that is, if you could do away with the wanting? With the wanting of new cars, new clothes, new CDs, new stereos, new appliances and amusements, new gadgets and gizmos;[1] with the ceaseless, endless torrent of stuff. What if you could give everyone what they wanted?—make them content and end the wanting. What would happen?"

The answer, of course, is simple: Life as we know it would end. Without the wanting, there would be no malls, no factories or design studios working feverishly to replace one hot item with the next. None of the associated jobs. Except for the producers and purveyors[2] of necessities—bulk flour and Soviet-style clothes—the economy would stop. Which means in turn that contemporary American culture is based on unsatisfied want. On unhappiness, really. People have to be unhappy for our way of life to continue. For if we didn't ceaselessly want new things, there would be little to sell or cart about.

Depressing though it is, this is not an unfamiliar concept to some people. I first realized this on hearing the editor of a women's fashion magazine interviewed on the radio. "Why," she was asked, "don't your models look like your readers? Why not foster a definition of beauty that most women could meet? Wouldn't your readers be happier if they weren't encouraged to aspire to physiques they will never have?"

"Yes," she replied. "But then we would have no advertisers. Because our readers wouldn't need their help to be beautiful."

The true business of her magazine, the editor understood, was the manufacturer of desire—of unending discontent with one's present circumstances. If the magazine's readers were to believe they could be beautiful without the advertisers' products, the readers would have no need for the advertisers, and the advertisers none for the magazine. Therefore, the readers must be kept unhappy, always in quest of a goal that must always be kept out of reach.

I was reminded of all this when my son, then twelve, was invited recently to "go to the mall." This meant joining a small group of similarly aged young people that would converge with other convening groups into an amoeboid mass that would then roam the corridors and concourses[3] for hours. Occasionally the mass would stop before a storefront to gawk at the window display. Occasionally it would send in an emissary to make a small purchase. Occasionally it would surge into a fast food outlet. Often it would giggle. Perhaps it would visit a theatre to watch a few hours of death and disfigurement.

Recently, the trendsetting Mall of America[4] in Minneapolis imposed a

---

[1] **ESL gadgets and gizmos:** Small mechanical or electronic devices often thought of as novelties.

[2] **purveyors:** Suppliers.

[3] **concourses:** Major walkways.

[4] **ESL Mall of America:** The largest retail and entertainment complex in the United States, located in Bloomington, Minnesota.

curfew on parentless teenagers. More generally, I am told that shopkeepers profess annoyance at the hordes of roving kids outside their windows.
But I do not believe this. I do not believe the protestations are real. Or, if
they are, I believe the mallkeepers are short-sighted in their irritation. For
the malls are the temples of our culture, and "going to the mall" is in
truth naught[5] but an initiation rite. The shopkeepers should be glad of
this behavior, for as the children gaze through the windows at the well-
stocked shelves within, they are learning to want, learning to ache for
things, supplied by others and of which there can never be enough.

My immediate inclination to my son's request ("Dad, can I go to the   9
mall?") was to say "no." But my wife said that she too had gone to the
malls when she was young and that it had merely been a safe place she
and her friends could go, a place to socialize without the tyranny of
parental oversight. Other parents said it offered a benign environment for
prepubescent "boy-girl stuff," our version of the *corso*—the street or
square where young Italians gather and stroll for the purpose of being
seen.

Certainly for social creatures such as ourselves these are important   10
functions. But why does it have to happen at the mall? There are myriad
other venues and activities at which young people can meet and practice
the skills of *homo teenageus.* There are sporting events, both participatory
and not. There are parks and museums. There is the beach. There are
clubs and societies. There are volunteer organizations—help teach a
young child to read or work to clean a littered piece of landscape. But of
course, none of these suggestions has the lure, glitter, or ease of the mall.

I will grant that the mall is safe, that kids need time away from par-   11
ents, that they need a place to be together. So why then do I object to my
son's "going to the mall"? Why does his request evoke in me such visceral
opposition?

In part, because an activity that affords safety is not of itself innocu-   12
ous. It can, for instance, displace more valuable activities. When I was
growing up my father used to tell me and my siblings to turn off the TV
and find something to entertain ourselves—read a book, play in the yard,
play with a friend, daydream. Do anything, but do it of your own initia-
tive, generate it from within. Because if you provide for yourself from
within you will never be bored, never be lonely, never need rely on the
amusements of others. But now, when I say these words to my son they
sound as anachronistic as if I'd told him to hitch up the horse. For our
culture today has no use for reflection, for solitude, for that which you
can provide for yourself—for a rich inner life. These are things that cannot be sold and they are antithetical[6] to a society that sees people primarily as customers or market share.

But as important, "going to the mall" is a part of a long and many-   13

---

[5] **naught:** Nothing.
[6] **antithetical:** In direct opposition to.

pronged courtship, a part of the relentless and powerful seduction of our children by that portion of our culture that accords human beings no more value than the contents of their wallet. It is a part of the initiation into a life of wanting that can never be sated, of material desires that will never be satisfied, of slaving to buy and to have, of a life predicated on unhappiness and discontent.

And why would I want that for anyone? Much less my son?   14

EXERCISING VOCABULARY

1. Shepherd compares a group of teenagers at the mall to "an amoeboid mass" (para. 7). What is an amoeba? How does an amoeba move? How effective is this unusual analogy?

2. In paragraph 8, Shepherd labels going to the mall "an initiation rite." What do initiation rites in most cultures symbolize? In what ways could going to the mall be considered such a rite of passage for our culture?

3. What is an anachronism? What example of an anachronism does Shepherd offer in paragraph 12? Why is he so certain that his son will not heed his advice to "do anything, but . . . generate it from within"?

PROBING CONTENT

1. How does Shepherd justify his assertion that "people have to be unhappy for our way of life to continue" (para. 3)? What would happen if this unhappiness vanished? Why does the magazine editor Shepherd quotes in paragraph 5 agree with Shepherd?

2. How do Shepherd's wife and some other parents view the mall? What other places does Shepherd suggest for teenagers to gather? Why are malls more attractive to young people than these other places?

3. Does Shepherd offer any reasons why teenagers *should* be allowed to go to the mall? If so, what are they? What is the basis of Shepherd's opposition to his son's spending time there?

CONSIDERING CRAFT

1. Not only does Shepherd compare a group of teenagers to "an amoeboid mass" in paragraph 7, but throughout the rest of that paragraph he refers to the group as "it." What message is Shepherd sending? How does his language choice further his purpose in this essay?

2. Shepherd calls malls "temples of our culture" (para. 8). What is the purpose of a temple? What activities take place in a temple? Reread the first six paragraphs of this essay and then evaluate the appropriateness of this metaphor.

3. What is the author's tone throughout this essay? How does this tone affect you as a reader? To what extent is the tone suited to Shepherd's thesis and its development?

RESPONDING TO THE WRITER

Do you agree with Shepherd that malls are dangerous for young people? Why or why not? Do you think that mall owners will attempt to prevent groups of teenagers from meeting there? Explain your answer. What other locations might replace malls if they were no longer available for teens? How well would these other locations fulfill the same purposes?

For a quiz on this reading, go to www.bedfordstmartins.com/mirror.

Tying the Score

KATE ROUNDS

Women's magazines have existed for years, ranging from *Ladies' Home Journal* to *Ms.* Only in the past few years, however, have women's sports magazines hit the racks. One in particular, *Sports Illustrated Women/Sport*, which launched its inaugural edition in April 1997, has met with mixed reviews. Gracing its first cover is a pregnant WNBA star, Sheryl Swoopes, with a basketball in one hand and the other hand on her basketball-shaped belly. In big print is the cover line, "A Star Is Born: Sheryl Swoopes and the WNBA are both due in June." What is getting more attention here, Swoopes's athletic ability or her ability to have a baby? What is your reaction to this cover? Do you find it arresting, clever, amusing, or objectionable?

Kate Rounds is not shy about giving us her reaction in this article from the July/August 1997 issue of *Ms.* magazine, a feminist publication. She says, "I just wanted to make the point one last time, that feminism is not about prudery — it is about equality." The writer has been a news editor at *Ms.* since 1993. She has a black belt in judo and currently lives on a boat in New York harbor.

THINKING AHEAD

The magazine *Women/Sport* was launched by *Sports Illustrated* in April 1997 and was the first magazine devoted to women's sports. What kinds of articles would you expect to find in such a publication? How would you expect men and women to be represented? What would the swimsuit issue look like?

INCREASING VOCABULARY

confer (v.) (3)

teaser (n.) (4)

trailblazers (n.) (6)

asinine (adj.) (8)

prude (n.) (8)

How come I enjoy reading about women's sports about as much as I   1
like reading about, say, beard-trimming techniques? The stories never seem to be about shooting baskets or hitting line drives. In one way or another, sportswriting about women is often about men. Take the inaugural issue of *Sports Illustrated Women/Sport*, which was unveiled in April. *SI*'s spin-off for women is as high-test as the Indianapolis Speedway. On the cover is WNBA star Sheryl Swoopes pregnant as a basketball, with the cover line, "Sheryl Swoopes and the WNBA are both due in June." Of course we see Swoopes in the one condition she couldn't have achieved without a man, or at least his sperm.

Peek inside *Women/Sport,* and you see the Editor's Letter illustrated   2
with some *SI* covers that featured women. One shows tennis great Chris
Evert, racket resting on her shoulder like a parasol,[1] with the cover line,
"I'm Going To Be a Full-time Wife." Yet another thing you can't be without a man.

Cut to a story about Olympic figure skater Nancy Kerrigan in her role   3
as "new mom." Comparing Kerrigan with the troubled young gold-
medalist Oksana Baiul, writer E. M. (Ed) Swift lectures, "At the same time
that nineteen-year-old wild child Baiul was drunkenly skidding her
$100,000 Mercedes off a Connecticut road at ninety-seven mph, twenty-
seven-year-old Kerrigan was up giving Matthew his 2 A.M. feeding."
Nothing like becoming a mother to confer sainthood.

Jump to a hysterically homophobic piece called "Sex, Lies, and Soft-   4
ball." After the teaser, "The stereotyping of female athletes as lesbians has
been a significant barrier to the growth of women's sports," we get soft-
baller Dot Richardson describing the horrifying moment during a tenth-
grade softball game, "when I learned for the first time that one of my
teammates was gay. That can't be, I said to myself. . . . I made a lot of errors in the next few games because I was distracted." What was distracting you, honey?

Turn to the story billed on the cover as "Why I Fell for Grant Hill." I   5
didn't even know who Grant Hill was. I discovered that he's a Detroit Pistons
player whom a writer named E. Jean Carroll apparently went gaga over.

To be fair, at least half of the stories in the women's mag aren't half   6
bad—e.g., one on the personal tragedies overcome by Rutgers basketball
coach Vivian Stringer, a follow-up on what's happened to the players on the
United States Olympic basketball team, an exposé about a top volleyball
coach accused of sexually abusing his young team members, and a salute to
six Title IX trailblazers. So why bury the good stuff under a pile of horseshit?
Women/Sport could be a trailblazer. It could be the publication that benches
homophobia, uncovers the inequities in judged sports like figure skating, and
helps get women's pro baseball out of the archives and onto the Astroturf.

A quick sprint through the May 5 issue of *Sports Illustrated* (Men/   7
Sport) reveals a magazine that contrasts sharply with its female counterpart. There are no articles about "new dads," or about a male athlete becoming a full-time husband; no guy reporter swoons in print over a
WNBA player; no confessional story about the first time a player learned
that one of his teammates was gay. What gives here!

The problem with *Sports Illustrated Women/Sport* is not that it's an   8
idiotic dunderhead[2] of a magazine for women but that men don't get
equal time. It's the same principle at work with the *Sports Illustrated* annual swimsuit issue. It's not that it features female models in swimsuits
who are not athletes but that it doesn't feature male models in swimsuits
who are not athletes. If you're going to make an asinine issue of a maga-

[1] **parasol:** A light, usually small woman's umbrella used to keep the sun off the face.
[2] **dunderhead:** A dunce; numbskull.

zine, you should at least be coed about it. Call me a grim feminist, but let's have two great sports magazines or two lousy ones. Call me a prude, but let's put male models bulging out of their Speedos in the swimsuit issue. Fasten your sports bras!

EXERCISING VOCABULARY

1. You know what the inauguration of the president is and thus what inaugural parties or celebrations are. What then would an "inaugural issue" of a magazine be (para. 1)?

2. In paragraph 6, Rounds discusses an exposé about a volleyball coach accused of sexual abuse. Knowing what *exposé* means, what then is an author's intent when writing an exposé?

PROBING CONTENT

1. Rounds says that "sportswriting about women is often about men" (para. 1). How can that be? What does she mean?

2. In paragraphs 2 through 5, Rounds gives four examples of photographs and features from *Women/Sport*. List these examples. What effect do these have?

3. What effect, according to the writer, could the "good" stories in *Women/Sport* have on women's sports? What examples does Rounds give of these potential benefits?

4. In what ways, according to Rounds, does the male version of *Sports Illustrated* differ from the female version? What is the problem with both the male and female versions of these magazines?

CONSIDERING CRAFT

1. Rounds uses sports jargon, or the unique language of sports, on numerous occasions in the essay, including in the title. Find three such examples. Explain what effect this use of sports jargon has on the reader. Did you recognize these words?

2. Describe the author's tone or attitude toward her subject and her readers. What effect does her tone have on you?

3. At times the author uses slang in her essay. Find several examples. What effect does the inclusion of slang have on the way you read this essay?

RESPONDING TO THE WRITER

What points does Rounds make that you consider effective? Find any portions of the essay that you would change or omit. Explain your reasoning.

For a quiz on this reading, go to www.bedfordstmartins.com/mirror.

Girls Will Be Boys

KIMBERLEY A. STRASSEL

Since Title IX — a federal law prohibiting gender discrimination in school sports programs — was enacted in 1972, female athletes are being taken more seriously. In 1970, a mere one of every twenty-seven girls played high school varsity sports. Today, that figure has dramatically risen to one in three, and girls can more realistically dream of becoming professional sports stars. This is a positive trend, right? Not in Kimberly A. Strassel's opinion. In "Girls Will Be Boys" she writes, "Title IX helps turn female athletes into dumb jocks." Citing a recent study, Strassel says that an increase in the number of athletic scholarships awarded to women — largely due to Title IX — has triggered a decline in female athletes' academic performance. More women now see college in the same way some male athletes do: a ticket to the pros, rather than a place to learn. Furthermore, Strassel argues that Title IX unfairly takes resources away from men's sports. Do you agree? How do you feel about gender equality in sports?

Before becoming an editorialist for the *Wall Street Journal*, Strassel wrote about real estate for its news section and also spent four years in London covering technology for the *Wall Street Journal Europe*. "Girls Will Be Boys" first appeared in the April 19, 2001, issue of the *Wall Street Journal*.

Title IX states: "No person in the U.S. shall, on the basis of sex, be excluded from participation in, or denied the benefits of, or be subjected to discrimination under any educational program or activity receiving federal aid."

THINKING AHEAD

How popular were girls' sports at your high school? How equal were the sports opportunities for boys and girls? Were the facilities equal? Describe any differences. Did girls sometimes play on boys' teams, or were all the sports separated by gender? What rules should apply regarding the gender equality of sports in high school? At colleges and universities? Professionally?

INCREASING VOCABULARY

mandating (v.) (2)

instill (v.) (6)

mortified (adj.) (6)

groped (v.) (6)

extol (v.) (9)

prattle (v.) (9)

sway (n.) (12)

steroids (n.) (15)

proclamations (n.) (17)

heady (adj.) (17)

adage (n.) (18)

So much for the weaker sex.

It's been nearly thirty years since Congress passed that little law mandating equal resources for the sexes in school sports programs. Any school intending to cash a federal check has to pledge to give all the little girls as great an opportunity to get sweaty and spit in front of crowds as all the little boys.

And now, decades after Title IX was introduced, women truly are coming even with men. A new study explains that we now have a crop of female university athletes who are just as dumb and academically lazy as their male counterparts. Way to go, girls.

Like all equalization initiatives Title IX was, in its broadest and most enlightened spirit, meant to give women more opportunities. And like all equalization initiatives, it instead turned into a way of punishing and discriminating against other groups — in this case, boys.

Indeed, the regulation has been twisted and mauled by ponytailed pipsqueaks[1] and their passionate parents in ways no one could have imagined. Schools that couldn't afford to provide equal golfing and baseball programs for the Iron Girl brigade were forced to shut down their men's programs.

Most recently, newspaper stories have detailed girls demanding to wrestle with the boys. The parents, after laboring sixteen long years to instill in Tommy and Jimmy the proper way to treat a lady, are now mortified to see their sons being groped on the mat by the gals. Some boys won't wrestle because they feel uncomfortable — as they well might — about performing a half nelson[2] on unexpected female body parts.

And yet while women have more opportunities and successes than ever, discrimination suits continue to multiply, and the number of Title IX complaints filed nationwide with the Office of Civil Rights grew fivefold during the 1990s, to 129 in 1999.

The problem, of course, often isn't with the kids. Rather, it rests with that extremely well funded gender-equalization Mafia that comes screeching into town to offer legal counseling whenever girls are denied. This group has co-opted[3] women's sports as a way of scoring political points, with little thought of the consequences to the girls they claim to fight for.

A perfect example came after the U.S. won the World Cup in women's soccer. As the players went on air to talk about the thrill of a penalty kick or the joy of a saved goal, women's-rights activists and "gender-equity consultants" swept them aside to instead extol the virtues of federal regulations. Women like Donna Lopiano of the Women's Sports Foundation have little time to congratulate our professional basketball league or ace tennis circuit when they can prattle on about "sexism," "sexual harassment" and the lack of female "athlete heroes."

---

[1] **ESL** **pipsqueaks:** Derogatory slang term for small or young individuals.
[2] **ESL** **half nelson:** A wrestling hold in which one arm is thrust under the corresponding arm of an opponent and the hand placed on the back of the opponent's neck.
[3] **co-opted:** Took over and made one's own.

And these days, what heroes they are. For it turns out these gender   10
politicos,[4] in their drive to turn girls into boys, have done a better job of it
than they might have supposed. Women jocks[5] are increasingly looking at
college in the same way as men, as sports factories—places to lift weights,
meet trainers, flunk a few courses and then head on to the pros.

This comes out in *The Game of Life: College Sports and Educational*   11
Values, a new book by William Bowen, a former Princeton president, and
James Shulman of the Andrew W. Mellon Foundation.

Messrs. Shulman and Bowen look at the records for thirty selective   12
schools in the U.S. over fifty years. One of their key findings is that with
sports programs holding so much sway in admissions, female jocks are the
biggest beneficiaries of affirmative action.[6] At one unnamed school in
1999, a black student had an 18 percent advantage over a white student
with the same SAT scores. Children of alumni had a 25 percent advantage. Male athletes had a 48 percent advantage. Female athletes had a 53
percent advantage. Talk about preferences.

But here's the best part. In the 1970s, female college athletes tended to   13
excel academically and be leaders in their classes. In contrast, their male
counterparts had already started underperforming academically. Today,
as Mr. Shulman put it recently, women have "caught down" to men.
Women athletes are entering schools with appreciably lower test scores
and high-school grades than classmates. The proportion of male athletes
who graduate in the bottom third of their class is 58 percent; the number
of female athletes in this category has risen to 39 percent. Girl jocks increasingly sign up for soft majors—that's right, psychology—right along
with the helmet heads from the football and hockey teams.

The authors point out that this academic performance is subpar[7] not   14
only when compared with that of classmates, but also given what the athletes would have been expected to produce given their admission test scores.
Time pressure isn't the excuse: Classmates who took part in other time-
intensive school activities tended to overperform academically. Rather, the
poor results seem to stem from a female sports culture that no longer values
academics as much as gym lockers and the party after the big game.

Other studies suggest the situation isn't as bad in high school, where   15
competition is less intense. Female high-school athletes tend to do well
academically and have lower pregnancy rates than nonathletes. On the
other hand, in a recent study of teenagers by the Women's Sports Foundation, highly involved female athletes are more likely than nonathletes to
drink and drive, twice as likely to use steroids and three times as likely to
chew tobacco.

The reasons seem pretty clear. Women used to go to school to, well,   16

[4] **politicos:** Politicians.
[5] **ESL** **jocks:** Athletes, especially college athletes.
[6] **affirmative action:** Government mandated effort to improve the employment or educa-
    tional opportunities of members of minority groups and women.
[7] **subpar:** Below standard.

go to school. The big-sports dream, the million-dollar contract, was a boy thing. But politics made competitive sports—whether in professional leagues, in the Olympics or in coaching—not only an option for women, but a duty. Being good at athletics is no longer a bonus, or a healthy well-rounded approach to school; it is a primary statement on womanhood.

Sadly, too, it is an unrealistic dream. Despite the charged rhetoric[8]   17 and grand proclamations of the women's-rights groups, professional women's sports will never rival professional men's sports in terms of audiences or revenues; they aren't compelling or exciting enough. Yet riding high on these heady dreams and political promises, a lot of young women will sacrifice college for a shot at the WNBA, and in the end get paid a little bit more than a dishwasher for the effort.

Sports are good, and it is great that women play them and play them   18 well. But it might also be a good time to start taking stock of where they fit in the bigger scheme. Meanwhile, some of those new female coaches out there might take a moment to remind their girl charges of that old but increasingly overlooked adage: It isn't whether you win or lose, it's how you play the game.

EXERCISING VOCABULARY

1. Strassel obviously has serious objections to what she calls the "gender-equalization Mafia" (para. 8). Who are these people, and what do they do? Who are the Mafia in the usual sense of that term? What is the connotative meaning? What kinds of activities are implied by such an association? Is Strassel in favor of or opposed to gender equalization? On what do you base your answer?

2. In paragraph 10, Strassel blames some of the ills in women's sports on "gender politicos." What is a politico? Who are these people? What is their interest in women's sports?

PROBING CONTENT

1. Why may the idea of girls competing on teams made up largely of boys require some basic shifts in our culture's notions about gender and appropriate behavior? What effect might such shifts have on areas of our culture beyond sports?

2. According to Strassel, what has changed about the way female athletes view college? What has been the result? To what can these results be attributed? How do female athletes in high school compare to nonathletes?

3. Why does Strassel consider women's professional sports "an unrealistic dream" (para. 17)? Why does she find female athletes' dependence on this dream so disturbing?

---

[8] **rhetoric:** The art of speaking or writing effectively.

CONSIDERING CRAFT

1. Strassel's tone is often sarcastic. Cite several specific examples of language that reflects this tone. How effective is this tone as Strassel presses her argument?

2. How does the adage Strassel quotes at the end of the essay summarize her position? How effective is her choice of this very frequently quoted statement? Is this choice more effective than ending with her own words? Why or why not?

RESPONDING TO THE WRITER

What kind of picture has Strassel painted of the prospects for female athletes in high schools and colleges? From your own experience or using your observations of others, use examples to refute or support her position.

For a quiz on this reading, go to www.bedfordstmartins.com/mirror.

DRAWING CONNECTIONS

1. Kate Rounds argues in "Tying the Score" that stories in women's sports magazines "never seem to be about shooting baskets or hitting line drives" (para. 1). Kimberly Strassel agrees in "Girls Will Be Boys" that female players never seem free "to talk about the thrill of a penalty kick or the joy of a saved goal" (para. 9). The two do not agree, however, on the factors that are preventing these conversations. Compare and contrast their views about who or what is responsible for the lack of focus on athleticism itself in women's sports.

2. Now that female university athletes are apparently "dumbing down" to the level of their male counterparts, what could a well-written women's sports magazine possibly do to help reverse this undesirable trend? How popular do you think such a publication would be? Explain your response.

Wrapping Up Chapter 9

REFLECTING ON THE WRITING

1. Using either "Wrestling with Myself" or "My Farewell to Fandom" as a model, write an essay in which you explore your own relationship to one particular sport. Be sure to examine how you became attracted to the sport, how long your involvement has lasted, the degree to which you feel committed, and any pressures you may ever have been under to reduce that commitment.

2. Reread the essay "Loving Las Vegas." Select one other city in the United States that captures the American spirit and attracts great numbers of tourists. Write an essay in which you discuss why this city is a major attraction. Why do people decide to visit? What occupies their time there? What dreams do visitors bring with them, and how does your chosen city fulfill their dreams? You may also wish to include references to this city from television shows, movies, or music to underscore its special appeal.

3. With Steven L. Shepherd's essay "Mall Culture" in mind, spend one afternoon or evening at a nearby mall. Keep some notes on the people you see there, what they are doing, and how they interact with each other. What social lessons are being learned or taught? By whom? Write an essay in which you evaluate the results of your research.

CONNECTING TO THE CULTURE

1. Watch a sporting event on television. Take notes on the advertisements that are aired during the event and analyze them in an essay. Consider the kinds of products being marketed, the type of audience targeted (considering such things as age, gender, and buying power), and the quality of the commercials themselves. How are these advertisements related to the televised event?

2. Consider a new trend in sports like extreme sports or snowboarding. Do some research by reading magazine articles, conducting interviews, and watching sporting events. In an essay, explain the intricacies of the sport and analyze the reasons for its popularity.

3. Write an essay in which you explore the influence of some aspect of the Internet on our culture. You may select role-playing games, email, chat rooms, message boards, online shopping, or any other aspect of the Internet. Be sure to include information on which populations are most likely to participate, at what time most people are online for this activity, and the impact that their Internet time has on their lives. You may wish to do some library research or interview friends and acquaintances to inform your writing.

FOCUSING ON YESTERDAY, FOCUSING ON TODAY

On Easter Sunday, April 1, 1934, three hundred thousand New Yorkers and visitors entertained themselves at Coney Island, at that time a state-of-the-art amusement park. Based on this picture, would you be wowed by this roller coaster? In the 1930s, entertainment was serious business, leisure time was scarce, and when a family had some time and some cash that wasn't needed for the rent, they all went out together to enjoy themselves. Today many of us take our leisure time in fits and starts, whenever we can grab five minutes between classes or meetings.

Coney Island Roller Coaster, 1934

This Puma ad shows three young people at ease — very relaxed, very informal, wearing Puma clothing, of course. Notice that the text tells us it's the two young women who are "conquering the universe," a concept unheard of in 1934.

Compare and contrast these two images of leisure. What emotions are conveyed by the Coney Island photograph? What emotions are conveyed by the Puma ad? What effect does the text have on the message? Which leisure activity is more appealing to you? Why?

Chillin'

Evaluating and Documenting Sources

When you research topics of interest in popular culture, you are going to want to augment your own thoughts and ideas with credible sources that support your position. You may think that it will be difficult to locate such sources. On the contrary, for most topics, you'll find a wide array of potential material to incorporate into your work. You won't be able to use everything, so you will have to make some important choices in order to focus on only the best and most legitimate evidence.

As you begin, you'll want to remember two important things. First, because popular culture involves what's popular, it changes rapidly. Remember the Spice Girls? Old news, right? Consequently, the more recent your source of material, the more valuable that source is to your research. A *Rolling Stone* article on current music trends isn't current if it was written in 1997, although it may still be useful if you are seeking a historical perspective.

Second, all sources are not created equal. Some publications or Web sites are created specifically to further the writer's own agenda. Material on the Internet is often unevaluated and unsubstantiated before it is posted. Let the researcher beware. You will want to establish certain basic information about any source you plan to rely on for information—for example, date of posting or publication or who is responsible for the veracity of the site's or the magazine's content. Learning to recognize and properly evaluate the bias embedded in some potentially useful material may require a little detective work, but it is essential to the authenticity and credibility of your own research.

In Chapter 1 we suggested a list of questions to ask as you deconstruct media images. Let's start with a similar list of questions to help you learn to accurately evaluate the potential of possible sources. These questions can be applied whether your source is electronic or in print.

1. Where is the source material located?
2. What is the publication or posting/update date?
3. Who is the author?

369

4. When the material was written or posted, who was the intended audience?

5. Is the material a primary source or a secondary source?

Just as we do when deconstructing a visual image, let's take the more "up front" and easily answered questions first.

Where Is the Source Material Located?

The first important consideration is where you have located the potential source material. If the article or advertisement is in print form, in which magazine or journal does it appear? What can you find out about this publication? Has it been in circulation for a long time? Who publishes the book, newspaper, or magazine? Who sponsors this Web site? What's the purpose of the Web site or print source? Check the titles of other articles listed in the table of contents. What patterns or similarities do you see? Are different viewpoints represented?

Answers to most of these basic questions can usually be found on a page near the front of the publication. Journals, whose articles are generally closely scrutinized before inclusion, are even more likely than magazines to provide such particulars. Remember that scholarly journals, unlike popular magazines, are published less frequently and are often written for a select audience of professionals.

If your source is electronic, you may not find this information as readily. Some Internet sources are affiliated with journals, magazines, newspapers, or professional organizations; these sites are generally very reliable and may include relevant dates as well as helpful biographical information about the author and about the site itself. However, remember that anyone can host a Web site and post whatever he or she chooses, accurate or not. Wouldn't it be embarrassing to find out you've quoted a seventh grader's Britney Spears site in a college paper? You'll want to reference only reliable Web sources that clearly reveal ownership and other factual documentation.

What Is the Publication or Posting/Update Date?

How recently was this information written and published? Magazines and journals are usually dated right on the cover. With popular culture topics, naturally, weekly publications give you more current information than monthly ones, and daily newspapers stay ahead of both. Some journals are published only once or twice a year, but they may still provide important background for your research.

Articles on the Internet may have the date of the site's creation or most recent update, or there may be no date at all. Then you will have to use clues to judge how recently the information has been gathered. Check the information against other, dated sources. Read carefully for dates and events mentioned within the article itself.

Who Is the Author?

Book authors' names are readily available; sometimes a note on the book jacket will list important biographical data. Periodical authors who have established reputations will be identified by name either close to the title of the article or at the end of the piece. A few lines about the author may also be provided—other articles or books written, current position held, any literary recognition received, or other specific information that makes the author more credible than others on that subject. Tiger Woods's writing on the best golf courses, for example, would automatically carry more clout than the average weekend golfer's. Journals generally offer a great deal more specific information about their authors, often going into detail about accomplishments and affiliations.

On the other hand, many magazine articles are written by staff writers who work full time for the publication, providing material on whatever topic they are assigned. Still other articles are written by freelance writers, hired by the publication or Web host to contribute one article on one particular topic at a time. Such authors may or may not even be named. Whoever the author, famous or not, whatever you can learn about him or her will help you to read the article more accurately, keeping an eye out for any particular bias or viewpoint. Clues about the author's angle and tone may also present themselves in the writing. An author who professes in the opening paragraph of a review to be a great fan of Julia Roberts is not likely to pan one of her movies.

Internet sources should list at least the writer's name. We suggest treating with caution any Internet article that lists no author at all.

As your research on a popular-culture topic progresses, chances are good that a few authors' names will appear as references in several different sources. This is testimony to the author's credibility and an indication that this author's thoughts and opinions on this topic are generally sought after and respected.

When the Material Was Written or Posted, Who Was the Intended Audience?

Do readers of the source belong to a particular age group, ethnicity, interest group, or occupational group? *Teen Magazine*, for example, is clearly marketed toward a certain age group, as is *Modern Maturity*, one of the publications of the American Association of Retired Persons. Perhaps the publication or site is intended for a special-interest group. Publications like *Dog World* fit this category. Some magazines, such as *Time, Newsweek, People,* and *Reader's Digest,* are written to appeal to a much wider audience. Knowing the target audience for a publication will help you evaluate any common knowledge, vocabulary, values, and beliefs that writers expect most readers to share.

Journals tend to direct themselves to very specific target audiences, which frequently consist of people in the same profession. Often in such publications the language and style used will be baffling to the outsider and yet easily understood by members of the profession. Perfectly common medical terminology in the *American Journal of Nursing* may sound like unintelligible jargon to someone outside the field of medicine. Remember, if you don't understand what you are reading, that material may have little value to you as a source.

In some cases, if the specifics of a complicated journal article are important to your research, you may want to consult a specialized dictionary. These references will help you decipher language unique to one field of study like law, psychology, or engineering.

Is the Material a Primary Source or a Secondary Source?

Making this determination may not be as easy as finding the date of publication or the author's name, but this distinction isn't really difficult. When you see *Star Wars: Attack of the Clones* and then describe in a paper how George Lucas employs technology to develop the character of Yoda, you are using a primary source (the movie itself). When you read an article that compares George Lucas's use of technology in the *Star Wars* trilogy and in the prequels in *Entertainment* magazine and then quote the author of that article in your own work, you are using a secondary source (the article about the movies).

Let's take one more example. If you watch a television interview with Denzel Washington about the role of black actors in American films and refer to that interview in your research, that is a primary source. You saw the interview yourself. However, if you miss the television show and read a review of it in the next day's Life and Arts section of the newspaper, you'll be using a secondary source when you incorporate information from the review in your paper.

With primary sources, you are in direct contact with the music, film, novel, advertisement, or Web site. You develop your own interpretation and analysis. With secondary sources, someone else is acting as a filter between you and the CD, the play, the short story, or the painting.

Both types of sources are valuable—after all, not many of us saw the Beatles's last live concert in person. But with secondary sources you will want to be alert for any bias or viewpoint of the author's that could affect the credibility of the source material.

Practice in applying these questions will help you to become confident about the value and validity of the sources you use to support your own ideas.

Here is an example of a Web page you might consult during your research into a topic in popular culture.

A) Item A identifies the group as a company (.com), not a school (.edu) or an organization (.org).

B) Item B offers a link to the Web site's home page.

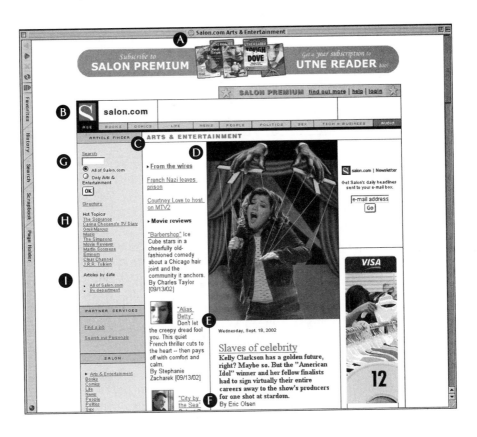

C) Item C provides a heading letting you know what part of the site you are viewing.

D) Item D uses engaging graphics related to the subject matter of a general topic.

E) Item E provides a date for the issue.

F) Item F provides the names of authors underneath article titles.

G) Item G allows for a search function.

H) Item H provides links to other topics within the site that might be of interest.

I) Item I provides links to additional articles.

EXERCISE

After closely examining the Web screen shot above, answer the following questions:

1. Who is the intended audience of this Web page? What aspects of this site provide clues to help you identify the audience?

2. What elements of this Web site indicate the reliability or unreliability of its information?

3. What aspects of this site let you know that this Web-based company wants its audience to return to the site often?

Documenting Sources

Now we are ready to take those sources for which we have established relevance and the proper credentials and think about using them in a paper or other research project.

Attention, please! Always write out a complete citation for any piece of material that you are seriously considering as a source for your research. That way, days after you put the bound volume of periodicals back on the shelf, you won't have to go through all fifty volumes to locate one article that contains just the right quotation or statistic. Also, always print out a hard copy of anything from the Internet. The fact that you knew the URL today doesn't mean you'll know it a week from now or that the same information will be posted again in exactly the same place.

Here are some examples of the correct ways to document your sources as references in your paper. We will also provide some examples of listings of sources for your works cited page at the end of your paper. This is only a brief listing. If you need additional information on documenting sources, go to *Research and Documentation Online* at dianahacker.com/resdoc. All the citations here follow the Modern Language Association (MLA) format.

MLA Format for In-Text Citations

You should provide an in-text citation every time you quote from, paraphrase, or summarize an outside source. Your citation should directly follow the sentence or sentences in your paper that refer to the source information. Please consult the following models when you cite sources within your essay.

BOOKS OR PERIODICALS

One Author

"The fact is that much of advertising's power comes from this belief that advertising does not affect us. The most effective kind of propaganda is that which is not recognized as propaganda" (Kilbourne 27).

Kilbourne states that "much of advertising's power comes from this belief that advertising does not affect us. The most effective kind of propaganda is that which is not recognized as propaganda" (27).

Two or More Authors
Every day, the average American spends nearly an hour watching, listening to, or reading advertisements (Jacobson and Mazur 193).

ELECTRONIC SOURCES

Web Site
Before Title IX's implementation in 1972, fewer than 300,000 high school girls played competitive sports. By 1997, that number had increased to 2.4 million (United States Dept. of Education).

MLA Format for List of Works Cited

At the end of your essay, you must provide a list of the sources from which you quoted, paraphrased, or summarized. Put the entire list in alphabetical order using the author's last name and the title as it appears on the title page of the source. If your source has no author, alphabetize it by the first main word of the title. Double-space your works cited page and indent the second line of each entry five spaces.

BOOKS

One Author
Kilbourne, Jean. Can't Buy My Love: How Advertising Changes the Way We Think and Feel. New York: Touchstone-Simon, 1999.

Two or More Authors
Jacobson, Michael F., and Laurie Ann Mazur. Marketing Madness: A Survival Guide for a Consumer Society. Boulder: Westview, 1995.

PERIODICALS

Signed Magazine Article
Tyrangiel, Josh. "The Three Faces of Eminem." Time 3 June 2002: 67.

Unsigned Magazine Article
"Women's Dissatisfaction with Body Image Greater in More Affluent Neighborhoods." Women's Health Weekly 21 Mar. 2002: 12.

Signed Newspaper Article
Jones, Allison North. "Strong Views, Pro and Con, on Ads Linking Drug Use to Terrorism." New York Times 2 Apr. 2002: C7.

Unsigned Newspaper Article
"Putting a Limit on Labels." Wall Street Journal 14 June 2002: W12.

Signed Editorial

Cohen, Adam. "America's Favorite Television Fare? The Normals vs. the
      Stigmatized." Editorial. New York Times 2 June 2002: WK18.

Journal Article

Birmingham, Elizabeth. "Fearing the Freak: How Talk TV Articulates
      Women and Class." Journal of Popular Film and Television 28.3 (2000):
      133-39.

ELECTRONIC SOURCES

Web Site

United States. Department of Education. Title IX: Twenty-five Years of Pro-
      gress. 9 July 1997. 29 July 2002 < http://www.ed.gov/pubs/TitleIX/>.

On-line Magazine Article

Goldberg, Michelle. "Flag-draped Voyeurism." Salon.com 9 July 2002.
      1 Aug. 2002 <http://www.salon.com/mwt/feature/2002/07/09/
      ground_zero/index.html>.

OTHER SOURCES

Published Interview

King, Stephen. "10 Questions for Stephen King." Time 1 Apr. 2002: 13.

Broadcast Interview

Tarantino, Quentin. Interview. Charlie Rose. PBS. WGBH, Boston. 26
      Dec. 1997.

Personal Interview

Salomon, Willis. Personal interview. 14 Apr. 2001.

Print Advertisement

Eternity by Calvin Klein. Advertisement. Vogue May 2002: 61.

Television Advertisement

Nike. Advertisement. MTV. 11 Dec. 2000.

Sound Recording

Nelly. Nellyville. Universal, 2002.

Television Program

"Miss America." American Experience. PBS. WGBH, Boston. 27 Jan. 2002.

Radio Program

"Natural Santa Claus." All Things Considered. Host Robert Siegel. NPR. WGBH,
    Boston. 29 Nov. 2002.

Film

Black Hawk Down. Dir. Ridley Scott. Perf. Josh Hartnett, Ewan
    McGregor, Tom Sizemore, and Sam Shepard. DVD. Columbia, 2001.

Speech or Lecture

Mahon, Maureen. "This Is Not White Boy Music: The Politics and Poet-
    ics of Black Rock." Stanford University, Stanford. 30 Jan. 2002.

Rhetorical Table of Contents

The rhetorical strategies—analysis, argument, cause and effect, comparison and contrast, definition, description, evaluation, illustration and example, narration, and process analysis—are listed alphabetically for quick reference.

Cause and Effect

Comparison and Contrast

Definition

Description

Evaluation

Illustration and Example

Narration

Process Analysis

ACKNOWLEDGMENTS (continued)

Fred Baldwin. "The Only Game *Not* in Town." From US Airways *Attache,* June 2001, pp. 57–59. Reprinted by permission.

Dave Barry. "The Ugly Truth about Beauty." From the *Miami Herald,* February 1, 1998. Originally titled "Beauty and the Beast." Copyright © 1998 by Dave Barry, Columnist, *The Miami Herald.* Reprinted by permission of the author.

Kate Betts. "A New Day: Fashion Contemplates Fresh Icons." From the *New York Times,* Sunday, October 28, 2001. Copyright © 2001 The New York Times Company. Reprinted by permission.

Gloria Borger. "Barbie's Newest Values." Copyright © December 1, 1997, *U.S. News & World Report.* Reprinted by permission.

Lauren M. Brackbill. "Safety in Sales: Advertising after September 11th." Copyright © January 2002. Reprinted by permission of the author.

David Byrne. "I Hate World Music." From the *New York Times,* October 3, 1999. Copyright © 1999 by The New York Times Company. Reprinted by permission.

Damien Cave. "The Tyranny of 'Abercrappie.'" Published in *Salon.com,* March 3, 2000. Reprinted by permission.

Jay Chiat. "Illusions Are Forever." From *Forbes ASAP,* October 2000. Copyright © 2002 Forbes, Inc. Reprinted by permission of *Forbes ASAP* magazine and Jay Chiat.

Nick Chiles. "What Men Say When We're Not Around." From *Essence* magazine, November 2001, p. 146. Reprinted by permission.

Delia Cleveland. "Champagne Taste, Beer Budget." Originally appeared in *Essence* magazine, March 2001. Adapted from an essay published in *Starting with "I"* (Persea Books, 1997). Reprinted by permission of the author.

Stephen Corey. "A Voice for the Lonely." Originally published in *In Short: A Collection of Brief Creative Nonfiction,* edited by Judith Kitchen and Mary Palmer Jones. Published by W.W. Norton, 1996. Copyright © 1996 by Stephen Corey. Reprinted by permission of the author.

H. D. "Dying to Be Bigger." From *Seventeen* magazine, December 1991. Reprinted by permission of the author.

Dan DeLuca. "Loving Las Vegas." Originally titled "Is gaudy, greedy Vegas a national symbol?" From the *Philadelphia Inquirer,* May 18, 1997. Reprinted with permission.

Carolyn A. Edgar. "Black and Blue." *Reconstruction,* vol. 2, no. 3, 1994. Copyright © 1994 by Carolyn A. Edgar, "Black and Blue." Reprinted by permission of the author. All rights reserved.

Quinn Eli. "Flagging Enthusiasm." Originally printed in the *Philadelphia Weekly,* October 17, 2001, vol. 30, no. 42. Copyright © 2001 by Quinn Eli. Reprinted with permission of the author. editmail@philadelphiaweekly.com.

Jamilah Evelyn. "To the Academy with Love, from a Hip-Hop Fan." From *Black Issues in Higher Education,* December 7, 2000, vol. 17, issue 21, p. 6. Copyright © 2000 Cox, Matthews & Associates. Reprinted with permission from *Black Issues in Higher Education,* December 7, 2000.

Mick Farren. "The Motorcycle Jacket." From *Icon Thoughtstyle* magazine, February 1998. Reprinted by permission of *ICON* magazine, New York City.

George Felton. "Wrestling with Myself." From the *Baltimore Sun Magazine,* November 11, 1990. Copyright © 1990 by George Felton. Reprinted by permission of the author. gfelton@columbus.rr.com.

John Follis. "Mad Ave." From *Adbusters,* Winter 1998. Copyright © 1998 by John Follis. Reprinted by permission of Adbusters Media Foundation.

Maggie Ford. "School, Girls, and the Information Age." Published in the *Austin American Statesman,* November 27, 1998. Copyright © 1998 American Association of University Women Educational Foundation. Maggie Ford is President of AAUWEF. Reprinted by permission.

Max Frankel. "Let's Be Chromatically Correct." From *The New York Times,* December 6, 1998. Copyright © 1998 by The New York Times Company. Reprinted by permission.

Laura Fraser. "Thigh Anxiety." From *Mother Jones,* March/April 1999. Copyright © 1999 by the Foundation for National Progress. Reprinted by permission.

Ellen Goodman. "'Going Thin' in Fiji Now that Television Has Arrived." From the *Austin American Statesman,* May 28, 1999. Copyright © 1999 The Washington Post Writers Group. Reprinted by permission.

Lois Gould. "X: A Fabulous Child's Story." Originally published in *Ms.* magazine, "Story for Free Children" in 1972. Copyright © 1972 by Lois Gould. Reprinted by permission.

Jeanne Albronda Heaton and Nona Leigh Wilson. "Tuning in Trouble." Adapted from *Talk TV's Destructive Impact on Mental Health* by Jeanne Albronda Heaton and Nona Leigh Wilson. Copyright © 1995 Jossey-Bass, Inc., Publishers. This article appeared in the September 1999 issue of *Ms.* magazine. Reprinted with permission.

Bob Katz. "My Farewell to Fandom." From *Newsweek,* January 25, 1999, p. 16. Copyright © 1999 Newsweek, Inc. All rights reserved. Reprinted by permission.

Jon Katz. "How Boys Become Men." Originally published in *Glamour* magazine, 1993. Copyright © 1993 by Jon Katz. Reprinted by permission of Sterling Lord Literistic, Inc.

Hayley Kaufman. "Belly-Baring Fad Not Cute as a Button." From the *Boston Globe,* February 11, 2002. Copyright © 2002 by the *Boston Globe.* Reprinted by permission of the *Boston Globe,* via Copyright Clearance Center, Inc. All Rights Reserved Worldwide.

Louise Kennedy. "Barrier Between Adults' and Children's Entertainment Is Breaking Down." From the *Boston Globe,* January 13, 2002. Copyright © 2002 the *Boston Globe.* Reprinted by permission of the *Boston Globe* via Copyright Clearance Center, Inc. All Rights Reserved Worldwide.

Stephen King. "Why We Crave Horror Movies." Originally published in *Playboy* magazine, December 1982. Copyright © Stephen King. Reprinted with permission. All rights reserved.

Naomi Klein. "The Brand Expands." Excerpt from *No Logo: Taking Aim at the Brand Bullies* by Naomi Klein. Copyright © 1999 by Naomi Klein. Reprinted by permission of St. Martin's Press, LLC.

Susan Brady Konig. "They've Got to Be Carefully Taught." From *National Review,* September 15, 1997, p. 46. Copyright © 1997 National Review, Inc., 215 Lexington Avenue, New York, NY 10016. Reprinted by permission.

Alex Kuczynski. "Women's Magazines Flip Past Feminism." Originally titled, "Enough about Feminism" from the *New York Times,* March 28, 1999. Copyright © 1999 by The New York Times Company. Reprinted by permission.

Ruth La Ferla. "Latino Style Is Cool. Oh, All Right: It's Hot." From the *New York Times,* April 15, 2001. Copyright © 2001 by The New York Times Company. Reprinted by permission.

Richard Lacayo. "Rock of Ages." Originally titled "Rock of Ages: Pop music used to be what divided the generations. Now it's what is drawing them together. If you don't count Eminem." From *Time,* February 26, 2001, vol. 157, issue 8, pp. 64+. Copyright © 2001 Time, Inc. Reprinted by permission.

Lewis Lapham. "Is There an American Tribe?" Copyright © 1991 by *Harper's Magazine.* All rights reserved. Reproduced from the January 1992 issue by special permission.

John Leo. "The 'Modern Primitives.'" From *U.S. News & World Report,* July 31, 1995, p. 16. "The Selling of Rebellion." From *U.S. News & World Report,* October 12, 1998. Copyright © 1996, 1998 *U.S. News & World Report.* Reprinted by permission. All rights reserved.

Patricia McLaughlin. "Venus Envy." From the *Philadelphia Inquirer,* November 5, 1995, p. 27. Copyright © 1995 by Patricia McLaughlin. Reprinted by permission of the author.

Tara Parker-Pope. "Custom-Made." From the *Wall Street Journal,* September 30, 1996, R6-R9. Copyright © 1996 Dow Jones & Company, Inc. Reprinted by permission of Dow Jones, Inc., via Copyright Clearance Center, Inc. All Rights Reserved Worldwide.

Leonard Pitts. "Value of Life Lost." Originally titled "Value of Life Lost in Gangsta Rap's Refrain." From the *Austin American-Statesman,* November 14, 1999, p. H3. Syndicated from the *Miami Herald.* Copyright © 1999. Reprinted by permission.

Katha Pollitt. "Why Boys Don't Play with Dolls." Originally published in *The New York Times,* October 8, 1995. Reprinted with permission of the author.

James Poniewozik. "Soaking Up Attention." From *Time,* December 17, 2001. Copyright © 2001 Time, Inc. Reprinted by permission.

Kate Rounds. "Tying the Score." From *Ms.* magazine, July/August 1997. Copyright © 1997. Reprinted by permission of *Ms.* magazine.

Richard Schickel. "Soldiers on the Screen." From *Time,* December 17, 2001, pp. 74-76. Copyright © 2001 Time, Inc. Reprinted by permission.

Read Mercer Schuchardt. "Swoosh!" From *Re: Generation Quarterly,* Summer 1997. Copyright © 1997 by Read Mercer Schuchardt. Reprinted by permission of the author.

Steven L. Shepherd. "Mall Culture." Originally published in *The Humanist,* November/December 1998, p. 40. Copyright © 1998 by Steven L. Shepherd. Reprinted by permission of the author.

Christina Hoff Sommers. "The 'Fragile American Girl' Myth." From *American Enterprise,* May–June 1997. Adapted from a speech at an AEI conference, December 1996. Copyright © 1996 by Christina Hoff Sommers. Reprinted by permission of the author and the AEI.

Debbie Stoller. "Brave New Girls." From *On the Issues,* Fall 1998. Reprinted by permission of *On the Issues,* c/o Choices Women's Medical Center, P.O. Box 3000, Denville, New Jersey 07834.

Kimberley A. Strassel. "Girls Will Be Boys." From the *Wall Street Journal* Eastern Edition, April 19, 2001. Copyright © 2001 by Dow Jones & Co., Inc. Reproduced with permission of Dow Jones & Co., Inc., in the format textbook via Copyright Clearance Center. All rights reserved Worldwide.

Grace Suh. "The Eye of the Beholder." Copyright © by Grace Suh. Reprinted by permission of the author.

Garry Trudeau. "My Inner Shrimp." From the *New York Times Magazine,* March 31, 1997. Copyright © 1997 by The New York Times Company. Reprinted by permission.

Alisa Valdes-Rodriguez. "Crossing Pop Lines." Originally titled "Crossing Pop Lines: Attention to Latinos Is Overdue, But Sometimes Off-Target." From the *Los Angeles Times,* June 11, 1999, p. F2. Copyright © 1999 *Los Angeles Times*. Reprinted by permission of the Los Angeles Times Syndicate International.

Nina Willdorf. "Reality's Fight." From the *Boston Phoenix,* September 6–13, 2001. Copyright © 2001 Boston-Phoenix. Reprinted by permission of the Phoenix Media Communications Group.

Teresa Wiltz. "Playing in the Shadows: Popular Culture in the Aftermath of Sept. 11 Is a Chorus Without a Hook, a Movie Without an Ending." From the *Washington Post,* November 19, 2001, p. C01. Copyright © 2001, The Washington Post Company. Reprinted by permission of The Washington Post Company.

ART CREDITS

Chapter 1: Photograph of a mother and child in front of the smoking Twin Tower site, by Alex Web/Magnum, from *Time* magazine.

Mallard Filmore cartoon by Bruce Tinsley, from the *Austin American-Statesman,* January 27, 2002. Reprinted with special permission from King Features Syndicate.

Chapter 2: "What Are You Wearing" Secret advertisement, © 2001 Proctor & Gamble "le plus beau jour de la vie" from *Doubletake* magazine, Fall 1997. Courtesy Jean-Christian Bourcart.

Photograph of Laila Ali by Jeff Kowalsky AFP/Corbis.

Chapter 3: "Nice Altoids" advertisement from *Newsweek,* January 26, 1998, p. 14. © 1999 Callard & Bowser-Suchard, Inc. Reprinted by permission.

Renoir painting, Kobal Collection, The Art Archive/Jean Walter & Paul Guillaume Collection/ Dagli Orti (A).

Body Shop ad campaign, The Advertising Archive.

Chapter 4: "What Do You Look Like?" cartoon by B. Ant, Copyright © 1999, Creative Syndicate, Inc.

"United Nations Do Unto Others as You Would Have Them Do Unto You" painting by Norman Rockwell, *Saturday Evening Post,* The Advertising Archive, Ltd.

Photograph of a mother and daughter by Joe McNally, *National Geographic,* vol. 196, no. 2 August 1999.

Chapter 5: "Where Should We Put the Logo?" cartoon by Peter S. Mueller. From the *Utne Reader,* March 4, 1998, by P. S. Mueller. Reprinted by permission.

Lee Jeans advertisement, The Advertising Archive, Ltd.

"Body Rites" advertisement by Chris Kane. From the *Austin Chronicle.* Reprinted by permission.

Chapter 6: "Is There a GAP in Your Life?" from *Adbusters* magazine (www.adbusters.org), Spring 1997, vol. 5, no. 1. By permission of the Media Foundation.

Kuppenheimer fashion advertisement, The Advertising Archive Ltd.

Tommy Hilfiger Freedom Fragrance advertisement, The Advertising Archive Ltd.

Chapter 7: Bunny Hoest and John Reiner, "Role Models" (cartoon), © 2002. Reprinted courtesy of Bunny Hoest and *Parade* magazine.

Psycho movie still, The Picture Desk, Kobal.

Scream movie still of Drew Barrymore, The Picture Desk, Kobal Collection/Moir, David M./ Miramax.

Chapter 8: VW ad, Russ Quackenbush/virtu.

Elvis photo, Bettmann/Corbis.

Britney Spears at Wembley photo, © Rune Hellestad/CORBIS.

Chapter 9: "No Pain, No Hockey" advertisement, *Sports Illustrated* "Hockey" advertisement featuring David Klutho photo from *People,* January 25, 1999. © 1999 Time, Inc. Reprinted by permission.

"Coney Island Roller Coaster, 1934" photograph, © Bettmann/Corbis.

"While Bob Was Being Grandmaster Bob..." Puma advertisement from *Nylon* magazine, March 2002 pg. 6, © Puma International.

Index of Authors and Titles